God

&

Mr. Godfrey

Asrar syed

PublishAmerica
Baltimore

First printing

ISBN: 1-4137-3739-0
PUBLISHED BY PUBLISHAMERICA, LLLP
www.publishamerica.com
Baltimore

Printed in the United States of America

To My Mother

PART I

GOD

CHAPTER (1)

'O Lord!' I said below my breath, addressing myself to Allah, my eyes shut and my hands raised heavenwards, "I begin this new day with Your name, for Yours is the Beginning and Yours is the Culmination. I acknowledge that You are the Creator of the Universe, You are the embodiment of Mercy, You are the ultimate in Compassion and You are the pinnacle of Munificence. By Your leave alone does the sun rise, bringing light into the darkness, separating the glare of day from the veil of night, bestowing sweetness on fruit, giving fragrance to flowers, providing the hungry with nourishment. By Your leave alone do the seasons change, the rains soak the parched soil, seeds sprout and yield vegetation; the breeze wanders around breathing life into the lifeless; migrant birds find new abodes, trees spread their hefty branches to support tiny nests, earthlings mate and multiply, the cycle of life goes on revolving forever and ever. By Your leave alone do the volcanoes hold back the molten lava, mountains control their landslides, clouds moderate their storms, oceans restrain their tides, rivers remain within their frontiers, so that life which You have introduced upon the earth is not cast against the wrath of hostile elements and destroyed. Forgive me my failings and shortcomings, free my mind of impious thoughts, cleanse my heart of indecent desires, keep my hands from evil deeds, lead me to the path of righteousness—the path of those who tread upon it and found everlasting repose in Your love, and not the path of those who strayed away from You into troubled horizons and forfeited Your grace—for in Your worship is my earthly affluence, in Your Will my destination and in your Kingdom my Paradise. *Ameen!'*

On that note of complete submission to His will and full of hope in His kindness and generosity, I concluded my prayers at the end of the morning

Congregation in our local mosque, put the Qur'aan on the shelf from where I had borrowed it for my regular recitation, shook hands with the priest and came out. The time was still only half past six in the morning, the neighbourhood was hushed, a lucid veil of mist had covered the surroundings, the slate grey sky was getting ready to welcome the impending dawn, crows clamoured on the branches of the tamarind tree, quiet gushes of breeze gathered up litter from the pavement and blew it around, a thin scattering of traffic on bikes and rickshaws occupied the street; the coffee shop on the other side of the road was busy serving cold buns and hot drinks to its first round customers. Unlocking the chain on my battered bike I had left in the front yard, I suppressed the shivers sent down my back by the cool breeze, hopped on the seat, peddled all the way to the Nampalli Railway Station for the morning edition of *the Deccan Chronicle*, purchased two bunches of fresh flowers from the florist for my sisters and, after a brief stroll down the vegetable market to pick up a few bits and bobs for lunch, came back to my house.

By then the dawn had broken; the twilight of the waning night was overlapped by the golden hue of the rising sun; the lingering layers of mist were burnt up by the advancing rays of sunshine; butterflies had emerged from their nocturnal repose and were busy flirting with pubescent blooms; squirrels raced around in search of windblown nuts; the superb midwinter dawn was as spectacular as I could ever expect it to be. In accordance with our normal family routine, my parents and my two younger sisters had gathered on the lawns to soak in the atmosphere: to watch the ascent of the glorious sun on the horizon and have their coffee as well as a pleasant chat in the garden. Wishing them a courteous good morning, I put away my bike underneath the stairs, tossed the bag of vegetables in the kitchen and joined the others just in time to catch Mamma's remark.

"A milkmaid who doesn't cheat is as rare as a ..." she said, and then, for some reason, left the sentence unfinished.

"As rare as what, Mamma?" I asked her, hoping to hear one of those delightful *originals* she comes up with from time to time.

"As a washer-man who doesn't cheat," she replied, dashing all my hopes.

"What's one got to do with the other?" Papa asked. "What can the common denominator be between dairy products and laundry service?"

"Well," replied Mamma with a sardonic smile, "I hate them both."

"Ah!" Papa said, reconciling too quickly, which was rather uncharacteristic of him; he had always been a fighter.

"There's a famous saying," my youngest sister, Roxana, pointed out, "which runs like this: 'if milk is cheap, why rear a cow.' True or false?"

Objection to that proverbial remark came from the least expected side.

"False!" Papa declared, "When your mamma planted the guava tree, hawkers were selling guavas a dozen per *Paisa*. Yet she planted it."

"Meaning, if guavas are cheap, why plant a tree?" I asked, seeking some clarification on the issue.

"Yes, why?" my younger sister, Shabana, enquired, somewhat puzzled by the entire line of conversation.

"Because they both cheat," Mamma stated.

"Which both?" Papa wanted to know.

"Cows and guavas?" I asked.

"Milkmaids and hawkers?" Shabbu asked.

"Hawkers and washer-men?" Papa asked.

"No!" said Rox, dismissing all the combinations and putting an end to the wild speculation, "That isn't what Mamma's taking about."

"Being cheated by a fourteen-year-old milkmaid day after day is an insult to the Quraishi stock," Mamma remarked, dragging family pride into it.

Papa was so sensitive to the topic, he reacted swiftly saying, "Good grief! We can't have that!!"

"Wait a minute," Shabbu intervened, "The grocer around the corner adds at least a quarter kilogram of stones to every kilogram of *Patna Rice* and cheats all his customers, including the Quraishis. I know this for a fact because I'm the one who picks the stones from the rice every day. It's beginning to affect my eyesight, you know."

"Which, in turn, is beginning to damage my teeth," said Rox, teasing her sister as usual.

"We can't have that, either," said Papa.

"We can't have what? Stones in rice?" I asked, raising a query.

"Danger to my eyes?" Shabbu asked, raising her hopes.

"Havoc on my teeth?" Rox asked, raising her eyebrows.

"*Chambeli*," Mamma insisted at that stage, "is the answer to all our problems.

I failed to see how. To the extent to which I knew, '*Chambeli*' happens to be the name of a delicate, spotless white and sensuously fragrant summer blossom. Where exactly did it fit into our conversation confused me.

"What've you got in mind, dear?" Papa asked, equally confused, "You aren't planning to stick a cluster of Chambeli in the milkmaid's bun and then get her to distract the grocer, are you?"

"Mamma isn't talking about flowers, Papa," Rox finally clarified, "She wants to buy a cow and then name it *Chambeli*."

"Why *Chambeli*? Why not *Gulaab*?" Papa asked her.

Gulaab means a rose and automatically implies *pink,* which made Mamma shudder. "A pink cow? How absurd!" she said.

"I don't think it's a good idea," Shabbu began once again, but quickly shut her mouth, presumably falling short of courage.

"What isn't a good idea?" I asked, propping up her courage, "A pink cow?"

"Any cow—pink or green or blue. They're just like monsoon in *Assam.* They give too much milk when you don't need it, and none at all when you desperately do."

"I've already lined up three customers in the neighbourhood for selling away surplus milk at an excellent price. Which, by the way, makes *Chambeli* a self-financing proposition," Mamma claimed.

"How much does this cow cost?" Papa asked her.

"About seven hundred and fifty rupees," she replied.

"I didn't mean the entire herd, my dear," he said.

"She isn't talking about the entire herd, Papa," Rox pointed out.

"I see," he said with slightly deflated enthusiasm, "But since you're planning to merchandise surplus stocks on a profit-making basis, why not spread the cost evenly over—shall we say—two years? There ought to be some such scheme available at the *Narsanghi Fair* as sell-the-milk-now-but-pay-for-the-cow-later?"

"There is no H. P. available on perishable goods," Rox categorically ruled it out.

"Seven Hundred rupees is a lot of money, Mamma," Shabbu courageously intervened once again, "Papa can't borrow any more than what he already has."

Her casting aspersions upon his borrowing powers upset him. "I can too!" He challenged her, suddenly turning hostile.

"I know you can, but you mustn't," Shabbu suggested, now meekly.

"What's this? Some sort of a counter-challenge? Are you calling my bluff? Which one of the two has a question mark over it: my creditworthiness, or my strength of endurance? Eh? Eh?" he demanded.

"Sorry, Papa. No offence intended," Shabbu said, hurriedly withdrawing the objection.

"No offence taken. If your mamma wants *Chambeli,* she gets *Chambeli.* She can have a whole cluster of them on a string, if she likes. Don't you agree?"

Before poor Shabbu could either agree or disagree, our little family tête-à-tête was interrupted by the arrival of a Morris Minor. As soon as they saw it enter the drive, all three ladies rushed into the house on account of *PURDAH* restrictions. Although Uncle Mohsin, who had driven in, was Papa's doctor as well as a close friend, segregation of sexes was observed in our households so strictly that men and women outside the family circle seldom got to see each other.

'*Kalim Immanzil*', an aging manor in which all of us lived together, was a very large dwelling. Situated in the semi rural neighbourhood of Asifnagar and surrounded by two acres of grounds, it often conveyed a misleading impression of affluence. A keen gardener and blessed with green fingers, Mamma had raised an eye-catching garden around the house. Several mature trees stood in prime positions, offering sanctuary to numerous colourful birds. Roxana, who was very fond of pets, had introduced a peacock into it. He mostly fed himself and did not need any attention, but like everything else in sight, he too added a false air of well being to the surroundings. We, however, were anything but well off.

A long time ago, the *Nizam of Hyderabad* gave the house to our grandpa as a gift because he worked at the palace as his head huntsman. In addition to the comfortable house and a lavish salary, he was also given a large estate of landed property on the outskirts of the city, which he leased out to local farmers, camped there once a year to collect his revenues and returned home loaded with money as well as gifts. But shortly after India became a Democratic Republic, things began to turn sour on him. The Nizam was stripped of his throne and his title was scrapped. As a result, the palace was shut down and the entire royal staff made redundant. Grandpa was no exception; he too lost his income and his estate, except the house in which he lived.

After his death, Papa inherited the crumbling manor. A decent education had ensured a decent job in the civil service and he settled down to raising his own family to the best of his ability. Mamma belonged to ordinary folks and did not have any formal education but she more than made up for it with her love, dedication, devotion, her impeccable manners and her graceful bearing. She was a brilliant housewife, an excellent cook and a keen gardener with an inborn passion for flowers. She kept the house in a spick and span condition even without proper upkeep or maintenance due to shortage of funds; extended its hospitality to all and sundry without discrimination, laid many a feast for Papa's friends, played the perfect hostess, gave alms without restraint and never missed her prayers or fasts, except on days of abstinence. Later on, after we were born, she did an immaculate job of parenting too by imbibing in us, especially in the girls, each and every one of the virtues with which she herself was imbibed by her own parents, taught them to be good Muslims first and only then be good wives and good mothers. Under her watchful eye and constant attention, coupled with a modern education that Papa enabled them to have, they grew up into desirable young ladies of whom any parent would be proud. Because of her strong sense of affiliation and spirit of solidarity, Papa loved her so much that he never had a harsh word for her in his entire life.

It was not as though finding a reliable job and a caring partner was the long and short of his troubles. If anything, it was only the start of a series of tests and trials in his life. The first of those materialised only a year after his marriage when Mamma had several successive miscarriages. According to the doctors, it was due to an incompatibility of the *RH Factor* in their blood and they were advised not to plan on having a family; in fact, Papa was asked to consider an hysterectomy done on her to avoid further risks to her life; but according to the *Ulemas* and the *Moulvis,* it was Allah's will and hence must not be interfered with. Their advise to them was to wait until the next pregnancy and then set out on a Holy Pilgrimage of all the prominent Muslim Shrines in the land. On account of their orthodox upbringing, together with their firm faith in Divine Compassion, they decided to ignore the former and accepted the latter; as soon as Mamma became pregnant again, they set out on their Pilgrimage as resolved. Amazingly enough, their prayers were not only heard but were also answered. I was born first, safe and sound, followed by Shabana and Roxana!

Being blessed with a lively family at long last meant so much to them they began to look upon us as 'Divine Gifts.' All parents love their children, but in their case, it had a different note to it altogether; we were too special for words. Allah already had a big share in their lives, but our arrival added a whole new dimension to it. They offered worship more regularly, adhered to the teachings of the Qur'aan with utter fanaticism and always remained within the perimeters of religion. When each of us reached the age of one, our heads were 'shaven' ceremonially; I was barely two when I got circumcised; on our fifth birthday respectively, we were made to memorise the first *SURAH* of the Qur'aan, which is considered to be the Doorway to Islam. We were taught how to pray and how to observe fasts; we knew our routine prayers by heart—what to say before food and after; before going to bed and upon waking up; during 'ablution' or during 'cleansing'; upon sighting the new moon; when confronted by a burial party and lots of other routines. Instead of fairy tales at bedtime, they narrated to us Parables from our Scriptures, which are not only interesting but are also indoctrinating. So finicky were they in their adherence to religion that the endless task of shaping our lives according to its concepts was never relaxed.

A few years after Roxana was born, Papa fell victim to the political, social and economic forces by which the small city of Hyderabad was rocked. On account of spending cuts implemented by the state government, the department where he worked was declared superfluous to requirements and wound up. As a result, he too was 'retrenched' and thrown out of his job without any compensation. It not only landed him in a rather sticky civil litigation with the government, but it also took away from him his only source of livelihood. His commitments remained the same while the means of meeting them abruptly disappeared. Round about the same time, due to a sudden influx of population from across the state, the cost of living shot up disproportionately and added further fuel to his worries. With five mouths to feed, finance the full time education of three children, two of them girls, buy us clothes, buy our school uniforms, pay for books, find money for fees and for rickshaw fares, not to mention medical bills for himself and for Mamma, he reached the end of his tether. He could not afford to simply carry on living from day to day, but had to devise a long-term strategy, not only for the present and the immediate future but also for the distant future when today's young girls would grow up into tomorrow's young women, with a different set of new and pecuniary priorities.

He did come up with a plan, which, if successful, could have provided him with the peace of mind he sought as well as the long-term financial stability he so desperately needed. By then, with the afflux of time and the economic changes taking place in the fast developing metropolis, his crumbling manor, situated in one of the most affluent areas of the city and standing in about two acres of vacant grounds, had become a prime target for property developers on the look out for rich and easy pickings. Raising a secured loan on it from a safe lender posed no insurmountable problems. Even though practising Muslims are not allowed by Islam either to take or to pay interests, he ventured to borrow a big loan from the State Bank of Hyderabad and invest it on a couple of projects he had in mind; one of them was to construct a small shopping precinct on the land that ran alongside the main road, and the other to grow a vineyard on the rest. Using the borrowed money, he went ahead with both and managed to get them completed in a matter of six to eight months. Twenty neat and tidy shops in the middle of a rapidly expanding neighbourhood, and a large, state of the art vineyard with trellises mounted on stone pillars and irrigated by a massive pond within easy access, should have seen us through for the rest of our lives. But in his case, the dream turned sour when a corrupt bureaucrat in Hyderabad City Corporation decided to play it rough on him for a large bribe. Although Planning Permission was obtained before starting the work, he came up with a few nasty loopholes in the application, had it sent back to the commissioners for a review and somehow got their original decision overturned, without even an apology, let alone compensation. On account of it, Papa had to abandon the entire project just as he was beginning to receive genuine offers from merchants interested in renting the shops.

That just about broke his back. Having sunk such a large sum of money into it, he was precariously stranded between an irredeemable debt on one hand and a worthless row of shops on the other, all but waiting to be devoured by squatters. And as if that was not enough, he faced yet another disaster from the vineyard too. For one thing, it was a long-term proposition that needed a constant supply of funds for several years before the vines could be expected to return their first yield. And for another, it was a job for experienced growers who were simply not available on hire. They either had their own plantations, or offered terms that rendered the proposition unviable. As an alternative, he had to rely upon casual labourers with no specialist experience in growing hybrid grapes, as well as manage the show by himself, also without any experience. The only son of a royal courtier, and then an officer in the Indian Administrative Service, he was not cut out for the task. The vagaries of the weather alone took away what little chances of success he had. In a matter of a few years, after swallowing up every penny he had put aside for emergencies and plagued by successive crop failures, the vineyard too stood abandoned just like the shops, swamped by weeds and nettles, of no real use to anyone but the children from the neighbourhood to playing hide and seek in!

His only material asset thus irretrievably stuck in the clutches of the bank, he was hand-to-mouth once again. Only, in addition to running the household, he now had to worry about the repayments on the debt too. Without an income, he could not cope with either of them so he resorted to borrow more and more and sink even deeper into debts. Since the property was not at risk of depreciating, the bank manager let him borrow without any hassle, but kept adding unpaid interests to the loan and making it even bigger. Papa knew what was happening, how he was being manipulated by a profit-orientated financial organisation and what was going to be its end result, but he did not have much of a choice. The costs of living continued to escalate; full time education of all three of us put a severe drain on his limited resources; infirmities resulting from stress added an extra dimension to his expenses, and with both the girls reaching the age of puberty, their priorities also turned a different corner. But in spite of all those overwhelming odds, keeping the darkest of his secrets under covers from us as well, not even letting a dent appear on his brow, he kept going, as charming and humorous as ever, as loving and dedicated as always.

At that stage, just like the economic changes around us had once turned *Kalim Manzil* into a gold mine, the social changes resulting from the osmosis of cultures between the Muslim families of Hyderabad and the non Muslim migrants from across the province lit up a new and unexpected light at the bottom of the tunnel for him. Until then, the Muslim community had been conforming strictly to the ordinances of the Qur'aan in matters of dowries for their children at the time of their marriages, which happens to be an agreed sum of money given by the bridegroom to the bride as a gift; but the symbiosis of contrasting cultures, coupled with severe shortage of boys as opposed to girls, reversed the process. Instead of giving dowries to the brides as per the Qur'aanic recommendations, parents of eligible and well-placed youths began to put price tags on them, often amounting to staggering sums of money, payable by the bride to the bridegroom instead of the other way around, in addition to many unreasonable demands for ornaments, gifts, home contents and spectacular wedding ceremonies. In fact, the better the match, the bigger the demands; sons turned into *assets* and daughters into *liabilities.* As luck would have it, being quite good-looking, fairly intelligent, resourceful, loyal, obedient, God-fearing and without any major vices, together with an enviable social standing, I was fast becoming a rare commodity in the *marriage market.* If I also had a good education and a decent job, I could easily fetch enough money in return for my hand to get both the girls wed in decent homes.

Quick to spot my enormous potential, he decided to exploit it to the utmost by making an even bigger investment in me than he had in the house, full of hope that, being his blood rather than a possession, I would yield him a more realistic return one day. In fact, turning away from everything else, he concentrated on the education of all three of us. Even though degrees were mere ornaments for the girls, he did not flinch from getting them aptly *adorned*; to make them self sufficient in the event of the unexpected as well as to enhance their chances of finding better matches. However, in their case, whilst he allowed them to choose their specialities according to their preferences, in my case, he insisted that I pursued only the courses that were aimed at improving my career prospects. On account of my theocratic upbringing, I had developed a passion for religious studies and was keen to get a Master's Degree in Comparative Theology with scope for research, but he would not let me. The oil industry in the Middle East was booming; not only did the desert represent material affluence but also spiritual uplift by reason of our common religious bond: our prophet was born there and Islam had begun there. To a visionary like Papa, the very idea of my setting up home in either Mecca or Medina became obsessive. Whether I liked it or not, he compelled me to take up Oil Technology as my speciality, believing that, as soon as coming out of the university, I would land into some lucrative job. By and large, the *plan* turned into a *passionate dream*: Shabana and Roxana married well; I prospering in the oil fields of Arabia and he and Mamma shunting between Bombay and Riyadh! Though it was only a dream and just a dream, it did not seem beyond the scope of accomplishment; and looking at the way the marriage market was shaping up in our city, a lot more realistic than growing hybrid grapes or building shopping precincts were!

Thus, next to Allah, I became his one remaining hope. If I got myself a decent job and married well, Shabana and Roxana were in with the chance of getting good husbands. But if I did not, their degrees alone could turn into shackles and strand them in the endless twilight of spinsterhood. That was the real litmus test—my marrying into wealth. As far as the debts were concerned, he was not too bothered about them. Once the three of us were off his hands, he could sell the house, settle his debts and move into smaller accommodation. It was as simple as that. Besides, he knew we would always be around to take care of our aging parents when they need us, just as they had taken care of us when we needed them.

And that year, somehow huffing and puffing, his *train* arrived at its first station before steaming up the hill towards its intended destination when Shabbu and I took our exams and passed with good grades—she her First Degree and I my Master's, while Rox also was not too far behind. Would his train make it to the crest? It remained to be seen … .

CHAPTER (2)

Spring always arrives in Hyderabad with the majestic grace of a fairy queen. It sprinkles stardust everywhere; bestows a new shimmer on the Milky Way; adds an extra colour to the rainbow; appends a novel dimension to our dreams. Gusts of refreshing breeze come from far-off vales laden with the fragrance of wild blossoms, carrying passionate messages of love, mirthful tidings of joy, priceless gifts of hope. They bring colours and contrasts; they bring glamorous butterflies, illusive dragonflies and vagabond bluebottles. They whisper sweet nothings in the ears of pubescent maidens and expectant youths; they rekindle relationships, tie new knots and match fresh pairs; they carry on their wings tears of grief and turn them into dewdrops and lodge them back on rose petals; they heal wounds, exacerbate joy and suppress pain; they take away the old and the spent, the sore and the hurtful, the pungent and the acrid, and give something new in its place, something full, something sweet, something pleasant; they pour nectar down parched throats, ignite sparks in gleaming eyes, put a flush in bashful cheeks and lay smiles on moist lips! They tarry, they tease, they tantalize and then they go away until another spring!

That year, like all other years, Mamma's garden was in full bloom. The *Chambeli* was gone with the summer but the *Juhi* had taken its place. The delicate roses, washed in dew, enriched with fragrance, unsurpassable in beauty, untainted by seasons, unharmed by time, untouched by thorns, tossed their heads with glee and excitement each time a gust of breeze passed by, tickling their sensitive petals. The heavy stems of marigolds, cajoled by wayfaring bluebottles swung with mirth, danced with ecstasy and made passes at each other. Beetles and ladybirds clung amorously to rippling grass-blades; the lilies in the pond tripped into each others arms in quest of furtive hugs and stolen kisses; toads squatted on lotus leaves and parleyed; even the timid snails found consenting playmates in the laps of the coy touch-me-nots! Spring had come into her garden too with magic mingled in its folds, scattered bliss on her lawns, breathed a new life in the barren tendrils of poison ivy as well as in the fragrant clusters of the cherry blossoms.

So was Papa's field of hopes, farmed on tough soil by the sweat of his brow, his tireless toils, his courage in the face of adversity, the sacrifices he had made, the risks he took, the storms he braved and the scars he bore. After withstanding many a drought, many a flood, many an invasion and many a disaster, it had given him its first yield; dropped in his empty bowl a long awaited and much sought after reward; filled his arms with hopes for the future of his children and his heart with gratitude for the real Provider in Whom he had never lost his faith.

Friday, the 28th March—an important date in the Quraishi calendar. The front lawns of our Osmania University were neatly mowed and watered; a collapsible stage was erected, comprising the podium, a row of tables covered with white cloth and an array of vases on them laden with imaginative floral arrangements. An assortment of cups and shields stood gleaming in a corner; immaculately dressed guests of honour sat relaxed in the chairs behind the tables, holding pleasant conversations in muted whispers, while members of university staff, given the responsibility of organising the prestigious convocation, briskly went about their business.

Facing the stage, the temporary auditorium erected to host the dense gathering of pupils and their families was crammed to capacity. Many young men, wearing smart suits or *Sherwanis,* and as many young ladies, clad in glamorous *saris* or *Shalwar-khamis* under the academic cloak, had come to claim their hard-earned degrees, their coveted cups, their cherished shields, their merit certificates and their adulations from the hands of the highest designate of the university, in the presence of their proud parents or their guardians. That evening, a total of one hundred and seventy-three young women and young men from all around the state were gathered there, to be congratulated, to be thanked, to be honoured, to be launched under the threshold of a new life in order to make their mark, to compete with one another in a strenuous race for careers, for success and for advancement; for erecting new goals in ambition and reaching them; for setting up new standards in excellence and accomplishing them; for taking both victories as well as defeats in their stride; for learning to live with their triumphs and their disappointments with equal fortitude.

Among them Mamma and Papa, surrounded by the three apples of their eyes, smiles of contentment on their lips and tears of joy rolling down their cheeks, come to hear their children's names echo on the loudspeakers, to watch Shabbu and me walk up to the podium amidst loud applause and receive our scrolls of honour, to hear us be complimented and congratulated, to realise their long-awaited dreams and to fulfil their most cherished hopes. It was a great day in their lives as well as in ours, a day of crops and harvests, a day when gardens of pride bloomed in the sunshine of victory, when Angels and mortals rubbed their shoulders to share a common bliss, when Allah reached out His hand and added an extra portion of Divine Compassion to the mixed fortunes of His grateful Creation!

After the convocation, Papa invited a few of his closest friends and their families to break bread with us. It was not just a feast to celebrate our graduation but also a public relations exercise to show off his children to the close community, especially his pretty daughters who were fast approaching the most crucial age. On account of it, he had also wanted the house to look its best. Half a day's hard labour by all of us ensured spectacular results; the antique furniture dusted, the chandeliers hung in their place, the porcelain vases gleaming with lustre, the tapestries and wall hangings rearranged, the mosaic floors washed, it did reflect some of the glory from its bygone past.

The feast was also a grand success. The combined culinary ingenuity of Mamma and the girls produced a mouth-watering meal, which everybody ate and enjoyed. After the feast, according to our family traditions, Shabana and I were asked to sit on the settee, garlanded by all the invitees and blessed. Attired in glamorous clothes, nicely titivated and in high spirits, the girls made quite an impact upon the women. Wherever they went, they received adulations from all the guests, some praising their looks and others praising their manners. Roxana, younger and also more naughty between the two, repeatedly tried her hand at matchmaking for me by creating several unexpected opportunities of bringing me face to face with her girlfriends, but without much luck. I turned away from them, feigning surreptitious shudders, just to tease her. But her pranks and wisecracks did enhance the exuberance of the get-together as usual; we all had a fantastic time.

After the departure of the guests, the five of us sat in the lounge for a family chat. While Shabana occupied herself with making tea, Roxana attended to Papa's *betel-rolls* and *hukka*. With so many of her duties and domestic chores being attended to by her daughters, Mamma could afford to relax. Exhausted by the daylong activity, she excused herself for her night prayers and went away. The room quickly filled up with the mellow aroma of tobacco coming from the *hukka*. As usual, a swarm of mosquitoes invaded us from the windows and commenced their nocturnal persecution. Crickets squeaked in the grass, owls hooted, toads croaked, all sorts of weird noises festered the quiet night outside. A stream of cool breeze began to flow in, driving out the body heat left behind by the guests and altering the room temperatures. Fetching Papa's shawl from his room, I wrapped it around his shoulders and sat down.

"Who can tell me what's the difference between a sparrow's nest and a beehive?" he asked, settling down in the easy chair and looking at us turn by turn.

The question obviously puzzled me, but I knew there had to be a sensible answer to it and a sagacious reason for its being asked.

"One is made of straw and the other is made of wax? One contains chicks and the other bees? One is clumsy inside and the other symmetrical?" Rox fired the three questions at him like pebbles from a slingshot, as usual in a big rush to claim all the laurels for herself first.

Shabbu, on the other hand, in the habit of thinking twice before opening her mouth even to ask for a glass of water, did seem to formulate a suitable answer mentally, but failed to put it into words.

"You tell us, Papa," I said, playing safe and throwing the ball back in his side of the court, "What *is* the difference between a sparrow's nest and a beehive?"

"Sparrows mate," he explained with a meaningful smile, "they lay eggs, they hatch them and they tend to their nests tenaciously. But once their fledglings grow their wings, they fly away, seldom to meet again. On the other hand, bees are born for the hive, they live for the hive and they die for the hive. Even when they part, they do not part to serve their own interests but only to serve another queen in the making of a new hive, for which they live and for which they die. That's why our Prophet (saws) exhorted all good Muslims to follow the example of the beehive rather than of the sparrow's nest."

"How true!" Rox could not help endorsing, quick to absorb the context in which the analogy was drawn, her sparkling eyes dwelling upon me.

"Well, Roxana," Papa said, looking at his pet daughter with an accentuated smile, "Next year, it will be your turn to hold the scroll of honour in your hand and to wear the garlands. For now, you channel all your energies in only one direction, and you know which direction that is."

"Yes, Papa," she said, sobering up at once.

"As far as you're concerned, Shabana," he said, shifting his attention upon Shabbu, "I did not educate you to gather honey for this *hive*; you can do it when you have a hive of your own, and only if those whom you serve require you to. For the time being, you head towards the kitchen where your skills are needed the most. As you know, too many people have started cheating your mamma—the milk is being adulterated by the milkmaid, *Patna Rice* are being tampered with by the grocer, the guava tree is in full bloom and a 'Chambeli' on her way! One pair of extra hands in the midst of it all would be most welcome!"

"Yes, Papa," agreed Shabbu, suppressing a smile.

"In your case, Yusuff," he said, looking at me, "A degree is not just a scroll of honour in your hand but a *MISSION* on your shoulders, as it were. What I would like to see next are those strings of roses elevated from your neck to your forehead—in the form of a bridegroom's *Sehra*.'

"Yes, Papa," I too said, agreeing with the obvious.

"Hear! Hear!" Rox added below her breath, surreptitiously poking her elbow into my ribs.

"Did you say something, Roxana?" Papa asked.

"No, Papa, I didn't," she replied, and then added as an afterthought, "But I might have something to say on the subject later on. I'll put my hand up when I do."

"So, as of tomorrow," he resumed his address to me, "we'll begin the task of looking for a bride for you, unless, of course, you have your own preferences. If you do, now is the time to speak up."

"No, Papa. Your choice is my choice."

"If it was up to us, we would have settled for a pretty and Godfearing bride from within our own wider family, regardless of her financial status. But then, Shabana and Roxana's prospects are just as important, and there's no shortage of pretty brides amongst the upper crusts, either."

At that stage, as threatened, Rox did put her hand up to say her piece.

"Yes, Roxana?" he asked her, his attention momentarily diverted.

"Besides," she said, her words addressed to him but her eyes rose in my direction, "What's in a face, Papa? Beauty, they say, lies in the eye of the beholder!"

"Indeed!" he applauded, looking at me once again.

"Indeed," I too agreed, if only to nip the issue in the bud.

"In which case," he carried on, relieved, "shall we move on to the next most important topic of a job and of employment prospects for you?"

"Yes, Papa, we can. Is there some news about it?"

"Yes, there is, though not particularly exciting."

"What is it?" I asked, quite excited nonetheless.

"A temporary clerical vacancy in the I.G.P.'s office, who happens to be a close friend of mine, just so you gain some work experience instead of wasting time. Not much of a salary, though, but then again, seven hundred rupees is seven hundred rupees, and you can buy a lot of postage stamps with it for sending off your job applications abroad."

"Yes, Papa, you're right, that would come in quite handy. Besides, there are some people I know who are getting pretty desperate for a set of glass bangles from *the lovers' arcade*," I said, my second sentence addressed to him, but my eyes dwelling upon Rox.

"Well, that's settled then," he said, wrapping up the conversation, "I'll pass on the details to you in the morning. Let's call it a day now. I'm tired and my *hukka* has also gone cold."

"I can get it going again," offered Rox from the goodness of her heart, but he said no, wished us all a good night and left.

As soon as his back turned, she pounced upon me for a fuller explanation of glass bangles at which I had hinted. But instead of elaborating upon it, I caught hold of one of her snake-like plaits and gave it a hard tug.

"Ouch! It hurts!" she complained.

"That's the idea," I said, without easing up the pressure.

"Let go! Let go! Or, I'll scream."

"Beauty lies in the eye of the beholder, eh?" I repeated her words without relaxing my hold on her plait, "If you think I'm going to settle for one of the ugly sisters just so you can find yourself a fancy Prince Charming, you're living in cuckoo land, Cinderella!"

"May you be lumbered for life with the ugliest of the ugly sisters," she cursed first, then bit her tongue and hugged me affectionately, saying, "I didn't mean that! Honest, I didn't! My dearest Bhaijan! My sweetest Bhaijan! May Allah bless you with a *pure companion*, here on earth instead of up there in Paradise, a real *HUR* with large black eyes and eternal youth, ya? And for that, I won't even ask you for any bangles!"

"Ameen!" said Shabbu, gently releasing her plait from my grip out of sheer compassion.

The morning after the feast saw us all occupied with the priorities allocated to each one of us by Papa while he became absorbed on the phone, contacting marriage brokers in search of some decent proposals for me; Rox got dressed and dashed off to the college; Shabbu began her tireless struggle separating *Patna rice* from stones and Mamma commenced preparations for the arrival of *Chambeli* from the *Narsanghi Fare*. As for me, without any adequate experience in the complex field of career hunting, I needed solid guidance and went looking for it to the only person whose advice and judgement I trusted. He was Sal—short for Saleem—my childhood friend. We had gone to the same schools and colleges until graduation, where our paths parted. The only son of a rich and successful barrister, he had no need for jobs; his father's thriving practice was large enough to absorb him as well. So, unlike me, he took a degree in law. In fact, he had done his utmost to persuade me to follow the same course, but since it meant going against Papa's *dream*, I had bowed out. He sorted out my C.V., got a professional correspondent to draft all my letters, showed me where to look for names and addresses of potential employers in the oil industry, not just in the Middle East, but on a global scale, and helped me launch my mission in every way he could.

In the mean time, the date for starting work at the I.G.P.'s office caught up and I went there on tenterhooks. My battered desk was situated in a large room shared by nearly thirty clerks, working for various departments but underneath the same roof. We had a common boss in the form of Mr. Swami, who sat like a king on his throne facing the entire team, watching, supervising, observing, sometimes helping us as well as doing his own work. He had no idea why and by whom I was chosen for the job nor was he aware of my fancy qualifications; and as there was no need for me to publicise either of these, I too kept quiet.

The job itself was not too difficult. Twice a day, stacks of mail arrived from the post office in special delivery vans, all of which came to me for sorting. After going through the letters, I despatched them to their respective destinations through the network of internal couriers known as *chaprasis*. That aspect of the job was called *inward mail*. And on its heels came the *outward mail* , which comprised letters going out. My duty was to make sure that the addresses on the letters matched the addresses on the envelopes in which they were going, and that there were no mistakes made by the *typing pool*. Neither of the tasks required brains, but just speed and presence of mind. There was no room in it for errors; one slip of the fingers could build up piles of brought forward mail. I did not like it and neither did the boss.

Getting accustomed to the work posed no problems. Being a quick learner, I soon gained the knack. By and large, I also picked up speed. Mr.Swami, the had clerk, was a reasonable man and a good guide. We got along quite well. The surroundings were fairly pleasant and most of my colleagues amiable chaps. We got to know each other during lunch breaks and had a few laughs. Time passed quickly. On the whole, it was not half as bad as I had initially expected it to be—except, of course, for the boredom.

At home, Papa, Mamma and my sisters often asked me how I was getting along. There was not much to say; the quality of the job hardly mattered. Money at the end of the month was all I cared about. In fact, I eagerly looked forward to the first pay packet, as it would be my first salary, and hence my first opportunity to do something for those whom I loved dearly. I made all sorts of plans. Oft and on, lying in bed at night, I pictured Shabbu and Rox wearing new *gharara* suits and pure silk *saris*, as if the measly salary could buy all that! I even thought in terms of gold chains around their necks and gold bangles on their wrists. If it was silly, it was just as stimulating; the imagination itself brought me a great deal of comfort.

My toils became worthwhile when I got my first pay packet in hand. Retaining only one hundred rupees out of it for charity and alms, Papa gave the rest of it back to me with his blessings. I knew exactly what to do with the *dosh*; I knew Mamma and the girls had only one pair of decent clothes, which they wore again and again on *special occasions* and then locked them away in their wardrobes. I also knew that six hundred rupees could easily add an extra pair to them, not to overlook the passionate subject of glass bangles from the *lovers' arcade* still waiting to be addressed. No doubt, as promised, Rox did not make any more references to it, but I could distinctly see the shimmer of hope light up in her eyes as soon as the words salary and shopping were mentioned. So, we made special plans for that Sunday, went to *Chaar Minaar*, then to the arcade, and blew away the whole lot on shopping as well as on some delicious *Biryani* at Medina Hotel. Thus I got value for money, hard-earned but well spent, which sufficiently motivated me to slave away for one more month.

Frankly, I would have carried on working for as long as the job lasted, were it not for a funny incident that occurred at the office round about the middle of the fourth month. One fine morning, as I sat sorting the outward mail, the boss approached me and, without uttering a word, began to go through the pile of envelops on my desk.

"Is there something you want, Mr. Swami?" I asked him, trying to be helpful.

"Ah!" he replied, scratching his head and yielding to a distinctly guilty smile, "Somewhere in this mess there must be a letter addressed to one P.C. Habeeb. Find it and then ground it."

"You mean, you don't want me to despatch the letter?"

"Just obstruct its progress until further instructions, that's all."

Who was I to decline the boss? Wasting my entire lunch break in search of the aforementioned item, I finally tracked it down and, without even bothering to look at what was inside, put it away in the bottom draw of my desk.

For the next three to four days, no more reference was made to it; in fact, the level of indifference was such that I even forgot all about it, until another day when a burly stranger arrived at the office, looked around, found the *monarch*, rushed over to his *throne* and had a surreptitious conversation with him. I also noticed some sort of a stealthy transaction take place between them, but as it was none of my business, I withdrew my attention and reapplied it to the job in hand.

Sometime later, as soon as the burly stranger stepped out of the office, Swami approached me once again, still wearing the smile, but no longer guilty. In fact, it was one heck of a smile of contentment, if I ever saw one!

"Boy!" he said, choking with delight, "Where's it?"

"Where's what?" I asked him and then blinked my vacant eyes several times, pretending complete innocence.

"The envelope! Remember?"

"No. Which envelope?"

"You know? That one. Ha?"

"Sorry, I don't. Which one?"

"That one! The white one with a window."

I knew precisely what he was after, but deliberately played dumb. "Nope," I insisted, "I don't have the foggiest notion what the heck you're talking about …."

"Ahm!" he mumbled, suddenly going pale in the face.

"Not this one, by any chance, is it?" I asked him, producing the envelope after teasing him long enough.

"Aha!" he said with immense relief. "Fantastic! The addressee is waiting for you outside. I mean, P.C. Habeeb. Give him his letter and you keep this. This is yours."

So saying, he forced another envelope into my hands. Eyeing it with a frown, or to put it more accurately, with solid suspicion, I looked inside. Upon sighting the contents, a series of strange noises echoed inside my head. Flares dazzled my vision, a loud gasp came out my mouth, the ulna of my right hand suddenly refused to cooperate with the radius, a dozen or so butterflies fluttered in my stomach, and finally my legs went to sleep. For, safely tucked inside the envelope were five crisp one hundred rupee notes, adding up to a cool five hundred *bucks*!

Connecting P.C. Habeeb with the money, the money with the mislaid letter and the letter with the burly stranger was not difficult, but resisting the temptation to look inside it was. As a matter of curiosity, I took a surreptitious peek.

To my extreme discomfiture, it turned out to be a Re-instatement Order from the I. G. P., addressed to Constable Habeeb, and giving him a date to resume duties.

Usually, Re-instatement Orders presuppose suspension, and suspension in turn presupposes guilt. By and large, the suppositions became so alarming, I ran out of breath.

As Mr. Swami was not there to shed some light on the matter, I came out of the office and looked around. P.C. Habeeb, who was restlessly pacing the floor in the corridor, saw me and came running.

"*Assalamu alaikum!*" he said with a broad grin.

"*Walaikum assalam,*" I replied, reciprocating the warm greetings equally warmly.

"I'm P.C. Habeeb, " he said, introducing himself first, and then asked, "Have you brought it?"

"Yes, I have," I said.

"Oh, great!" he applauded, "I've given it to Mr. Swami ..."

"Given what to Mr. Swami?"

"You know ... That!"

"No, I don't. 'That' what?"

"Ah!" he exclaimed after some figuring out, "You're new, aren't you?"

"So?"

Gulping a few sour lumps down his throat, he explained to me what it was all about. Apparently, three years ago, he was suspended from duty on grounds of graft and corruption. In my country, all corrupt policemen are usually tried and invariably exonerated. So was he, and the papers rustling in my hip pocket were his *chapatti* and *daal*, in the form of the Re-instatement Order.

"Well, my friend, I've kept my end of the bargain," he declared with a great deal of pride.

"You gave Mr. Swami some money?"

"Yes, I did. A deal is a deal."

"How much?"

"Two thousand rupees."

Postage seemed to be getting pretty expensive! Such a heavy financial blow to a police constable suspended from duty without pay for three whole years could be crippling. Yet, he had managed to find the two thousand rupees! No wonder Mr. Swami looked like a fox smacking his lips after a succulent kill; if he gave me five hundred rupees just to keep my *trap* shut, he must have helped himself to a good thousand for doing nothing.

"Do you have a family?" I asked him, just out of sympathy.

My prying into his private affairs seemed to puzzle Habeeb.

"Yes, I do," he replied with a deep dent on his brow. "But why? What's that got to do with you?"

"Any kids?"

"Yes."

"How many kids?"

"B...B...But ..."

"How many?"

"Thirteen ..."

"Good grief! That's a lot of kids!!"

"What? Between five wives? Some people seem to think it's a sad reflection upon my virility!"

"Five wives as well? All those mouths to feed and no job or salary for three whole years? Wasn't it tough, laying your hands on two thousand rupees at a time like this?"

"No money, no Re-instatement Order. Do I have a choice?"

Maybe he was right. But I had no wish to soil my hands with such wages of sin. My share of the loot was still rustling in my other pocket. Giving him the order first, to the delight of my conscience, I also returned him the money, to the dismay of my mind, none of which made any sense to P.C. Habeeb.

"But why?" he asked, absolutely baffled by my gesture, "If you're not happy with your share, just tell me. I'll give you some more."

"No, I don't want more. I don't want this, either. Buy some clothes for your wives and kids from the lovers' arcade. Give them a treat at the Medina Hotel too. They serve superb Biryani and don't charge a fortune for it."

I said so, remembering the extent of joy I had myself derived from doing precisely that. But instead of lifting his spirits, the recommendation seemed to plunge him into further confusion. After eyeing me for a while as though I was some kind of a freak, he worked things out in his mind.

"I get it!" he said, brightening up at long last, "You're feeling sorry for me, aren't you? You think Mr. Swami has taken me to the launderers? Thanks very much, but don't worry. When on duty, I can easily recover two thousand rupees within a month or two. My beat happens to be exceptionally prosperous, crammed with unlicensed hawkers, fruit and vegetable stalls, sugar cane juice, bangles and what not. I let them make money and keep my cut, on a *live and let live* basis."

Forcing the money back into my hand, he thanked me once again and left. For a long time after he was gone, I stood plunged in deep thought. The police, doing precisely what they are employed to prevent; Mr. Swami, himself an incorrigible corrupt, corrupting the others. What was a nice guy like me doing in a dump like that?

Frankly, it was all just a storm in the teacup. By then, I had come to hate that office and the job so much, I was looking for a good excuse to jack it up. Quite by chance, P.C. Habeeb provided me with that excuse,

"Trouble, young man?" Mr. Swami asked me, jumping me from the rear and breaking my chain of thoughts.

"No, Mr. Swami," I replied, returning to reality. "By the way, how often does this sort of thing take place here?

"Getting greedy already, are we?" he replied with a curious glint in his eye, the raised eyebrows and the sarcastic smile well matched, "As often as you like. But why?"

"Just wondered. As far as I know, it has happened only once in four months."

"That's because you're only a temp. But then, for another two grand, I can make you a perm. Interested?"

"I'll think about it and let you know."

He nodded and went in. I too returned to my desk, my mind more or less made up. I had been working there for a worthy cause. I could not even think in terms of buying food for my family with that kind of dirty money. So, I decided to quit. Without making any reference to the unfortunate incident, I scribbled a brief note of resignation and handed it to Mr. Swami, together with my share of P.C. Habeeb's bribe.

"Is anything the matter?" he asked, browsing through the note.

"Nothing, boss," I replied casually, "Just fed up, that's all."

"And what about this?" he asked next, pointing at the envelope that contained the money.

"You keep it, Mr. Swami. I was only a temp, anyway," I replied.

When I left him, he looked a bit uneasy. My timing of the resignation seemed to have scared him; the *mob* does not like its *hit-men* dropping out of sight on the heels of a *hit*! But there was no need for him to worry; I had no intentions of taking the matter anywhere beyond that office. Such rubbish lies all around us and it was not my job to sweep it up.

Seeing me home unusually early, my folks were taken by surprise. I told Papa what happened; I had to, because the job was his choice and the I.G.P. was his close friend. But after listening to me, and quite contrary to my fears, he burst into hysterical laughter. So did the rest of the others.

Having gained enough work experience in course of those few months to last me over an entire lifetime, I dug in for a long haul towards reaching my real goal. In a way, coming out of that dead-end job did seem like a good move as it gave me plenty of free time to concentrate on finding one in my speciality, whether in my own country, in the Middle East, or any other part of the world for that matter. The importance of my getting a proper job quickly could not be stressed enough; for Papa's strategy to succeed; for his squeaking *train* to reach the crest of the hill; for his field of dreams to survive until the next harvest; for Mamma's garden to await the return of a new spring; for Shabana and Roxana to repose on beds of roses; in short, for us to be able to live underneath the egregious shelter of our own house with self respect and dignity, I desperately needed a rich wife, and to be able to get a rich wife, I desperately needed a well-paying job.

During the four months I was at work, response to my first round of applications was beginning to arrive in tiny trickles, mostly full of regrets for the present but hopes for the future. Without getting too despondent by those negative replies, I discovered fresh venues to explore, got more addresses of potential employers from libraries and embassies, gave a facelift to my c.v., had a new covering letter drafted by someone else and sent off a second round of probes. On that occasion, I also got in touch with some recruitment agencies in Bombay who specialised in the Middle East job market. My professor at the university, who had banked a lot of his hopes on my success, gave me several leads to peruse, which I did, but without much luck. Even if I did not have worthwhile contacts of my own, Papa knew quite a few big shots here and there and pulled all sorts of strings. That too did not work. No employer in the West was willing to consider making even a formal offer without an interview first, which was quite expensive as well as risky. Some recruitment agencies in Bombay did put forward a few proposals, but with too many strings attached: Their offers stipulated enormous commissions, payable in advance, and assignments in the Middle East usually lasted for only three years, subject to extension, which put me off. In spite of shelling down such a lot of money in commissions and fares, I could still be back to square one if the employment contracts were not extended for any reason. Eager as he was to make a success out my life and recover at least some of the investment he had made in me, Papa tried to raise more money, even from *loan sharks* if necessary, and give me another shot in my arm, but I did not let him. Whatever else I did, the one thing I was determined to avoid was to make him sink deeper into debts in order to finance for me such dodgy propositions.

Like the best laid plans of mice and men, Papa's began to run aground once again. Without a sound career or a suitable job leading to it, my *popularity ratings* in the *marriage market* plummeted rapidly; the chances of my securing the sort of bride that he had envisaged for me became remote, and together with it, the future of the girls also turned bleak. Having already kissed goodbye to the job at the I.G.P. Office, and together with it, to the seven hundred rupees I got at the end of each month, we were hand to mouth again. At such a critical juncture, as soon as the debt reached two hundred thousand rupees, the bank manager abruptly introduced severe restraints on further borrowing. It hit us the hardest. The unfinished shops carried on gathering moss and cobwebs; the vineyard kept dying day by day from lack of irrigation and upkeep; there were no more silver linings in the clouds, no pretty brides for me, no Prince Charmings for the girls, no pennies left in anyone's piggy bank, no work, no earnings, not even as a porter at the Nampalli Railway Station!

At a time like that, after an unusually long gap, Sal phoned me from right out the blue and asked me if I could see him on a matter of some urgency. My time being completely free, I went to his house right away.

CHAPTER (3)

That being a Sunday, Sal was home. The maid came into the *Ping Pong* room upstairs where we sat and served us with thick, creamy and delicious almond shakes, flavoured with rose water and cooled with crushed ice. By then, summer had arrived in Hyderabad, introducing clear skies, bright sunshine, hot winds, crowded ice parlours, mango and water melon stalls, sugar cane and orange juices, an explosion in the population of stray dogs, marauding bulls, buzzing flies, clamouring crows and soaring kites. Summer blooms replaced spring blossoms with onus on fragrance rather than on colour. Living habits of people had also changed with the season; electric fans came out, mosquito nets went up, hot drinks gave way to fruit juices, the emphasis shifted to out of doors activities, cinema halls drew denser crowds, parks saw an increase in the volume of visitors, children thronged the swings, film songs echoed on loudspeakers in restaurants and tea-houses. Just like the spring, the summer brought with it a distinctly carnival atmosphere, with a scattering of Exhibitions, touring theatres and open-air markets.

"Any progress?" Sal asked me halfway through the drinks.

"In the lives of twenty thousand chauffeurs, barbers, cobblers, carpenters, nurses and engineers from Hyderabad, yes, there is; they all got jobs in the Middle East and are living happily ever after! But in my case, eighty applications have produced six lukewarm invitations to attend interviews, with no guarantees of employment."

"Which could be a rather expensive way of discovering that you're crossing swords with Oxford and Harvard graduates?"

"Precisely."

"What about the recruitment agencies in Bombay?"

"I've heard some hair-raising rumours about their real game, though without any proof."

"Oh? What sort of rumours?"

"According to my informant, *flesh trade*, would you believe? It seems they procure teenage girls from hard-pressed homes here and fill the *harems* of degenerate oil barons there, in return for franchise on manpower. They're each given a quota of vacancies per year, depending upon the number of concubines they supplied, and are allowed to do a roaring trade. They recruit workers left, right and centre, charge them commissions in advance equalling an year's gross pay, often *herd* the *victims* and the *beneficiaries* on board the same plane and go laughing all the way to their own banks! They are okay for bread and butter jobs, but certainly not for careers or for futures."

"And what's happening about the wedding bells?"

"Not much just now. It's something I'm determined to avoid. I don't want to get hooked to a rich heiress, make lots and lots of babies and then turn into a henpecked husband, taking orders either from her or from her parents. I've seen it happen to the others and I don't want it to happen to me. I'm not cut out for that sort of life."

"Can't blame you."

"I don't give a toss whether she's a *Hur* from Paradise with large black eyes as described in the Qur'aan, or one of those cross-eyed *ugly sister* as described in fairytales, but I won't touch her money until I'm satisfied that I too can deliver the goods; I too can measure up to expectations; I too can fulfil my end of the bargain. I've already told Papa about it in clear terms."

"What did he say?"

"With his kind of respect for morality and righteousness, he can say only one thing and he already has. He said he would never ask me to do anything which goes against the very principles by which he's taught me to live."

"Good."

"A much safer way out for him would be to sell the house, move into smaller accommodation, get the girls off his hands and then dig in until I find myself a nice job. Sooner or later, I am bound to get both—a nice job and a rich bride."

"Why doesn't he do that?"

"I only recently came to know from Roxana that he's facing a few newfangled problems there as well. Although he doesn't allow anyone to tell him how to run his affairs, he does take her into his confidence sometimes."

"Did she tell you what sort of problems?"

"Yes, with the outbuildings. During Gandpa's time, when he had loads of servants, he got some living quarters constructed for them in the grounds.

Over the years, servants have disappeared but squatters have moved in, some truly homeless, but others nasty customers. Papa doesn't want to throw them out because it goes against the preaching of the Qur'aan. Allah exhorts good Muslims to refrain from turning a fellow Muslim out into the streets, regardless of the academics of right and wrong."

"Which, I guess, is affecting the price?"

"Phenomenally. On current offers, after paying off all his debts, he might be left with just enough to purchase a smaller house in a reasonably decent area, but not enough to finance two weddings as well."

"And if he doesn't sell up quickly and settle the debts, he might not be left with enough even to purchase another house?"

"You said it!"

"Gosh! You do have some big problems, brother!"

"Yes, I know. Only, I wish I hadn't grown old enough to hear about them and worry over them. Maybe that's the reason why Papa never talks about these matters in front of the family. He keeps them to himself and hardly ever allows his worries to reflect in his behaviour or in his attitude. One heck of a reason for having a Coronary Thrombosis, don't you think?"

"Well, look, " he said, letting out a deep sigh, "Except taking the squatters to court with the help of my dad, provided your old man lets me, there isn't much else I can do to help. But as far as an immediate income is concerned, a sound proposition has come my way in which I thought you might be interested. You won't get rich on it, you won't build careers with it, you won't find rich brides because of it, but you will certainly be able to keep the wolf from the door for as long as you want to.

"What is it?"

"Have you ever heard of an exam called the *Aligarh Matriculation?*"

"Only briefly. Why?"

"It's a high School examination conducted by the Aligarh Education Board. For sitting it, there are no restrictions on age nor are there any requirements to produce proof of full time attendance in a state registered school."

"What's the catch?"

"So far, the qualification did not lead to higher education because it wasn't recognised by colleges, universities or even employers, and hence wasn't worth the paper on which it was written. But as of now, this situation has changed."

"In what way?"

"Under the new rules, Aligarh Matriculation Certificate holders are to be treated the same as Secondary School Certificate holders, both for higher education as well as for jobs. This means, all those thousands of youngsters who got stuck at high school for one reason or the other now get the chance to sit the exams without being entered by recognised schools. All they need is a little bit of coaching by way of home tuition, and most of them are prepared to pay handsomely for the help."

"I see. "

"I have a list of pupils who desperately need this help, and I can give you more names in due course. My cousins, who gave me this list for want of time, are also university graduates like you, stuck for jobs and kicked around. But now, they're making as much money from tuitions as you'd be in Trombay's Oil Refineries, or so they tell me. The guys I'm referring to are Anwar Ali and Akbar Ali, and I think you know them both."

"Yes, I do, though not intimately. They were senior to me by two years."

"Well, what do you say? It's a decent vocation and there's plenty of money to be made. Any day, a heck of a sight better than sorting mail at the I.G.P.s."

"Aren't there some moral issues at stake here? I mean, all said and done, I'm not qualified to teach, am I? I don't have the necessary training."

"You don't have to split hair. We're only talking about some help at home. If the parents had some time and some knowledge, they would give it to their kids for free."

"What about the fees? How do I know how much to charge and on what basis?"

"The list does contain some guidelines about it. You can either follow them verbatim, or make up your own mind as you go along. You can charge some of them more than the others; you can coach for free where there are mitigating circumstances; you can drop those who aren't easily accessible; you can do what you like. Take the list home, read it, talk it through with Shabana or sleep on it for a while. There's absolutely no rush and you don't have to decide right away."

I took the list, thanked him, promised to phone him in a couple of days and returned home, rolling everything he said over and over in my mind, trapped between opposing extremities of worldly needs and religious doctrines; between bread on the table and reward in the hereafter; between money in the pocket and mnna in heaven; between pangs of hunger and pangs of conscience. Sal was quite right in saying that it was better than sorting mail at the I.G.P.s—anything was—and if I could really begin to make as much money in tuitions as I could in the oil refineries, most of our problems could be solved at a stroke. We could afford a square meal a day and some decent clothes; we could start repaying our debts; I could break the financial shackles on my parents' legs and set them free; I could save up for investing in my future too by taking a few calculated risks, and who knows, we might even find good bridegrooms for the girls who preferred their breeding over their bank balances; their inner qualities over their outer ornaments; their ethics over their economics; willing to marry them for what they were rather than what they brought. All that was possible, and yet, somehow, I felt uneasy about the proposition. My sense of reluctance had more to do with my conscience than with rules and regulations. For one thing, I was neither qualified nor trained to teach. Having a sound academic background and knowledge of the subjects was not enough; good aeronautic engineers do not make good pilots any more than good referees make good boxers. Besides, imparting knowledge in return for financial rewards, and basing the quantum of those rewards on the circumstances of pupils rather than their needs, went against the preaching of the Qur'aan. There is nothing wrong with it; all teachers work for a living, but their dealings are with the school and not with the pupils. They do not decide whom to teach and whom not to because of their financial standing, the distance of their abode, the colour of their skin, the veracity of their faith, the choice of their hairstyle, the coordination of their apparel!

I got home in time for lunch. Shabbu had made a delicious fish curry with tamarind, which was the only non-vegetarian dish we could afford. As usual, we sat around the dining table, and as usual, Rox served the meal, deciding at the point of a ladle who should eat what and how much. That day, only a head and a tail of the fish appeared on my plate—the head later on swapped for a succulent cutlet with an indulgent smile. One cardinal rule in our house was never to let the dining room conversation dwell upon topics that were likely to ruin the appetite. Food, Papa always insisted, was a very special benediction from Allah and must be consumed both with relish and gratitude. Our chats, therefore, tended to centre around how sweet the mangoes were that season; what contribution does ginger and garlic make to our digestive system; why should burping not be considered a sign of contentment rather than a show of bad manners; or around other food-related topics, preferably with a religious flavour, such as the significance of oblations; how to consecrate game on the spot; how did making vermicelli pudding on *Eid-ul-*

Fitr day enter into our native Islamic traditions. Completely shutting myself off to the controversy still raging in my head regarding Sal's proposal, I too made a solid contribution to the pleasant conversation and concentrated on eating alone.

A couple of days later, Papa asked me to see him in his room. When I went in, his usual cheerful mien was replaced by a ponderous one, clearly indicating that he had something heavy on his mind. Without mincing his words, he told me that the grocer around the corner from whom we bought our provisions had refused to supply them on credit any longer until the previous bills were settled, and Mamma had already cautioned him that her storeroom was nearly empty, with rice stocks down to the last two kilograms. He had, no doubt, borrowed a small hand loan from one of his friends to tidy him over for the time being, but he would not be able to do the same again and again. He also confirmed what Rox already told me that the house, together with the land, was in the hands of property brokers to sell, but there were no offers in the pipeline. Most investors knew we were in serious financial trouble and were simply waiting for the right moment to go for the kill. The bank being one of them, the manager was quietly tightening the financial noose on Papa's neck to speed up his capitulation. On top of all that, one of the squatters occupying the largest outhouse was causing him grave concern by attempting to build an extension to the premises without permission. Apparently, he was also encouraging some of the slum dwellers to set up their shacks on our land and move in.

"So, what're our options, Papa? Are we going to stop them, or are we going to let them do what they like and get away with it?"

"Civil litigation happens to be a long drawn affair and damned expensive too. Anwar Khan knows I'm vulnerable and is getting up to all sorts of mischief."

"Who's Anwar Khan? The one you didn't want to throw out on compassionate grounds?"

"No, that was Badr-ud-din. After he fell ill, his sons came from Bidar and took him back. That's when my problems began, really. He was loyal and had kept the entire area under his firm control, without letting anyone trespass."

"Is money the only thing which is holding you up from taking action against Anwar Khan?"

"No, not the only thing. I don't want to rub him on the wrong side right now and escalate hostilities. Besides, we have two young girls in the house whose safety could easily be at risk from such riffraff."

"Is there something I can do to help?"

"The property broker thinks that, if we divide the site into smaller plots, he might be able to get rid of them more quickly and more easily."

"Do you need a hand with the measuring and the dividing?"

"Yes. At least, we can make a start. If we get rid of even one plot, it would be enough to ease my cash flow problems."

"Do you also need a hand with tackling Anwar Khan?"

"What can you do? I don't want you entering into frays with people like that."

"I wasn't exactly thinking of entering into frays with him, Papa. Sal said he would be able to tackle them legally through his dad, if you wanted him to. We can settle the legal costs later on, after you've sorted out everything else. We can make a start on it too. "

After giving it a brief thought, he agreed. In spite of the grim plight of his finances, far worse than they had ever been before, I did not breath a word to him about the tuitions. Before making it known to anyone, I wanted to fully satisfy myself both about the morality as well as the viability of the proposition. It was not the sort of time to raise his hopes and dash them, even though the conversation did strongly persuade me to consider its positive aspects more keenly than the negative ones. For the time being, leaving it at that, I picked up the measuring tape and the clipboard from his table and followed him.

Before embarking upon his disastrous ventures, Papa had, as usual, planned ahead and got a brick wall raised around the house, setting aside a small plot of land for Mamma's garden, with two access points to the yard, both doors firmly kept under lock and key. Whilst on the positive side, such a partition did ensure us complete privacy and security, on the negative side, it also prevented us from finding out what was happening in our own backyard, unless someone from our house made a special trip to go and check. So far, on account of my preoccupations with my education, that someone had invariably been Papa, as the ladies were never allowed to cross over because of the *Purdah* restrictions as well as the presence of squatters. That was how nasty characters like Anwar Khan had been able to trespass into our premises and run amok without any restraints. Hence, even if I did not wish to have any confrontations with the riffraff, I made up my mind to visit the yard more often in the future than I had in the past and let my presence be felt, instead of leaving it forever unattended, as if it did not belong to us.

After stepping on the derelict site for the fist time in many years, looking at the rough blades of knee-deep grass that had covered every inch of the land; the overgrown bines of hybrid grapes supported by the crumbling trellises; the rust laden winch and pulleys over the so-called *lotus pond,* which was once used for irrigating the wines but now lying idle; prurient street dogs chasing bitches on heat; lazy hogs from the slums rolling in the mud; mosquitoes and tadpoles breeding in puddles of stagnant rain water; children from the neighbourhood playing hide and seek underneath the dangerously encumbered trellises; I felt a sharp constriction in my heart. Measuring the site *in situ* while it lay abandoned in such a pitiful state of wanton neglect and then breaking it into smaller plots seemed to me like a job for the professionals, either the estate agents or their surveyors, but realising that nothing moves without money, I kept quiet and concentrated on helping Papa.

It took us two hours, a couple of tumbles in the brushwood, some scratches and bruises resulting from them, not to mention the muddy clothes and gallons of sweat, we somehow managed the measurements near enough to divide the plots. All through our hard toils, I noticed we were being constantly watched by the dwellers of the clandestine shacks that had sprung up all over the place, without a single soul coming forward to lend us a hand. As neutral as the hogs soaking in the mud; as engrossed in themselves as the dogs chasing the bitches and as proliferate as the mosquitoes breeding in puddles, they all just stood and stared. But then, why should they help, anyway? We were not partners in the same venture but were opposed to each other; we were a threat to them and our interests were in conflict. If they could, they would have probably done their utmost to get together and prevent us from doing what we were, but only a lack of guts stopped them.

Round about four p.m., just as the sun began its downward journey, shadows slanted, dogs finished with the bitches, wild birds roosting in the thickets homed in one by one with food in their beaks, the hot afternoon wind gradually turned into much cooler and fresher gusts of evening breeze, Papa got called away by Rox in order to answer an important phone call. As soon as his back turned, all those children who had disappeared from sight on our arrival there to play some other game somewhere else returned in a big bunch and resumed the hide and seek underneath the shady trellises, breaking into loud bursts of laughter and screams from time to time. Ignoring their distractions, minding my business, not even looking at them, I rearranged all the loose sheets of paper containing the measurements in the right order, carefully clipped them together, gathered up the tools we had used for the job and headed towards the communicating door.

Half way through, I felt some sort of a magnetic pull slow me down and then force me to stop. I stopped and looked around. The only objects in motion being the children engrossed in play, my attention automatically shifted on them. But after a while, my roving eyes came into contact with the player in the blindfold and froze. For one thing, she was not a child but a teenager. For the other, in sharp contrast to the rest of the children, she had an incredibly fair complexion. Because of the blindfold, she was unable to see me, but I could see her clearly. She had dark hair that were woven into two plaits and tied at the bottom with red ribbons. Her flawless features were absolutely breathtaking! As a result of physical exercise from running around in the sun, blood had drawn to her pretty face and flushed the rosy cheeks. The tender lips, as delicate as the petals of the rose she wore in her hair, had turned red, presumably from chewing *betel-rolls*. Clad in a white *Shalwar,* a white *Khamis* and pink *Dopatta,* she was devastatingly beautiful. I had never seen anyone as beautiful as that in all my life. She looked like some sort of a celestial being who had somehow strayed into our grounds straight from Paradise, or had deliberately wafted in. A HUR on earth, indeed—strangely exuberant, irresistibly vivacious, mystical, magical, caged within a heavenly aura and cast in a divine mould, transmitting signals that turned into invisible chains and tangled in my legs!

I became so impelled by her arresting magnetism, I could not help changing course and heading towards her, as if in a trance, as if in a dream, as if under a spell. Upon noticing me come towards them, the rest of the players put an end to the laughter and screams, hushed up completely and disappeared from sight, leaving her alone, slightly confused by the abrupt cessation in activity, at the mercy of her ears, her sensors, her instincts. She kept using them tenaciously to detect the whereabouts of her playmates, concentrating on every sound, of random footfalls, snapping twigs, gasps of breath, or rustle in the brushwood, changing the direction of her invisible antennas inch by inch, her attention fully focussed upon the only moving object in her near vicinity—me—drowned in amazement, overwhelmed by awe, close enough to see even the tiny beads of perspiration glistening on her flushed face, to pick up the exhilarating perfume of incense emanating from the tufts of her silken hair, to be enveloped by her sensuous body odours mingling in the breeze, her slender hand still stretched out to seek her illusive targets, her dainty fingers getting tantalisingly close to me, her hesitant legs slowly moving towards me, cutting down on distance, bridging the gulf, setting me ablaze, accelerating my blood flow, making my heart flutter like a wild bird caught in a hunter's trap! Throwing manners to the wind, forsaking the principles and disciplines of a lifetime within the batting of an eyelid, abandoning each and every one of my self imposed restraints, I stood still, deliberately waiting for the fumbling hand to get closer, to concede a touch, to unleash the avalanche locked inside me and let it come bursting out!

When it got within a hair's breadth of me, I broke out of every moral barrier and held it for a flash of a moment; felt the opulence of marble and the softness of velvet at the same time; felt an electric charge rock me; felt currents of heat travel through the length of my body; felt an invisible stranglehold choke my breath; felt the crest of a tidal wave sweep me off my feet and take me away into unknown distances, into voids, into vacuums, into puffs of cloud! Realising that something was wrong; that the flames she touched had to have some viable explanation; that the noisy gasp which escaped my mouth needed a rational interpretation; that the breathtaking hush by which she stood surrounded could not be taken at face value, she broke into a honey-soaked smile first, revealing a perfect set of pearl-like teeth, pulled away the blindfold and emerged into the light. Together with it, somewhere inside the secret recesses of my mind, a full moon cast off its veil of clouds and woke up; somewhere in the galaxy, planets collided and exploded; somewhere on the earth, gardens of bliss bloomed and swung. Her opulent eyes, gleaming with lustre, glittering like gem stones, piercing the gullets of shadows, slicing through the darkness, setting off flares, chasing fireflies, scattering stars, settled on my face briefly, widened with surprise, drowned in moisture, vacillated from shyness, drooped with modesty, took shelter behind the welter of her lashes to escape the heat of my gaze and finally forsook me. Soon, her playmates came to her rescue, surrounded her from all sides, cordoned her off, prevented her from being visually trespassed, being covertly adored, being secretly worshipped, being inaudibly eulogised! Cast inside the protective pentacle they had formed, travelling with the grace of a crescent on the wheels of rain clouds, she gradually receded into the distance and disappeared from my field of vision completely.

Who was she? Where did she come from? Where did she go away? What was the purpose of her brief excursion into our desolate territory? What were the mysterious messages concealed in her eyes? What was the language in which her enigmatic entelechy conversed with me? If I climbed on board her chariot of dreams drawn by the unicorns of bliss, which unfamiliar destination would she take me away to? To which distant paradise did her abode belong; whose life blood was surging in her veins; what was her secret; what was her definition; what was her connotation? Would that brief encounter between us transcend into a longer lasting bond? Was that wordless exchange of feelings a propitious prologue to the story of our lives, being written by the Scribe of Destinies? Was her name enmeshed in the complicated fate lines on my palm? If we did meet again, on which celestial plain would our next encounter take place?

The chain of my pleasant thoughts abruptly shattered by my sister's urgent summons, I woke up from my reverie with a start, responded to the summons, reluctantly moved away from the soil on which her pretty feet had left their indelible prints; from the breeze still laden with the perfume of her silken locks and her fragrant breath; from the dereliction still singing odes to her glamour! After emerging on our side of the wall, and while locking up the door, I could not help surrendering to the dismal feeling that I was locking away something mine on hostile territory; I was forsaking a precious treasure to the mercy of bandits; I was casting away my soul in that haunting wilderness and taking my body too far from it; I was drowning my raft in the middle of doldrums and throwing away the oars; I was forcing myself awake from an unrepeatable dream before it came to an end!

Suddenly scared by the unknown direction towards which my crazy heart was dragging me, reminding myself of the chains of loyalty in which I was shackled; of my responsibilities to my parents and my duties to my sisters; I rushed into the bathroom, cooled underneath the torrents of a cold shower the fierce fires of passion raging inside me, changed into clean clothes, went into my room, spread the mat on the floor and stood on it to pray. The blazing sun, hurtling down the crimson horizon to make room for the impending dusk, had not yet soaked up the daylight. Just in time for *ASR*—a crucial moment for remembering Allah; a moment of introspection cast between the brightness of day that was ending and the darkness of night that was beginning; between good and evil; between cleanliness and filth; between self restraint and self surrender; I offered *Namaaz* first, then repeated the *Surah az-taghfaar* one hundred times on the rosary, and finally, raising my hands heavenwards, addressing myself to Allah from the bottom of my heart, I begged Him to lead me out of temptation; to give me the strength to stay on the right course through the maze of perdition; to be a loyal son and a dutiful brother first before being a steadfast partner; to drive out of my erring mind all those thoughts which could deter me from my avowed goals; to cleanse the impurities with which my conscience was tainted; to make me raise my eyes only upon the virtuous; to seek only the purest; to surrender only to the upright; to expend my energies only in deeds of honour; in deeds that would make my parents proud of me; that would give my sisters strength in their love for me; that would rest the souls of our dear departed in peace and in tranquillity!

My commitment thus regenerated, my resolve thus reinforced, my faith thus re-asserted, I felt like a new man, enjoyed my supper more than I had enjoyed the dinner although the latter was merely a left over from the former, entered into a fierce competition with Rox in cracking *Birbal's* jokes, lost it to her, came back to my room, offered the final *Namaaz* of the day in a less ponderous mood, sought a few earthly rewards on top of the heavenly ones— to help me succeed in bringing home our daily bread without breaking moral codes; to help me help Papa with his problems and preoccupations; to help me build a future for all of us with earned money rather than with borrowed money. After that, I switched off the ceiling lamp, switched on the spot light, which enabled me to lay in bed and read and sat up with Mary Coreli's *Sorrows of Satan* … .

CHAPTER (4)

Having heard from Papa about the real gravity of our plight, the ultimatum he was given by the grocer regarding future credit, his having had to resort to the humiliation of borrowing hand loans from his friends, and having seen with my own eyes the pitiful state of neglect into which our most precious material asset was abandoned, I made a few justifiable compromises with myself. Allah had blessed us with a loving and supportive family, provided us with a decent shelter, ensured us our daily bread in our own backyard, and yet, for want of simple management skills, we were throwing away everything, borrowing loans, paying interests, running up credit bills and missing meals, which was all wrong. While Qur'aan stipulates restraints, it does not encourage fanaticism. Muslims are entrusted with the responsibility of ensuring the well being of their families, next in importance only to worship. A man who neglects his family neglects Allah; a man who fails his family fails Allah; a man who does not light a candle in his own house is not welcome to light a candle in His house; a man who does not feed and clothe his family according to his means stands naked in the eyes of Allah. It was, therefore, of primary importance that we used our discretion in our choice of principles; used our good judgement in their application and our conscience in their adherence. Nothing can possibly be wrong with imparting knowledge in return for material rewards, so long as the knowledge imparted is righteous, the manner of imparting it is competent and the rewards sought are reasonable.

Encouraged by such positive thoughts, I rearranged Sal's list of addresses according to my knowledge of the streets where they were located, got ready quite early in the morning, had a full breakfast, sought Allah's blessings, got on the bike and set off on my crucial mission, without breathing a word to anyone about it out of sheer expedience. Even though Sal had obtained the list from his own cousins—and knowing him as well as I did—I was quite confident that he would never have put it in my hands without being sure about it himself, I still decided to play it safe. We were a desperate family struggling for survival, and in our precarious circumstances, nothing could be more cruel than raising their hopes and then dashing them. At that moment in time, I was merely exploring an opportunity. If it really turned out to be as good as thought, I would not even dream of making a start without the blessings of my parents; without bringing a basket of sweets from *Hamidi* confectioners; without it being consecrated by Mamma before we touched it; without its being accompanied by fresh clusters of *Chambeli* for Shabbu and Rox; without conceding few promises of nose studs and bangles to the latter! The sun was hotter than usual that morning; the wind was lesser than normal; the strain of pedalling the old bike through the traffic and the crazy ups and downs of our city roads squeezed every ounce of liquid out of my system; sweat drenched my body and soaked my clothes; my throat parched from thirst and the dazzling sunlight blurred my vision; but I kept going thinking about all those *cycle rickshaw* lads who not only had their own weight to cope with but also the weight of the *rickshaw* as well as passengers travelling in it, in the knowledge that if they did not soak their clothes and drench their brows, there would be no fire in their ovens that night; no rice in the saucepans; no milk for the baby; no cosy bed to stretch in; no kisses and cuddles from the wife; no hope for the morrow! That one inspiring thought alone kept recharging my flat batteries; rejuvenating my spent energies; daubing my wet face; slaking my prickly throat; clearing the blurring from my vision.

By the time the sun turned the corner and began its descent, its fiery rays retracted, the heat rescinded, the shadows slanted and the breeze cooled, I too completed all nine calls on my list with propitious results. From talking to pupils as well as their parents, I realised that there was definitely a demand for the service; youths of both sexes, mostly over sixteen and under twenty, too old to start school all over again but too young to give up hope, write off the prospects of improving their lot, bettering their future, getting admission in vocational courses, venturing abroad, competing for jobs, all because of not having crossed the vital hurdle of high school graduation, were crying out for help. The door of opportunity was there in front of them, and the key of hope to unlock it in their fists, but what they did not know was how to turn the key. Amongst them were girls with fiancées already abroad, lads with *green card* holders in the States and *sponsors* in Britain, contacts in industry or capital for trade, ideas of their own or the ability to explore other people's ideas, some filled with profound regrets for having wasted their irreplaceable childhood in trivialities, and some who had never had a decent childhood but were more than willing to make up for it, all in desperate need of coaching for the exams, prepared to invest in their future, in terms of time, effort as well as money. The thought that, apart from making an honest living, I would be able to help a new generation of youngsters caught up in predicaments not too dissimilar to our own, gave me renewed impetus to look at the heaven sent opportunity with a greater resolve than I had in the morning.

That evening, I came home blessing dear Sal from the bottom of my heart for his concern and his sincerity, thinking about me when the chips were down, putting the proposition my way just when I desperately needed a break like that, something with which I could cope, with confidence, with competence and with a clear conscience, something I could plan on my own, could expand or scale down according to changes in my circumstances, hopefully making enough money to keep the fire in the oven going; keep the rice in the saucepan boiling; keep the bangles on Rox's wrists shingling without our having to take a mouthful from the grocer, without Papa having to go around with a begging bowl, perhaps even get the site cleared of weeds, get it measured by qualified surveyors, get the riffraff out with the help of solicitors and keep them out. The possibilities were limitless, and for a dreamer like me with such fertile imagination, I could go on imagining without limits. I did too; sang a romantic *Ghazal* or two in my discordant voice throughout the shower (to the heckles of Rox coming from kitchen, if I might be allowed to add!), washed off the grime of sweat and dust on my body, changed, fumigated my room with the refreshing fragrance of jossticks and, having thus rendered unto Caesar whatever belonged to Caesar, I settled down to rendering unto Allah what belonged to Allah, rendered it with my *NAMAAZ* and followed by my solemn thanksgivings.

After that, I phoned Sal to apprise him of my progress. Just back from the courts, he too was anxiously waiting for my call. I told him whatever transpired in course of the long and tiresome day, including my first impressions as well as my renewed enthusiasm towards the project resulting from them.

"Even though I haven't made any firm commitments but only promised to go back next week to finalise matters, I want you to know that I'd like very much to go ahead with it," I said.

"What's stopping you?" he asked.

"Only two things. One is, what happens next? And the other is, how much do I charge?"

"The answer to your first question is that, I have a second list of no less than eighty candidates and increasing day by day. By the time you covered them all, you'll have so many referrals, you'd be passing them back to me to help others in a similar situation like yourself."

"No kidding!"

"No kidding. As far as fees are concerned, it's up to you. Where possible, I'll try and jot down on my list an outline of the parents' financial circumstances. If not, you can find it out for yourself. In this vocation, Allah is your boss and your conscience is your guide. In the case of some, you might want to insist upon the dictum 'value for money,' and in the case of others, you might want to do it for free. Like they say, horses for the courses. It's your show and you run it the way you want to."

"Great! That would suit me just fine."

"Got a pen and paper on hand?"

"Yep, shoot."

Giving me more names, he asked me to go head with finalising the tuitions as well as the fee without any qualms, treating it like a full time job at least for one year, with decent, regular and reliable earnings. It was good enough for me; his word was good enough. It seemed the time had come for breaking the news; bringing home some sweets for *Fateha*; setting Papa's mind at ease about our immediate needs; assuring him of some solid help from me towards his financial problems; towards sorting out the site as well as handling the riff raff with a firm grip, but above all, buying for Rox a second set of bangles from the *lovers arcade*! I made up my mind to bring all those goodies next evening and relaxed. Sticking to our routine of spending the pleasant summer evenings out of doors, she had sprinkled water on the lawn, laid out the chairs, fed her peacock and was sorting out Papa's *hukka* when all of us emerged and sat down. The evening had turned quite pleasant; the departing sun had left its embers smouldering underneath the ashen crusts of clouds; a steady flow of breeze was blowing in laden with the fragrance of *Chambeli* thriving so well on its trellis; the fresh buds waiting to be picked and threaded—yet another chore for Rox, which she enjoyed doing the most. Mamma triggered off her pet conversation centred around her other heart throb *Chambeli*—the white cow; how much milk she was giving every day and how much money she made from merchandising the surplus stocks, completely omitting to mention how much money she had cost so far in maintenance. I sat listening to her, a load off my mind, building castles in the air, making plans on how to spend the money before I even earned it; how to organise my list of priorities; in which bank to open my account; how many hours per week to set aside for tuitions and how much time to devote on continuing with job hunting; whether to resume the job hunting at all or to pack it up for good.

As I sat rolling all those pleasant thoughts in my mind, a faint noise in the distance distracted my attention. It was only the neighbourhood children playing with the children from our outhouses, laughing and screaming as they were on a prior occasion, but the memory of that pretty girl in the blindfold entered my head at once, took charge of all my thoughts and threw out everything else from it. Her dark hair, the wild tufts scattered on her face, the intoxicating fragrance of incense emanating from them, the two loose plaits tied with red ribbons and undulating like snakes at play, the rose tucked in the clip looking as salubrious as the face it adorned, the almond-shaped eyes housing the large and lustrous pupils afloat in the glistening fluids of life, the tender lips wallowed in red from chewing a *BETEL-ROLLS,* the set of perfect teeth looking like succulent pips cushioned inside a ripe pomegranate, her gorgeous smile setting off glares and storms, her graceful body clad in simple clothes, her vivacious personality, her enigmatic aura, her matchless exuberance, packed up and tucked away in the brevity of a dream and yet as abounding as the imagination of a poet, they all got together and crashed into my head, demolishing every one of my restraints and refusing to go away. I could no longer sit there with my family, with my own blood, with my kith and kin, enjoying their conversation, sharing their peace, taking part in their wisecracks, breathing in the fragrance of *CHAMBELI* and breathing out the freshness of dusk. I had to get up and go looking for her, whether underneath the decrepit trellises of our vineyard, or on the floating puffs of clouds, or in the copious distances of the horizon, or on the canopies of the faroff hills, or in the opaque contours of paradise, riding on her chariot of dreams, racing away her unicorns of bliss!

Giving Papa a lame excuse that I had dropped my Parker pen in the yard while measuring the plots—my first white lie to my own father in an entire lifetime—I borrowed the key to the door and, my heart throbbing, my breath bated, my mind drowned in a spate of hopes, I opened the lock with a trembling hand and slipped to the other side, without making the slightest noise to ensure that the children did not suspend their play and go into hiding, including her, assuming she was also there with them. But too engrossed in their blithesome preoccupations, they did not even notice me. Walking on tiptoes, I reached the spot where our unforgettable encounter had taken place; where I had held bliss by the hem and tugged it towards me; where I had touched the acme; where I had taken the veil off the face of perfection and marvelled at the limits of Divine excellence; where I had witnessed how our dreams could sometimes blend with reality and then become immortal! The hallowed ground on which she had stood was still there, untouched and undisturbed, bearing the indelible contours of her footprints, purified by her contact, clinging to her mementos with fondness, wearing her coronets with pride, waiting for her return with hope, reproducing her images with fervour, wallowing in her memory with passion. Bending upon my knees, I touched her footprints, picked up a fistful of soil from the dents, kissed it, stroked it, and then let it flow through my fingers like cascades of expectations.

At that particular moment, when my emotions were trapped in the grip of an uncompromising whirlwind; my mind was getting ready to wear the shackles of lifelong captivity; my heart was succumbing to the onslaught of an unfamiliar storm; an invisible hand had picked up its quail to scribble a new presage on my forehead; a gentle whiff of breeze blew in from somewhere, brought with it a priceless gift and left it clinging to my face, suddenly flooding my inner seclusion with a strangely stupefying fragrance; lifting me up into the clouds; setting me afloat on the beams of moonlight; sprinkling dew upon all the burgeons of my innate garden and ushering into it a new spring! It was the pink scarf which she had wrapped around her eyes like a blindfold, into which the twinkling beads of her perspiration had trickled and soaked; the flush of her cheeks had inalienably transferred; her enigmatic ambience had infused; her scent unalterably trapped, and which had, therefore, become such a part and parcel of her pith and core, I felt as though it was her cheek brushing against mine; her breath smothering my face; her eyes scanning my inner entelechy; her soul bonding itself to mine. Holding it tightly in my worshipful hands; exalting it from a piece of chiffon into a celestial benediction; treating it like a parchment from heaven proclaiming our bonds sacrosanct; brought to me by the bewildered *Hurs*— bewildered by the intensity of my passion, the extent of my capitulation, the entirety of my surrender. Making sure I was not being watched by spoilsports, idle minds and wagging tongues, I carefully treasured it in my pocket, as a tangible reminder of an intangible moment, as a visual emblem of an invisible image, as a material link with an immaterial longing. It was going to remain with me right through this lifetime and the next, until its owner came wearing floral garbs and pledged herself to me forever and forever!

I had no idea for how long I stood there, sliding my thought buds on strings of gold, but at some stage dusk began to take over from daylight and thin out the brightness. Before the Call of *Mo'azzam* for Men of Faith to congregate and offer worship echoed on the loudspeakers and altered our priorities, I stopped thinking and decided to concentrate on finding out who she was, where did she live, why was she not there that evening to dazzle me with the glare of her eyes, to bewitch me with the magic of her smiles, to ensnare me in the tangles of her looks, wearing the blindfold, seeking the hiders, gathering the strays, guiding the wayfarers and capturing the targets. So, with the best of intentions, without counting the real cost of my folly, I spotted the oldest girl at play and signalled her to come to me. That bit of harmless intrusion into their activities abruptly put an end to their fun and frolics, stopped their laughter, muffled their screams and hushed them up. They gathered together in one bunch, each holding the other's hand and thus gaining strength from proximity, from contact, from unity - they against me—as though I was some sort of an evil tyrant who had gone there to castigate them for having a good time. But in a big rush to find some quick answers to the questions exploding in my head before the sound of *Azaan* echoed from the mosque, I ignored the kids and beckoned to the older girl once again.

She came, walking in slow, hesitant and reluctant strides. Around fifteen or sixteen, clad in somewhat dirty clothes, the pouting chest barely covered by the soiled and crumpled *Dopatta,* giving out an odious odour of sweat and grime, of foul breath, of unkempt hair, dark in complexion, hostile in disposition, she defiantly stood facing me with a querulous look.

"What?" she said.

"What's your name?" I asked her, trying to be polite.

"Why?" she demanded in a rude tone.

"Do you know who I am?"

"Everybody knows who you are! What do you want from me, anyway?"

"Why are you talking to me with a chip on your shoulder, eh? I didn't tell you off; I didn't shout at you, I didn't stop you from playing. Cool it, girl! We don't have to be at odds with each other, do we?"

"But you did call me here, didn't you? So, what do you want?"

"I wanted to ask you about the girl in the blindfold yesterday. Remember?"

"Why? What has she got to do with you?"

"Nothing in particular."

"Then why do you want to know who she is?"

"Well," I said, foolishly showing her the scarf, "I found this here. I know it belongs to her and I just want to return it. That's all."

"Give it here. Give it to me, I'll return it."

So saying, she grabbed the scarf and tried to run. But as I had no intentions of letting go of it so easily, I tightened my grip and tried to wrench it off her by force. Unfortunately for her, being stronger and far more determined to keep hold of the scarf, I must have given it a much harder tug than she expected; for, losing her balance, she tripped over and toppled straight on to me. However, in view of the undesirability of physical contact with a member of the opposite sex, especially with the time for *Namaaz* approaching fast, I hurriedly pushed her away from me. Staggering on unsteady feet as a result of that unceremonious shove, she lost her balance once again, fell on the ground, got back to her feet, landed a nasty slap on my face with all her strength, broke into needless sobs and ran towards her folks who stood in the background watching the scene, followed by the entire bunch of her friends and siblings, everyone screaming and weeping as if the skies had begun to fall upon their heads!

Suddenly, a very simple error of judgement escalated into a crisis of major proportions. I had no idea what conversation exchanged between her and the grown ups and what sort of blame she impugned me with, but just as the Call of the *Moazzan* began to echo on the loudspeakers, I noticed Mr. Khan take over from her, signal her to go inside the outhouse, pick up a nasty looking bamboo cane lying nearby and head in my direction, unambiguously demonstrating his intentions to castigate me for my uncivilised behaviour towards the girl, whoever she be. At such a critical juncture, regardless of how important it was for me to put aside our earthly quarrels and run to bow to my maker, I could not run, I did not dare run, I could not afford to abandon the battlefield in the wake of such truculence, such audacity and such a menacing gesture. It occurred to me that skipping the *NAMAAZ* for the time being and catching up with it later on in my room was a better option to take rather than show signs of weakness to a man whose very presence on our land was an inexcusable trespass. So I held my ground, waiting for him to do whatever it was that he intended to do, either let loose his nasty tongue on me, or go one step further and use his cane.

"Nice one, Mr. Quraishi," he began, electing to do the former rather than the latter, his breath smelling even fouler than his daughter's from the adulterated liquor he was consuming, his speech badly slurred and his gait unsteady, "Just because you belong to the manor and we dwell in the slums, you are a man of letters and we are dumb illiterates, you go to work in made to measure *Sherwanis* and we get up our cycle rickshaws in smelly rags, your friends come to visit you in cars and we don't have any friends, your sisters go around in *purdah* and our daughters run around bare faced, you don't think we have any honour and self respect, do you? If I manhandled your sisters the way you assaulted my daughter, I have no doubt your father would gun me down like a dog. What did she do to you to be treated like that, like filth, like a pig, eh? She happens to have the same red blood in her veins as you do, sir! If you cut her, she bleeds; if you kick her, she cries; if you tickle her, she giggles; if you fuck her, she gets pregnant. She is just an ordinary fifteen-year-old girl like all the other fifteen-year-old girls under the sun, trying to lead as decent a life as her father could afford to give her by the sweat of his brow! She could do without the affronts and the humiliations, thank you very much! So, in the future, kindly keep your hands and legs to yourself instead of using them on those who cannot defend themselves. On this occasion, as this happens to be your first invasion into our privacy and your first assault on our integrity, I'll let you off with a simple verbal warning. But if it happens again, you'll have to deal with my stick and not with my tongue. So, watch where you tread. Have I made myself clear?"

After delivering that lengthy, acrid, asinine warning in a reverberating voice, he gave a demonstration of how good he was at the use of his stick and went away. I did not open my mouth, did not defend myself, did not try to apportion blame. I had no wish to convert that monologue into a dialogue in case he stopped to ask me what started it all, nor had any intentions of dragging that poor girl into the slush. I did not know who she was, what was she doing on our premises, what was her connection with those children. Although I doubted it very much, there was always the chance that she could turn out to be his own daughter, or a stepdaughter, or a close relative. Without making sure of it, I did not wish to even remotely associate her with the dispute. Apart from that, if the scarf crept into the conversation and he demanded it to be surrendered to him, it would not be as easy for me to put him off as it was to put off his daughter. Even if he so much as asked to see it, I would have a big problem declining him without compounding the argument. To me, that scarf was no longer a piece of rag to be looked at and cast off. It had suddenly become more important than life, more valuable than all the treasures of King Solomon put together, more sacrosanct than any amulets and talismans, next in importance only to Allah's written word. It contained her perfume, it had rubbed on her skin, touched her eyelids, her brow and her nose, soaked in her sweat, run through her locks, it had been tied and untied with her own hands. Everything about it was not just precious but irreplaceable. I needed to keep it somewhere hidden, under Allah's protective eye, in the safekeeping of His Angels, guarded by my life, looked after with resolve, watched over with care. So, without giving a toss about Mr. Khan's nasty innuendos and nastier threats, I held my ground until he disappeared into his quarters, presumably to replenish his spent energies with a few more pegs of the booze, returned home, locked up the door, left the bunch of keys in Papa's room and joined the family, desperately hoping the slap dealt on my cheek by the stupid girl had not left any visible marks, such as a bruising, a swelling or a black eye, enough to send Papa's blood pressure soaring, resulting in a heart attack, or a stroke or something even worse.

"Did you find the pen?" he asked, thankfully dwelling upon the least of my worries.

"He seems to have found trouble with a capital T," Rox remarked, knowingly or unknowingly plunging into the worst of them.

"What was all that about?" Mamma asked, reminding me that the tongue unleashed by Khan in such a loud pitch had not missed their attention after all.

"Nothing important, Mamma," I replied in a passive tone, making a bid to nip the matter in the bud, "I noticed some kids picking the *chambeli* buds from our creeper and asked them to be careful with the trellis, but they took offence and complained to Mr. Khan."

"And he took offence and shouted at you?" Papa asked, looking irritated.

"I don't think he knew what he was saying. He's already had one drink too many for an evening."

"Why didn't you take offence too and shout back at him?" Rox snapped, her face beginning to flush with indignation, "That's no way to talk to a gentleman."

"Shut up, Rox," Shabbu intervened swiftly and bridled her mouth, "It takes a gentleman to know a gentleman. Don't expect blood out of brick walls."

"I think you better have a serious chat with Saleem about getting rid of the squatters," Papa added, "Flare ups like that could plunge the entire family into disrepute—with two unmarried girls in the house. Listening to him, it almost sounded as if he was accusing you of fooling around with his daughter."

"Leave it with me, Papa. I'll sort it out with Sal pretty soon."

"And until you do," he said, putting his glasses on and looking at me with a curious expression on his face, "better stop going there, unless you have to. Imputations, true or false, tend to stick like nettles. That's the whole reason why Allah reminds us of the story of Joseph and *Zulayqa* in the Qur'aan so that we guard ourselves against senseless gossip."

"Okay, Papa, I won't," I said and left it at that.

Having missed the congregation for the evening prayers, and with little time left between then and supper, I rushed into the bathroom, performed ablution, went into my room and spread the mat. Suddenly, quite a lot of weight had gone up my mind. For one thing, I had lied to my parents twice in course of the same evening; the mislaid Parker pen was just a fib and so was the *chambeli* picking by the kids. At that rate, I could pretty soon lose respect for myself as well as fall out of Allah's grace. And for the other, my infatuation with that irresistible stranger in the blindfold seemed to be getting the better of me, which made me quite uncomfortable. I did not know who she was; where she came from; what was her story; what were her secrets; was she real or just an apparition; would I see her again or was that only a one off encounter; how often did she grace our vineyard with the magic of her presence; how many more of her footprints were scattered on our soil; how many gusts of breeze that passed through the bines of wild bluebells and bougainvilleas came laden with the exhilarating fragrance of her locks! For a person in my precarious circumstances, my chosen one being merely pretty was not enough; in addition to it, she also had to have wealth as well as *pedigree*. If she was in some way related to Mr. Khan, the stain on her could prove too hard to come off. But if she hailed from a decent family in the neighbourhood, even if not particularly rich, and had only gone there to play with the kids, it would be a different matter altogether. Her beautiful face, her budding youth, her charismatic personality, her irresistible charm and her stunning grace were wealth too, more unique and matchless than all the gems lying concealed on the beds of oceans across the world. Deep down my heart, I knew she was just the sort of bride that Mamma and my sisters were secretly pining to find for me. But with all those restrictions imposed on my movements by Papa, how would I manage to find out anything about her at all, about her family, her antecedents, her horoscopes, her secret identity, her mysterious lineage? How would I find out whom she belonged to and whom she did not belong to—both equally important now?

Much more gruelling than the fibs itself, that was the other weight lying on my chest I needed to alleviate. Hence, after *Namaaz,* I turned to Allah; the best friend any frail human could hope to have; the strongest ally in times of need; the wisest guide in moments of confusion; the brightest light in the midst of darkness; the ever-present support for the unsteady, the ever-sharing partner for the distressed, the ever-giving benefactor to the needy, the ever attentive companion for the lonely. Coming clean, I made Him my confessions, begged His forgiveness, sought His blessings, asked for guidance, described the tussle that was going on in my mind, told Him all about the mysterious seed of *love,* which had taken route inside me, then about the storms by which it was surrounded and about the imminent need of a new spring for it to bloom and to flourish.

Sufficiently relieved by the prayer, and before summons for supper arrived from the dining room, I put away the mat, took out the crumpled scarf from my pocket, sniffed it again, kissed it again, stroked it again, as though it was not a piece of fabric but a part of her, and carefully concealed it inside my chest of draws. What were the chances of my running into her one more time; hearing the melodious sound of her laughter from across the wall; picking up a whiff of her perfume mingled in the breeze; being able to gaze into the helical depths of her mesmeric eyes; hold that elegant hand; feel the opulent texture of her skin; envy her bangles the luxury of embracing her dainty wrist; envy her ring the bliss of clasping her delicate finger; envy the rose its proximity to her beautiful face; envy the ribbons the luck of holding on to her tufts; envy the ground the bonanza of her feet; envy the simple suit she wore the bounty of treasuring her body? What were the chances of my being at the right place at the right time? Of my finding her seated in a chair right next to mine inside a cinema hall? Or travelling in a rickshaw with its curtains open? Or choosing a new set of glass bangles in the *lovers' arcade*? Or selecting some material for a *Gharara* suit to be worn on the next *Eid*? Fifty fifty? One in a million? Next to none? Who knew! It all depended upon strokes of luck, the casting of the dice, the conjugation of the stars, the whims and fancies of Cupid! Or, the veracity of my faith in Allah, of my belief in Destiny, of my reliance on Fate. If He Who brought us together also willed us to remain together, to unite and to multiply, to flourish and to prosper, to stand underneath the cashew tree and feed the nuts to squirrels, walk hand in hand in Mamma's garden picking the jasmines and the rosebuds, launch the Quraishi stock into the next generation, then no power on earth could stop us. And if not, no power on earth would be able to nurture those seedlings of love in us regardless of how expectantly we sowed them! It was as simple of that.

On that conciliatory note, I had my supper, bade good night to everybody and retired to bed early. I had a big day coming up in the morning.

CHAPTER (5)

Some time ago, when I was at the Osmania University, my professor, Abdul Wahaab Bukhari (may Allah bless his soul), had given me a piece of invaluable advice on how to be successful in life which I never forgot. His philosophy was that, "A successful life is full of successful days, and a successful day is full of successful deeds." If we accomplished as simple a target as that, he said success would come rolling to our feet. And to be able to accomplish it, all we needed was to draw up a realistic list of *things to do* before setting out of the house, begin the day with *number one* on the list and try not to go to *number two* until completing *number one*. That way, by the time we return home, we would have a list of *things done* to replace the list of *things to do*, together with the taste of success in our mouths!

Keeping that golden rule in mind, I charted out my tasks for the day in my diary with clear vision, firmly determined not to return home without finalising at least ten tuitions. At the same time, I prepared for myself a self regulatory code of practice too that I intended to follow under all circumstances. According to it, I decided not to take pupils on board without the consent of their parents or their guardians; not to refuse any assignment because of the distance of their houses from mine; not to base my remuneration upon anything other than the extent of coaching undertaken, and as far as possible, not to name a fees nor harangue over it but leave it to the discretion and financial capabilities of their parents, or guardians, or in the case of a self financing pupil, the pupil himself. To that extent, my thinking was based on the *Ahadith* of our prophet in which he does permit a *voluntary Hadyah* as opposed to a *pre-negotiated fee*. It kept my conscience clear, which was very important to me. At the end of each day when I rest my head on the pillow, I wanted to be able to sleep in the knowledge that I had done a day's honest work, and that, the bread my earnings bought for my family was not tainted with greed or with unfairness.

It took me all day, including the best part of the evening, but I managed to finalise eight out of the ten pupils on my list, without making any compromises in my code or sacrificing any of my principles. Two out of the eight pupils were completely non-paying because of their extenuating circumstances, but I did not mind it. Some appeased my conscience while the others appeased my pocket. Frankly, not naming the fees turned out to be an advantage rather than a hitch; most parents I met were decent people and came up with their own offers, some generous and some even lavish, the well-to-do thus more than making up for the not-so-well-to-do. In each and every case, I assessed their standards first and only then decided how much time to spend on whom and how often in the week. At that stage, with an open calendar in front of me, it did not make much of a difference whether they were close by or far off. Later on, after workload built up to an optimum level, I could take into account the distance and travelling time too for my plan of action.

Satisfied—in fact—absolutely delighted with the way things turned out, I finished my rounds in time for the evening prayers, went straight to the *Hamidi confectioners* as planned, purchased two baskets of sweetmeats, one for us and one for Sal, together with a pack of jossticks for *Fateha* and got home. Frankly, the news I had to break to my family was not just great but fantastic. Based upon aggregates, my commitment that day amounted to mere sixteen hours per week but my potential earnings to eight hundred rupees, nearly half the salary of a full time teacher! If work was there—and I had it on reliable authority that it was—I could manage anything up to fifty hours per week; I had the energy as well as the motivation for it. No wonder Sal's cousins were making a bomb and sticking to the job; I could fare even better.

Without telling anybody what it was for, I put the basket of sweetmeats in Mamma's hands and asked her to consecrate it with *Fateha.*

"And what shall I tell Allah it's in aid of?" she asked me with an affectionate smile, "That, you've found a *Zulayqa* of my dreams?"

"Not *your* dreams, Mamma," came a petulant voice from not too far, "*His* dream! But he'll have to wait until Sunday for that."

"Why?" I asked the petulant speaker, somewhat intrigued by the disclosure, "What's happening on Sunday?"

"Your tongue is always wagging like that flour mill up the road, Roxana!" Mamma chided her good-humouredly. "Nonstop."

"Sorry, Mamma," Rox made an instant retraction, "Statement withdrawn!"

"The vice of a statement," my sagacious sister Shabana intervened from inside the kitchen, "lies in its being made."

"All right!" I calmed them down, "But the fact remains that I still don't know what's happening on Sunday."

"And I still don't know what am I supposed to tell Allah about this basket of sweetmeats," Mamma interposed

"Allah knows what it's for, Mamma. He's opened a new door of opportunity for us and we all need to thank Him for it. I'll fill in the details over supper when Papa is also here. *Now,* will somebody tell me what's happening on Sunday?"

"We're going bride-hunting for you!" Rox replied.

"Who's '*we*'?"

"The entire female population of the Quraishi household."

"Really? Where?"

"In Fairy Land! No more questions, please, or I'll be in trouble with Papa."

Unwilling to get her into trouble with Papa, even though it was often he who got into trouble with her for forgetting to turn off the taps after use, mislaying his rosary, misplacing his wallet, dozing off with a live Hukka, I stopped asking her any more questions. But it became obvious that something was happening on Sunday, something quite portentous, which threw my heart into palpitations. In course of the time that could take Mamma to perform the *FATEHA* and for Rox to serve our supper, I went into my room, got rid of the *sherwan*i and fetched that mystifying scarf from the chest of draws, still rampant with its owner's undying perfume, her unending recollections, her unrivalled images, her unsurpassable vestiges. The temptation to plant a kiss on it did entice me, but I resisted it. If the entire female population of the Quraishi household was going on a bride hunting spree for me on Sunday, presumably arranged by Papa with the help of his favourite marriage broker, *Ali Janaab* Moulana Saheb, even before coming to know about the swift progress I had made in becoming a financially productive member of the family, then it seemed to me my *goose* was as good as *cooked*. So, what was the point in my prostrating before a goddess who was destined to grace someone else's shrine; bowing to a queen who was not going to wear my crown or share my throne; building up a thirst without knowing in which neck of the desert lay the oasis? Why raise my hopes, see all those untenable dreams, build all those castles in the air, beguile myself with the unattainable, deceive myself with the improbable, bind myself to the inaccessible, row my raft in the midst of doldrums and let it be capsized, walk blindfold on live cinders and get blisters, wound my heart, scorch my soul, destroy my life? Besides, I did not know anything about her, whether she was for real or a *HUR* from Paradise who had perchance strayed into our yard one hot Sunday afternoon to while away the time; if she was free and available; if her heart belonged to herself and not to somebody else; if her hand was her own and had not yet been pledged away! I did not know if there were any insurmountable barriers in existence between us, any inaccessible distances, and any unbridgeable gulfs!

Rolling all those uneasy thoughts in my mind, I put the scarf back where it belonged, inside the anonymous recesses of a sparsely used piece of furniture, away from view, inaccessible to touch, beyond the scope of recollections. With Rox's summons for supper already reverberating in the dining room, I could not do much else other than respond to them. Besides, the presence of sweetmeats on the dining table would unequivocally declare that someone around that table was a harbinger of blithesome tidings and an explanation would be awaited with considerable impatience by all and sundry. So I rushed. A few moments later, as expected, we did assemble to break bread amidst an air of expectation, every look raised on me, the ladle in Rox's hand for once arrested in mid motion, her glittering eyes shining like beacons!

"Is someone going to say something, or are we going to wait until *poor* Roxana' s hand drops off?" Papa said, looking at her with soft and sympathetic eyes

"Cheers, Papa!" said his *poor* daughter, looking at the rest of us with raised eyebrows, serving steaming Patna rice on his plate first, followed by the rest of the items, "As you can see, I do not get much sympathy around here."

"Doesn't look like it," said Papa, knowingly spoiling her some more.

I told them all about the tuition as well as the potential for making a good living out of it. Without finding out whether the grocer's ultimatum regarding future credit and the somewhat embarrassing situation into which it had drawn Papa was common knowledge, I did not broach on the subject openly, but made sure he got the message that such a contingency was not going to repeat itself in our lives ever again for as long as I breathed. As a result, I could distinctly see the creases of tension recede from his face and his eyes glisten with a thin film of moisture as he asked me one or two questions regarding the details of the venture. Then he narrated to us an enlightening episode from the life of Prophet Moses, which occurred on the first night of his people's mass exodus from Pharaoh's land. As he sat alone underneath a big tree, worrying over how he was going to find sustenance for all those hundreds of thousands of people who had forsaken their homes and their belongings to follow him, Angel Gabriel appeared by Allah's command and asked him to strike the ground with his staff. When Moses struck it, the ground split open and revealed a river underneath its surface. Then Gabriel asked him to strike the water with his staff. He did, and the water split apart, revealing a solid rock at its bottom. And finally, when he was asked to strike the rock with his staff and that too split apart, Moses saw a tiny insect emerge from one of its crevices, carrying some food in its mouth. So the Angel admonished Moses to have faith in the love and compassion of the real provider of sustenance, who does not neglect even the tiny creatures that dwell in slits of rocks at the bottom of rivers flowing beneath the surface of the earth!

"And there I was, worrying over where the next morsel of bread was going to come from on this table!" he concluded.

"Hear! Hear! Papa," Rox chirped as usual, her comments addressed to him but her naughty eyes dwelling upon me. "What an inspirational episode! And it was only the other day, as I stood ironing my last *sari*, I too had wondered over where the next lot of *saris* for me were going to come from! But see how Allah takes care of the needy?"

"The needy, yes. But not the greedy," I mumbled below my breath.

The repartee plunged everyone into laughter, leaving dear old Rox flushed. Papa, thrilled by the good tidings and the prospects of some desperately needed financial relief, got into high spirits and began making plans about how he was going to spend the money, which I was yet to earn, starting with some saris for the ladies. Getting the site cleared of grass and weeds, getting it plotted by surveyors and doing something about the squatters featured in them, as did making a clean start with the grocer and the butcher on future credit. Frankly, if my efforts really bore such fruit and I brought home a regular income, from the dusty streets of Hyderabad and from the pockets of my contented pupils, if not from the oil fields of Arabia and from the pockets of rich oil barons, I could not ask for anything more. The honest and hardworking ladies of our egregious household were welcome to buy as many *saris* as I could afford, and Papa to ease as many of his burdens as he wished. In fact, if he could clear away all the tangles from his property affairs, get rid of the squatters, break up the site into smaller plots, sell them and pay off his debts, we could all relax and take things easy. He would no longer have to link his daughters' matrimonial prospects with his son's; instead, he could set aside a modest sum for each girl, find two decent men for them who sought their hands rather than the wallets they brought, find me, too, a simple girl from a simple home, simple enough to wear simple cottons, play hide and seek with kids from our neighbourhood, her real wealth concealed in the richness of her smiles, in the brightness of her eyes, in the softness of her hands, in the joy she spread, in the candles she lit, in the dreams she stirred!

After supper, and before going to Sal's house with his share in the sweets and in my success, I knocked on Shabbu's door for a quick word. After having finished her household chores, earned her family's blessings in an unsurpassable measure, washed her face, combed her hair and still weaving them into a neat plait, she let me in.

"I'm so pleased for you about your project, Bhaijan," she said, her eyes twinkling with delight and her face brightened up, "Frankly, it couldn't have come at a better time. Papa's really up the creek."

"I know. He did drop a few hints about the state of the poll only the other day."

"It was really nice of Sal Bhaijan to care and to share."

"That's what friends are for."

"I wish he could come up with some such suggestion for me as well. Papa's spent such a lot of money on educating me, at times I feel totally helpless and inadequate. I wish I, too, could make some worthwhile contribution towards discharging our common dues."

"You are already making more than your fair share of the contribution, dearest! Without you taking half the burden on your young shoulders, Mamma would have been simply crushed. Besides, I need some help too, I need a working partner, I need to form a team. I can't think of anyone better suited for it than you."

"Tell me what you want me to do, and it is yours for the asking."

"Thanks. Sal's talking about a lot of pupils and I haven't even scratched the tip of the iceberg. When I reach the peak, I'm going to need some solid backup. Especially with setting homework and doing the markings. If you could share the workload with me, you would be gathering a lot of *honey* for this *hive* without even flapping your wings. A deal?"

62

"A deal! It'll be my honour, my pride and my joy."

"Thanks. I'm going over to Sal's place with his basket of sweets and inform him about our team too. Now, what exactly is happening on Sunday?"

"What Rox told you. We're going *bride hunting* for you. Moulana Saheb has lined up three *viewings* for us."

So, it was not a joke made up by Rox on the spur of the moment to pull my leg. My heart took a sudden dip in the sea of despair that surrounded me and sank. The enigmatic *Haseena* in the blindfold suddenly emerged from out of the voids, rearranged her *Dopatta*, straightened her windswept locks, broke into a dazzling smile and knocked on the door of my mind. By then, it had become quite impossible for me to forget her or to rub off her image from my thoughts. What would happen on Sunday evening if the *bride hunters* come home and report a *kill?* If they ran into a bride rich enough to satisfy Papa's needs as well as pretty enough to measure up to their specifications? And what would I do if, after everything was finalised with someone else; after the *deal* was signed, sealed and delivered, I came to know that my anonymous *Haseena,* too, could have matched everything; could have, perhaps, even excelled all the others?

"Is anything the matter, Bhaijan?" Shabbu asked me, obviously noticing the vacuous expression on my face, "You look like you have seen a ghost!"

"Marriage is a lifelong commitment, Shabbu, and a damned serious one at that. Whenever you people talk about *bride hunting,* I always feel as though a judge who had sat in judgement upon my fate had gone into his chambers to consider a verdict. It scares the hell out of me."

"Listen, Bhaijan, no matter how many judges sit in judgement on you; how many laws are applied; how many juries are consulted, *Fate* is a verdict that no one can alter or misinterpret. The lines on your palm with which you were born, they can never be changed, can they?"

"No, they can't."

"We can look at her palace, see the ornaments around her neck and hands, hear the shingle of gold sovereigns in her money bag, measure the length of her eyelashes, admire the slant of her eyes, count the teeth in her mouth, but what we can't do is to unfurl the top layer of her skin and see what sort of metal she's made of underneath, what sort of a person she turns out to be or what sort of a partner she makes."

"Of course not."

"The only thing we can guarantee you is this. We love you, we won't settle for anything less than the best for you, we know your taste and you know our choice. What Rox says about beauty lying in the eye of the beholder is just for fun and merely to tease you. But when it comes to putting her finger on a bride for you, she's the real fusspot. Nobody is good enough for her *one and only* Bhaijan. Still worried?"

"No, I'm not. Only, sometimes, while gazing at the faroff constellations, we tend to overlook the tiny flame prancing right underneath our eyes!"

That was the closest I could get to a confession, but it did not escape her attention. Her gleaming eyes pinned to my face with complete concentration, her face changing colours like a chameleon; she studied me for several hushed moments.

"Is there someone close by whom we're missing out, Bhaijan?" she finally asked me quite pointedly.

"I didn't say there's."

"If there is," she emphasised, still devouring me with those incisive eyes, "*now*'s the time to tell us. At least to me. Papa can always find alternatives for coping with his financial needs, but what he would never be able to find is an alternative youth to replace his only son's ruined youth, and he knows it."

What she was offering me on a silver platter was a golden opportunity to come clean; to pour out my heart; tell her about my mysterious *Haseena*; dive for the pearls; head for the shore; place the crown of my love on my queen's head; get on board her chariot of dreams and ride off with her to the never-never land! But I could not. I could not tell my own kid sister that, one hot and humid Sunday afternoon, when butterflies were flirting with pubescent summer blooms; when the young cuckoo was getting ready to build her first nest on the tamarind tree; when Rox's peacock on our roof had flared his turquoise feathers and was cooing for a mate; our derelict yard had suddenly turned into Paradise; fountains sprang to life and replenished all the silvery brooks with water; clouds came down from the sky and smothered the roses with their kisses; the rainbow tipped and turned into a swing; songs of love sung by invisible mouths echoed everywhere; and an uncrowned queen, attired in the spotless whiteness of the *Juhi* and the *Chambeli,* filling the garden with a strangely intoxicating perfume; spreading the freshness of spring through the medium of her sparkling eyes and honey-soaked smiles; stood in front of me for a glorious moment, let me hold her hand, let me kiss her scarf, let me touch her feet, let me tie a knot, let me incise her image on the inner layers of my mind. I just could not tell her that much and walked out of her room chained to my principles.

By the time I reached Sal's house and knocked, he had just finished supper and was getting ready to go to bed. Both of us went into their unoccupied rear lounge and sat down for a brief chat. After giving him his basket of sweets with thanks from all of us, I filled him in on what happened in course of the day, my first day of concrete efforts and positive results, including my voluntary code of practice, my views on the issue of fees, how I translated them into action and what was its propitious outcome. Then I told him about my chat with Shabbu towards forming a team. Delighted by the success of my mission so far, he approved the idea of involving her in work and once again assured me that my airborne *kite* was not in any danger of *nose diving*, and that, on the strength of my workload, which he already had in his hand, he would be able to keep me going with a constant supply of leads until I either ran out of time or began to build up my own. Finally, broaching upon the subject of Papa's plans to break up our vacant site into smaller plots for a quicker sale, I told him all about my nasty confrontation with Mr. Khan a few days ago and asked him if he could set the ball into motion about tackling the squatters before they planted themselves on the plots as well and started putting up their shacks in them. He said he would have a quick word with both our fathers soon and take the matter on board. I did not, however, mention anything about the unexpected storm that had gathered on my horizons and was threatening to strike at my peace with its recurring flares; it seemed to me the time for making those sort of confessions was not yet ripe.

The rest of the week passed away like a flash. I came across no hurdles, no tripwires and no pitfalls. My circle of contacts kept widening and I enrolled more and more pupils day by day. Shabbu stood by me as promised; most of my free time got swallowed up; my fame spread like the fragrance of musk; my pupils loved me, their parents respected me, I became so completely engrossed in work, the only time I could spare for fond reminiscences was at night; after everybody fell asleep; in the obscurity of darkness; in the loneliness of my room; in the quiet flux of the moon; in the hushed flight of the glow worms; in the tragic wails of the nocturnal *chakore*; the pink scarf pressed on my eyes or on my lips, its immortal perfume waking up the sleeping blossoms in the secret garden of my emotions; its feel and its touch opening up countless doors leading to a maze of dreams; its proximity breaking down all the locks on my self restraint!

Soon it was Sunday, the only day of the week that I had kept in hand to plan the following week; to catch up on errors; to finish the unfinished; to lend Papa a hand with his work, and sometimes, to pause and to ponder as well. But that Sunday was not anything like the Sunday I had hoped it to be. I wanted to take my sisters out, have some fun in the public gardens, stroll through its florid glades, lick ice cream from cones, play on the swings, feed the swans in the lake, pick the lilies, chase the squirrels, go to the *lovers arcade* and *Charminaar*, blow the last of my savings on sets of glass bangles: on *Hena* and *Shikakai*, on incense and jossticks, on sandalwood and bath oils, on *Dopattas* and *Ghararas*, on earrings and nose studs, on amulets and anklets, on hair bands and mirrors! But that Sunday turned out to be one of those awful days when I woke up and wished I had not woken up to it, because on that Sunday, dressed up in smart *saris*, reeking of perfume, chewing *betel-rolls* and showing off their pride, my family had gone away on a bride hunting spree for me, to shatter my peace, to break my slumber, to snatch my dream, to plunder the garden of my bliss, to trample upon all my hopes. And left to myself, I accompanied Papa into the vineyard under the pretext of supervising the clearing up operation he had organized, but in reality to keep persecution at bay, stave off my odious thoughts, overcome my unpalatable forebodings, to escape portents and presages, but above all, to rebuild her images, to revive her recollections, to resuscitate the hope of seeing her one more time before chains of morality went up my limbs, to breath in the breeze rampant with her perfume, to touch the soil enriched with her footprints, to conquer the distances that existed between her and me. I was there in body only and not in mind; it kept wandering across the infinite distances of the azure sky, above the woolpacks of silvery clouds rolling in its lap, in the obscurity of the hushed bines, underneath the shades of the unkempt trellises, behind the camouflage of shrubs, on the wings of butterflies, in the fragrance of the roses and the jasmines, anxiously looking out for a dash of white dappled with a flash of pink, for a face that could bestow youth upon every yawning bud, for a figure that could carry the sun up one of her sleeves and the moon up the other, for two dazzling eyes cluttered with a myriad twinkles of the milky way, for a magical personality vivified by the exuberance of spring!

Then, suddenly, a miracle took place; an invisible hand came down from the sky and rolled up the curtain of mystery; a gust of wind arrived from somewhere and blew away the veil of secrecy! I saw her, slim, slender, petit, a shy poppet of the invisible fairies, born to the wild wind and raised inside the dew drops, ushered into the perimeters of my own private world on the wings of dreams, wearing different clothes this time; in colours intended to draw attention; to knock off breath; to arouse adulation; to test restraints; to break pledges; to conquer hearts; to stir up passions! I felt as if the entire sky blacked out first and then lit up in an amazing luminance of gold; my body seemed on fire; my heart fell into uncontrollable poundings; a sudden current of excitement rocked me; a seizure of amazement arrested me, a spate of joy swept me off my feet. I felt so utterly overwhelmed by her aura, I did not know what to do. Surrounded by her friends and playmates, she emerged from Mr. Khan's dwelling, spotted me, recognised me, reacted to my presence, blessed me with a divine smile, demolished my restraints, messed up my priorities, ignored my principles, put cuffs on my wrists and pulled me towards herself. I yielded to that magnetic pull without any resistance; I succumbed to her charisma without protestations; I accepted her bondage without stipulations, I forfeited everything mine and pawned myself off to her; I left even my shadow behind me and surged towards her without it!

Probably because of our proximity and our activity, their fun and play did not begin, it could not begin. They simply stood and watched us, which was a big disappointment to me. I could not ask Papa and the labourers to go away from there because they were holding up something crucial; they were stopping my bated breath from resuming; they were standing between me and my salvation; they were demolishing the crystal palace of my dreams; they were preventing me from drinking the elixir of eternal life! For as long as they were there, the blindfold would not go up on her dreamy eyes; the moist lips would not relax into cherubic smiles; the soft cheeks would not flush; the playful laughter would not come out of her mouth; the delicate feet would not leave any prints on our land; the fragrance of her breath would not run wild across our garden; the elegant hand would not reach out for me! Oh, what a loss, what a waste, what a mess! What could I do to stop time in its tracks; halt the earth from revolving; change my fortunes? Where would I find the magical remote control with which I could direct her movements without stirring from my place; make her put on the blindfold and burst into laughter, jingle her glass bangles; stretch out her hand and come towards me, come closer, and closer still, until I could hold that dainty palm, press my lips on it, press my eyes on it, rub my forehead on it, worship it with my eyes!

The stalemate carried on for a while; neither we moved nor did they. I could not do anything; with Papa so close to me, I could not stand there, devouring her with my eyes, even if his mind was on his own business. But I could pray, and I did. I kept repeating Allah's name with my motionless lips, begging Him to make that moment last forever; to persuade her to stay and wait for me until I was freed; to give her the patience to let me catch up with her—in play as well as in life; to explain to her that patience happens to be a great virtue and waiting is the quickest route to accomplish it; to reassure her on my behalf that if she was patient and waited for me, I would make that wait worth her while; I would pluck the stars from the sky and sprinkle them on her *Dopatta;* I would bring the crescent down and wear it around her neck; I would load up her chariot of dreams with an equal share of joy from me; I would match mirth for mirth, smile for smile, heart for heart; I would pledge her my eternal bondage in return for just one moment of her companionship!

Either Allah heard and answered me, or she herself read my thoughts; for, the group did not disperse. Instead, I noticed her summon Mr. Khan's daughter to her side with a quiet signal and whisper something in her ear; her attention focused on me but her lips giving way to a devastating smile; the head cocked up, the eyes glittering. And Mr. Khan's daughter, no longer hostile as she was a week ago, came towards me smiling and walking in hesitant steps. It threw me into a sudden panic. If she brought a message for me from her friend, regardless of what it was, and it was delivered to me within Papa's hearing, it would put me on the spot. He had taken such exception to her father's language and lecture only a week ago as to deviate even from the path of the Qur'aan and agree for the eviction proceedings to be commenced against him. Now, if he noticed a covert communication take place between that same man's daughter and me, it could cast serious aspersions upon my integrity. But unfortunately, the arrow had left the arch and it was only a matter of time before it reached the target. Keeping my fingers crossed, I did the only thing I could to avert the catastrophe, I simply moved as far away from Papa as possible, beyond the range of his hearing, if not the field of his vision.

"My mother asked me to apologise to you for what happened last week," said the girl, "I'm sorry I was rude to you."

"Apologies accepted and you're forgiven," I replied, without making a song and dance about it.

Frankly, if that was all she came to say, it could have helped if it was uttered within Papa's hearing; it would have satisfied his ego and made him rethink his decision about going to court—people like Khan were better bought with money than challenged by law. But it seemed there was something more to come from her, which saved my soul by a whisker.

"She wants her scarf back," she said, slightly lowering the pitch of her voice and pointing at her friend with her eyes.

"And who's she to you?" I asked her the sixty-four-dollar question that was long overdue, making the risk worth its while.

"She's my cousin."

"Hasn't she got a name?"

"I'm not telling you."

"Does she live with you?"

"No."

"In the same building?"

"No."

"Does she come visiting you every Sunday?"

"Not every."

"Every other?"

"Why?"

"Because I gave the scarf to my sister for safekeeping and she's gone out. If you tell me when your cousin would visit you next, I'll bring it and give it to her myself."

"Next Sunday."

"Fine. Next Sunday it is, then."

By the time I got through that, my shirt was drenched with sweat. But I was so thrilled by the progress made so far, every step a step in the right direction; her initiative combined with my resourcefulness; her courage hand-in-hand with my brains; her swift response to my passionate prayers; they brought us closer to each other by the smallest of margins, which was good enough; better than parting without that link; better than separating without the hope of meeting again; better than drifting in mid-ocean without a shore in sight. It meant I had eight days in which to make up my mind, to tell Shabbu all about the prancing flame close by they were missing out in their flight for far-off constellations; put an end to the bride hunting sprees; put an end to the secret torment; come out into the open fighting for my share of luck; for my right to have a say in my own future, and their duty to respect that right; at least find out what *Haseena* had to offer me apart from a pretty face; how well she, too, could compete with the others; how well she could measure up to their expectations too; what was her story; was she an earthling or a celestial stray; did her heart belong to someone else or was it still available for occupation; was her hand pledged to someone or was it still up for grabs; what sort of a breeding and upbringing she had, even if she was in some way related to Mr. Khan? With so many new doors thrown open, I felt like a prisoner set free after a punitive confinement; I could feel the heavy shackles come off my legs and enable me some much needed movement; I felt the lock on my cage snap and release me into the infinite vastness of the clear blue skies.

"That was Khan's daughter talking to you just now?" Papa asked, breaking the chain of my thoughts.

"Yes, it was."

"What did she want?"

"It seems her mother asked her to apologise to me for her misbehaviour last Sunday," I said.

"Did she, really? That's a step in the right direction."

"It is, isn't it?"

"Yes, it is. But if I were you, I'd take it with a pinch of salt. She isn't her husband's keeper. He drinks, and when you're drunk, the devil takes over your senses. So, watch it."

"Yes, Papa, I will."

He went back to the other side of the yard. With him so far away from me, I was able to steal a few surreptitious glances of the children at play. That day, instead of hide and seek, they chose something else and became engrossed— all, except her. She kept looking in my direction now and then, sending sparks through my system. The gorgeous plaits flung around whenever she tossed her head; the bangles on her wrist shingled; the coils of loose hair fondly caressed her soft cheeks; the florid *Dopatta* rippled in the wind, the *Kurta* clung to her shapely figure and discreetly accentuated the supple contours of her body; the random smiles on the lips precipitated a collision of planets inside my head; our looks clashed from time to time; a strangely endearing state of affairs prevailed on the weed-ridden grounds; she and I breathing the same air; drowning in the same ocean; running on the same track; heading for the same goal; meeting and parting, again and again, exchanging silent messages, making wordless pledges, tying invisible knots, coming closer and closer still, cutting down on distances, building new bridges, bridging old gulfs!

CHAPTER (6)

Later on in the night, tired and washed out from their daylong exertions, the ladies returned home. As soon as I heard the noise of *cycle rickshaws* stopping outside the gate, my heart fell into loud pounding. For me, it was like a moment of reckoning. If they brought with them the news that they found the ideal bride for me, it would trigger off a civil war within the family perimeters; it would set me up against my own kith and kin; it would mean their choice as opposed to my choice; their needs versus my fancies; heart versus mind; love versus duty; emotions versus common sense. It would also start a nasty race between two non-participating contestants: who was better than whom, who was richer than whom; who was prettier than whom; who had cash as well as looks; who had looks as well as breeding; who had breeding as well as accomplishments; who had *Green Cards* and *Sponsorships*; who could heap gold Sovereigns on a silver platter and make a greater contribution to the family weal; who would make a better partner for the Quraishi stock between the niece of a drunkard and the grand daughter of a title holder; between the outer family of a *rickshawalla* and an heiress to the estate of *Khan Bahadur Mukarram Jah*; between a simple girl who played hide and seek with slum dwellers on someone else's land, and a lady who grew up on the laps of trained nannies, rocked in sandalwood cradles, walked on marble floors, slept in the cosy comfort of net curtains and goose feather eiderdowns, wore pure silks and *Dhaka muslins*, went to public schools, played with equals, taught by the *Moulvis* and disciplined by the *Ulemas*!

But matters did not come to that. Allah was on our side; on the side of the plodders; on the side of the dreamers; on the side of the *admirers* of the Taj Mahal and not its *builders*; on the side of thirsty hearts; restless souls and unfinished dreams. With Him on our side, we had no pitfalls to fear, no perils to contend with, no tests to face; with Him on our side, we were home and dry, we were basking in sunshine, we were underneath our goal posts; with Him on our side, we had no battles to wage, no races to compete in, no rivals to match and excel. From the tall tales my sisters had to tell about the brides they had seen, a sore splinter came off my thumb. Although I never had any reason to doubt their sincerity, to impeach their integrity, to put their love for me through the litmus test, my faith in them was reaffirmed, our bonds were strengthened, and our goals were reasserted. It was no longer I against them, but *we* against *the rest of the world*! We were a family, bonded with tassels of love, together in moments of need, equals in sharing and in caring. Rox's hilarious description of the brides they saw kept plunging her captivated audience into bursts of hysterical laughter, including Papa.

"Like I said, Papa," she told him, thoroughly enjoying the limelight, "what's in a face, ya? We all have different tastes on account of which wisdom dictates that *beauty lies in the eye of the beholder*. What looked to us like the flattened nose of a water buffalo, Bhaijan might see it as the very pinnacle of feminine excellence; what looked to us like the big ponch of a voracious rhinoceros, he might see it as the curvaceous waistline of an *Apsara* from the *Ajanta-Ellora* sculpture; what looked to us like the beady eyes of a *Langoor* poaching upon another *Langoor's* patch, he might see them as the repository of his dreams; what looked to us like the mouth of auntie *Gul-Chaman's* badly vandalised money-purse, he might see it as the starting point of a melodious *Thumri!* Who can tell? There are as many bride hunters and bride gazers as there are brides ..."

"So, nobody left any positive markings on your touchstone, eh?" Papa asked her emphatically, enthralled by the hilarious conversation.

"Nope," she replied without a flinch.

"Not even one?" he pursued.

In answer to it, she came over and sat on the hand rest of the chair in which I was sitting, circled her arms around me and blessed me with an affectionate hug first.

"Well," she declared, "if I had more than one Bhaijan, maybe I'd have picked one of those, regardless. But not for my *one and only!* She'd either have to be the pinnacle of perfection by *my standards*, or the very pit of absurdity by *his choice!*"

"And what about you, Shabana? You didn't like any, either?"

"Just glitter, Papa, but none gold. Yes, they were all rich, lived in pompous palaces, wore brocade *Ghoongats* and real pearl necklaces—and if we had the chance to get to know them, they might even turn out to be gentle souls—but this is one game in which we've to get everything right the first time. There are no second chances. You're either right or you're not right. There is no middle ground for making compromises."

"Of course not."

"We're all Allah's creation, Papa, the beauties as well as the beasts, and Allah doesn't like conceit, so it is wrong to make fun and to ridicule. All I can say is, in looks alone, not one of them measured up to our expectations."

"Doesn't speak much for Moulana Sahib's choice, does it?"

"With his kind of a fatal squint," Rox could not help taking a potshot at the most revered marriage broker in the trade, "you can't expect him to concentrate both on *looks* as well on *dosh* at one and the same time, Papa!"

"Hush, girl!" Papa chided her good-humouredly; "Don't ever let him catch you with that remark. He happens to be very partial to his squint, you know, and I'm going to have to rely on his services towards finding a match for you too."

"Good thinking, Papa! Those who live in glass houses should refrain from pelting stones at others!"

"They should. One day, it could be *you* under the hammer and someone else inspecting the merchandise. It's a wicked world."

"Yes, Papa, it is!"

"And last but not the least," he said, addressing himself to Mamma, "What about you, Kulsoom? Anything new to add?"

"I agree wholeheartedly with Shabana. It reminds me of what my father used to say. If you're trying to pick a winner on the race track, go by its mane and not by its teeth."

"What sort of a horse are you looking for? A *winner* on the race track or a *jewel* in your stables?"

"A *Jewel of jewels* in my stables!"

On that optimistic note, the conversation came to an end, at least for me; I had a very important task to attend to: I had to spread the mat and say thanks to Allah for transforming what seemed like a miserable Sunday morning when I got up into such a propitious Sunday night when I was ready for bed. In fact, it had turned out to be a day of revelations, a day of blessings, a day of miracles, a day of good omens. It was a day when I found out that my queen of hearts was neither a *HUR* from Paradise nor was she a stray from fairy land; she was an ordinary human being, belonged to an ordinary family, visited her cousins now and then, played around with her friends, laughed when provoked into laughter, wept when drawn into tears, spoke a known language, sent secret messages, responded to darting looks, cast spells with her bewitching eyes, captured hearts with her charismatic smiles, inspired adulation from her adoring fans. It was a day when I found out that the flames leaping out of me had set fire to her as well; that she, too, was feeling the same way towards me as I was towards her; that it was her initiative more than mine that ensured one more meeting between us; that not only did she toss on the surface like a dream boat but also caused ripples and dared undercurrents. It was a day when I found out that I was not being looked upon by my family merely as a *flotation* on the *marriage-market* for raising capital, but as a person with an identity of my own; my own likes and dislikes; my own tastes and choices; my own principles and disciplines; my own hopes and my aspirations. It was a day when I realised that even if money did feature on their portfolio of priorities, it did not feature at the very top and did not swallow up all their other priorities. And finally, it was a day when I realised that it is not a sin in Allah's eyes for two members of opposite sexes to look upon each other as reincarnations of Adam and Eve; that chaste love is not tabooed in heaven; that humans are allowed to err and Divinity is ready to forgive; that when Allah promises to keep *true pairs* forever together, His concern towards abiding by His promise begins right here on earth!

For the next six days, work kept me occupied. I had so many pupils on my register, my time got booked up choc-a-block and I could not afford to take on any more, especially those living too far from the area where I concentrated. So I retained only some who were within easy reach for me and passed on all the others back to Sal so that he could organise someone else local to that side of town and get things rolling. Besides, I also needed some time for preparing work. After running around all day, I tackled it during the night with Shabbu 's help when she, too, could free herself from her domestic preoccupations. We sat up until the midnight hours, going through the syllabus, choosing text books, drawing up schemes of work, organizing lesson plans, finalising time tables, sorting out home work, keeping track of weekly progress, the lot. It was the most tiring and demanding aspect of the job but we enjoyed doing it, with Rox also lending us a hand, sometimes with work, sometimes with mugs of revolting hot drinks she made, and sometimes with her wise cracks.

On Friday of that week, the ultimate in miracles happened to me when the course of events took an abrupt turn with a rather fascinating incident. It was another of those hot and humid days with a cloudless sky, a fiery sun and gusts of scorching breeze. A thin film of dust, raised by endless human activity going on all around, hung in the air and simply refused to budge. Stray bulls mingled with the chaotic traffic dominated by *cycle rickshaws* and cyclists, all seemingly in a big rush to get to their respective destinations as if the Day of Reckoning was upon them and the world was drawing to an end. Street dogs ran amok, dodging accidents and frustrating the road users; oft and on, marauding pulses of wind picked up litter rolling in the streets and then blew it around from one end to the other. I carried on with my task, undeterred by the heat, in spite of the streams of perspiration drenching my clothes, ignoring the thirst built up by the strain of physical activity and pangs of hunger resulting from a lack of timely nourishment.

Towards the end of the day, almost winding up the list of pupils given by Sal, I reached the neighbourhood of Aghapura for my final call. The person I needed to see was Mr. Saleh Ansari, who worked at Union Paper Mills as a maintenance engineer and lived in one of the prefab family quarters rented by the mill to their permanent employees. Sal had already given me full details of his domestic circumstances. He had a wife and eight children to support on a very modest income, seven of whom went to school, except his eldest daughter Azra, who stayed at home and helped her mother run the household. Understandably, feeding so many mouths as well as financing their education on a single person's salary was getting to be tough. Besides, his eldest son Vaseem was offered a place at the City Polytechnic towards his Diploma in Mechanical Engineering, which ensured him better prospects of employment in the future; and to help out the family accomplish their goal, the manager of the paper mill had promised Azra a clerical job, provided she passed at least the Aligarh Matriculation Examination. If she managed it and started work, Vaseem, as well as the other children, would have a better future to look forward to; but if she did not, then some would have to give up theirs for the sake of the others. Hence, the need for a tutor to coach her, and a desperate one at that.

Leaning the bike against the trunk of a large *neem* tree in their front yard, I knocked on the door. It was answered by my host, a middle-aged gentleman in a white gabardine *Sherwani*, his short beard just beginning to turn grey and his head concealed underneath a tatty fez. Greeting me with a cheerful smile, an affectionate handshake and a warm *Assalamu alaikum,* he took me into a small room he used as his reception. It had a window overlooking the street, a three-piece suite made of cane but well cushioned, and a choir mattress covering the slabbed floor. In one corner, there was a bookshelf full of neatly arranged volumes of *Mirzan Ghalib's* poems, a coffee table in the middle of the room and two picture frames on the wall containing calligraphy inscriptions from the Qur'aan. The room reeked of perfume from spirals of smoke released by jossticks burning somewhere out of sight. Apart from the nonstop chatter of their parrot, there were no other voices or sounds in the background

After we sat down, he triggered off a pleasant conversation about general matters and then, without beating around the bush, gave me more or less the same details of his circumstances as I had already gathered from Sal. Obviously, his needs exceeded his means and his plight was as bad as ours was; so there was no question of my negotiating a fee; if I could be of any help to him, I was at his disposal for the asking.

"So much depends upon Azra passing this exam, I feel guilty putting such an enormous burden on the shoulders of a very young girl. But what else can I do? Either I get help from one, or I give up on the others," he said, concluding.

"Don't worry, Mr. Ansari. We're all sailing in the same boat. Leave it to me and I'll do my best to help her out."

"Thank you. I can't afford a fancy fee, but I, too, will do my best towards it. I gather you're not like the others in money matters?"

"The same Allah who provides for you provides for me too, sir, and I'm grateful to Him for whatever He puts my way."

"*Subhaan Allah!* What a noble sentiment! Indeed, we all should be. How soon can you start?" he asked, looking at me with anxious eyes.

"On Wednesday next week? At eleven in the morning?" I said, suggesting a day and a time that I had already pencilled in for them in my appointments diary.

"Smashing. Once a week?"

"Twice, to begin with. Same time on Fridays. If necessary, we can always alter the number of visits later on. As far the fee is concerned, please don't give it another thought. You want your daughter to succeed for your reasons as a father, and I want all my pupils to succeed for my reasons as a teacher. Money isn't amongst them."

"May Allah bless you! In that case, let's get on with the introductions," he said and rose to his feet.

Amongst pupils I had enrolled so far, not all were boys. There were girls, too, with whom I had talked and whose standards I assessed, but in every instance they invariably sat on the other side of a thin curtain on account of *purdah* restrictions, obscured from view. I saw vague silhouettes, heard muffled voices and suppressed giggles, caught scent of perfume and flowers, but never came face to face with any of them. Hence, when Mr. Ansari prepared to introduce my pupil to me, I naturally assumed he would do it in the same way, draw a curtain of some sort in the room, or put up a partition first and then fetch her from inside. But he treated me to such an unexpected surprise, it knocked off my breath. At his signal, the inside door opened and someone entered. My eyelids instinctively drooped, blood raced in my veins at an unfamiliar pace and my heartbeat shot up. I forgot everything else except that I was in the presence of a person at whom I was not permitted even to look directly by my religion and our traditions. I wanted to; I was being allowed to; and yet I could not. The strangely permeating fragrance that arrived into the room along with her and crept into my lungs worked like a fast acting intoxicant. In the profound hush that ensued, I could distinctly hear the rustle of her clothes, the snapping of her bones, the chink of her glass bangles and the squeak of her sandals; I heard Mr. Ansari tell me who she was; heard her clear her throat before the greetings; heard her say *ASSALAM ALAIKUM* in a voice that sounded like music; became vaguely aware that father and daughter occupied two chairs facing me; became conscious of the fact that they were waiting for me to speak; and I knew how important it was that I did, yet my breath remained bated in my throat and my vocal chords gave up on me completely.

"This is Azra, Mr. Quraishi," said Mr. Ansari, breaking the awkward spell of silence, "and this, Azra, is the gentleman who has agreed to coach you for the exams."

"*Assalamu alaikum,* master saheb," she said once again in a slightly louder voice.

At that stage, I had no choice but to look up, which I did, with tempestuous consequences. For, seated in the chair directly facing me, her mesmeric eyes registering recognition and slightly widened with surprise, lips bathed in a ghost of a smile, the flushed cheeks rosier than I had ever seen before, filling up the room with a strangely euphoric perfume, stirring invisible ripples in air, raising storms of excitement in my system, causing mayhem inside my mind, knocking off my breath again and again, there sat the very person for whom my heart had been pining all week, whose face my eyes had been scanning the earth to see, whose memory had been clinging to my mind with tentacles of love and longing, whose dreams I had been switching on and off through my sleeps and catnaps, whose scarf I had exalted into a parchment from paradise and been secretly worshiping, whose fragrance I had been trying my best to wipe out of my lungs but without much success, whose name I had been struggling to read in the lines on my palm, and above all, for whom I had been vexing and nagging Allah at least a couple of hundred times a day, with my eyes shut, with my eyes open, outside in the streets, inside in the mosques, awake and asleep, alone or in company, begging or exhorting! To be brought face to face with the same idol in such a way, closer than I had ever thought possible, as often as twice a week guaranteed, not to say anything about chance encounters in our vineyard, to work together, to sit together, to talk to each other without the fear of being pried, being criticised, without breaching restraints, without any sense of guilt, without remorse or self censure, sharing a common goal, moving in the same direction, aiming for the same finishing line—it was terrific, it was absolutely miraculous, it was simply incredible!

"*Walaikum assalam,*" I reciprocated to the melodious greeting without giving a toss about how my voice sounded, without giving her father even the slightest hint that we had already met before, on some other day, on some other plain or planet, in some other life or existence, "glad to meet you, Azra, and to be of some service to you and to your father."

I could not have come any nearer to the truth even if I bid for it a hundred times. That initial exchange, of greetings, of aspirations, of mutual resolves, of well-conceived intentions, of implicit deals and promises, threw the element of indecision out of my system, giving me an abundance of courage to take the rest in my stride.

"Thank you, *master saheb,*" she replied, the address 'master saheb' from her lips adding a whole new dimension to my status; flying me into endless vacuums and then bringing me back in a new mould each time; drowning me in a spate of joy and pulling me out again; testing me on the tight rope of restraint without giving me the space to breath.

"Before I can set a timetable for her," I said, addressing Mr. Ansari, secretly desperate to make that moment of togetherness last for as long as possible, forever and forever, if possible, "it would help me if I could assess her standard first."

"Don't tell *me*, Mr. Quraishi," he replied, quickly getting to his feet, "You take it from here; you are the expert. Next only to Allah, I'm putting the future of my son in her hands as well as in yours. I'll try to see you next time you come. I've got to be going now. My shift begins in an hour."

So saying, he shook hands, thanked me for accepting the pleasant mission and went away, leaving us alone and together in the small room, though under the weight of an overriding moral responsibility. The room plunged into silence, their talkative parrot carried on chatting, my heart kept pounding inaudibly, my eyes played host to a million dreams, my mind threw open all its doors and began to think every unthinkable thought it could.

"When did you last go to school, Azra?" I asked her, if only to trigger off a conversation.

"Three years ago," she replied, turning a little red in the face from shyness, "long enough for the clogs to rust ..."

The cute reply touched the cords of my heart. So, it had fallen into my share of luck to remove the rust off those clogs! It was a beguiling task in which I had absolutely no intentions whatsoever of failing.

"That's what we have to try and accomplish together," I said, laying a subtle emphasis on the word *together*, and secretly ingratiated by its note of cosiness, "I mean, get the rust off those clogs."

"Can we?" she asked, making the word *we* sound so sweet, I could almost feel the taste of honey in my mouth.

"That depends upon the *both of us*."

"Does it?"

"Yes, it does. Have you got anything to write on?"

"For now, only my sister Mahjabeen's slate and pencil," she replied, picking it from her lap and passing it on to me, along with the pencil, the action inevitably resulting in a very slight brushing of our fingers, which sent a series of electric shocks running through my body. If I could, I would have carved out that part of my skin that touched hers with a sharp knife and preserved it forever inside a pouch filled with nectar! Accepting the slate and the pencil from her, I wrote on it the sentence 'Shuja is a good boy' and gave it back to her.

"In this sentence," I said, watching the expression on her angelic face with animation, "I have said something about SHUJA. How many other things can *you* say about him?"

Accepting the slate, making a deliberate attempt to avoid contact, blushing even more intensely than before, fidgeting in the chair, snapping bones in her ankles, breathing hard, her eyes downcast and dug into the slate, she became absorbed. Letting her concentrate, I made use of the opportunity to study her face in greater detail. The more I looked at it, the more convinced I became that she could not belong to the fraternity of mankind—such enigmatic features, such perfection, such grace, such silken wisps, such a flawless forehead, such a slant of the eyes, such a welter of lashes, such pencil sharp eyebrows, such a classic nose, such rosy cheeks, such delicate lips, such a dreamy smile on them, such attention to detail, such artistry and such accomplishment—they could only belong to the Celestial, to the *HURS* referred by Allah in the Qur'aan, to those bred and brought up on *Manna and Salva*, to the occupants of the *Garden* underneath which flow sable streams of Eternal Tranquillity, to those that are blessed with nearness to Him, only to those *Perfects* who are in attendance upon the *Most Perfect of All!*

"I can't do this," she finally said, interrupting my study, my thoughts, and my silent adoration.

"Why not?" I asked her, returning to earth.

"Because I don't know anyone called SHUJA," she replied quite bluntly

"I see," I said, rather nonplussed by the reason, "What if I changed it to *Sakina*?"

"Pardon?"

"What if I changed the sentence to *'Sakina is a good girl'?*"

"You mean, my cousin?"

"Your cousin?"

"Yes."

"I didn't know you have a cousin called Sakina."

"Pardon?"

"I said I didn't know your cousin is called Sakina."

"Yes, she is, and I know quite a lot about her. Can I do it as my homework? I work better on my own."

"Tell you what," I said, inwardly despairing at having to bring my visual feast to an end so soon, "I'll prepare a timetable for you and drop it in through the letter box on Monday."

"You mean, you're willing to help me take the rust off my clogs?" she asked, the gleaming eyes pinned to my face, cheeks flushed as before, the devastating smile back on the lips.

If only there was a way in which I could tell her all those impossible things I was willing to do in order to dip and drown in the helical depths of her eyes one more time; the improbable tests I was prepared to face and win in order to gain access to her heart; the incalculable amount of bliss that I experienced in her company; the indefinable conflicts of loyalties into which I was plunging myself ever since I had set eyes upon her.

"Yes, I am," I replied, emphatically enough to eliminate even the slightest risk of misunderstanding anywhere along the line.

"Thank you, *master sahib,*" she said, seeming to suppress a surge of emotion, to overcome a tide of joy, to swallow a gasp of relief.

With that, it was time to part. She seemed more affected by that painful inevitability than I was; the dazzling glitter in the eyes toned down a little; the pretty face shed much of its breathtaking exuberance; a succession of unspelt messages of farewell appeared and disappeared on it; the mind succumbed but the body reeled; she put away the slate on the bookshelf and got to her feet to see me to the door, unfurling her figure in front of me like a rosebud unfurling its petals to transcend into a flower. The petit body wrapped in a simple *Kurta* and *Shalwar,* her chest and shoulders covered by a matching *Dopatta,* both her plaits tied with satin ribbons and hung to the front, a cluster of *Chambeli* clipped to the hair, she stood in front of me like a dream personified!

"Instead of dropping it in through the letter box," she said at the door in a deliberately lowered voice, "why don't you knock for me?"

The invitation was irresistible and I did not resist it. Once again, it was her initiative and resourcefulness, as opposed to my dumb stupidity, which ensured us an extra, an unscheduled, a welcome meeting.

"Sure, why not?" I said, biting my tongue so hard, I could almost feel the taste of blood in my mouth.

That, by far, was the happiest day of my life. Unexpected spring had arrived in my garden; tickled the night queens awake; brought the rosebuds to youth; scattered pearls of dew on lotus leaves; released fragrance from the pouches of perfume concealed in secret stems; re-sprayed the wings of butterflies with new colours; added an extra fluorescence to the peacock's tail; set up cradles for the cuckoo's chicks and sung them lullabies; changed around the hues of dawn and dusk; polished the glitter in all the twinkling stars; accentuated the halo around the moon; rekindled the embers smouldering in the midnight sun; pulled the veil of anonymity off my queen's face; escorted her into my lonesome kingdom; put the crown of my love on her head and sat her on the throne, which belonged to her alone, her alone, her alone!

The unexpected arrival of Azra into my vacuous life, investing it with a new identity; transforming its dimensions; earmarking its frontiers; redefining its connotations; reinvigorating its proportions; giving it a clear purpose was a great boon to me. I had never been in that kind of a situation before; never been in love; never come so close to anyone; never wanted anyone all to myself; never had a house guest residing inside me; taking away my sleep; dominating my dreams; putting me on pins and needles; exacerbating my thirst; increasing my palpitations; making me feel alone in the midst of crowds; locking me up in the kingdom of flowers and perfumes and turning me into a total stranger to myself.

The Saturday following the Friday when I took leave of her and the Sunday when I was going to see her again in our vineyard to return the scarf turned out to be a day stuffed with too many idle moments, too many tedious hours, too many boring tasks. The one task more entertaining than others was preparing a timetable for her and I completed that task before all the others, picturing us sitting together in the small room, separated by a short and yet insurmountable distance; her melodious voice pouring honey into my ears; the chink of bangles setting cords of music in my heart; the euphoric fragrance of flowers she wore purifying my inner seclusion; the shimmer of her eyes lighting candles in its every dark corner; the proximity of her arms putting me on crests of emotional tides. Then, having done it once, I returned to it again and again; making a few changes here; a few changes there; giving it finishing touches; extending the span of an hour into the span of a lifetime; elongating the span of a lifetime to the very outer limits of after-life; prolonging the 'after-life' into eternity; still not satisfied, not content, not satiated, not gratified!

Somehow, dragging myself with brute force; staggering under the weight of expectations; besmirching my conscience with white lies and excuses; breaking every stipulation drawn in my code of practice and rewriting my portfolio of my priorities, I counted the long and dawdling moments until supper time, my mind crammed with no other thoughts but hers; my eyes absorbing no other image than her pretty face and her comely figure; my ears strained to pick up only the sound of her voice, her laughter, her words, her *Assalamu alaikum,* her *Khuda Hafiz,* her welcomes, her goodbyes, her invitations, her questions, her answers, her expectations, her thanksgiving! For the first time ever, I did not laugh to Rox's wisecracks, did not enter into any tongue in cheek repartee with her, did not grasp her conversation, did not respond to her questions, did not put forward any suggestions, did not enjoy the meal one bit. If my unusual and uncharacteristic reticence was noted, it was not underlined by anyone, put down merely to my preoccupations with work.

After a constantly disturbed night; sleep invaded by dreams; dreams invaded by swinging plaits and satin ribbons; secret hopes in combat with secret fears; expectations encumbered by doubt; mind at loggerheads with heart; conscience at war with emotions, I woke up like a stranger to myself, had a rigorous shower rubbing sandalwood oil on my skin, changed three sets of clothes in the pace of twenty minutes; brushed my hair again and again; calmed down my high-strung nerves with rose-flavoured milkshakes; drove out all the butterflies fluttering in my stomach; borrowed the key to the vineyard from Papa's room without his knowledge or consent and waited for the noise of children to begin on the other side of the parapet wall, very much like a nervous bridegroom on the verge of making his inviolable conjugal vows!

At about 1 p.m. just as we assembled around the dining table for lunch, the first echoes of laughter and screams rang in the vineyard, triggering off nonstop shivers of excitement down my back, locking out my appetite and my craving for food, blocking my ears with invisible cups and tempting me into doing something outrageous: change the dining room protocol; drop a plate, stop eating, get up and go, tear open my heart and show everyone the metamorphosis taking place inside its secret seclusion, shout the name Azra at the top of my voice, pledge myself to her in the presence of all those witnesses, pin tassels of gold to the word *love* within their eyeshot and exonerate it! But tied down to traditions, shackled to morality, imprisoned inside the cage of restraints, prevented by duty, governed by principles and muffled by etiquette, I could not leave; could not so much as turn away from my plate; could not divert my attention, could not concentrate on any of those delightful sound waves travelling towards me, recognise the sweetest of all and absorb it in my eardrums, until the last morsel on Papa's plate was eaten; one more round of thanks were given to Allah for the conclusion of a well-deserved meal; the assembly terminated and freedom of movement and action finally declared to one and all.

Without making any fatal mistakes, without getting caught by prying looks, without attracting needless attention, without giving anyone the chance to suspect my motives, I quietly dropped out of sight and slipped into the vineyard with a throbbing heart, with racing blood, with bated breath, and looked around. They were all there, children big and small, engrossed in playing hide-and-seek once again, with a different seeker in blindfold this time. Azra was also there, now a hider, slinking behind a variety of ideal camouflages, hiding not only from the seeker but also from the rest of the world, herself seeking someone else without the blindfold, the glittering eyes scanning the derelict trellises, cheeks flushed, hair windswept, plaits swinging, ribbons rippling, chest heaving, fists clenched from tension, sweat pouring down from strain, driven by hope, slowed down by disappointment, revived by expectation. Taking cover behind a shrub, I just stood wide-eyed watching her, the matchless beauty that was hers, the elegant figure that was hers, the precision-based proportions of the modestly wrapped body that was hers, an acme of sheer perfection, an icon of feminine excellence, running around like a juvenile gazelle ahead of her herd, unaware of the storms she triggered off, unmindful of the heads she rolled, unconcerned with the hearts she crushed. It was not her fault; her Maker had made her like that, cast her in the mould of *Hawwa, Zulayqa* and *Bilquis,* to test the nerve of Prophets, to lead Emperors into temptation, to turn saints into sinners, to raze thrones, to relinquish crowns, to topple kingdoms! I, my secret infatuation, my passive obsession, my silent quest, my pitiful thirst were nothing compared to all those capitulations!

Long before my explosive thought waves subsided, she spotted me, her eyes lit up, face flushed, lips relaxed, fists unclenched, a newfound alacrity electrified the body language, she looked from me to them, and from them to the door of the outbuilding, presumably to make sure we were not being watched. While she did so, the tiny earrings in the slender lobes swung, the stone on her nose stud twinkled, the plaits undulated, the ribbons rippled, and each of the movements—of the head, of the hair, of the nose, of the chin, of the lips—raised a million storms in my heart, tossed me around like a kite with a broken string and sent me crashing somewhere away in some distant wilderness. Keeping the misty eyes pinned to my face, leaving the door to a feast of her smiles wide open, extending irresistible invitations with her swinging arms, she returned to the arena of her divine charms, to the theatre of her triumphs and my capitulations, to the tiny patch of our land consecrated by her feet, and either accidentally or deliberately bumped straight into the *seeker* in blindfold, getting caught, giving rise to a volley of hysterical screams, generating such unanimous adulations even in defeat! The myriad satellites floating around the focal planet changed their trajectories at once and drew to her—like a cluster of twinkling stars surrounding their luminous moon—adoring her, admiring her, loving her! And she, too, as exalted as the celestial body, glowing against the background of the vacuous sky, casting her light on the face of darkness, shackled them in the orb of her halo and anointed them with her aura!

Then the gentle tide of mirth swung in my direction as they clasped her hands and dragged her towards me, by then her scarf held by me like a flag of surrender, or of truce, insisting that she wore her blindfold with my hand! The very invitation, however blithesome, however irresistible, however unrepeatable, threw my heart into loud pounding, hyped up my blood flow, turned me upside down. If I was to meet their fervent demands and carry out the delightful task, she would have to cut the distance between us right down to a few inches, even less, and stand with her back to me, the evocative fumes of the *Rita Shells*, of *Shikakai* and of Incense emanating from her silken wisps mingling in my breath, creeping into my air stream, evaporating inside my inner space, setting my senses ablaze, razing my restraints to the ground, driving me crazy! I could not dare embark upon such a daring adventure without caution, without controls, without safeguards, without drawing lines, without setting perimeters, without erecting barriers.

Probably going through the same emotional turbulence, caught up in the same undercurrent, rocking in the same tremors, she, too, dug her heels in, clung on to the straps of modesty, checked herself from easy capitulation, pulled upon the bridles of pride, held her horses, resisted the pressure and staved off the gentle persuasion, without seeming to be rude, without display of impropriety, without conveying any ambiguous signals, without being seen as a person of easy virtue, and yet without causing offence. But her adamant playmates, now determined to set her off on the road leading to our illusive goals, did not yield, did not let her postpone the moment of our coming together until some other auspicious date, did not agree to delay our metaphoric conjugation under any circumstances. Bit by bit, inch by inch, step by step, moment by moment, the distances began to shrink, Apocalypse held its breath, earthquakes paused, landslides stood aloof, my heart ticked away, my arms extended towards her, the scarf fluttered, all the jasmine buds came to life and bloomed, butterflies changed course and returned, the peacock on the roof stood still and cocked up its crowned head, squirrels abandoned their race and gazed in our direction!

Eventually yielding to the pressure, she stopped, turned round, bent her head, shut her eyes, held her breath and stood still, waiting for me to do the honours like a queen awaiting her investiture. Holding the scarf in my trembling hands, totally lost to the rest of the world, nothing else visible to me except her head, her lustrous locks, the back of her ears, the tiny earrings, the cluster of *Chambeli*, the middle parting separating the two strands of her gorgeous hair, the slender neck exposed in between the plaits, the imbroglios of her *Dopatta*, the buttons holding up her *Kurta*, her presence, her nearness, her ambience, her entelechy, and nothing else, and nothing else, and nothing else, I fastened the blindfold over her eyes and tied the knot with the utmost gentleness, without bruising the petals of that tender bud, without smearing her moral rectitude, without taking her for granted. As if the tying of that knot meant something more than what it was, much, much more than the apparent, the visual, the obvious, the prima facie, our animated audience broke into a noisy applause, clapping their hands, bursting into laughter, letting out screams of delight, leaving her to deal with the consequences of wearing that blindfold—she, groping in the dark with her hands outstretched; they, mischievously tugging at her *Kurta,* or at her *Dopatta*, or at her *Shalwar,* teasing and tantalising her, throwing friendly challenges at her, daring her to win her round; and I, making my own solemn resolves to hold that slender hand in mine forever and forever, bring her out of darkness into light, out of confusion into coherence, out of loss into gain, and never to let go of that hand for as long as I lived, never to let the light in her life fade, never to let her wander alone in pursuit of joy, of freedom, of success and never to let her lose anything hers!

CHAPTER (7)

The midsummer dawn broke at five. The magnificent dome of the *Shrine* rose against the background of a spotless sky, taking on the azure tone of the day from the misty grey of night. Merry flocks of pigeons flew around in fearless freedom, as though exchanging messages of goodwill between the dwellers of the earth and the occupants of Paradise. The *Peepal* tree in the vast forecourt played host to a large colony of crows. They sat on its branches, some making nests, some hatching eggs, some feeding their fledglings, some settling their feuds and others merely guarding their shelters. Underneath its shadow, almost as numerous as the crows and just as noisy, sat a multitude of beggars, cripples, lepers, orphans and destitutes, some hungry, some blind, some sick, some in pain, some in need, some just avaricious, making their bids for alms from the large crowds of visitors to the Shrine, attracting attention, demanding charity, seeking priority, lavishing blessings, in the name of Allah, in the name of the Saints, in the name of all the blessed and the exalted, wherever they may be. Wreaths and flowers, together with baskets of sweets and bunches of jossticks for *Fateha,* in big demand at that time of day, were changing hands outside the busy stalls of florists scattered around the path. Despite the rush and the dense gathering, the air was laden with fragrance, with human expectations, and Divine mercies.

Locking up my bike in the cycle stand, I went into the adjacent mosque first, joined the congregation, offered *Namaaz,* then bought some flowers, together with the basket of sweets and the pack of jossticks, emptied out my pockets for giving alms, stepped inside the shrine, handed over my offerings to the High Priest for consecration, paid my respects to the two majestic tombs, collected my basket of sweets from him, sat in a quiet corner, recited a few passages from the Qur'aan below my breath and stretched my hands in front of Allah. The one thought uppermost in my mind being the tuition I was starting, I addressed it first. I begged Him to help me earn an honest living, impart knowledge to the best of my ability, give the right guidance to those who sought guidance from me, respect and be respected, reward and be rewarded, share and be shared with, never expect to reap any more than what I had sown, always practice what I preached, negotiate darkness with vision, win hearts with compassion, forgive those who err with tolerance and with forbearance.

For Papa and Mamma, I begged Him to give them some peace of mind from a speedy and satisfactory resolution of the endless worries in which they were still entrenched; to help them find compatible partners for the girls and see them off to their destinations; to put their past behind them and look in the direction of Mecca and Medina; to rest their aging bodies in His Peace and in His Praise; to sit back at long last and watch with contentment the new generation take over from the old, harnessing the virtues they had inherited at birth and carry forth the mantle of traditions into the future.

For Shabbu and Rox, I begged Him to enrich their lives with success; give them strength to be bold in the face of adversity; to be honest to themselves and faithful to others; to give back in a much greater measure than what they receive; to endure life's injustices with smiling faces; to be patient in hardship; to be generous in charity and compassionate in attention; to be paired with loving mates and flourish alongside them; be sincere to those who have a right to bank on their loyalties and never sway away from the path of righteousness laid down by Islam.

And finally, for the one whom I had recently entered on the list of people closest to my heart; I begged Him to give her good health, a long life and a happy future; protect her from the evil eye; give her the resolve and tenacity to live up to her parents' expectations; to earn their love, their esteem and their respect; take light into the life of the man she would marry one day— whether me or someone else; imbibe in her offspring such matchless virtues as Loyalty and Self Sacrifice; structure her family in the framework of Islam as preached and promoted by the Holy Qur'aan and the *Ahadith* of our Prophet; turn her home into a flagship for her siblings to follow; find peace in Allah's love on earth and find Salvation in His grace beyond the earth.

With that, my homage to Allah paid with candour, my heart laid bare, my concerns expressed, my needs sought, my spirit comforted, I came home, put a bit of the consecrated sweets in everybody's mouth, had a pinch for myself and saved a pinch for Azra, already a part and parcel of my close family in my mind at least, skipped our regular assembly on the lawns and got ready. While Rox arranged all my paperwork in my briefcase and Mamma busied herself with packing my lunch box, Shabbu sorted out the homework for my pupils that we had prepared together in course of the week. As far as Azra's timetable was concerned, *she* and *it* had both been at the forefront of my mind all the while. Even though the idea of knocking for her with the timetable instead of dropping it in through the letterbox was not mine, I was glad that it had sprung up and was agreed. On a day when I was setting out to commence a crucial project, which might even be instrumental in the realisation of my secret dreams about us later on, making her house my first call, hearing her sweet voice, gazing at her salubrious face, watching my reflection on the sheen of her moist eyes was, indeed, a most welcome suggestion.

Taking leave of my family midst a volley of blessings, I got on my bike and headed for Aghapura. Barely ten minutes' ride from my house, I managed to get there before the hot sun and the strong breeze could rage too much havoc on my clothes and on my face. Leaning the bike against the trunk of the same tree as before, my heart beating like a drum, my breath speeded from the strain of pedalling up the steep hill in order to get there, and from the excitement, from expectations, and from nerves, I knocked on the door. Within a minute or two of my knocking, it opened and she stood in it, wearing a crumpled *Kurta*, a soiled *Shalwar* and an equally soiled *Dopatta*, her ruffled hair hurriedly pressed in place, one plait hung to the front and the other to the back, no fragrance of flowers on offer nor flowers in sight but some paddy husks and coriander leaves tangled in the loose tufts, hands reeking of dough and pure ghee, the smell of ginger, garlic and firewood smoke on her clothes, a charcoal smear on forehead and another on chin, cheeks flushed from the heat of the wood fired oven if not from blushing. As soon as her eyes came into contact with me, I could distinctly see a swift change take place in them; they lit up with sparkles of joy; the lips eased into a cosy smile of welcome; the pearl-like teeth gleamed. Quickly readjusting the *Dopatta* around the shoulders, she touched the centre of her brow with the middle finger of her right hand, said *Adab arz* in a soft voice, and then held the door open for me to enter.

I did, like a somnambulist walking a tight rope, so utterly lost for composure by the magic of a single look from her it was unbelievable! Barely managing to reciprocate to those cheerful greetings, I followed her into the lounge, thrilled at the prospects of spending a few golden moments in her company; of basking in the luminance generated by her presence; of bathing in the spells cast by her dazzling eyes; of drowning her inside me; of diluting her into my bloodstream; of locking her up in the secret chambers of my heart; of taking her away from the clutches of the world and keeping her all to myself.

"Your timetable, Azra," I said aloud, getting on with the inevitable, "I hope this isn't too inconvenient."

"Thanks, *master sahib*," she said and stopped.

When she stopped, my heart also stopped beating; the world stopped revolving; the clocks stopped ticking; the sun stopped moving; everything that mattered to me, that progressed in my life, that moved and marched for me, came to a standstill! I, too, stopped in suspense, waiting to see what happened next; how the situation developed. Having ventured to set up our meeting by her own initiative, there was no need for her to terminate it so quickly; she could sit with me for a while; scrutinise the timetable in greater detail; come up with some problems, some pointers, some objections, some alterations, some suggestions; make a few changes here, add a few ideas there; let me quench my thirst; let me give my heart some contentment; let me muster enough courage to live for another day; let me caress those honey-soaked lips in my mind; let me hold those gentle wrists in my hand; let me wave a magic wand and put my life back on track and get things going again—the earth, the clocks, the sun, the clouds and the breeze!

"Would you terribly mind taking your seat and waiting for a quick moment, *master saheb?*" she did say with her blessed lips, giving me a new lease of life, ushering into it an unexpected spring and changing my fortunes. "My saucepan is simmering on the oven and Ammijan is in the bathroom. I'll just give it a stir and be right back."

"Sure, go ahead," I said.

She hastily rushed inside the house and then popped her pretty head back into the room with an absolutely divine smile.

"One sugar or two?" she asked, without putting the offer of a cup of tea into so many words.

For tea made by her, there was no need to add any sugar. Her touch and her hospitality was enough to make any beverage she offered taste like pure nectar, like ambrosia for Gods, like an elixir of eternal youth, but I said two and let it rest there. The head disappeared behind the curtain as quickly as it had appeared, depriving the day of its brightness, the room of its dimensions, the breeze of its volume, my heart of its vigour, my breath of its flow. I slumped in the chair, counting moments, building castles in air, making wishes, waiting for her to come back with the sun and the moon rolled up her sleeves, flood the surroundings with her ambience, bring along with her a piece of eternity, put it on the pedestal of love, adorn it with unending dreams and squander it all away on me!

Within a few moments of restless waiting, by which time I managed to build up a mental scenario of what I was going to say to her, she returned with a tray balanced on the palm of her right hand like Venus balancing the universe on her little finger. It had a pot, a mug, a sugar bowl and biscuits on a plate. Putting it on the coffee table, she kneeled, bent her head, tossed behind her back the plait which had dangled to the front, filled the mug with the golden decoction, filled the room with the mellow aroma of the Orange Peco, added two sugars to the tea with a spoon, added a million beats to my heart with her look, pointed at the biscuits with a subtle movement of her chin, topping up the hospitality with a generous helping of the most disarming and winsome of her smiles, conversing only through the medium of her animated eyes, the multiple expressions on her face, the subdued body language, her invitation as well as her acknowledgment of my thanks both gift-wrapped in the same look!

"If this is for me," I said, swapping the biscuits with the consecrated sweets I had brought for her, "then this is for you!"

"*Laddoo!*" she exclaimed with cherubic glee, as if I had unwrapped in front of her the treasures of *Salar Jung*, "How did you know?"

I did not; but if it was a confession of her partiality to *Laddoos*, then I could kiss the hands that made them, the hands that sold them to me and the hands that consecrated them!

"If they're for a wish come true," she added before I could respond to the remark, the smile accentuated, the body language unscrambled, the sparks in the eyes multiplied and the expression on the face intensified, "then all the best to you!"

She could not have come any closer to the truth. The sweets were, indeed, intended to celebrate an event of success, but in my book, there was no other success worthy of celebration than the triumph of her charms over the surrender of my heart! I only wished I could tell her that, squeeze the enormity of my passion in the brevity of words, give her a glimpse of the turmoil going on in me, acquaint her with the unspoken language of my heart, share with her the storms into which I was plunged, put a piece of the *Laddoo* in her mouth with my own hand and let her taste the syrup of my secret success in the duel of love! But I could not open my mouth; I could not take the veil off the sacrosanct; I could not give expression to the withheld; I could not betray the hidden.

"Now, about the timetable," she said, coming down to brass tacks, "I had a look at it while making tea and it suits me fine, except for one slight alteration from Abbajan. On Wednesday, at the start of the first lesson, he wants you to come at five p.m. instead of eleven a.m.—just for that one day— if it isn't too inconvenient."

"Not at all. Five p.m. it is," I confirmed emphatically, put the biscuits in my mouth while she helped herself to half the *Laddoo,* presumably saving the other half for her mum, drank the tea without wasting a single drop, my eyes dug into her face, enjoying the first taste of her hospitality, hoping to drink many more cups of tea made by her precious hands in the future; hoping to spend every moment of my life in the joy of her company; hoping to live forever within an earshot of her cheerful voice; within the purview of her dreamy gaze; within reach of her bountiful arms, at her beck and call.

The sound of pots and pans in the kitchen, indicating her mum's return to the culinary preoccupations, inevitably brought those blithesome moments to an end. Both of us got to our feet and made for the door, she walking ahead of me to see me off, and I laboriously dragging myself to take her leave. Holding the door open to let me out, she did her best to hide the creases of disappointment on the face; the slight dimming of dazzlers in the eyes; the almost invisible toning down of smiles on her lips, the words *Khuda Hafiz* ringing a distinct note of optimism; the words 'see you soon' heavily laden with the weight of unspoken promises; and the words *Fi Aman Allah* the most potent amulet I ever wore around my neck!

Leaving her there standing in the door, without daring to look back, without sinking in the deluge of despair chasing me; without getting irretrievably lost in the maze of unpredictable events; without losing track of my sensibility and my better judgement; without letting go of caution, I picked up my bike and rode out of there, biting upon my lips, hating myself for running, castigating myself for the cowardice, for turning away from her before she turned away from me.

My resolve, however, did not last for long. As soon as turning the corner, I stopped pedalling, came to a complete halt, rested my foot on the kerb and looked towards her house. It put her living room window in my purview, and together with it, a part of her petit figure too, standing there and watching me, for some reason the *Dopatta* covering her head. On account of the distance, I could not see if the smile was still clung to her lips or had forsaken them; I could not see if her eyes were glittering like gemstones or had drowned in moisture; I could not see if her chest was heaving from anxious breaths or had left her out of breath; but she was still there, holding the curtains apart, looking out for me, letting me know how she felt, spelling out her wordless messages of affiliation, wedging my courage, carrying the torch, banishing the darkness and bringing in some light.

The rest of the hectic day passed away in running around. I coped with my first six tuitions in six hours, not counting the travelling time. No doubt, the strain exhausted me, but I managed to break the ice. Everything went according to expectations; my pupils were there waiting; we managed to establish a healthy rapport between us; they understood me and I understood them; we were on the same wave lengths; all the parents were polite and courteous; the lessons were deliberately kept light for the first day; homework targets set by Shabbu were modest; and as a matter of principle, any offers of refreshments made by my pupils were firmly declined. Thus, by half past five, day one of the project drew to a successful close.

I came home, physically a complete wreck but mentally very much at ease. All those tenterhooks on which I was ever since rolling the project disappeared at a stroke. I knew I could do the job and give full value for money. No doubt, things were going to get tougher from the second day onwards, as the target of six tuitions a day would have to be increased to eight in order to cope with the volume of work I had booked up, but it did not put me off. With only twenty-five pupils on my books, my potential earnings were already in excess of the salary of a head teacher. If I expected to make that sort of money, I should be prepared to work like a bull. I was, and so was Shabbu. It was about time we teamed up and prevented Papa from sinking deeper into debts. The house played a significant role in our lives. Without it, we could easily end up in the streets, and hence, it was of the utmost importance that we protected it from the clutches of the bank, or any other loan shark for that matter. Besides, if we made sure that our liabilities did not increase, Papa stood a fair chance of raising enough capital from the sale of the vacant site to settle his debts as well as to finance the weddings of both his daughters, setting me free to shape my own destiny without any sense of betrayal. So, hard work, even very hard work, was the least of my worries. I had the brains as well as the body to cope with it; I had the backing of a loyal sister like Shabbu and a loyal friend like Sal to help me out. So, what was I afraid of? Why should I shatter my dreams? Why should I waver in my resolve?

Just as I sat in my room, mulling over all those thoughts, in preparation for a shower to wash off the grime and dust, two friendly heads poked in through the door.

"Hi, Bhaijan," said Shabbu, "You okay?"

"No, he isn't," Rox took the lead and answered her on my behalf.

"Why not?" Shabbu asked her

"Because if he was," replied Rox, "he wouldn't be looking like the last pumpkin in the hawker's basket which the poor old hawker couldn't sell."

"I see," I said, suppressing a smile at the cheeky analogy, "Is that how I look?"

"Isn't that how he looks, *Baji?*" she asked Shabbu.

"And doesn't she look like a piece of cheese in the mousetrap which the mouse didn't touch, *Baji?*" I retaliated.

Aggressively bursting into my room, she pinched me in the arm quite hard. In answer to it, I, too, pinched her, not so hard. She screamed at me and Mamma shouted at the both of us.

"Stop it, you two!" she said.

"Price of progress, Mamma," Rox retorted, "Bhaijan has just left his boy's world and entered into a man's world. It shows on the face!"

"Shut up, Rox," Shabbu shouted in a deliberately lowered voice, "you know Papa isn't in a good mood."

"Why? What happened?" I asked, feeling concerned at once.

She gave me the depressing news that his plan to divide the site into smaller plots had run unexpectedly aground; apparently, before putting the plots up for sale for construction of domestic properties, he needed to obtain planning permission from the local municipality ahead of sale, and in order to obtain permission, he would have to invest thousands of rupees towards getting all the plots connected to the three main amenities: electricity, water and drainage. That was the law and there were no short cuts to it.

"Besides," Rox said, sobering up a bit, "something else has also happened which's raised his temperature quite a bit."

"Oh? And what's that?"

"A marriage proposal Moulana Sahib was trying to swing in Shabbu Baji's favour fell through. It seems the bridegroom's dad suggested that, if

Papa didn't have access to instant cash, they'd settle for a *Promissory Note,* which has thrown him into tantrums."

"Where is he?"

"On the lawns, waiting for his cup of tea and for us to join in so that he could get things off his chest."

Rushing through the shower, I changed into a pair of freshly laundered casuals and joined the family. No doubt, Papa did look a bit put off, but not as flustered as the impression I had been given. Frankly, he seldom lost his cool, especially at someone else behaving like an imbecile. Even if he did get into tantrums, he had a right to it; the very suggestion that he could give the bridegroom a promissory note in the place of cash was singularly preposterous and any father would take offence from it.

"You heard?" he asked me straight away.

"Yes, Papa, I just did," I replied, getting into my chair.

"Islam," he mused in a soft voice, "happens to be a way of life to follow and not a badge of honour to wear and show off."

"You mean, like the Victoria Cross?" Rox prompted him.

"Precisely," he said, his eyes lighting up with admiration for his clever daughter's clever analogy, "Some cheek, asking me to replace the cash with a promissory note! How ludicrous and how very *un-Islamic!*"

"What does Islam have to say on the subject of dowries?" Rox asked him.

"According to the Qur'aan and the *Shariyyah,* " he replied, addressing all of us turn by turn, "the only money—either in cash or in kind—that changes hands at the time of marriage is *Mehr,* to be given by the bridegroom to the bride, not the other way around—and a strictly, *means-tested affair!*"

"And what did you tell them?" I asked him.

"I could never bruise my daughter's pride by stooping to such levels. I told him to go take a hike!"

"That is," Rox explained to us on his behalf in much greater detail, laying due emphasis on the three *ASKS*, "Papa *asked* Moulana Saheb to *ask* this brat of a bridegroom to *ask* his father to go take a hike! Right, Papa?"

"Right."

"Hurray!" she applauded him, "makes me proud to be your daughter!"

"The reference," I tried to correct her, "is not to *this* daughter but to *that* daughter."

"So what?" she rammed in her opinion with sheer brute force, "What's good for the goose is good for the gander! I am not going to marry a dirt merchant who's quite prepared to pick up coppers straight out of cow dung with his own mouth? Yak!"

With that, the issue of marriage proposals was nipped in the bud. Mamma caused a diversion by asking me to tell them how my first day at work passed. With the exception of Azra, I told them everything, for the first time openly disclosing how much money Shabbu and I were expecting to make from the job, what sort of a future potential it had and what were we planning to do with our earnings, dwelling at length upon the imminent need to stop the rot, start repaying the interest to the Bank, keep the wolf from the door by keeping the grocer's account up to date, relax, have a good time, let matters take their own course, let us make our contribution to the family weal too, let us not forget that we were *five* now and not just *two plus*, let us not rush into things and regret later. If the site could not be broken into plots without sinking more money into it, it could be sold on its own; if one marriage proposal fell through, there could be another around the corner; if no proposals were forthcoming because of inadequate funds, Papa could always revert to his original plan of *flogging* me in order to raise the capital. I said all those things without causing him any offence because I felt he needed to be reassured about the future; he needed to realise that he was not on his own anymore, that we, too, were there to share his worries and to alleviate his burdens. The message sank in and the optimist in him instantly surfaced as the witty father and the witty daughter joined hands to banish the gloom and usher in a pleasant mood of exuberance.

Preparations for the second day's work became a joint effort by all three of us, occupying the best part of the evening until supper, and then going well into the night. Full concentration, coupled with Rox's endless jokes and potshots at both of us, made the time pass quickly. But soon after everybody retired to bed and I, too, hung up the gloves, my mind became victim to all sorts of persecuting thoughts. The sultry night refused to budge; moths and mosquitoes invaded the room; a fat gecko crawled on the ceiling and had its feast; there was absolutely no wind; nothing was visible outside the window except swarms of glow worms; the crickets squeaked listlessly in the grass, toads croaked, owls hooted, a stray bat, which had somehow wandered into the house, kept bashing on the living room windows rapaciously. Soon Azra entered my head and took control of everything; my words of solidarity to Papa rang a hollow note in my ears; I realised with a bleeding conscience that I had not been entirely honest with him; I was not yet ready to give her up, as soon as that, as easily as that, for as little as that; to throw her out of my system; drive her out of my life; bang the doors in her face; drop the curtain on her role; rub her image off my mind; pretend she did not exist; scorch in the flames of distress to the end of my living days!

Frankly, she *crashed* into my thoughts with such force that I felt I did not belong in that house any more; my breath began to choke; my heartbeat began to weaken; the bonds of blood and human love with which I had been tied to my family started to snap one by one; Shabbu and Rox kept fading into obscurity; Mamma and Papa looked like two unfriendly demons waiting to swallow me in their gory mouths; the house felt like a dungeon closing in on me from all sides; the buzz of the mosquitoes sounded like muffled wails; I felt I was being crushed to death underneath the weight of a massive toad; I was being bled to the bones by a hostile swarm of fireflies; I was being chased by grotesque geckos; I was being sucked out of my juice by marauding vampire bats; my entire life was being turned upside down, being beaten into a pulp, being churned and destroyed. Unable to stand the sheer horror of it all, almost on the verge of hysteria, drenched to the bone in sweat, gasping for breath, I came rushing out of my room into the hall, which gave access to the entrance door. But plunged in dark, in a nerve-racking hush, reproducing the echoes of snoring from all sides, it was of little comfort to me. Escaping from its oppressively claustrophobic dimensions at once and breaking into the freedom of spaces, into freshness, into some life giving breeze seemed like my best bet, and I came out without making any noise.

Once in the open, I fetched my bike from the garden shed and quietly slipped outside through the gate. The feeling of being locked up inside a metal jacket with no room to manoeuvre became overwhelming. I needed to do something to break out of its fatal grip; I needed to find a haven of peace and take shelter in it. There were only two places in town where I could find such a haven—one was Azra's house in Aghapura, and the other was the *Holy Shrine* farther beyond. At that time of night, there was no question of my finding her in the window looking out for me, her head covered by her *Dopatta*, her anxious eyes raised on the street, her lips sealed, her body motionless, her mind drowned in thoughts, but nevertheless, I made for her house, her physical proximity the next best thing to a visual encounter. I could breath the same air that she, too, was breathing, I could kiss the gusts of midnight breeze coming out of her house with a bit of her ambience mingled in it, I could sneak into her secret dreams and make new pacts with her; I could cajole my *Ka* to creep into her room with my messages of love; I could turn into a moth and burn my wings in the flame of her bedside lamp; I could become a glow worm and watch her restlessly tussle in bed for me; I could build notional temples and tabernacles on her footprints and enshrine her in them; I could violate the code of monotheism and worship her for a while; I could, for once, commit a sin for the sake of love and blister my soul! By going to her house, there were so many things I could do to gain some comfort, to feel alive, to bid for relief, to levitate, to transcend.

As expected, it was plunged in darkness and hushed. Resting my foot on the pavement across the street, I pictured her asleep in her room; dreaming or not dreaming; about me or about someone else; aware of the doldrums in which I was caught or oblivious to them; sharing my hopes or standing aloof; aiming for the same goals or at her own goals; walking alongside me or on a journey of her own; a thought in her mind to spare for me or engrossed in other thoughts; the sparks in her eyes triggered off by the passions I aroused or merely a part and parcel of her general makeup; the smiles on her lips inspired by the magic I made or simply a public relations exercise; the blushes and the body language intended for me alone or for the rest of the others too! I wished I knew; I wished I could figure it all out; I wished I could enter into a dialogue with her on the subject of having an open *affair* and negotiate its *stipulations*; I wished I could tell her I loved her and ask her if she loved me too; I wished I could hold her hand, tie the ribbons on her plaits, put a *betel-rolls* in her mouth, watch her lips turn red, adorn her with clusters of *Chambeli* and roses, wear a new set of bangles on her wrists, make beautiful patterns of *Henna* on her hands and on her feet, sit her down on a pedestal, put a tiara of diamonds on her head, let her watch her reflection on the sheen of my worshipful eyes. But the teacher in me woke up and splashed cold water on all my thoughts; the son in me, the brother in me, the Muslim in me, the cynic in me, they all joined hands and rebelled against me, took me captive, put shackles on my arms and legs, cut off my tongue, removed my eyes, threw away my heart and replaced it with a stone!

Soon, the much awaited Wednesday, treasured in a precious ivory cask along with a bunch of hopes and expectations, written down in the diary of my heart with my soul's pen, set aside from other dreary days of the week, embossed in gold, asterisked with diamonds, washed in dew, consecrated with faith, hung around my neck like a holy amulet, caught up when I was time-tabled for Azra's first lesson, my first test in self-control, her first opportunity to raise the stakes. A deliberate gap between my previous appointment and hers served nicely to recuperate from physical fatigue, repair the damage a day's hard work had done to my appearance, cool off the steam, recover the nerves, refresh the face, change the drenched clothes, put on something decent, something different, something new, something designed to get noticed, something from Yusuff to impress Azra, a covert message, a secret hint, a signal that was not intended to be picked up by anyone else other than her.

For the third time in course of only one week, my heart in my throat, my future in my fist, my joy at its peek, I knocked on that door again, which had, by then, assumed the significance of a doorway to paradise for me, and stepped back, reciting below my breath all the beautiful names of Allah mentioned in the Qur'aan. Not too unexpectedly, Mr. Ansari, clad in the same old sherwani and wearing the same fez, but a new expression on his face and a new spark in his eyes, answered it. After an exchange of warm greetings on the doorstep, he shook my hand and welcomed me to his house with unconcealed zeal and gust. The living room into which he escorted me also looked different from other days; the floor recently polished; the mattress on it rigorously dusted; the old purple curtains replaced with green, the book shelf given a facelift, a bouquet of wild summer blooms neatly arranged in the vase, two or three jossticks burning on the stand and filling up the room with soul stirring fragrance, all of which, if managed by a special person to receive a special guest on a special day for a special reason, then the rewards for all my toils stood paid in full already! Masking well the currents of excitement leaping out of my eyes, drawing blinds on the lines of expectation lurking on my face, I sat down and looked at him; at the face of the man who had brought my love into being; the face which partly reflected her own face and her features too, and had, therefore become quite precious to me.

"Thank you for coming in the evening instead of the morning, Mr. Quraishi," he said, triggering the conversation.

"At your service, Mr. Ansari," I responded, matching his politeness and his manners.

"I had one or two reasons for troubling you at such short notice," he began, dwelling upon the same subject, "and I'll get down to them straight away. First of all, I would like you to meet the rest of my children, who're seldom around at eleven in the morning."

"The pleasure is entirely mine, Mr. Ansari."

"Secondly, I do realise that, if you accepted refreshments wherever you went in course of the day, you could be getting yourself into serious problems with your digestive system, but could I urge you to make one exception today?"

"If you do, I won't say no, regardless of consequences, sir!"

"How very nice of you! With regards to your fees, I've decided to follow the example of a close friend of mine whose son you teach—no naming names—to put a sealed envelop in your hands at the end of each month, reflecting both your trouble as well as my ability. Would it be okay?"

I wished I could tell him how insignificant money was to me in that context, and that, the countless gifts of bliss his daughter could offer me on the tips of her eyelashes were gifts that I could not find in the treasures of King Solomon, but modesty prevented me from taking such a liberty.

"You couldn't have made a better offer, Mr. Ansari," I said instead and left it at that.

"And finally," he said, shifting his weight in the chair indicating a subtle degree of discomfiture, "Azra said she saw you once or twice in Asifnagar, next door to Mr. Quraishi's residence. Is he your father?"

"Yes, he is. Do you happen to know him, Mr. Ansari?"

"No, I don't. But I know the man who is squatting in his outhouse. His wife and Azra's mother are sisters, which is the real reason why there is this social intercourse between our families. I don't like the man; I don't like his way of life; I don't approve of what he's doing to your father; but unfortunately, blood being thicker than water, I can't stop my wife from seeing her sister. Neither can I ask Azra to stay away from her cousins. But I want you to know that, whatever Mr. Khan does with his life is his own business and has nothing to do with me."

"Of course, I'm conscious of that, sir."

"Thank you. And now that Azra has put her head on the anvil for the sake of her brother, I doubt very much if she'd find the free time to spend her Sundays with them, anyway."

"But if she does, she's more than welcome to drop in at our place and meet my family. I've two sisters about the same age as her who would be absolutely delighted to make friends with her."

Letting it rest there, he excused himself briefly and came back along with all his children, the eldest girl among them carrying a tray and struggling to say *Adaab* to me, until he relieved her of it and placed it on the coffee table. Fresh and fragrant, smartly dressed and behaving with impeccable manners, all eight of them surrounded me, introducing themselves without any formalities, without feeling coy or bashful, without any artificial pretences, or any deliberate show of restraints, one cuter than the other in looks as well as in behaviour. Mahjabeen, Vaseem, Nargis, Ayesha, Saberah, Aliah, the list went on and on. A little bit of Azra was concealed in every one of them, in their refreshing smiles, their pearly teeth, the bright eyes, the same toss of the head, the same lift of the chin, the same swing in the earrings, the same flight of the plaits, the same poise and bearing. Talking to them felt very much like talking to her; some sort of a quiet empathy flowing out from me and enveloping them; a strong rapport; a sense of belonging; of togetherness; of firm bonds; of affiliation; of mutual respect and of love.

"If this is your wealth, Mr. Ansari," I said with honesty, "then you are, indeed, a very rich man!"

Looking pleased with the way my compliment was phrased, he checked his time, gently dispersed the crowd, shared the snacks and refreshments with me, once again expressed his pleasure at having come to know me, wrapped up the hospitality and left. The room and the house plunged into complete silence, broken only by the parrot's endless chatter, repeatedly calling the name '*Azra! Azra! Azra!*', drowning me in an ocean of envy for being closer to her than me; for being able to roll that sweet name on his beak without the fear of reprimand; for being able to watch her get on with her daily chores without restraints; for being able to be fed his share in her *chapattis* without having to ask for it!

A few moments after Mr. Ansari had left, I heard the sound of footsteps and braced up to watch how dreams become realities; how imagination transcends into facts; how abstract images transform into concrete visuals! Azra entered the room with a few books in her hands, wearing her usual *Kurta, Shalwar* and *Dopatta*; her hair slightly dishevelled; the alert eyes raised on me; the tender lips relaxed in the exuberance of her magical smile; the tiny ruby on the nose-stud glittering; the glass bangles on her wrists making music; the rhythm of her breath sending vibrations through the air; crashing bolts of lightning upon me; raising tempestuous storms; drowning me in turbulent straits of emotion without any mercy at all. Even the ritual of *Adaab*, given a whole new outlook by her inimitable style, also had its own tale to tell. When she bent her head and touched the centre of her brow with the middle finger of her right hand, laying out a feast of smiles, I felt as though the winged unicorns drawing her chariot of dreams paused in that room for a fleeting moment to take me aboard before getting back once again up the rainbow track! I reeled; hurriedly searched for my voice; found it and returned the greetings, wondering within myself how on earth was I going to take charge of the situation; deal out the cards; set up the rules; start the game; change over from a doter to a teacher; keep my pangs aside; segregate my duties from emotions; give her father the value for money which I had guaranteed him.

"The list," she said in a husky voice, as always the first to break the ice; the inveterate protagonist between us; the resourceful one; the brave one; the articulate one!

"Pardon?" I said, having forgotten all about the homework she had offered to do during our previous meeting, and which had, by then, begun to seem like a million years away—a day without her as long as eternity; a day with her as quick as a flash; my sense of timing lost; my sense of balance shattered; my sense of duty in a mess!

"The list of things about Sakina you asked me to prepare," she elaborated, putting a sheet of notepaper in my hand.

Holding it with great veneration as if it was one of the tablets containing the Ten Commandments given to Prophet Moses by Allah, I looked at it. She had written a few lines about Sakina as promised, but not quite what I had wanted. 'Sakina my cousin, Sakina go Safdar Jung school, Sakina no English, Sakina play good, Sakina sing good,' it went on and on, in virtually illegible handwriting.

"How is it?" she asked, biting her tongue.

"Well," I said, at a loss for words, unwilling to hurt her feelings; to disillusion her; to associate dissatisfaction with anything she did; to assign to her anything that is less than perfect; anything she said; anything hers!

"No good, am I?" she said in a somewhat dry tone, reading the expression on my face, preferring self ridicule to criticism.

"No need to get disheartened, Azra," I said, making a bold bid to salvage her wounded pride, "as they say: 'from tiny acorns grow the mighty oaks' …"

"What does that mean?" she asked, the large eyes glowing like beacons and boring holes in my face.

"It means: 'from tiny *Nimbolis* grows the mighty *Neem,*'" I rephrased the idiom, deliberating using a tree and its seeds with which she was quite familiar; and which, in fact, stood right there in her front yard.

"Oh yes, how true!" she exclaimed, catching the sense in the saying without any difficulty.

"Don't worry about the English, Azra. Some pupils I teach don't even know the alphabet. It's my job to prepare you for the exam and let me worry about it. Now, let's see how you fare in maths."

It turned out to be an even poorer choice. Maths seemed to strike her like a disease, for she hurriedly changed the topic saying, "Do you mind if I called you '*master saheb*', master saheb?"

"No, I don't. How about maths …"

"Nice *master saheb!*" she said barely louder than a whisper and then hastily added, "I mean, you're a nice master saheb."

"Thank you."

"What did you think of the sweetmeats, *master saheb?*"

"Delicious! Now, then …"

"I made them myself, you know?"

"You did, eh? Well, now …"

Her nose wrinkled at that, but below it the smile became tenfold sweeter.

"What's the matter? Don't you like maths?" I asked her.

"I don't have a head for figures. They make me dizzy."

"I see. How much have you learnt so far? Multiplications? Subtractions? Additions?"

Her head cocked up but the eyes remained fixed on my face. I could see she was trying to suppress her laughter.

Making a start on additions, I took two mangoes from the tray brought by her sister, put them side by side on the coffee table and asked her how many mangoes there were. She said 'two' quite sensibly, but broke into such an unnerving smile after it, I lost my composure at once.

"What would happen if I added these custard apples to the mangoes?" I asked her, adding two custard apples to the mangoes, as there were no more mangoes on the tray.

"Pardon?" she said, blinking her eyelids several times and putting a dazzling glitter in them.

"What would happen if *you* added two custard apples to the two mangoes?" I asked, instead of asking 'these two to those two', just to get a two-plus-two-makes-four out of her.

"Who? *Me?*" she said, pointing at herself with her index finger, "why would I do a silly thing like that?"

"Come, come, Azra! You know what I mean?"

"Well," she said, drawing a deep breath, "I will either end up with a messy paste of mango pulp and custard apple cream, or a bad case of indigestion."

I had it coming! No one in his right mind adds mangoes to custard apples.

"I know subtractions better than additions," she claimed.

"Really? Let's see," I said, taking her up on her claim.

In reply, she extended her slender hand towards me, the texture of her skin as opulent as marble, the red bangles on the wrist enhancing its elegance, the long and shapely fingers moulded to sheer perfection, wordlessly inviting me to reach out for them; to take charge of her life; to be partners with her; to walk alongside her; to set her a goal and lead her to it!

"If I broke two out of these eight bangles, I'd be left with only six," she said, proudly looking into my eyes.

"Brilliant! And how many would you need to make them eight again?"

"Eight."

"Eight? Why?"

"Because," she replied with a great deal of relish and looking at me askance, "they are only sold in sets of eight, which is the big difference between making calculations here at home and being out there in the street!"

The sagacious remark, though passed in the most matter of fact manner, made me realise that, underneath the exterior of bashfulness and innocence, she had kept hidden quite a complex personality too.

"Abbajan …" She started to say something but broke off.

"Yes? What were you saying?"

"He doesn't seem to know what he's doing."

"Oh? What makes you think so?" I asked her out of mere curiosity.

"Well," she replied, drawing a deep breath again, "Taking the buffalo to the marshland is one thing, but making it wallow in the mud is quite another."

"I see," I said, staring at her, totally perplexed, "In other words, we're both wasting our time?"

"No! No! No!" she almost screamed, the emphasis on the 'N' gradually increasing, the pretty head shaking more and more rigorously, "I'll learn if *you* teach me."

"You mean, you won't mind wallowing in mud?"

"It doesn't matter whether I do or I don't. The important thing is, Abbajan is counting on me."

I breathed a sigh of relief. Her willingness to learn guaranteed our meeting twice a week at least for one year.

"All right, let's both try," I said, "Where there's a will, there's a way."

"Maths again?" she asked, shooting a disconsolate look in my direction.

I nodded, watching her keenly. She wrinkled her nose again, which seemed to be a habit with her. But on her face, even that looked absolutely gorgeous.

"Or, any other subject, for that matter," I said, making a generous concession, "You choose."

"Will you help me with this, *master saheb?*" she asked, pushing a leather-cased diary towards me from amongst the books she had brought along, the eyes still alight, but the smile gone.

I picked it up and browsed through the pages. There was a poem written in Urdu on each folio with a neat and firm hand. I read a few, quite struck by the sensitivity of her thoughts. The theme seemed to be the worship of perfection, but there was also something else concealed in every lyric she wrote—a scream of agony desperate to break out. The work was not only brilliant, but it was also original, individualistic and stirring. After skimming through several pages, I shut the book and stared at her. She sat watching me without the slightest hint of vanity or self-approbation, almost afraid to discover my reaction.

"Excellent!" I applauded sincerely, "Absolutely brilliant!"

"Do you really thinks so, *master saheb?*"

"Yes, I do."

"In that case, will you help?"

"How? If you're considering publication of the poems, I'd be glad to put you in touch with the right people. I know one or two personally. Would that do?"

"No," she said, registering disappointment on the face, "Something's wrong with my perspective, something missing, something off. I can *feel* it but I can't *find* it. That's where I need help."

The poems being the outcome of her thought process, if she felt so strongly that there was something missing, then there must be. "And you think I can help you find it?" I asked her.

"Can you?"

"I don't know, but I'll try."

"Thanks."

"Tell me one thing, though. As a matter of curiosity, that's all. Why are you so obsessed with perfection?"

The question put a deep frown on her brow. "Do you think Allah would have taken away one Paradise from Adam and Eve only to give them another?" she asked, staring at me with penetrating eyes.

"I daresay He wouldn't."

"There you are! We live in an imperfect world that won't last beyond a given point. We are told about the *end* at the *start* itself. Why then all the fuss? Why make the rose so beautiful and then commit it to autumn winds? Why create only to destroy? Why make and then break?"

Her questions made me sit up. For a young person of her tender years, the philosophy seemed too stout and heavy. "May I borrow this for a few days? At least until next Friday?" I asked her.

"For as long as you want to," she replied.

Leaving it at that, we returned to arithmetic once again. I soon found out that her knowledge of the subject was equally abysmal, but she stuck to it with firm determination. We worked for a whole hour, making no more reference to poetry or to mangoes and custard apples. Time just flew. She was terrific. Her sharp sense of humour filled every moment with fun. I could spend an entire lifetime in her company without experiencing a single dull spot.

After the lesson, I returned home, fully satisfied and thoroughly pleased, wearing a grin so broad, it stretched from one earlobe to the other!

CHAPTER (8)

"Hi, Bhaijan! You okay?" Shabbu greeted me as soon as I stepped into the house

"Yes, thank you," I replied.

"No, he isn't," Rox once again gate crashed into the conversation.

"Why, may I ask?" Shabbu queried it as usual. "What makes you think he isn't?"

"Because, if he was," Rox replied, "he wouldn't be looking like a joke at which no one laughed."

(How wrong she was! I had been laughed at in big doses … .)

"Is that how I look?" I demanded of her.

"Isn't that how he looks, Baji?" she asked Shabbu.

"I don't think so," said Shabbu, positively disagreeing with her. "If anything, he's looking more like a prayer that has just been answered."

(How very right she was! Whether or not I looked it, I certainly felt like it.)

"And doesn't she look like a burp that leaves a bad taste in the mouth, Baji?" I asked one sister, pointing at the other.

"Yes, she does," agreed Shabbu, bursting into laughter.

"I don't know about how you look," Mamma shouted from the kitchen, "but the three of you are beginning to sound like three ducklings orphaned in the *Narsanghi Fare*. All the time Bak! Bak! Bak!"

"And if you've chanced upon a *Zulayqa* in the midst of your pupils, Aali Janaab Yusuff Saheb," Rox quietly whispered in my ear, getting dangerously close to the truth, "and are keeping her hidden in a basket of *Laddoos*, I'll soon find out."

"Is that a threat?"

"It's a promise."

"Godrej locks happen to be *thief proof*. Didn't you know?"

"Some thieves happen to be *lock proof!* Didn't you know?"

"Roxana! On the double!" Mamma shouted again, "Your kettle is boiling and we need the oven."

It put an end to our challenges and counter challenges. She went away to make tea and I went into my room to prepare for the shower. Mention of tea reminded me at once of the tea I was given in Azra's house; brewed by her; brought by her sister; served by her dad; and together with it, the sweets which she said she had made herself, the mangoes, the custard apples, the buffaloes in the marshes, bangle sets, the jokes, the blithesome conversation, the furtive smiles, the surreptitious glances, the lingering looks, the occasional brushing of hands, the speeding of breaths, her responses, my thoughts, the black diary containing her feelings, her philosophy, her lyrics, her talent, her writing, a part of her ethos and her essence captured in the inflexibility of ink and paper, a visual reflection of her invisible self—so much that went on in that tiny room in so short a time, possibly the writing down of a *preface* to the story of our lives!

Ending the endless flow of my thoughts there, I opened my briefcase, took the diary out, held it in both hands, kissed it, pressed it on my chest, my eyes, my cheeks, did everything else except reading the contents before hiding it in a safe place because of implicit threats of espial made by certain *unpredictable characters* in the house! Read it I would, sooner or later, absorbing every word written, caressing each and every line, extrapolating the hidden, exploring the complex, enjoying the obvious, eulogising the exemplary, but not while perils of exposure were hovering around right outside my door. Luckily for me, there was a genuine piece of antique furniture in my room in the form of a medieval chest of draws containing a secret compartment, inaccessible to bungling hands, which could easily store not only Azra's diary, but also a diary of my own I intended to keep from then onwards and record in it the progression of events, now that I had found a new pivot to revolve around.

However, later on in the night, after everybody retired to bed, just as I crept out of mine, switched on the bed lamp, fetched the diary from its hiding place and settled down to read it, several unnerving thoughts entered my head and disgruntled me. Ever since I set eyes upon Azra in our vineyard, I had fallen a prey to such intense emotional turbulence as I never knew before; I had been tempted into drifting away from my responsibilities, ignoring my blood bonds, trifling with my conscience, overlooking all moral perimeters, trespassing into the forbidden, breaking every rule in the book. And as though that was not bad enough, the dictates of my destiny had given the story of my life an unexpected twist by bringing us closer together in the unlikely roles of *the teacher and the taught*; introducing extra temptations in my way; setting up new goals in self restraint; erecting hurdles hitherto unknown to me; forcing me to take difficult tests of endurance. The question in front of me was, if it came to the crunch, how well would I measure up to that challenging role? What would I do if things went wrong? If my expectations did not bear fruit and my dreams shattered? If the tide of adversity swept me off my feet and abandoned me in the midst of doldrums? If destiny remembered to deal out only punishments and forgot all about rewards? If her infatuation with me turned out to be just a teenage crush which would wear out with time? And above all, one bright and breezy Sunday afternoon, if Moulana saheb dropped in with the *ideal* proposal for me from a bride who could not only lay golden eggs but also make the roses blush? Who would bother to look inside a little house in Aghapura belonging to the Union Paper Mill and take my passion for Azra seriously, regardless of how pretty she was and how many other things she could offer me except a fat dowry?

Besides mine, she had a few problems of her own, too, to contend with. At sixteen, she had more responsibilities straddled on her young shoulders than I ever had. Like she herself said, whether she relished the idea of wallowing in the mud or not, she had to, because her Abbajan, her Ammijan, Vaseem, Saira, Mahjabeen and etcetera were counting on her. Even if I broke out of my oaths of solidarity and pledges of loyalty, it did not mean that she would do the same. The ripples by which her paper boat was surrounded were not the same as ours; we at least had alternatives; we had a large house; a massive vacant site smack in the middle of a rapidly expanding metropolis; I had a master's degree and both my sisters were grown up. Put together, we were quite capable of looking after our parents and ourselves. But her circumstances were different. With so many mouths to feed and only one breadwinner in the family, the odds were stacked high against her. In such precarious circumstances, if ever the tests of loyalties were forced upon her, by me or on account of me, I could never forgive myself for driving her into a tight corner; I could never instigate her to choose sides against her own kith and kin.

Taking all that into consideration, it seemed safer to use some caution in our relationship rather than haste. If the few poems I already read were anything to go by, there was enough ammunition in that diary to demolish all my defences completely and force me into lifelong captivity, whereas I was not yet ready for such lasting ties. Besides, as things stood, we seemed to be doing quite fine. Without a sound career or an appropriate job leading to it, the chances of my getting the *ideal* match were as remote as pie in the sky; no matter how much money I was making, a tutor is just a tutor, and hence my poor *popularity ratings* on the *matrimonial market* did not hold the prospects of a sudden rush for *shares*. As her tutor, I was able to see her at least twice a week without any problems, and if *the lovers' blues* smote us sometimes, there was always that derelict vineyard for her to visit and a game of hide and seek to beguile ourselves with. Hence, I put away the diary back in its safe spot, tuned in to some moody film songs on the radio, reduced the volume to its lowest, shut my eyes and escaped into the never-never land.

Time began to pass with lightning speed. Shabbu and I worked relentlessly. No doubt, the strain wore us out, but it also had its own rewards. For one thing, we were able to afford a better standard of living; the quality of food we ate rose and we never missed another meal. The part-time maid and the gardener were made full-time; some of the old furniture and curtains were replaced; the house was given its first whitewash since Papa inherited it and the garden had never looked better. Mamma hardly bothered with the kitchen, which enabled her to give Papa some much needed personal attention. She also recited the Qur'aan twice a day instead of once and offered *NAMAAZ* on time.

Regular income helped Papa too. He no longer had to borrow money from the bank or accumulate unpaid interests. With the stress gone, his health improved, restoring much of his personal charm. Watching our parents go to the shops and buy whatever they wanted to gave us a great sense of satisfaction; being able to see the result of our toils made all the difference to us. I, too, helped myself to a small luxury and bought a motorcycle on hire purchase. While teaching itself was not so hard, going around from house to house on the bike certainly was. It made life a lot easy.

From a very special person, Azra became the most important person in my life. Though I never put it to her in so many words; never violated the codes of morality in which I truly believed; never made the most sublime of my emotions common by putting them under a common caption; never dared to trifle with traditions; lose track of modesty; ignore manners or overlook etiquette, it was only too obvious that I had taken Cupid's darts smack in the chest and was reeling in its aftermath. The four working days of the week when I was not timetabled for her lessons turned into dark days of grievous punishment imposed upon me by cruel fate. I could not concentrate on the job; I behaved like a cat on a hot tin roof; I became broody and absentminded; became too sentimental; listened to love songs from Indian movies on every channel of the radio; stuffed the pages of my diary with my romantic writing; filled up all the empty spaces in it with her name; kept it hidden along with her poems and away from the unkind hands of *nosy parkers* in the house; lost my appetite; lost my taste; lost myself; lost the cool and confident *man* behind the man! But on Wednesdays and Fridays when I was timetabled for her, I did very little other than preparing her lesson; preparing her homework; rehearsing my piece; choosing my clothes; grooming my hair; scrutinising my reflection in the large mirror; talking to it; smiling at it, improving upon it; doing all sorts of crazy things I had never done before; never thought it possible that I would do them; never even felt embarrassed at having begun to! Love had come to me in big doses and changed everything.

On those two glorious and blissful days, come rain, come sunshine, come the Day of Reckoning, when I went to her house, spring accompanied me; Angels protected me; fairies guided me; her memories turned into amulets and hung around my neck; her blessings took over my bike's handle bars; her *Fi Aman Allahs* and *Khuda Hafizes* restrained its speed; her henna-soaked palms kept the rest of the traffic under firm control so that I reached her house safe and sound; the lessons progressed as planned; our targets remained unchanged; our paths did not part; our journey did not terminate; our goal did not change; her delicious beverages trickled down my throat; her snacks and sweets kept my hunger appeased; her smiles quenched my thirst; her conversation beguiled me; her laughter entertained me; her mother welcomed me; her dad respected me; her family adored me. I never forgot to take bunches of *Chambeli* for her and her sisters; she never refused to wear them; I never treated her with disdain; she never took me for granted; I occupied a place of esteem in her heart; she permeated my entire life and my soul; I was for her what she was for me, even though we never told each other that.

There was no longer any need for me to dodge reading her poems, either. In the beginning, while browsing through the diary, I had completely misjudged her theme. Upon revision, I realised she was not eulogising perfection but lamenting its inevitable decay; her quest was the *purpose* of perfection without *perpetuity*. She admired the fresh rose at dawn, but underlying the admiration, there was always a cry of anguish for the one that withered in order to yield it a place; she could not praise sunshine without weeping over the sunset; she could not postulate peace without mulling over the storms. Such negative thoughts made her poetry unduly depressing and was also in sharp contrast to her own cheerful nature; for one so full of life, the direction seemed wrong. But before I could point it out to her, she changed course herself; at some stage and for some reason, the *quest* began to turn into *acceptance*; concern into contentment and the question became the answer. Evil hypothesised good, pain reflected relief, sorrow coexisted with joy, ends culminated in beginnings.

In course of those weeks and months of unparalleled happiness, I had many moments of immense anxiety too. Unaware of the storms in which my boat was caught, Papa was still on the lookout for an ideal match for me. It was, by far, the most convenient and speedy solution to his problems; I needed a good wife and the girls needed good husbands both of which could be accomplished in one stroke. At the same time, it would also remove the chains on his legs, setting him and Mamma free to concentrate upon their spiritual obligations, such as Pilgrimage to Mecca and Medina before death overtook them. Having money for fares and expenses was not enough. Islam prohibits Muslims from contemplating on a *Hajj* whilst there are outstanding debts on hand or unmarried daughters at home; based on the thinking that redemption of worldly liabilities must take priority over redemption of the spiritual dues. So, they were inescapably trapped from all sides. Even if the site were sold, it still would not mean freedom to them; their marriages were of crucial importance to their planning. And it was such a sensitive issue, I dared not even postulate what would happen if the tide took a turn and caught me unawares. Allah was my only hope, my only bastion, my only friend. I went to sleep with His name the last word on my lips and woke up with His name the first thought in my mind in the hope that, having brought us together, He would take charge of our lives; protect us from the adversities of fate; help us reach our goals. All five times in course of every day, after each *NAMAAZ*, I repeated His Titles on my rosary and prayed only for one thing: to spare us the test of loyalties; to make our dreams come true; to bless us with success in our secret aspirations; in our love; in our happiness!

Soon, the month of *RAMADAN* caught up with us when our resolves in moral rectitude and righteousness were put to the ultimate test. It is a month that sits in the Islamic calendar like a jewel; it is a month when the Qur'aan was revealed to our Prophet, when all Muslims are called upon to make sacrifices for Allah; to endure hunger and thirst without grumbling; to give alms without any restraint; to keep their bodies clean and their minds chaste;

to refrain from any form of cruelty, misdemeanours or imbalances, not even anger; to set up a strict code of self discipline and adhere to it; to impose self restraints and abide by them; to observe a punctual schedule of fasting without any excuses, not only in food, but also in thought, in action, in speech, in behaviour, at home, at work, in travel, with family, with friends, with strangers. It is the only month in which restrictions are imposed even upon conjugal relationships—a month of endless tests, a month of total dedication, a month of utmost self sacrifices.

At the same time, Ramadan is also a month of rewards and blessings, when Allah too is in a charitable mood; when prayers are heard as well as answered without discrimination; when human congregations in mosques for worship are thronged by angels; when after each solicitation for divine mercy a million cries of *Ameen* are echoed by invisible mouths; when the meek are protected; when the hungry are fed; when the naked are clothed; when the destitute is sheltered; when battles are brought to a standstill; when hostilities are abandoned, when truces are drawn, when nursing breasts are filled with milk of human kindness; when cradles of sick babies are rocked by healing hands; when the dimensions of graves are stretched to their widest limits, when Allah steps out of His Throne of Glory and rubs shoulders with us mortals; when tears of grief are dried; when cries for help are heeded; when sins are contained; when souls are redeemed; when the doors of Paradise are thrown wide open; when Allah takes us all to His bosom and embellishes us with His resplendence. In such a great month, such a wonderful month, such a glorious month, there is no room for grief or for any disappointment, for loneliness and recantation, for despair and hopelessness!

Right through the first three weeks of the month I carried on with my work uninterrupted. Even though the cycle of activity is never brought to a halt because of fasting—and the Qur'aan makes sure that it must not be—the volume of work, in my case, did reduce a bit, all my pupils being Muslims, fasting and joining congregations five times a day, followed by additional sessions of *Taravaeeh* late at night. Concessions were made on both sides, lessons were shortened, homework targets became modest, attendance was made voluntary and timekeeping relaxed. No doubt, it made life a little easy for me, but that was the least of my worries; hunger and thirst hardly bothered me because, with so much work to do, time passed quickly. Where my faith was put to the litmus test was during Azra's lessons, and by an entirely different aspect of fasting, which imposes severe restraints on what we behold, what we think, what we touch, how we conduct ourselves. Strictly speaking, since we were not related to each other, we should have been observing *Purdah* and sitting behind curtains. No doubt, on account of her father's indifference to it, we were able to dispense with the restriction, but that did not mean we were free to do what we liked. Even when sitting face to face, one had to behave as if the other did not exist, as if both of us were not present in the same room at any one time. We were expected to refrain from coming into physical contact with each other, not even the slight brushing of the hands while exchanging books, from holding any sort of conversation except what was necessary for teaching and learning, from loud outbursts of laughter, from entertaining unbecoming thoughts in our heads, from indulging in trivialities, from being deliberately amorous, from looking at any part of the body other than the face exposed to the naked eye through a firmly drawn veil. Even though no one was standing watch over us and telling us how to behave, that was the approved protocol and we were supposed to know it as well as expected to observe it.

I tried, both of us did, but it would be less than honest on my part if I claimed that I succeeded. I could not possibly look at her face without admiring her beauty; I could not admire her beauty without stirring my soul; I could not stir my soul and yet behave as if she did not exist. If I made a resolute effort and avoided looking at her, I could not stop her perfume from going into my lungs; if I avoided talking to her, I could not avoid hearing her voice; if I avoided laughter, I could not escape the charisma of her smile; if I avoided confronting her directly, I could not avoid the imprints of her image engraved upon my mind. I could not be so deeply immersed in her and yet breathe; I could not touch the flames leaping out of her and yet not burn; I could not go to the oasis and turn away without quenching my thirst; I could not fall asleep without letting my *Ka* wander through my field of dreams! In short, I could not live without breathing; I could not grow without living; I could not run without standing. That was how indispensable she was to me, the other side of my coin, the light that shone to brighten my darkness, the day that broke to end my night, and the melody that rang to negate my silence! It was a battle I could not win, I did not even try to wage, and I conceded defeat without picking up the arms. It was, therefore, entirely up to Allah to judge me, and if He found me guilty of emotional excess, to let His Divine forgiveness prevail over my human error!

Winning a few tests and losing a few, proud of a few of our accomplishments and ashamed of the others, sometimes letting our bodies be ruled by our minds and sometimes letting our souls be governed by our hearts, we entered the fourth and the final week of Ramadan, which contained the *Shab-e-Qadr,* then a special day on Friday, and finally the night of the New Moon marking the end of Fasting, all three days of equal significance. Hence, for that one week, by the unanimous desire of all parents and pupils, I was persuaded to take time off and concentrate on my own family's preoccupations. It helped a lot because the twenty-seventh day of Fasting is considered the most important day of the month, to be followed by *Shab-e-Qadr,* when special prayers begin after *Taraveeh* and last until *Sehri.* On that day, all those Muslims who can afford it feed all those brethren who cannot, by preparing good quality food and sending it to local mosques for mass consumption after breaking one fast and before starting the next. Having adhered to that tradition even when the chips were down on us, we managed to fare better this time and delivered a lavish meal, to eat, to enjoy, to give thanks to Allah and to bless those who hosted it. The backbreaking preparation that went into it, coupled with the Friday Mass, the *Shab-e-Qadr* and the *Chaand-raat,* was one good reason why taking time off work really helped.

But there was another reason too for the generous gesture, and it was the preparation for the blithesome occasion of the *Eid-ul-fitr* itself, which follows the sighting of the New Moon, marking the end of austerities and the start of festivities in appreciation of Allah's bounties, celebrated by Muslims all over the world with great enthusiasm. Rich or poor, from out of our savings, or from our incomes, or, in some cases, even downright borrowing, most families tend to break records in spending for the festival. As far as possible, we all wear new clothes, we distribute new clothes to those who cannot afford to buy them, we eat well and we feed well. For the ladies, it is a license to dig into their men's wallets and blow away the last copper remaining. They rummage through the *lovers arcade* for cosmetics and jewellery, they buy glamorous clothes, they buy large packs of *Shikakai* and *Rita shells,* Henna and bath oils, false hair and hair bands, sari borders and embroidery, ribbons and hair clips, silver and golden threads, wives to please their husbands; girls to please their sweethearts; the affianced to please their fiancés; the gentler sex to please their secret admirers; a bit of over indulgence discreetly conceded in order to compensate for all the austerity which had thus far been voluntarily endured.

With an inveterate spender like Rox in the house, and some additional funds already earmarked for that purpose, shopping turned into quite a hectic affair. Thrilled to bits that I had the time to spare, she dragged me everywhere.

For the first time since she grew up into a young woman of exquisite looks, we had the capacity to let her loose herself in the shops with but few restrictions. I did not mind it and neither did Shabbu. Only, they went into the shops where each and every one of the gorgeous displays reminded me of a person who was missing from the group, who was not part of the group, at least not yet. She, too, was about the same age as Rox, had the same likes and dislikes, same looks and airs, the same needs and cravings, the same choices and selections. If she was there, and if I could, I would have sat her on one side of the scales, put the entire stocks of the *lovers arcade* on the other and given it all away to the beggars lined up outside the *Holy Shrine*, to take them home for their women folks. But she was not there, I was not entitled to buy her any gifts, she was not eligible to accept them from me.

Nevertheless, whenever the girls disappeared into shops of their choice hunting their own bargains, I, too, sneaked into other shops and looked around. Without any idea of her sizes nor any experience in shopping for girls, all I could do was to gaze at the spectacular displays and picture her wearing one of those exquisitely tailored *Gharara suits*, or her favourite '*Shalwar, Khamis* and *Dopatta*', or the pure silk *Banarasi saris* with superb golden borders, which I had never seen her wear, the lustrous strands of her dark hair washed and brushed, woven into plaits, tied with ribbons, the elegant feet hidden in red sandals, the silver bells on her anklets jingling, the delicate palms adorned with patterns of henna. It turned out to be such a fascinating pastime, I forgot all about Shabbu and Rox for a while, bought a couple of dresses for her, based entirely upon guesswork, got them gift wrapped and hid them in the small glove compartment of my motor bike. I had no idea if I would see her before the festival, and even if I did, would I be able to lavish on her such gifts without attracting attention or inviting comments, and even if I dared, whether she would break the protocol and accept them, but it remained to be seen. For the time being, I could lock myself in my room after nightfall, scatter the packets on my bed, gaze at them, kiss them, her gifts if not her hands, her footwear if not her feet, her image if not her self, her memory if not her core. After all, it had been a few long and lonesome days since I last met her, when she saw me off at the door with moist eyes, with her lips engaged in the arduous task of saying goodbye, with her hands unwilling to shut the door after me, with her feet desperate to walk away along with me!

However, after returning to the pavement near where I had left the girls, just as I stood waiting for them and ruminating, someone said "*Adab Arz, master saheb!*" from not too far away and startled me. When those familiar words, spoken in a gentle voice for which my ears had been starved for days, rang in the midst of all that hustle bustle, I could not believe my ears, I could not believe my luck, I could not believe such a delightful miracle had taken place for me and put me within a striking distance of the only person in the world whom I wanted to see and be with at that particular moment in time. Having somehow spotted me in the midst of the dense crowd, she had torn herself away from her family and come rushing to greet me, to make my day, to fill my lungs with a fragrance far richer than all the perfumes of *the lovers arcade* put together, to wear around my neck a chain beaded with the gemstones glittering in her eyes, to bless my soul with the unique wealth concealed in the richness of her smiles, to banish my loneliness with the joy of her company, however brief it be. My quest for her throughout the last week of Ramadan, the sweet and sour pain of separation in my heart, the unendurably intense thirst in my eyes, they all disappeared at a stroke. I felt so repleted and revived, it was like leaving behind me a desolate wilderness and crossing over into lush pastures, into green fields, into living gardens, on to a new plane arrayed with the blessings of Spring!

"Azra!" I gasped, overwhelmed and short of breath, the only word that could express my inner excitement, the only name that could do justice to my fervour, the only acknowledgment that could speak for the enormous storm triggered off inside me by that unexpected encounter.

"Just wanted to wish you an *Eid Mubarak*, master saheb!" she said, looking deep into my eyes and adding a hitherto unseen connotation to the exuberance of her smile.

"*Eid Mubarak* to you too, Azra," I reciprocated, choking with a sudden upsurge of emotion, "May Allah fill your life with all the joys of this world and make your smile last forever!"

My wish, made from the bottom of my heart and delivered with utmost sincerity, seemed to have touched a sensitive chord inside her and cause an invisible upheaval, for she put the tips of her fingers between her teeth and gently bit upon them in order to mask the interaction. As she stood there, half drowned in the endless tide of shoppers, staring at me with intent eyes, the thick welter of lashes flapping from time to time, cheeks flushed from a combination of sunlight and blushing, raising a million questions by herself and finding her own answers to them, trying to set up a link between her thoughts and my words, to interpret the complex expressions on my face, to decipher the odds and to place her bets, the rest of her sisters also arrived and mobbed us from all sides. In the turmoil that followed, her response to my emotive blessings muffled. Courtesy demanded that I divided my attention between them equally, and I did, but my impatient look kept returning to her again and again, sometimes to the silence of her eloquent eyes, sometimes to the neutral smile sealing her lips, sometimes to the impenetrable mask covering her face.

"Will you come to see us on *Eid*, master saheb?" she asked me in a trembling voice just before joining her sisters and leaving, loud enough for me to hear but not to be heard by the others.

"If I can't, or if I don't," I replied, also caught up in the same invisible tremors in which she was rocking, "will you meet me in the vineyard?"

Although I had not intended to extend such an invitation to her, strewn with perils and complications, I did, and without regrets. So far, in spite of being so irretrievably immersed, so firmly bonded, so deeply enamoured, we had only communicated with each other through the medium of our eyes and our body language, without once giving expression to any of our passions, without resorting to the spoken word, without coming out into the open, not yet. Whatever be her reasons for it, mine were fairly obvious: my circumstances had not yet changed; half of my moral dues were still outstanding, my conscience was still trapped in secret pangs, a *Damocles' Sword* was still precariously poised on top of my head. Besides, if I had made a mistake in interpreting her feelings for me, if I had misread the messages in her eyes or on her face, if I had made an error of judgement, a confession of such sensitivity by me at a time like that could easily affect our entire relationship, take her away from me for ever, shatter my dreams, ruin my life, even kill me. With so much at stake, and under the threat of such serious ramifications, it was silence that was gold and not speech. I could carry on loving her until eternity without telling her, I could reconcile with what little I had in my hand than go for the sweepstakes and lose it all, I could be happy living under her shadow than have that shadow taken away from me, I could drive around her house again and again just for one glimpse of her in the window than have that window walled. But it was something I had to do sooner or later, I had to brave the risk, I had to take the plunge. So, why not on a day when Divine mercy and compassion were rampant upon earth, when Allah Himself was out there rubbing shoulders with us mortals, when all our self denials and self sacrifices were being rewarded with both hands?

Before she could say yes or no, her sister Mahjabeen rushed back and dragged her away, leaving me high and dry, neither accepted nor denied, neither answered nor evaded. Moments after their backs turned, my sisters also emerged from the shops, their shopping tucked underneath their arms, all their needs satisfied, their faces flushed, their hearts content, now engrossed more in discussing their bargains than hunting for them, making plans for the festival, what to wear, what to cook, whom to invite, where to go, which films were showing in which cinema halls, who acted in them, who gave a better performance than whom, what time did the shows start, how much scope they needed to beat the queues. Rather apprehensive of Rox nosing into the secret contents of my glove compartment, eager to get home before they did and hide the gifts in a safe place, I quickly arranged their transport in a *cycle rickshaw* and rushed home.

Two days later, it was the night of the New Moon and we all went up the terraces to sight it. On a clear and cloudless night like that, we had no difficulty in spotting the luminance of the thin crescent against the background of the grey sky despite the crepuscule of dusk. Sirens blew all around us, marking the end of Ramadan, followed by the call of the *Mo'azzan* on the loudspeaker, summoning the Faithful to proceed for the evening Congregation and offer thanks to Allah, leaving barely enough time in hand to make our wishes. I shut my eyes and dearly wished Azra was there for me to see her salubrious face when I opened them, I wished the time for her to be there was not far away, I wished I knew if she, too, was making the same wish, she was sharing my fervour from across the other side of our neighbourhood, she was conscious of the storms raging in my head, she too was praying for us to be together soon, she was getting herself ready to take over the reigns of my life. Then I wondered if she would come to meet me in the vineyard or not; if she would accept my gifts, my pledges, my love, my invitations; how would she react to them, would she get scared, get into a panic, be shocked, be angry, turn away, reject me, repulse me, forsake me? I did not know, and on that night, there was not enough time left for me to hypothesise, to postulate, to speculate. The dice was cast and it only remained to be seen on which side it settled!

On the following morning, the main *Qutbah* was held at the *Eidgaah*, followed by the special *Namaaz*. Once it was over and the congregation relaxed, I looked around to spot familiar faces for greetings. Sal was there with his father, frantically trying to catch my attention. I rushed over to him; we shook hands, hugged and wished each other *Eid Mubarak*, followed by a similar routine with his father. That year, I had made a lot of new friends by reason of my job. Most of my pupils were there, along with their fathers or guardians. I got busy shaking all those hands extended towards me for greetings, wishing them well and being wished well by them. Mr. Ansari was also there, accompanied by his son, Vaseem, and blessed me with a warm hug. Seeing them there reminded me of the one who was physically not there, but was yet there with me, hidden inside my heart, inside my eyes, inside my mind, holding my hand, walking alongside me, greeting those whom I greeted, shaking the hands I shook, repeating my words below her breath, looking at me, smiling at me, adding a whole new dimension to the blithesome festivities. If it was up to me, I would have got on my motorbike and gone straight to her house racing with the wind, but the standard protocol was, I waited for Papa to finish with his friends and then accompanied him to our house first, meet and greet the family, touch Mamma's feet, receive her blessings, wait for my sisters to touch my feet, bless them, break the final few hours of symbolic fasting on that day with *vermicelli pudding*, calculate the amount of charity we were required to give by way of *Fitra*, make sure it reached the right destination, feed all those beggars and destitutes whom Papa had invited, partake in the special festival meal, chew a *pan* made by the girls and only then think in terms of visiting my friends, whoever they be, provided there were no guests expected to visit us first.

By the time all those priorities were concluded, it was well into the afternoon. Smartly dressed in their new clothes, Mamma and my sisters looked smashing. So did Papa, showing himself off in his black *Sherwani*, white *Churidar*, the *Jinnah cap*, a smart haircut and a nicely trimmed beard. The house, with its recent paintings and decorations, new curtains and new furniture, neatly spruced and cleaned, reflected some of the affluence that the job, and a regular income resulting from it, had ushered into our lives. But away from the house, its occupants, its surroundings, its changing fortunes and mixed blessings, my mind was occupied by other thoughts, about how to break out of there before guests arrived and caused additional diversions, held me up once again, delayed me from driving over to Azra's house, look at her face without the strain of fasting on it, see what the removal of restrictions on wearing flowers in her hair had done to it, see the lips soaked in the red colouring of *betel-rolls*, the welter of lashes accentuated by strokes of eye shadow, the cheeks once again pink from an increased circulation of blood, the shapely contours of her body wrapped in something new, which she must have bought from the shops that day, a new set of bangles on her wrist, a new pair of sandals on her feet, new ribbons tying up her plaits, new perfume emanating from her body, new dazzlers in her eyes. I was so very desperate to make one quick trip to her house, take one quick look at her, whisper one quick word in her ear, hear just one beat of her heart in exchange for ten beats from mine, enrich the festival with the wealth of her greetings, adorn the hour with the coronets of her ambience, put her seal upon everything mine!

Unfortunately, I just could not. Ours being part of a very large outer family, both from Mamma's side as well as Papa's, not to mention the wide circle of his closest friends, guests began to trickle straight after lunch. I could not leave him on his own at a time like that and go away. Courtesy demanded that I stand shoulder to shoulder with him in receiving, looking after and entertaining them. I did, but with only half my mind on the job in hand, while the other half, the most receptive half of it, remained at bay, constantly tuned in to the nonstop shouts of children reverberating on the other side of the parapet wall, just in case it also contained one voice that was dearest to me, in case she did pick up my invitation, accept it, remember it, respond to it, and was waiting to greet me. At one particular point in time, when the gathering of guests in our house was at its densest and our side of the wall, too, became as noisy as the other, I could not resist the temptation to disappear from there, fetch the gifts from my room which I had bought for her, hidden in a carrier bag of some sort, sneak into the vineyard and look around. If she was there, I could greet her, talk to her, make my confessions, quench my thirst, rest my overworked heart, put the gifts in her hand, rush back and then celebrate the rest of the festive day with such rejoicings as our two hundred year old *Haveli* had never known before, not even during our grandfather's halcyon days! But if she was not around, I could make use of the opportunity to hide them in one of the empty shops and get back to them later, after she arrived.

Somehow, behaving like a thief in my own house, escaping the attention of many prying eyes, a lot sharper than Rox's, my heart pounding away, my knees shivering from the fear of getting caught and losing my face in front of all those big shots, I managed to smuggle the merchandise from my room undetected, pinched the key to the door and sneaked into the vineyard, prayers rampant on my lips, shadows gliding in my eyes, butterflies fluttering inside my stomach, my life on the line, my honour at stake, my fingers crossed. In the vineyard, no longer as derelict as before because of some extra work Papa had got the gardener to do, and hence, with less hiding places now, I did not need a miracle to see that all the kids were there, engrossed in play, except Azra. Neither won nor lost, neither in the plus nor in the minus, I checked the time on my watch and was relieved to notice that it was still only half past three, with plenty of time to spare for visiting relatives, especially aunts and uncles. So, without despairing or wasting too much time, I carried on with my secret mission, went into the most sheltered of the shops, found a safe spot, added to the gifts a special Greetings Card which I had bought for her on the very first day of Ramadan, containing an emotionally charged poem and addressed to her in my handwriting, hid the carrier bag, removed all visible traces of detection, begged Allah to send His Angels for guarding it, or to keep it under His own protective eye, let me successfully finish what I had nervously begun, let me make my confessions to my lady love that day, such a great day in His divine calendar too, let me revel in its bliss, let me attain my earthly salvation, let me enter the door to our *mortal Paradise* holding her hand!

To do all that, it took me only five minutes or less, not long enough for me either to be missed or to be searched. Back at my post, breathing a big sigh of relief, masking the silly smile of accomplishment on my face, I picked up the threads, crashed into conversations, said 'yes' to the elders, said *no* to the youngsters, went around passing fresh *betel-rolls* to those eligible to chew them, revitalised Papa's *hukka*, asked Shabbu to send us some more hot vermicelli pudding, asked Rox to mind her business, asked the maid to make a start on tea, all that without losing my nerve, without letting my inner state of mind reflect on the outer state of tranquillity, without looking too thrilled or too distraught, but above all, without taking my mind off any signs of progress on the other side of the wall, without letting my concentration drift too far away from it, without giving up hope too soon and without breaking into premature rejoicings.

Round about half past four, just as women gathered in the *ladies wing* began to send surreptitious signals to their men folk gathered in the *men's wing* to call it a day, my strained ears picked up the sound of a familiar laughter in the vineyard, heralding the arrival of good tidings for me, replacing my outer calm with shattered nerves, tearing up the mask of tranquillity on my face, introducing a queer tendency in my gait to trip over and keep falling, giving my speech an unbecoming slur, pushing me over the brink. Regardless of all that, no longer able to or willing to retain my existing priorities, to stick to a silly protocol and sacrifice a matchless attainment, to stay with farewells and forego the welcomes, I abandoned my post at once, rushed into the bathroom, freshened up with a splashing of cold water on my face, checked its state in the mirror, wiped all traces of fatigue from it, brushed my hair to a satisfactory style, put some scent on my handkerchief, made sure I still had the key to the door in my pocket, made sure I was not being watched, made sure I was not being spied upon from secret corners by certain *undesirable* elements in the house, and literally walking on tiptoes, slipped away from the crowd, stepped on the hallowed ground where our crucial rendezvous was going to take place and looked around.

As plain as daylight, my queen of hearts was there, the full moon surrounded by a trillion stars, a trillion satellites and a trillion planets, standing out, shining aloft, unparalleled and unsurpassable, the icon of feminine excellence, the Acme, the Apex, still clad in the *Shalwar,* the *Khamis* and the *Dopatta,* but one I had never seen her wear before, in a colour made to enhance her beauty a thousandfold, in soft cottons aimed at challenging the purest of silks, in simplicity designed to defeat all the prints and patterns ever innovated, a lovely combination of peach and sandalwood, bringing out the opulence of her creamy skin, the windswept locks adrift, the two plaits undulating like snakes, the comely hands adorned with new bangles and fresh patterns of henna, her mouth red from chewing *betel-rolls* and the long lashes accentuated by strokes of eye shadow, her cheeks flushed in natural pink, her smile setting off tempestuous vibrations and adding glorious finishing touches to her consummate beauty, just like I had pictured it all!

Without yielding to distractions, without giving in to rush, without giving a toss about the rest of the world, be it Rox, be it Sakina, be it her uncle, be it the amorous butterflies, the envious roses, the spying jasmines, I carried on watching her, in amazement, in awe, in a daze, until she caught sight of me and at once metamorphosed from something to something else, like a young bud unfurling into a delicate bloom, waved to me, let the smile do the talking, let her eyes do the rejoicing, let her breath express her inner turmoil, let her legs do the catching up, let her hands demonstrate the fervour, let her body speak for her heart. As she prepared to bolt in my direction at top speed, triggered into motion by an irrepressible surge of joy, like a young gazelle heading towards its long-lost mate, everything in my personal universe came to an absolute standstill, the breeze stopped blowing, the time stopped ticking, the seasons stopped changing, the mist stopped swirling, the clouds stopped rolling, the sky stopped revolving. My heart was there inside my body but without its tick, my breath was there inside my lungs but without its flow, blood was there inside my veins but devoid of movement, incapable of taking life to my limbs, no longer in a position to perform its expected functions!

At that particular moment, before she could rush into my outstretched arms, before the circle could be drawn and exclude all the exits, before two mercurial beads could blend into each other and become one, something went wrong. An unexpected hitch got in the way, bound her legs with invisible shackles, snipped the circle, shattered the beads and sent them asunder. For some reason she stopped, hesitated, looked at the doors and windows of the outhouse, saw something untoward in them, shrank away from her course and gave in to retraction. Her face lost some of its colour, the lips shed their smile, the eyes forsook their gleam, and the body language faltered and became incoherent. From where I stood, I could not see who was there in those doors or windows, who was obstructing, who was posing the threats, but it hardly mattered. Suddenly, I remembered something that I had forgotten all along, I remembered the shadows that lurked, the perimeters that were there, the frontiers around us, the sign posts which barred our entries and accesses. It was not my parents standing in those windows or doors, it was not the palanquins for my sisters that were holding up the traffic, not my problems, not my obligations, not my moral dues, not the Damocles' swords hanging above my head. It was something else altogether, either something to do with she being an inexperienced young girl, I being a hot-blooded young man, the world being a crooked place, life being a pit of risks, walls having eyes, ceilings having ears, the wind having a voice; or, it was something to do with straps upon *her* freedom, demands upon *her* loyalties, a time for accountability, for taking new tests, for keeping old promises.

After only a few moments, the obstruction removed itself and let events take their course. She resumed her race to reach me, but because of the slight delay resulting from her hesitation, her sisters also came out of the outhouse shouting "*Eid Mubarak*, master sahib' and caught up with her. And when the rest of the children saw them, they, too, joined in, repeating the same slogan but without meaning a word. Understandably, to them, I was just a faceless, nameless, inconsequential scarecrow rolling under the caption of '*master saheb*', and to me, they were a bunch of stray heifers from the neighbourhood come to play in our backyard. No doubt, by way of mere courtesy, I responded to all and greeted them back, but my attention kept returning to her, now only one in a large crowd, unable to take the lead, switch on her charm, drown the rest in the cavalcade of her matchless exuberance, give eloquence to her eyes, widen the connotation of her smile, vivify the expressions on her face, put together the silent words of her body language and give them a firm voice, tell me that all was going to be well at the end of the day, that problems come and problems go but we would go on forever and ever! She could not do or say any of it because of the presence of company around her, especially her own sisters, as well as her proximity to the outhouse. But my share of the greetings were distinctly written on her face, diluted in her smile, reflected in her eyes. How I wished I could hold her hand and walk out of there, go away somewhere beyond the silvery horizon, where fairies pause to groom their wings, where dreams come and change their garbs, where dewdrops roll out of golden shells, where cherubs sit to play their harps, where rainbows begin and rainbows end!

Even before the noisy greetings subsided, someone from the outhouse shouted at the children to stop the play and return. They did, including she, my thirst unquenched, my heart assailed, my carefully rehearsed *confessions* wallowing in dust, under the leafless shrubs, under the bineless trellises, under the sunless sky. The only conversation that passed between us was, she asked me if I would resume her lessons on Wednesday, and I told her I was, *unless prevented by death alone*, which was as close to making any confessions as either of us could get to. Then she went away, leaving me alone, leaving behind the ever-rejuvenating fragrance of her breath, the images of an uncrowned queen wrapped in peach-coloured robes haunting the solitude. Mulling over the sharp reminder that, by *my* getting out of the woods, *we* were not yet going to be able to get out of the woods, unless *she*, too, got out of the woods at the same, I turned round and headed for the sheltered shop in which I had hidden her gifts, along with the greetings card, until then a harmless declaration of sacred love, but from then onwards a dangerous proclamation of guilt because of the amorous verses it contained, retrieve them, and either put them away somewhere safer and forget about making any confessions for the time being, or destroy them altogether. Whether or not my confession reached her ear, whether I burst the bubble or let it float, it occurred to me that my secret was best kept wrapped up in secrecy for a while longer; for, if her parents came to know about my passionate love for her before she herself did, and saw in me a threat to Vaseem's future, they might cancel the tuitions and take her away from me forever. After all, I was not the only tutor in town able to help their daughter accomplish her mission; they could get someone else to take over from me without giving a toss about how I felt, how much it would hurt us both, how much grief I would endure and how much distress she would suffer.

Unfortunately, however, by the time I reached the spot where I had hidden the gifts, I noticed with dismay that the shopping bag was no longer there.

What happened to it? Who stole it? Who knew about it? Mahjabeen? Sakina? Mr. Khan? Mrs. Ansari? Or any one of those idle kids who happened to see me hide it there? Had it fallen into the wrong hands, the greetings card more than the gifts, and given our game away? Was Azra cautioned by one of the concerned adults to stay away from me? Was that the real reason behind her hesitation, behind the simmering down of her passions, behind that subtle change in her attitude? Was that going to be the end of our love affair, the end of a beautiful dream, the decisive severing of our bonds?

Without any idea at all of what had happened, of what was happening, of what would happen, what would be its outcome in the morning, its grilling ramifications, its grim consequences, I returned home and plunged into family affairs, wearing a smile which had no business being on my lips on that miserable day!

CHAPTER (9)

That night, I had a strange dream. I saw myself walking on a beaten track, passing through an unfamiliar wilderness. Someone was following me, stirring up swarms of fireflies and scattering them around like fluorescent sparks in a dark tunnel. Somewhere ahead of me was the glare of light, illuminating the grey sky, postulating human activity. I was heading towards it in rapid strides, avoiding the potholes along the way, hopping on shrubs, skipping over dry tendrils and jumping across sharp stumps.

I finally reached the glare of lights. It was a familiar street, leading to the gates of the *Holy Shrine*. That night, in my dream, and to my surprise, there were no cries of anguish coming from the beggars assembled alongside the path, no cries for attention, and no cries for alms. They were there, but no longer in dire need. Some Angel of Mercy appeared to have visited them before I got there and filled up their empty bowls to the brim. I, too, had a bowl in my hand, but unlike theirs, it was empty, and I was anxiously looking around for the Angel of Mercy to come and fill mine too.

After a while, a stranger came towards me. He was a young person, about the same age as me, but tall and athletic, wearing a white turban, a white robe, a black beard and a winsome smile, generating a strange aura, exuding an amazing charisma, inspiring confidence. As he got closer to me, I felt shivers travel down my back. But wedging my courage with his talismanic smile, he quietly dropped a golden key in my bowl and then pointed towards the dome of the shrine. I looked up. A powerful beam of light was projecting from the sky, falling on the dome and illuminating it. In its brightness, I noticed that the dome was not a dome anymore but a mammoth cage made of gold and holding a prisoner inside it. She was a young woman, dressed in red like a bride, adorned with rose garlands, head bent, forsaken, quiet, lost, tears trickling down her cheeks like pearls flowing out of sea shells. I could not see her face clearly because of the distance and poor visibility, but she did look astonishingly similar to Azra. Her sad plight had such a profound effect upon me, I did not want to do anything other than scale the slippery slopes of the marble mausoleum, reach her, unlock the cage with the key given to me by my Guardian Angel, set her free, usher her into my world, take her away with me up the crest of a solitary mountain, pitch our tent on it and then live happily ever after!

Propelled into action by those impelling thoughts, I began to climb the stone structure. As soon as she saw me heading in her direction, she jumped to her feet, rushed as far as the cage allowed her, grabbed hold of the bars and stood shivering, her eyes fixed upon me, her hopes risen high, her heart ticking away. But suddenly, only a few feet away from her, the key slipped from my fist, hit the stone, rebounded and landed straight on the palm of someone else who was also climbing up the minaret right on my heals. Unless I was grossly mistaken, he was the same person who had picked up my trail near my house and been shadowing me since.

When that happened, the crowd watching us came to attention and their combined gasp echoed in the vast forecourt. The girl in the cage stood on her toes, bent her head and looked at the man who had taken possession of the key. So did I. In the beam of the light flooding in from the sky, I noticed with horror that he was a leper, afflicted by the worst kind of contagious leprosy. All ten of his fingers were consumed by the disease; he did not have a nose left but only two holes for respiration; his eyelids had also fallen off, laying bare the eyeballs. He looked fearsome and utterly grotesque. Terrified by his bizarre appearance, the girl in the cage let out a series of piercing screams. Ravens roosting on trees and pigeons sheltering in the shrine woke up and took off at once, adding more confusion to the fracas of screams with their cooing and flapping of wings. Helpless and forsaken, I just stood there stranded, neither moving nor frozen, neither dead nor alive, neither shouting nor dumbstruck. He, however, kept heading towards the door to the cage in leaps and bounds, his glazed eyes pinned on his target, his direction unchanged, his intentions unambiguous, his progress unchallenged, his goal guaranteed.

I had no idea what happened after that. Unable to watch her desecration at his filthy hands, I shut my eyes, sought Allah to intervene and save her, summoned the Angels to come to our help, exhorted the souls of the Saints lying in peace underneath us to prevent the leper from touching her, begged the mist to turn into rocks and inhume him; the wind to turn into a storm and blow him away; the moon to change its silvery beams into flames and set him ablaze; the stars to swap places with meteors and hurtle upon him; the lock on the cage to snap open and free her; the carpet of clouds to come flying and take her away. But nothing happened; Allah did not intervene; my Guardian Angel stood in the midst of the crowd and watched the show but did not respond to my pleas; the Saints in the shrine did not stir; the mist kept swirling on the back of wind; the moon lay sunk in the euphoria of sleep; the lock remained in place; the leper progressed unhampered; her screams of despair mingled with my screams of anguish and carried on reverberating in the open skies, until Shabbu, Rox, Mamma and Papa came running into my room, jogged me awake, drew the blinds on that nerve-racking scene, guided me back into the peace and quiet of my room, calmed down my rattled nerves, rebuilt my faith in mankind, in human love, in earthly bonds.

The faint recollections of that terrible dream hung at the back of my mind for the whole day. I had no idea what to make of it; how to interpret its implications and what lesson to learn from its occurrence. But I could not help feeling that it was either some sort of a warning about dangers looming over us, or a stern reprimand for me to step in line; to moderate my behaviour and to tone down my passions. I realised at once how wrong it was of me to have bought those gifts for Azra, addressed such a passionate greetings card to her and left the shopping bag in a place from where it could so easily be pilfered by any number of children playing around in the yard. If that shopping bag, by a stroke of bad luck, fell into the hands of a ruthless person like Mr. Khan and was exploited by him, either as a bargaining chip in his dispute with Papa over the squatting, or as a piece of damning evidence to get even with his brother-in-law in their domestic feuds, how would I feel? Or, if it fell into the hands of her parents and Mr. Ansari confronted her with it, how would she feel? Or, if he confronted my father instead of his daughter and told him how he trusted us both and how we betrayed his trust, what would happen to us, to our self-respect, our pride, our status? In the final analysis, if the secret of our affair somehow leaked out and reached the ears of gossip mongers in the community and her name was brandished about as a young woman of easy virtue, what would happen to her entire household, her brothers and sisters, her own future?

On Wednesday of that week, it was time for me to visit her for the first time since Ramadan break and I went to her house with mixed feelings. On one hand, I was quite thrilled at the prospects of seeing her, sitting close to her in the seclusion of her living room, holding an uncensored conversation with her at long last, laughing when laughter was provoked, responding when attention was sought, admiring when admiration was warranted, being a teacher when required by principles, being a human when justified by the occasion. On the other hand, I was also scared about the thought of the shopping bag, in case its finder already passed it on to her parents, leading to serious ramifications, perhaps a nasty reprimand from her father, or even a verbal Notice terminating the arrangement. But to my immense relief, no such thing happened; Azra did open the door to my knock as always, wearing the same splendid clothes which she had worn on *Eid*, hair gleaming with lustre from a slight application of coconut oil, a fragrant cluster of fresh *Chambeli* pinned to the hair clip near her cheek, one end of her *Dopatta* tied around her waist and the other covering her head, the face radiating even more against the background of the fabric, making her look like a doll carved in ivory. There were no signs of any stress or tension on it, there was no change in her attitude, no watering down of her zeal and enthusiasm, any regressions or inhibitions in evidence. I could see I was expected; the room was tidied up; a joss tick kept it fragrant and refreshed; her books lay on the coffee table; she looked pleased to be back on target again; the rigours of Ramadan and the festivities of *EID* left behind; recouped and recovered; blood drawn to the cheeks; lustre restored to the eyes; speed returned to the limbs, mind active, thoughts fluent, looks agile. A few moments later, refreshments also arrived from inside with her mum's blessings, reinforced by the addition of a greetings card for me from the whole family. Conforming to tradition, the tray contained a hot dish of vermicelli pudding too, which I picked up first, watching her blush, bend her head and bite upon her tongue. It was, indeed, gratifying to notice that her smiles were still there for me, and so were all the propitious signs; nothing had changed, nothing seemed different, nothing portentous or untoward had happened; the stealing of the shopping bag now a three-day-old mystery, with no casualties yet, no ramifications, no ill-omened after effects.

Nevertheless, its strange disappearance continued to bother me for a long time. I lived under a constant fear of its turning up in the hands of some evil person determined to stir up nasty storms, rock our boat and push us into the doldrums. Whenever I heard a louder than normal conversation between Papa and Mr. Khan in the vineyard, my heart fell into severe palpitations, my blood pressure shot up and my nerves shattered. I stopped going there and avoided running into Sakina in case it was she who stole the bag and, instead of either selling off the contents for pocket money or passing them on to her father, was hanging on to them in order to blackmail me herself. I had horrendous visions of our secret affair being publicly debated in our local mosque by old men with long beards; of Azra committing suicide from disgrace, her coffin being lifted, her mother bashing her head against the wall out of grief. At my own home, the pleasure of sitting around the dining table for a meal amid cheerful conversation was gone from my life. I barely concentrated on what was being said, hardly ever listened to Rox's jokes or enjoyed them as I used to. I just sat watching the expression on Papa's face with apprehension, scared that he might ask me into his room for a confidential chat and bring up the dreaded topic. Even when he did invite me for any tête-à-tête in his room for matters that had nothing to do with Azra and me, I broke into a cold sweat. Until not too long ago, going to her house for her lessons used to be the happiest aspect of my work. But ever since the disappearance of the bag, it turned into quite a trial of nerves. My secret fears persecuted me weeks on end, until the volume of work multiplied due to the proximity of exams and virtually drowned me in. Either owing to the acceleration in the pace of activity, or simply withered by the passage of time, I finally managed to get over the phobia and settled in.

Behind the facade of innocence and immaturity, Azra turned out to be lot more resolute than I had given her credit. All the coquetries and the playfulness were packed up to make room for astute preparations; attention shifted from mangoes, custard apples and bangle sets to fractions and percentages; from the romantic tales behind the building of the Taj Mahal to the harsh realities of Adolph Hitler and the concentration camps; from the alchemy of romancing to oxygen and hydrogen; from the passionate poems of Ghalib to English comprehension and punctuation; from the corn fields of Telangana to the equator and the North Pole; from jokes to serious discussions; from coy smiles to crowded brows. For a person who had not had much of a formal schooling, and who had spent most of her conscious life behind wood-fired ovens making chapattis and daal, they were extremely challenging targets, sometimes driving her to the brink of tears, but she stuck it out. If it were up to me, I would have asked her to toss the idea in air and forget all about it; there are better things to life than Aligarh Matric. But it was not. I was neither a part of her problems nor their solution. She took her mission so very seriously, and her father's reliance on her with such pride, she never once relaxed her determination nor wrote herself off.

Nine productive and rewarding months later, coaching season finished and exams began. As there was no need for me to stay with my other pupils anymore, I spent most of my time with her, helping her revise, giving her practice with sample question papers, wedging her courage, escorting her to the examination centre and back, assessing her performance, giving her as much encouragement as she needed, making myself useful to her in every way without attracting too much attention. All along, while her own concentration was firmly focussed upon doing her best in the exams, I was aware that, in a matter of days, our relationship of *Teacher and the taught,* would come to an end; my excuse to see her twice a week would no longer be valid; the merry sessions in her living room would terminate; no more cups of tea containing the sweetness of her magic touch in the place of sugar, no more *laddoos* and *pakoras* for me, no more clusters of jasmines and *Chambelis* for her, no meeting of looks, no blending of breaths, no brushing of hands, no soul stirring displays from her nor any lyrical adulations from me!

The examinations lasted for two weeks after which Mr. Ansari gave me my last pay-packet together with a bottle of the finest perfume he could afford, and his sincere gratitude for going out of my way to help Azra, for the hard work that had gone into the preparations, and for that one particular aspect of my assistance to her which, as he put it, no amount of money could repay: my honesty and my integrity. "*Hisaab-e-dostan dar dil*, Mr. Quraishi," he said in Persian, meaning, *"accounts for true friends are kept in the heart."* If only he knew how that modest valediction was affecting me; what sort of a havoc it was raging on my emotions; how difficult it was for me to endure even the vaguest hint of a farewell between her and me; how much joy I had derived from the fulfilment of the delightful mission that he entrusted to me a few months ago; what a wealth of memories I amassed and treasured in my heart in course of those unforgettable months; how much his daughter meant to me; how madly I was in love with her; how far I was prepared to go in order to realise my precious dream! If only he knew that, ever since I found his daughter, I stopped looking for Paradise, stopped searching for the shore, stopped fearing the waves; I was no longer hopping from branch to branch, I had taken repose on a tree, which had only one branch and that branch was all mine; I had begun to gather twigs and hay to build my nest; I knew who I was going to share it with; who was going to lay our brood in it; who was going to tend to our fledglings; who was going to be my true companion in life; and then in the *after life*, and then in the *Gardens underneath which flow the rivers of Eternal Life!* If only he knew that I had charted out the full course of my journey; I had found my fellow traveller too; I had finalised my goal and I was not erecting alternative goal posts any longer!

As he sat saying his piece, and I rolling all those pleasant thoughts over in my mind, Azra stood not too far away, resting her back against the wall, wearing a curious expression on her face which made no room for distress or pathos, which burnt out the thin film of moisture in her eyes with its heat, its radiance, its effervescence. She stood looking at me in spite of her father being there, making invisible promises, which I alone could read, binding herself with inviolable pledges, binding me with sacred vows, melting me into liquids and absorbing me in her bloodstream, adding me to the spirals of smoke emanating from the jossticks and breathing me in, locking me up inside her heart and throwing away the key, composing poems in her eyes and turning them into melodies with her furtive smiles. I read those poems too, tuned in to each and every one of those stirring melodies, acknowledged her pledges and reaffirmed my vows, made pacts with her and put my whole life on the palm of her hand to do what she liked with it, array it with golden tassels, bury it underneath heaps of buds, hide it in the ivory towers of her love, lay it in sandalwood cradles and sing lullabies to it—whatever!

The courage with which I said goodbye to her father and then took her leave at the doorstep lasted only until I got on my bike and turned the corner, after which, it suddenly fizzled into thin air. I felt as though, whilst I was gestating in the fluids of a claustrophobic womb, without any strength in my limbs to move, without any vision in my eyes to see, without any awareness in my mind to rationalise, someone arrived from somewhere and severed my umbilical cord; I felt as though I was heading for the mouth of an active volcano riding on a missile over which I had little or no control; I felt as though I was trapped in a sandstorm in the middle of an interminable desert, which displayed no signposts to the safety of its hidden oases. How I really felt, how long did that short distance between Aghapura and Asifnagar stretch at that moment, how full was my life when I was underneath her roof and how empty it became after I came outside, how rich was I in the proximity of her arms and how impoverished was I rendered away from them, it was better guessed than expressed. An endless stream of cyclists, scooters, rickshaws and pedestrians went whizzing past me, shops emerged and disappeared, electric poles jutted in and jutted out, trees suddenly materialised and dissipated, unexpected potholes gave the bike nasty bumps, the handlebar kept slipping through my grip again and again, I came within inches of terrible accidents and fatal collisions but finally got home, avoiding the crashes by the skin of my teeth.

From that day onwards, my life turned into an existence without an identity; an ocean without any waves; a spark without a tenure; a gust of breeze in a sealed tunnel; a thought trapped in an infant's mind; a random throb ticking in a failing heart! Every evening, I sat on the lawns with my family, eyes focussed upon my surroundings but my mind taken prisoner by the lifeless tendrils of our vineyard, or latched on to the tumultuous uproar of children at play, or clutching at the straps of my unanswered prayers, or drowning in the cascades of my unfulfilled hopes. I sat with them from the moment the sun tilted towards the horizon until it was soaked up by the skyline, participating in their conversation, listening to their questions, formulating their answers, matching up expressions, giving live performances, but neither my mind nor my heart in any of it. Azra was all I could think of, her name was the only word that sprang to my lips, her face was the only image imprinted on my mind, her recollections were the only thought-waves in which I drowned and surfaced. I circled around her house a hundred times a day, on my bike rather than on my motorbike to ensure anonymity; I went to cinema halls, hoping to bump into her in the endless queues behind ticket counters, I dragged Shabbu and Rox through the precincts of the *lovers arcade* in search of bargains that were simply not there, I hung around in the All India Congress Exhibition for hours on end, watching the spate of crowds rise and fall. Frankly, there was not a single spot of interest in the whole of Hyderabad that I did not stalk in the hope of catching one glimpse of her face, but without any luck. Driven to such infinite despair by pangs of separation, I tried several times even to seek an audience with my parents, tell them all about Azra, tell them I had fallen in love with her, make them understand how hopelessly I was trapped in a storm over which I had little or no control, a storm that smites its victims without mercy, takes over the heart first and then invades the mind, confiscates all the other priorities and establishes its own stipulations, but I simply could not muster the courage to tell them that I had chosen my partner in life without letting them have their say in it.

My torment carried on for a whole week and left me a total wreck. On Sunday, the first Sunday since our parting, I waited with a bated breath to see if she, too, driven by equal despair, would come along with her mum visiting her aunt, now that the pressure of exams was over and she had plenty of time to spare. No doubt, most of the trellises in our vineyard had gone and it was no longer convenient for playing hide and seek, but so what? She could always drown me in the profusion of her arms and seek me out with her thirst; she could lock me up in her heart and seek me out with her love; she could let me hide in the helical depths of her eyes and seek me out with her soul! So, I went to the yard on some pretext and waited for her, looked out for her, prayed and comforted myself, dreamed and beguiled myself, hoped and disappointed myself, expected and deceived myself; I pined for her, I prayed for her, I pined for her and I prayed for her, but she did not come. The sun tarried through his final sojourn for the day, dissipated into a thousand embers and got soaked up in the horizon; the lotus pond gyrated many a ripple, tossed the leaves, teased the stems, then subsided itself and went to sleep; the butterflies sat brooding on roses, fatigued by their daylong toils, making halfhearted attempts to gather more nectar before dispersing into anonymity; yesterday's jasmines, tired of waiting to be picked, drained of fragrance, discoloured by age, woke up today's buds from sleep to take their place. I hung in there, too impatient to await another day, too thirsty to give up hope, too distressed to turn my back, until someone from behind accosted me with unexpected greetings.

"*Assalamu alaikum,* master saheb!" said a somewhat familiar voice, though not of Azra, taking me by surprise.

Sharply turning round, I came face to face with Sakina and stared at her with blank eyes. After a gap of several months, she did look different, a lot rounder and fuller than before, grown up, mature, even sober. As a measure of courtesy, I returned her greeting with a polite *Walaikum assalam.*

"*Azra Baji* asked me to convey her *Adab Arz* to you, master saheb, " she said, cheeks flushed and eyes sparkling, making my day with that blithesome message.

"Did she?" I said, doing my utmost to mask the surge of joy, "When was that?"

"On Wednesday of last week. I couldn't tell you because you weren't around."

"That's all right. Thank you very much for the trouble. When you see her next, give her the same from me."

"She likes you a lot, you know?"

"I guess I do—now that you've told me."

"You're in love with her, aren't you?"

An intimate question, asked with such blatant callousness, without an iota of confidentiality, turned me hot underneath the collar, even though I knew she was only making a wild guess.

"You've been watching too many romantic movies, Sakina. Do you realise asking a silly question like that is dangerous and could hurt your own cousin more than it could hurt me?"

"I love her too, master saheb," she said, looking me in the eye and breaking into a beaming smile, "Everybody loves Azra Baji. She's a very loveable person. And besides, you don't have to hide it from me. I know everything."

"Pardon?"

"I read the greetings card you wrote to her on *EID* day. I found the bag which you hid in the shop along with her gifts and gave it to my mum after reading the card."

"What did your mum do with it?"

"She gave it to her mum."

"Does Azra Baji know about this?"

"I don't think so. My mum asked me not to talk about it anymore."

"You aren't going to, are you?"

"No, I'm not. Cross my heart and hope to die. I'd never do anything to hurt Azra Baji. She's my best friend."

That chance conversation, containing revelations of such sensitivity and magnitude, made me at once forget all about the purpose for which I had ventured to cross the wall. Besides, before I could say anything else, somebody from the outhouse spotted her talking to me and called her away rather loudly. I, too, returned home, went into my room, sat by myself and put on my thinking cap. If whatever Sakina told me about the bag was true, it meant both the mothers knew my secret and were yet keeping it wrapped up in covers. No doubt, only three days after it went missing, when I visited Azra for her first lesson since the festival, her mum treated me with the same courtesy and attention to which I had been accustomed, with absolutely no change in her attitude, but that did not necessarily mean she condoned my indiscretion. She might have decided to keep quiet for the time being for Azra's sake, or more than Azra's, for the sake of the mission she had offered to accomplish, so that she was not deflected from her course. Otherwise, a discovery of such significance was hardly likely to go unheeded or unresponded forever. As a mother, she had a responsibility towards her daughter, and as a wife, she had a much greater responsibility towards her husband. Even if she welcomed the idea of an alliance between Azra and me, it was not the sort of thing that she could keep to herself. Buying gifts and writing passionate greetings cards by themseves were neither sins nor violations, but they were enough to sweep an inexperienced girl off her feet; to fill her head with thoughts unbecoming of a young woman; to give her a taste of the forbidden fruit; to push her over the brink; to make her an easy prey to temptations. All said and done, they did not know much about me; they could not assess whether my feelings were for real or just aimed at taking advantage of her; whether I meant what I said and said what I meant or was merely trying to impress her; how sincere was I and how chaste was my love. Inarguably, Azra was at such a vulnerable age, even a scratch on her heart was enough to ruin her budding life.

The more I thought about it, the more complex my thinking became. The possibilities were limitless. It was possible she did not take anyone into her confidence and was, in fact, waiting for *me* to make my first move, talk to my parents and then send them to talk to her parents, either bring spring into the garden or take the garden into spring; give the young buds of love a chance to unfurl and bloom; let the merry notes of the *SHEHNAI* echo in their front yard; let the anxious maiden wear scrolls of bridal *Henna;* let her hands be held in the hands of a true companion; let her smiles flourish underneath the shelter of chaste love; let her untouched body be wrapped in unused muslins and silk; let the chain made with pearls of marital bliss adorn her neck; let her make her resolves of loyalty and breathe them in the ears they were aimed at. She must be waiting for all that to happen, a wait that was not going to last forever but be decisively short-lived, either to sink in a deluge of tears or to ride on the crest of joy; either to wither in the hot winds of adversity or to bloom in the sunshine of spring; either to reach its distant goal at the end of the journey or to go astray along the way.

Or, it was equally possible that she simply put the shopping bag in her husband's hand and left it to him to straighten it all out. If so, how did he react to it? Did my perfidious behaviour, rendered possible by his own indifference towards one of the most basic principles of chastity imposed by Islam—the *PURDAH*—offend him beyond redress? Did the news of my entertaining a few secret thoughts about my pupil whilst playing the role of teacher to her disillusion him? Did he also suspect his own daughter of complicity in the profanity; did he think she, too, abandoned her modesty in return for amorous adulations; she betrayed his faith in both of us by encouraging me to breach my restraints; she sacrificed her spiritual obligations on the road to emotional gratification, she put her heart above her soul, she flouted God's

Commandments in order to win a man's attention; she traded her place in the everlasting paradise for a place in her lover's arms? Did he lose his respect for her; did he recant her; did he ostracise us both; did he order his doors to be shut in my face forever; did he vow never to cast his eyes upon her unworthy face again; did he wish her eternal fire for leading me on; did he wish me damnation for leading her astray? Had she been forbidden to me and I to her? As her parent, would he refuse her hand to me, even if my parents sought it on my behalf? Had she been stopped from visiting her aunt, from going anywhere on her own, in order to prevent us from meeting; from tightening the knots on our bonds; from making new pacts of allegiance; from taking new oaths of loyalty? If I went to their house, would they turn me away, would they keep her locked up in her room, would they put shackles on her legs?

In due course, the results of the exams were published in the Deccan Chronicle. It was a big relief to me to see that over 90 percent of my pupils passed. Unfortunately, Azra was not one of them. I did not know whether it was good news or bad. No doubt, it was a serious blow to her ego as the taste of failure always goes bitterly down anybody's throat, but considering the circumstances in which we were both stranded, perhaps it was a good thing after all that she failed instead of passing. For, if she had passed, she would have had to take up the job at the paper mill whether she liked it or not, turn into a *bee* for her father's *hive* and embark upon the arduous task of gathering *honey* day after day, serve a master whom she did not herself choose; reconcile with priorities she did not draw up; be loyal to a cause which was not hers and spend the unrepeatable days of her youth in servitude. On the other hand, by failing, she had left her options open without taking the blame for it, she was free to swap loyalties to a different *master* without being branded a traitor, she had an open-ended prerogative to moderate the flow of her life according to the speed of her choice, and perhaps, in the final analysis, she could also keep the flame of our hopes alight for a while longer, buy me some breathing space, at least another year's time to sort out my problems too in the same way, without any blames, without any betrayals, without any sacrifices, and without our drifting too far away from each other.

A few days later I went to her house to say hello, on my motorbike instead of the other bike, if only to let her know I was coming; I had not forgotten her; I was standing shoulder to shoulder with her. Mr. Ansari answered my knock instead of her, for which there could be umpteen trivial reasons. Welcoming me with a warm handshake, he took me into his lounge and offered me a seat.

There was no evidence of hostility or dissatisfaction in his mien, absolutely no expression of any sort on his face. Either he knew all about the gifts and the Card and was masking his feelings, or he did not know a thing. If he knew and approved the idea of my seeking Azra's hand in marriage, he would certainly bring it up in course of conversation and say so: or, if he was unable or unwilling to consider the proposal for one reason or the other, he would offer his apologies and nip the matter in the bud. I was sure of that much. But deep down in my heart, my most ardent wish was, he did neither of those two but simply asked me to continue with the tuition for one more year.

"I'm sorry, Mr. Ansari. I wish Azra had passed," I said, broaching upon the subject myself.

"Don't worry," he replied with a genial smile, "but it's nice of you to drop in. I really appreciate it."

"What've you decided to do?" I went ahead and asked him, drawing courage from the fact that he was not hostile, at least not yet, "One more try?"

"No more tries," he said absolutely firmly, "I know both of you did your best. To tell you the truth, the fault was mine; my thinking was wrong."

"What about the job you had lined up for her? And Vaseem's education at the City Poly?" I asked him in the vain hope that a reminder of his priorities might force him to think again.

"Vaseem has decided to drop the idea of the Polytechnic," he replied without any change in his expression, "He can take up the job intended for Azra and help me raise the others. They're just as important. That's how it should have been from the start."

His thinking was the same as my father's; he seemed to have realised that Azra was a *bee* whose loyalties must lie elsewhere, and hence, his relying on her to gather honey for his own *hive* was a tactical error.

"Azra's a fine girl and we're proud of her," he continued, "what she really needs is a home of her own, a husband, some children and her own personal goals to reach. That's what we've decided to do, give her the best we can afford."

It was, no doubt, a sensible decision and the only one which made it possible for me to realise my own dream too: she, thus relieved of her responsibilities, the way could be paved for me to seek her hand myself. But unfortunately I was caught unawares. Failure in exams might well be a blessing in disguise for her, but it had done nothing to change my circumstances. She was free, whereas I was still in shackles, which suddenly pushed me against odds I had neither anticipated nor was equipped to face.

As a measure of routine hospitality, tea and snacks were served. Etiquette demanded that I ate, and I did, but without relishing a thing. The *Pakoras* turned sour in my mouth and the sight of *Laddoos* hurt me. Mr. Ansari maintained a steady flow of pleasant conversation about this and that while I simply listened to him, my mind miles away. Until that day, I had been keeping a leisurely pace at my affairs, but suddenly, unexpected hurry had crept into them. Rush always made me nervous. Even if there were easy solutions staring me in the eye, I became quite incapable of seeing them. Whatever he said might not amount to any more than just a casual observation, or even a deliberate attempt on his part to draw me into the open without seeming to do so, but his words toppled on my head like a tonne of bricks and deprived me at once of my ability to think straight. It was still early days; they had not pledged her hand to anyone yet; they had not found a suitable match; nobody was standing outside the door demanding an instant decision; I had not told Azra how much I loved her and how crazy I was about her; I had not asked her if she loved me too in an equal measure; I had not disclosed my pleasant secret to my parents and sought their blessings, but I felt as though I had been locked up in a metal jacket and dumped in mid-ocean. Such was the extent of my madness for her, I could not tolerate even a vague hint of her being considered for someone else. The thought itself felt unclean, sacrilegious, an abomination, a scourge!

Towards the end of the one-sided conversation, he checked the time on his watch, said he had to rush to work and saw me to the door, thanking me once again for all the help in the past, for dropping by to say hello, for caring about the results, for suggesting a second try, wishing me well, hoping we might bump into each other, sometime, someplace, somehow, without bringing up the topic of either my proposal or my intentions for Azra, giving me nothing from her, a *Shukrya*, an *Adab Arz*, a *Khuda hafiz*, a *Gustaqi maaf*—nothing.

I came out of the room, my ears blocked, my vision blurred, my legs unsteady, my mind obtuse, my heart stunned. Riding the bike with such broken nerves seemed perilous; I could so easily collide with a passing truck and die. I wished I did, I wished the ground split open and swallowed me, I wished the sky broke into pieces and inhumed me. My life, from that moment onwards, turned utterly punitive. There was neither a purpose to it nor did it have any direction. Papa and Mamma, Shabbu and Rox, the house, the debt, our struggle for survival, everything slid into the background. I had never expected to see the day when my own family and their needs sank so low down the bottom of my urgent priorities, but love had changed my thinking completely.

Just as I was about to get on my bike, her soft voice echoed in the poignant silence and arrested my movement.

"*Adab Arz,* Master sahib!" she said from somewhere and touched the cockles of my heart.

I froze first and then turned around. She stood in the door, clad in her working clothes—a slightly soiled white *Shalwar,* and *Khamis* along with the pink *Dopatta* that went with it—one end tied around her waist like a cummerbund, the other covering her head, hair parted in the middle, a plait to the front and a plait to the back in her very own inimitable style, the loose tufts left wild around the flawless face, eyes swollen, probably from weeping, looking like an Angel of Mercy, like a *Hur* from Paradise, a doll outside her dollhouse, a queen outside her throne, a marvel to behold even in such simple clothes! My heart took one big leap and sat in my throat.

"Hello, Azra!" I said, gulping down a bitter lump, "I just dropped by to…to…to say hello."

"Thanks. Won't you come in?" she replied with a smile.

The invitation was irresistible and I did not resist it. She took me back into the lounge and we sat facing each other. It had been a long time since we sat like that, together and by ourselves, which felt good. We old-fashioned Muslims, the most indomitable puppets in the hands of religion and tradition, are told never to stare at members of the opposite sex when in their company. In her case, I had banished the thought a long time ago. Looking at her was all I could do and I had been feasting my eyes to my heart's content. That day was no exception. And if it was going to be anywhere near being the last day of our togetherness, I was determined to engrave every vivid detail of it in my mind so that I would never lose it again.

"I'm sorry to have disappointed you, *master saheb,*" she said, "I didn't pass, but I did try hard. I mean, I did wallow in the mud!"

"Of course you did. Are you upset?"

"Not particularly."

"Why are you crying, then?"

"Who's crying? Those dreadful fumes from damp firewood got into my eyes. What about Abbajan? What has he been telling you?"

"He's so angry, he's contemplating life imprisonment for you."

"Is he?"

"Something on the lines of colouring your hands with Henna."

My choice of words was deliberate. In our community, 'dyeing a girl's hands with Henna' automatically implies marriage. She knew it. First, her head bent; then, a deep blush gathered in her cheeks; her eyes went downcast and her breath gently speeded. I could see she was biting upon her lower lip to suppress a smile. If there was anything I wanted to tell her, that was the most appropriate moment for it. She was waiting, she was ready, she was restless. If I threw open the doors of my heart, she would have walked straight inside and locked herself in; if I managed three simple words as 'I love you' to her face, she would have pledge herself to me for the rest of her life; if I took one step in her direction, she would have covered the rest of the distance in leaps and bounds. But as always, my courage fled just when I needed it the most. I knew how much she meant to me, I knew what would happen to me if I lost her, I knew what I must do to make sure that I did not. Yet I wavered. Probably surprised by my reticence, perhaps even disappointed, she slowly lifted her eyes and stared into mine; whatever was concealed in her heart, she conveyed it through the multiple sparkles in them. If what I thought was right, her impatient look was making quiet demands upon me; her heart was fluttering with anxiety; her breath was held in suspense. And what did I have to offer in return? A sigh too faint to be heard, a silence too resolute to be broken, an expression too complex to be interpreted!

"Your father said there's no need for me to come again," I informed her in a hoarse voice.

She simply nodded. Lustre forsook her eyes and the face shed much of its colour. I could see the tropic I introduced was not to her liking.

"You're by far the most fascinating student I've ever had the pleasure of teaching, Azra" I mumbled, more or less closing the book.

"I, too, enjoyed your company, *master saheb*. Thanks very much for all the help. I wish there was some way in which I could pay you back," she said.

There was. We both knew which. I certainly did.

"Azra ..." I said, almost on the verge of making the crucial confession, but still not succeeding.

"Yes?" she said at once, the large, almond shaped eyes aglow with expectation, the flush returning to the cheeks again but her breath suspended as before.

"Your diary of poems—I've still got it."

"Yes, I know."

"What do you want me to do with it?"

"Drop it in through the letter box next time you're passing this way ..."

"All right, I will."

"Wait," she said on second thoughts, "Why not bring it along with you on Wednesday at eleven o'clock?"

The suggestion was so welcome I grabbed it with both hands. It meant I had one more opportunity of seeing her, which was better than having none at all; it meant I had four clear days in which to assess my chances of marrying a girl of my dreams who had everything else to offer me except money; it meant I could come back to her either with a newfangled courage to say what I wanted to say, or with a reaffirmed resolve not to open my mouth ever again. It meant all that and much more.

"May I? Really?" I asked her, making no effort to conceal my joy.

"Will you?"

"Which means, we don't have to say *Alvida* today?"

"No, we don't. We can say *Fi AmaanAllah*, instead …"

On that exceedingly cheerful note I got to my feet. But for some reason she hesitated. There was a strange expression on her face, which made me uneasy. If it had anything to do with my show of reticence earlier, I could put things right on my next visit—hopefully. But if it was something else, I wished I knew what. I wished all our worries disappeared that very moment. I wished there was some way in which I could tell her whatever was going on in my mind without uttering a word. I wished marriage were as simple as my asking her to be my wife and her agreeing to it!

"*Master saheb!*" she said at the door in a husky voice, "You will come again, won't you?"

One more time, yes; there was no question of doubt about it. But after that, it all depended upon circumstances over which neither of us had any control. Would Papa agree to my bringing home a goose that knew not how to lay golden eggs? Would Mr. Ansari agree to her marrying a man who was not born with a silver spoon in his mouth? All said and done, if my father put his foot down, I would not dream of disobeying him; and by the same token, if her father refused consent, it was equally unlikely that she would consider eloping with me.

"Yes—unless prevented by death alone," I said and meant every word.

The expression on her face swiftly changed. The ponderous look was gone, replaced by sheer vivacity. Smile suited her so well she looked like an entirely different person. The large eyes lit up and a whiff of breeze sent the soft curls bouncing. Given a chance, I would not let a shadow of worry fall upon her ever; if I could, I would not let even a speck of dust settle on her face;

if I could, I would not let her grow a day older for as long as she lived; if it was left to me, I would not tolerate anything come between us.

"*Fi AmaanAllah, master saheb!*" she said finally, giving me a blessing so rich I could live off it until the day I died!

Under its auspices, I drove home safe and sound, without any crashes along the way, without falling victim to the unforeseen. The foreseeable itself was enough to keep my hands full for quite a while. The gracious look with which she saw me off was just the sort of motivation I had needed to fight for my hopes and dreams. Suddenly, nothing seemed beyond reach. There were a few problems and a few hurdles, but none felt insurmountable; there were only four days left in which to reorganize my priorities, but they seemed long enough. Never before had my passion for life been so intense as it was on that bright and glorious afternoon!

As soon as I reached home, Shabbu told me that Sal phoned and asked me over to his place for supper. It seemed Uncle Zama—his father—had something very important to discuss with me.

In all the years I had known Sal, there were only twelve occasions on which I ran into his old man, invariably by chance. A successful barrister, and consequently, a very busy man, he seldom had the leisure to socialize with his son's friends. So, his starting to express an interest in me all of a sudden addled my wits and I rushed to his house at once.

After a brief chat with Sal, which contained no auspicious or inauspicious revelations, I was taken upstairs into his dad's extremely large and fully air-conditioned office room. His massive desk, and his awe inspiring figure behind it made me nervous, but pulling myself together, I settled into a chair across the table and looked at him rather apprehensively. Putting my mind at ease with a polite enquiry about my family and me, he began by asking me if I had heard of the *JAMAYYAT-UL-ULEMA FOUNDATION*. I said I had. It was a very large educational fund set up by the renowned Urdu poet Allama Iqbal and maintained by the Muslim community to harness the spiritual, educational and cultural pursuits of Muslim children from all over the country. Apparently, a few years ago, the foundation launched an ambitious project of constructing an independent boarding school for boys and girls, but the scheme had to be abandoned because of opposition from local politicians who were unhappy about the funding of an exclusive Muslim school in a city which was no longer dominated by Muslim population as before. While the issue was still being contested in courts, the superbly equipped premises in Mogulpura were laying idle and gathering dust. Hence, the working committee of the foundation decided to put them to an interim use, and he being the chairman of the committee, it was left to him to come up with some good ideas and sound proposals.

'How would Shabana and you like to run a tutorial institute in it on behalf of the foundation for the same Aligarh Matriculation Exams?' he asked me, finally getting down to the point. There was room to accommodate one thousand children, strictly on grounds of no income or low income, without regard to cast, creed, race or religion, and no fee. All the refurbishing and maintenance costs would be borne by the foundation, including salaries to full time staff. Money was of no consequence as they had plenty of it and were keen to spend on such and similar projects. We would get an *open cheque,* with no supervision, except one quarterly progress report to the working committee. All the jobs would be salaried, including ours, one thousand rupees for Shabana and fifteen hundred rupees for me. No more headaches, no running around from house to house, strictly nine to five and five days per week. He did not think Papa would object to Shabana working along with me at the institute as all senior Muslims were well aware of the foundation and its aims, but if he did, I could always hire someone else in her place, he concluded.

What a bonanza to drop into the lap of an idealist like me and at a time like that! Barely fighting back my tears of joy, I thanked him for his faith and his confidence in us. After a firm handshake and a pat on the back, he asked me to see Mr. Raza, the secretary of the foundation, in the morning to sort out the paper work. Unable to believe my luck, I said "yes" and rushed out of the room before he changed his mind. It was not just a job for the two of us, but also a whole new future for a lot of us.

As soon as I hit the ground floor, Sal confronted me with a broad grin.

"Your pop," I whispered in his ear, still in a disbelieving state of mind, "hasn't taken to opium addiction lately, has he?"

"Nope," he insisted stoutly, "he's fit as a fiddle and still good enough for the Supreme Court of India."

"In that case, what's all this *Bakwas* about ..." I began but he cut me short. Apparently, the idea was his own brainchild. The whole thing had been simmering on low heat for well over two months, pending the publication of the results in order to assess our performance as tutors.

"And if you've any conscientious objections," he said quite jovially, "get stuffed. There're plenty of others besides you who are just as good, if not better."

145

A year ago, perhaps I would have, but not anymore. Now, I was an experienced man. I was also a pretty desperate man, on the verge of acquiring new responsibilities.

After a mouth-watering meal, I came home. Having finished supper without me, my family was gathered around the dining table and engaged in some lively conversation. Instead of interrupting, I, too, changed and joined them. Thrilled to bits as I was, I also made a solid contribution to the chat.

Later on, I took Shabbu into my room and told her whatever transpired in Sal's house. For a long time after I finished, she sat staring at me with incredulous eyes.

"No kidding?" she exclaimed as soon as finding her tongue.

"No kidding," I confirmed categorically, "but not without you joining hands."

"What about Papa?"

"First, what about you?"

"Wow! Did I ever say *no* to you?"

"There's always a first time. What the hell is it? Is it a *Yes*, or is it a *No?* "

"Yes, yes, yes—a million times yes. But Papa …"

"Don't panic, pretty face. Tomorrow night, you and I can sit with him in his room and somehow squeeze out a *YA*! Okay? "

"Okay. And one more thing. You said this is a permanent job. Does it mean you won't leave us here and go too far away in quest of livelihood?"

"Tell me one thing, dearest. How can I forsake you all to the winds and where can I go? For what, anyway? My whole life's here."

After rolling it over in her mind for a while she broke into a beaming smile. "Know something, Bhaijan?" she said in the end, "It couldn't have happened to a nicer guy."

"*SHUKRIYA!* Will you join hands?"

"With pleasure. So long as you won't drift away from us."

"But you will, one day, wrapped in red silks and muslins, won't you?" I reminded her.

That was when she told me something that I have never been able to forget. "This is where I belong, dear Bhaijan," she said, "this is my home. A part of me is diffused in its every brick and rock. If it's taken away from me, or if I'm taken away from it, I can never be a whole person again. When the rose buds bloom each dawn, one of them will be me; when the birds chirp at noon, you will hear the sound of my voice too; when the rains come, every cloud will scatter a few of my tears on this soil. Like the wild tamarind tree,

I might grow once again in someone else's patch, but here's where my seeds are sown and this is where I shall always return ..."

When phrased in Urdu, they sounded as sweet as any of Azra's superb poems!

CHAPTER (10)

I started Uncle Zama's proposed project with a visit to Mr. Raza who was the foundation's secretary and was expecting me. I gathered from him that a fair amount of preliminary work had already been done. The institute was named after Allama Iqbaal, a renowned poet, and the one responsible for setting up the foundation, and registered with the board of trade as a charity. The abbreviation A.I.M for the Allama Iqbal Memorial sounded very appropriate too. I was told that the ultimate *aim* of the foundation was to convert it into a full time secondary school for *under-privileged* children rather than for *Muslim children* only. A fresh application had also been made to the education board for the award of the status of a recognised school and, as acting principal of the institute, whatever I could do towards accomplishing that goal would be much appreciated, he said. Briskly dispensing with the initial paperwork, he wished me luck and saw me off.

Before getting too deeply involved into the project, I needed to have a chat with Papa, as there were several moral issues at stake. To begin with, were it not for his determination and his tireless efforts to ensure that all three us got good education, we would have probably been stuck in dead end jobs like the one I used to do at the I.G.'s office, either sorting mail, or sucking the juice out of vulnerable targets like P.C. Habeeb to make ends meet. It would, therefore, be inappropriate on my part to accept any job without seeking his blessings first. Then there was the issue of Shabana being spared for a nine to five job outside the house, and a few ramifications resulting from it. If she was to withdraw her *ornaments* from cold storage and go in pursuit of *honey* for a *hive* that was not hers, someone else would have to put away theirs and relieve her. That someone, obviously, was Roxana and hence, as a matter of principle, her consent was also needed. Taking all that into account, I preferred to make it a joint decision by the whole family, so that everyone had a fair chance to express their views and brought it up that evening when we gathered on the lawns to watch the sun go down. Upon listening to the full details, they seemed impressed by the prominent names behind the project; the idea of service to the community appealed to them, and our being entrusted with such a major responsibility at so young an age tickled their vanity too. In the end, when the question of Shabbu working alongside me as vice principal for the girls section was raised, Papa agreed to let her, with but one minor reservation.

"Provided, it is all right with Roxana," he said, eyeing her with a patronising smile, "I mean, picking stones from Patna rice, making guava marmalade and clearing *Chambeli*'s dung ..."

"For the time being," she replied without flinching, "there is nothing that a couple of *Kashmiri silk saris*, a ready made *Gharara Suit*, and a nose stud for this *regal* nose won't fix. But I'll have to look into it more carefully later on, when a real *fat cow* with a real *fat batwa* comes up for auction in the *marriage market* willing to wed our *Shahzada!*"

"A reasonable expectation, isn't it?" Papa asked, looking at Shabbu and me this time.

"The e*xpectation* is," I agreed without harangues, "but the *threat* that followed isn't."

"This *servitude* has to end sometime, doesn't it, Papa?" she said quite vociferously in her own defence, "I mean, somebody would have to swallow the frog in order for the snake to sleep ..."

"Roxana," Mamma addressed her with a confused expression on her face, "these bizarre sayings you come up with from time to time, are they real, or do you make them up as you go along?"

"Help! Help! Papa ..." Rox squealed

"Of course, they are!" Papa confirmed, quickly stepping in to her rescue, "It means, for as long as the toad is croaking, the snake can't sleep. That is, for as long as someone doesn't say 'yes' to the *fat cow* with a *fat batwa*, Roxana's lot won't improve! Am I right, child?"

"Bravo, Papa!" she said, clapping her hands, "In this house, you are the only one who understands and appreciates me."

"Thank you," Papa acknowledged.

"And by the way," Rox added, sufficiently encouraged by his solid backing, "that nose stud which I mentioned, it would have to have a real diamond set in it."

"Twenty-two carat?" I sought clarification at once, so that there were no differences of opinion later on.

"Fourteen would do nicely, thank you very much," she said and left it at that.

The rest of the evening was spent in some more conversation centred around *fat cows* and *fat batwas*—to them, mere jokes to while away the time, but to me, constant reminders of how quickly time was running out and problems were piling up. In my camp, the hunt for a golden goose was still very much alive, and in Azra's, the search for a *Nawabzadah* was about to begin. If I did not hurry up and make my intentions known to all concerned, one might soon be found and finalised on both sides, after which, it would be twice as hard to undo the damage. For as long as I was knocking around from house to house, coaching pupils, my popularity ratings in the *marriage market* might well have gone down, but in the case of the principal of an institution backed by the *Jamayyatul Ulema Foundation*, the odds were entirely different, regardless of the small print. And in Azra's case, her alluring beauty alone was enough to win her the attention of any Prince Charming on the look out for a Cinderella, with no strings attached. I knew there were plenty of them in town, born with golden spoons in their mouths, capable of looking after their own as well as hers for the price of her hand. I was, therefore, up against pretty tough competition. My only ace of trump was, I had the full backing of the bride—if at all I did. But did I? I did not know that for sure. Besides, she had not even looked around to see what sort of *heartthrobs* were there, all those handsome young men who could freeze Venus in her tracks, who could tempt the moon into their bed chambers, who could ignite crackers in any woman's heart, marble carvings straight out of dream galleries, icons of male excellence, wooed by roses, sought by jasmines, worshiped by lilies, adored by goddesses, desired by queens! They were all out there, flitting around in darkened glades and sunken gardens, visible and yet invisible, teasing and tantalising, in pursuit of pretty maidens to adorn their hearts, on the look out for fairy queens to occupy their thrones!

Before falling asleep that night and then falling a prey to all sorts of hallucinations and nightmares, I made myself a firm resolve—not the one that was going to be made at nightfall and then abandoned at daybreak, but the one I was going to stick to at all costs. On Wednesday of that week, Azra had asked me to knock for her, rather than drop the diary through her letterbox, and I knew it was a day of the week when her father was mostly at work. If so, we could sit together in the lounge by ourselves and have a quiet chat. I could tell her that I loved her and how much I loved her; that I was all alone in my journey through life and needed the helping hand of a caring companion; that my solitary journey was getting tough and my legs were beginning to wobble; that my paths were strewn with all sorts of thorns and I needed someone who could help me avoid treading upon them; I needed the glow of her eyes as my beacons to guide me to the shore; the sweetness of her smile to usher a new spring in my garden; the freshness of her breath to fill its blooms with fragrance; the shadows of her ringlets to attract the cuckoos and the nightingales; the skills of her hand to build our nest; her insight to forecast the storms and protect it from being vandalised by hostile winds. I could ask her if she was that companion whom I sought; if she was the answer to all my prayers; the outcome of my dreams; the elixir I needed to reinvigorate my aching limbs; the potion I sought to transform my fortunes. And if she was, would she agree to take me on board her chariot of dreams; would she say yes to my solemn solicitations; would she say yes to my parents as well as to her parents; would she agree to dress herself in the red Banarasi sari sent by me; to wear the *black beads* necklace stringed with pearls of marital bliss; to accept a short ride from Aghapura to Asifnagar in the red palanquin arranged by me; to enter the cosy world of my arms and rest her head on my shoulder?

The two seemingly endless days intervening my resolve and the day set aside for its accomplishment were occupied by work. Shabbu and I went to see the premises in Mogulpura for the first time, where Mr. Raza also came to meet us. Having emerged out of the house in pursuit of livelihood, it was no longer practical for her to stand on formalities and observe *Purdah*. If she was going to effectively discharge the duties of a vice principal, she would have to be prepared to communicate with colleagues, liase with parents, negotiate with tradesmen, and a lot more besides. Hence, her departure from tradition began with Mr. Raza himself to whom I introduced her first. Apparently, she and his eldest daughter, Shehnaz, were classmates at the women's college, which enabled her to address him as Uncle Raza and ushered an unexpected element of familiarity between them. After the hellos and how-do-you-dos we were given a guided tour of the premises. It was a very large structure covering two floors, standing on its own grounds of about three acres, comprising two identical wings, one for girls and the other for boys. Each wing had its own office, reception, assembly halls, laboratories, libraries, classrooms, dining halls, modern toilets, catering facilities, and basements, everything with no expense spared at all. Apparently, financed by *petrodollars* from the Gulf and intended for children from wealthy families of *Oil Barons* too, it was a thoughtfully planned and lavishly constructed establishment.

After taking us around the sports facilities outside the building, which included everything that was needed for entry to the Olympics, Mr. Raza sat down with us in one of the offices to go through the details of furnishing and refurbishing contracts which had been put to tender by the foundation, so that it could all be done with professional competence. The idea was to prepare the premises for occupation by the school later on, but to run the tutorial institute during the interim period, pending the decision from the education department about the granting of the status. The full details of the works contracts, which had been prepared by seasoned professionals at his behest, did not leave much to be desired. They took care of everything, including the stocking up of libraries and laboratories, in consultation with specialist organisations. Even the task of recruitment was given to professional staffing agencies with experience in the field of education. The target date for completion of the entire work and commencement of enrolment was four months, during which time, we were asked to attend our respective offices between nine to five on weekdays and make a start on planning. Since the requirements of a tutorial institute for the Aligarh Matriculation Exams were going to be different from those of a secondary school, which was what he asked us to concentrate upon. He said he would be always available on phone at his office during working hours, and if we could let him know what those separate sets of needs were going to be, he would make sure that we were provided with them at the earliest.

Soon, blessed Wednesday arrived and woke up all my anxieties anew. To me, it was going to be a *make or break* day. I had never wooed anyone before; never whispered oral confessions of love in anybody's ears; never been in that situation. On that day, Azra was no longer *just* 'Azra' to me—an animated mare in blindfolds, seeking out little foals hidden underneath derelict trellises; or a glamorous poppet running wild in our backyard; or a coquettish teenager doing her additions and subtractions in terms of mangoes, custard apples and bangle sets; or a kitchen-soiled maiden with ruffled pigtails and smeared clothes; or even an ivory doll wrapped in peach-coloured garments, casting upon me her magical spells with the charisma of her ambience. She was something else now; something new and something different; a life supporting oasis in the middle of desert sands; a fountainhead that kept my valley green; an anchor that prevented my boat from drifting into the doldrums; a guardian who kept the key to my paradise hidden in her fist;

a goddess enshrined in the temple of my dreams. I wished I could tell her those brilliant things about herself; make her know how important she was to me; set up for her a pedestal of glory; sit her on it; gather dew drops in lotus saucers and wash her feet; pluck stars from the sky and decorate her *Dopatta*; turn sunrays into tinsel and weave them in her *Khamis*; stand at the end of her suitors' queue and yet give her the most, be a pauper who could take on any prince for her sake; be a David who could throw the heads of ten Goliaths at her feet; be a Jason who could slay a hundred dragons to win her hand.

When I reached her house, serious trouble lay in wait for me. The cheerful palpitations drumming in my heart slowed down at once when her brother Vaseem opened the door to my knock, instead of she or even her father. Without asking me what I wanted, or who I had come to see, he politely said his *salaam,* took me into the lounge without a word and went away. There was no sign of Azra; there were no signs of human presence in the kitchen that backed on to their lounge; no sound of snapping bones; no chink of bangles or even a hiss of breath. All I could hear was their parrot *Jehangir* bringing the roof down with his excited shrieks of *'Azra! Azra! Master Saheb! Master Saheb!* Taken aback by the unusually frosty reception, on that day of all the days, I sat in a chair and waited, uncertain as to who would arrive from inside—he, or she—and wondering what to say if he came instead of she and asked me what I wanted. Obviously, a few days ago, when our meeting on Wednesday was set up by her, he had already left for work; and if her invitation was extended in the expectation that he was going to be out, I did not wish to tell him I was there at her invitation and get her into trouble. Hence, my hurried searches for a convincing excuse.

After an excruciatingly long wait in nerve-wracking tension, he arrived instead of she and extended his polite greetings in a voice that was far from cheerful, wearing an expression on his face which was next only to a scowl. I could see that something was wrong; there was a distinct change in his attitude towards me since our most recent conversation in the same room a few days ago. If his wife did not pass on that shopping bag with its incriminating contents to him until our last meeting, it seemed it had been, soon afterwards. Even such a supposition threw a nasty scare into me. Writing an enamoured greetings cards to a receptive and responsive sweetheart about the storms raging in my heart was one thing, but trying to take on an irate parent rubbed on the wrong side by height of stupidity was quite another. What would he ask me and how would I answer him? The situation had gone past the *sensitive* stage and was bordering on to the *incendiary*; I, a mature Muslim man, with outwardly unimpeachable pretences to respectability, and she, a young and inexperienced Muslim girl with an undeniable claim to innocence, masquerading in the roles of *the teacher and the taught*, either getting together to draw a blindfold over the eyes of their parents and their peers, or I on my own, trying to lead her on to the primrose path with cheeky gifts and even cheekier greeting cards! What was my defence going to be, my answer, my explanation, and my redemption? To what extent had I upset him? Was he angry because of what I did, or because of my being what I was and yet doing what I did? Was his anger aimed at my actions or at my intentions? Was it the renunciation of a principle that had hurt him, or was it my gall, my audacity, my contumacy? Would he seek his redress simply by turning me out of his house, or would he resort to humiliating me, perhaps even manhandling me? What exactly was he after, my soul or my blood?

It did not take too long for those disconcerting thoughts to race through my frenetic mind. However, a sudden sense of relief from tension overcame me when, instead of dwelling upon the core of my sin, he simply stretched his hand for the diary, as if he knew that was what had brought me to his house. I had no choice than to give it to him without uttering another word. Words were, no doubt, uttered in the room, but not from my mouth. He said it on his own accord that Azra had told him I would be dropping in to return the diary.

"I'm sorry your time was wasted," he added, forcing himself into an apologetic smile, "She shouldn't have troubled you like this. She had no right to take advantage of your politeness."

To me, the long and short of that brief communication was like *sudden death* in a game of chance; he could just as well have booted me out and banged the door in my face. Behind the simple excuse of returning the diary, I had gone there to do a lot more besides; I had gone there in quest of an oasis to quench my thirst; a fountainhead to keep my valley forever green; a beacon to guide me ashore; an anchor to protect my boat from drifting. Before pouring my heart out to my parents, that was my last hurdle. I desperately needed to talk to her that day, I needed to hear from her own mouth and in her own words how she felt about me, I needed to get a correct interpretation of her body language, her wordless signals, her effervescent looks, her enigmatic smiles; I needed to know what did her welter of lashes say to her eyes whenever she faced the mirror to put *Kajal* in them; what did the red ribbons say to her twin plaits when she tied up the strands; what did her wild tufts tell her rosy cheeks when a whiff of breeze sent them bouncing; what did her heart say to her mind when she lay in her bed and ruminate! I needed to put my finger on her pulse and feel its tick; I needed to address her entelechy and ask for some straight answers; I needed to be sure that she had kept the doors of her heart open for me; that I was welcome to take a stroll in her dreams and build my monuments in them; that she was willing to get into my *red palanquin* when it came along; that she had no intentions of turning away my *white stallion* from her doorstep. Frankly, my real mission that day was not to return something hers but to retrieve something mine; it was not for giving up but for getting back; the issue was not the diary but the hand to which it belonged—*her* hand, to wear *my kangan, her* finger, to wear *my* ring, *her* shoulder, to support *my* head!

"It's all right, Mr. Ansari?" I said quite boldly, "It gives me the chance to say goodbye to her and to wish her luck until we meet again."

"Listen, Mr. Quraishi," he snapped, staring at me with a somewhat stern look, "Forgive me if I sound a little harsh. I already told you that I've changed my mind about sending Azra to work. Right now, we're doing our utmost to find a suitable match for her. You may or may not be aware of this, but it's an uphill task. I'm not a man of either financial affluence or of social status. Self-respect is my only asset which, unfortunately, isn't enough to compete with for a good match. This is an extremely nasty neighbourhood and gossip travels fast. One adverse comment about her is enough to ruin what little chances she's got. I just can't afford to take such risks, especially at a time like this. So, please try and understand."

His pincer-sharp words, delivered without a trace of either ambiguity or indecision, made me sit up. I had been seeing Azra for the past nine months and no one ever said to me that I was bad for her image. But suddenly, I had become an embarrassment. Just when I plucked up enough courage to lay the cards out before her; put my feelings into words at long last; reveal my heart; tell her what was going on in my mind and find out what was going on in hers; either take my garden into the spring or bring the spring into my garden, I was being denied the opportunity to do it. What was my recourse? Tell him what I would have told her? Admit it to his face that, whilst he allowed me to teach his daughter without any *Purdah* restrictions, I had been abusing the prerogative, feasting my eyes, entertaining *ideas* in my head about her? How could I tell him in so many words that I was in love with his daughter? And if I did not, then what was the alternative? Get up and ride off? Having gone to the oasis for quenching my thirst, return home with an empty pail? I could not do it. The stakes had gone up too high for me to freak out. It had never been my intention to bypass standard protocol, but it looked as though the time had come for me to slay the dragon of tradition and go for the golden fleece. Everything I wanted out of life was right there underneath his roof, and hence, that was where I decided pitch my tent and fight back.

"Mr. Ansari," I ventured somehow, "I never thought I'd sit here one day and say this to you with my own mouth, but it seems I must. I love Azra and I cherish her. May I, please, have the honour of seeking her hand in marriage, sir?"

My words seemed to have unleashed a shower of live cinders on his head. He could not be more shocked if I had told him she was already bearing my illegitimate child! I failed to see what was so preposterous about the offer. Having allowed us to meet for so long without any formal restrictions, he should have expected some such thing to happen. After all, I was twenty-five and unattached, and she an extremely pretty teenager. I only said I loved her; I did not say I had seduced her. Yet he sat slumped in the chair for one heck of a long time staring at me with wide eyes as though I was a carrier of the Bubonic Plague! Silence in the room became so disturbingly deep I could hear the flutter of my own heart. But apart from waiting, there was nothing else I could do. I had spoken my bit; the rest was up to him. Azra was no longer in the picture.

"Does she know about this?" he asked me, finally recovering from his shock.

"No, sir, she doesn't."

"What about your parents?"

"They don't know either. As a matter of fact, no one does except me, and now you. But I was about to tell them, anyway. It still isn't too late to do things in the traditional way, if only you would let me."

"She's your student, for God's sake!"

"I know, sir. But please believe me, I had no control over my feelings."

"For how long has this been going on?"

"Nothing has been *going* on, Mr. Ansari. I'd appreciate it if you kindly refrain from making it sound dirty. Turn me down if you must, but please don't be in a rush to condemn me. Or her. We've done no wrong."

"What I do or what I say isn't important. The whole of this neighbourhood knows that you're her teacher, and also that I let you teach her without any *Hijaab*. Once married, she'll go away to live with her husband and his parents. But I've to spend the rest of my life here. She isn't my only daughter; I have others besides her. How am I supposed to face the neighbours? Walk that street with due dignity? Even visit the local mosque? Have you thought about it?"

Frankly, I had not. But even if I did, it would not have made any difference to me. How Azra felt was another matter. After all, he was her father, and those towards whom concern was being expressed her sisters. I preferred not to comment.

"Well, I don't know what to say!" he muttered in the end, "I'll have to thrash this out with Azra and her mother first. I am afraid you're going to have to wait until I do."

"I'm in no rush, Mr. Ansari. Not anymore."

"Before you go, let me make one thing clear," he said after some more thought, "I've nothing against you. Frankly, in our circumstances, I'm sure we couldn't have found a better match for her even if we searched the earth with a torch in hand. If there are no objections either from her or her mother, I'd be happy to say yes, in spite of the fears I expressed just now. But on the other hand, if turning down your offer becomes inevitable, I'd be doing it with a heavy heart. Will you bear that in mind?"

"Yes, sir, I will. There is one thing I, too, would like you to bear in mind before making a decision. Azra is a priceless jewel that can make any crown in which she is set twice its worth. I have no crowns either to wear myself or to place on her head. But I do love her so much, anyone in whose veins runs the same blood as runs in hers is equally precious to me. That, I assure you, will be a part of my marriage vows to her."

"Very well. Come and see me a week on Wednesday at the same time. I'll be home and I'll have an answer."

My fate thus hanging in the balance, I took his leave and came home. The next fifteen days felt like fifty decades. Having taken on a serious responsibility, I could not neglect work, but my mind was not on anything. If the decision lay with my parents alone, it would have been another matter. They were *my* parents, they loved *me*, they had my best interests at their heart. I could talk things through, negotiate, persuade, and even disobey if it ever came to that. I had a strong will; I had experience; I had taken the rough with the smooth; I had faced challenges; I had absorbed losses; I had erected goal posts; I had hoisted flags. But above all, I knew my mind, I loved her, I was committed to her; I was on board; I was not susceptible to outside influences; I was not trading in alternatives; I was not open to offers; not prepared to cut corners. I did not want money from them, no Green Cards, no Sponsorships, no *links* or *contacts* abroad. She was all I wanted; her hand in my hand; her head on my shoulder; her face in front of me; her dreams in my eyes; her name on my lips; her help in my need; her companionship in my sojourn; her guidance in my troubles. I wanted my chapattis to be made by her alone; my tea to be sugared with the sweetness of her touch; my hunger to be appeased by her culinary innovations; my room to be filled with the fragrance of her breath; my nights to flourish in her arms; my dawns to break on her lap!

But what about her? Young, fragile and impressionable, with blood in one cheek and mother's milk in the other; away from her stalwart and alone in her mission; too resilient to obstruct and too easy to break; torn apart between opposing loyalties and cast in the centre of extremities; uncertain of her priorities and unsure of her recourse; would she be able to take on all those formidable pressures single-handed and win through? Did she even remotely possess the resourcefulness to render unto *Caesar* what belonged to *Caesar* and save *God's* for *God* alone? Did she have a will with an impenetrable crust; a mind with an impermeable will; a determination with an impregnable mind? How much could she put up with before cracking; how far could she go before freaking; how many tests could she face before winning? Was it fair on her to be straddled with the onus of such magnitude; to be consulted in a matter of such sensitivity; to be cornered into such an unevenly cast trial of strength? Who was there to umpire for her, to ensure fair play, to safeguard her interests, to champion her cause? Would she get an impartial trial, an unbiased hearing, an untainted verdict? Would she manage the right words to protest in, the right strength to fight back with, the right help to reach out for?

A week on Wednesday, I went to see Mr. Ansari as arranged, a lot bolder than I ever was, determined to straighten it all out with him, battle bound, in full armour, swords drawn, provoked by my fighting spirits, protected by my faith, prepared for the worst. As promised, he was home and was waiting for me, but the grim expression on his face clearly indicated that all was not well. I was taken into the lounge, now unkempt and unattended, clearly bearing traces of neglect, books taken out of the shelf and scattered on the floor, everything in sight covered under a week-old layer of dust, the flowers in the vase wilted, burnt out stubs of jossticks wallowing in the ashes, crying out for some much needed attention from the cherished hands that used to keep it spruced. It was not my business, but its sad plight hurt me. That tiny room with its small window and modest furniture was of special significance to me. Everything in it had a profile, a tale to tell, a memory to awaken, an association to renew. That was where I had first encountered my dream; I had come across the Apex; I had learnt my alphabets of love; I had learnt to live;

I had learnt to laugh. That was where I was taught the language of the eyes; I was taken into the secret chambers of the heart; I was introduced to the fanfare of live emotions. Somehow, it belonged to us; it belonged to Azra and me; it was a part and parcel of our past.

Soon after we sat down, he picked up a thick wad of letters lying on the coffee table and put them in my hand without saying one thing or the other. Quite surprised, I simply ran my eyes over them. They were all in Azra's hand, addressed to 'My *master sahib!*', 'My dearest *master sahib!*', 'My very own *master sahib!*'. If I could count them and then count the number of days we had known each other, there could easily be one for one. Rendered utterly speechless by it, I sat staring at the ornate calligraphy on perfumed paper with bewildered eyes. It meant that, in all those long, lonesome and oppressive nights, while I restlessly paced the floor of my balcony counting the stars, she had been pouring out her heart to me; in all those nights, which were lost to speculation and self-debate, she had been sitting on her bed holding the answers to my complex questions on the palm of her hand. She had not only been writing those letters to me, but was also filling up her poems with the same sentiment. I should have realised that she moved away from grief to joy because she found a reason to be happy—I was that reason, love was that reason; and those were her letters, containing a rather simple message which she had been unable to convey to me by word of mouth out of shyness, out of meekness, out of modesty, out of respect. It just said that she loved me too and ended there. If only we had talked things over between ourselves whilst talking was still possible. But unfortunately, etiquette had prevailed and prevented us both; our preoccupation with being *teacher and pupil* had stopped us, our infatuation with principles had held us up. As a result, we were now at the mercy of others, being governed by a will that was not ours, by whims we did not particularly care about, by decisions beyond our control.

"How did you come across these?" I somehow made myself bold and asked him.

"I don't think it's of any relevance," he replied point-blank.

That shut me up. After spending some more time in complete silence, his hawk-like eyes glued to my face, he let go of his held breath, took out a snuff box from his pocket, helped himself to a generous pinch and sniffed it hard to clear his head.

"When Azra's mother found these letters in her room," he explained in a terse voice, for some reason changing his mind, "she brought them to my attention. It wasn't easy for me to sit down and read through these passionate love letters written by my own daughter, but I had to find out just how far this affair had gone."

I did not quite know how to cope with that observation and remained silent.

"Well," he carried on, "at this stage, I'm not trying to raise any moral issues. I know the score now, which's enough. If reading the letters was embarrassing to me, you can guess how unpalatable it must be to discuss them with you. But I have my reasons. Would you please skim through the first few and then compare them with the last three or four?"

I did not do his bidding right away. It meant they had been already scrutinized, which was quite unforgivable. They were her letters and contained her private thoughts and personal emotions. His reading them without her consent was most unfair.

"Go on, Mr. Quraishi. Read them," he insisted, getting a bit impatient.

If only because he ordered me to, I did. There was, indeed, something odd. In the beginning, her mood was frivolous, cheeky and entertaining. But as she came to the last few, the tone had changed significantly. The passion began to subside, the tide started to recede into ebb. For some reason, she was begging me to forget her, drawing blinds, banging doors, and breaking bonds. What happened? Why did she so abruptly begin to withdraw and to retreat? Why was she turning away? The letters themselves did not contain any clues.

"See what I mean?" he asked me, reading well the confused expression on my face.

I simply nodded.

"What's gone wrong suddenly?" he asked.

What, indeed! I wished he had found out. I wished he would tell me too.

He did tell me. Apparently, for the past several weeks, she had been having a strange dream, in which she saw an old man with white hair and a white beard, clad in green robes and wrapped in a black blanket, come out of the voids with a hurricane lantern in his hand and keep beckoning to her. She was so scared of the frightening vision, she was afraid to fall asleep!

I did not know what to say. I had never come across anything as fatalistic as that in my whole life. Besides, I had not seen any signs of fear or stress in her behaviour, not even during our most recent meeting. If anything, we had parted on an optimistic note, saying *Fi AmaanAllah* to each other instead of *Al vida*.

"What's it got to do with me?" I asked him, my confusion at its worst. "I mean, what's the connection between the dream and us?"

He explained to me that too. When she told him about it, he got scared as well and immediately took her to a friend of his who specialised in interpretation of dreams. After listening to the details, his friend told him that she and I were mismatched, our stars were in conflict, she was bad for me and would bring me plenty of misery. The dream, he stressed, was merely an oracular warning of things to come, and his recommendation was to break up our match at once!

"He also proved it," he concluded.

"Proved it! How?"

In answer to the question, he produced five split tamarind seeds from his pocket, rolled them in his fist for a while and then cast them on the floor. Four settled down on the shear side and one face downwards. No matter how often he cast them, the result remained the same, defying reason, defying logic, defying even the law of averages. It was so bizarre I had a job believing my own eyes.

"You try it," he said as I sat gaping.

If reluctantly, I did. The same thing happened. Ten times, twenty times— it hardly mattered. Rendered speechless, I stared at him with blank eyes.

"Don't just sit there staring at me, Mr. Quraishi," he said, evidently as flabbergasted by the strange phenomenon as I was. "Say something. What do you make of it?"

"Is this why she's asking me to forget her in her letters?" I stammered. "Because of the interpretation of her dream?"

"I suspect it's because of a strong sense of prognosis."

"What about asking her?"

"Her mother has already asked her, repeatedly. But she hasn't opened her mouth so far."

"May I talk to her, Mr. Ansari? After all, I've been teaching her until only the other day, and all being well, we'll soon be man and wife soon? Please?"

"I'm afraid, it isn't up to me anymore. She doesn't want to see you or talk to you. According to her, for your own good. What can I do?"

A few days ago, he turned me down, on account of neighbours, gossip, self-respect, his concern for his other daughters. And now, Azra herself was turning me down, on account of her dreams, forebodings and superstitions. Finding out that she, too, loved me did not resolve a thing. On the contrary, it complicated the matter even more. Giving her up now was tougher than it had ever been before. But my hands were tied. She was leaving me no room to manoeuvre.

"Listen," said Mr. Ansari after a while, reaching his own decision, "Now that I know the whole thing, I'll make you one promise: I won't take any steps toward her marriage until this issue is resolved. As her parents, we too want for her what she wants for herself. So, trust me and leave it at that for now. When she has done some thinking and cleared her head, I'll get in touch with you. What do you say?"

There was nothing for me to say. Until that moment, most of my misgivings had centred on my parents and her parents, my sisters and her sisters, my priorities and her priorities, my duties and her obligations. If they were, I could have tackled them all without letting anyone down. But, for the first time, it emerged that our real enemy was something else, something hidden and unexpected, something notional and intangible, its direction unpredictable, its strength incalculable and we too unprepared to take it on.

My fate hanging in the balance once again, I went home.

CHAPTER (11)

Out of goodness of his heart, Mr. Ansari let me keep the letters. Shortly after supper, as soon as everybody retired to bed and the house plunged into its usual hush, broken only by the sound of nonstop snoring, or by the muted tumult of nocturnal life rampant outside, I too locked myself in my room and settled down to reading them. They were all written in Urdu, a language in which her standard was exceptionally high. The magic moment in her life was the same as it was in mine.

'When Abbajan introduced you to me that day,' she wrote, 'I could not believe my eyes! I never thought such coincidences did happen in real life too. I had seen them happen in movies and I used to laugh. But, you see? When Allah decides to bring two strangers together, He acts in mysterious ways! Only last Sunday, when I went visiting auntie Ayesha, my cousin Sakina asked me to play hide and seek with her friends. I said yes and ended up in the blindfold. After tying the scarf on my eyes, she whispered in my ear, 'if you make a wish while the blindfold is on, it will come true when you take it off.' So I tried. I wished Allah to bring me face to face with the most handsome man in the whole world. Guess what? When I took off my blindfold, he was there right in front of my eyes! His complexion was fair; he had dark hair that rippled like silk; he wore a white *Kurta* and white *Churidar;* his bright eyes cast strange spells and his smile was irresistible. I rubbed my eyes and looked at him again and again to make sure he was real. Then I tore my eyes away from him with great difficulty and did not let them return to him with even greater difficulty. But he simply stood there staring at me, devouring me with his looks. I did not move, I could not move, I could not even breath until Sakina came and broke his hold. Later on, when I heard that he was manor born, he lived in that great big *Haveli* next door and owned all that land; I shrugged aside his memory because we were not in his league. He belonged to the other side of the gulf to which girls like us have no access.

'But only a few days later I was proved wrong when Abbajan introduced him to me as my teacher! He was no longer a shadow from the other side; he belonged to the same side to which I, too, belonged; he spoke the same language as me; he, too, showed his teeth just like us when he laughed; he, too, laughed like anyone else, but his laughter was somehow different from the rest of the others; it rose goose pimples on my skin; it stirred up storms and made me run for cover. No other laughter had ever shaken me up like that; no other man spoke to me the way he did; no one looked at me with his kind of eyes.

'And now, he is my *master saheb*! My precious *master saheb*! My special *master saheb*! See how Allah acts in mysterious ways? See, *master saheb?* He granted my wish without my having to do anything; He filled my lap with roses; He brought happiness to my doorstep. I still remember how you sat in the chair frozen like a manikin, blushing like a bride, not looking at me, not talking to me, and behaving as if I did not exist. What I can't remember is, how you look, which is good because I can give you a thousand faces and then choose the one I like the best. Fancy that! My heart going dharak! *dharak...dharak!* Over someone whom I don't even remember! When you come on Monday, I've every intention of taking a good hard look at you. I happen to be very partial to noses, you know? From a distance at least, yours didn't seem to have much of a future with me. Next time you come, I hope you'll bring a better one along ...'

It was her first—cheerful, casual, witty, humorous and brought back a lot of pleasant memories. Imagine, her *Abbajan* reading that! The first was not half as embarrassing as the one that followed was:

'My! My! My! What a lump of sugar candy you turned out to be!' she wrote in it, 'How many casualties have you accumulated, *master sahib?* Count me as one .... I'm crushed; by the way, why do you keep blushing? Do I bother you? Good teachers look their pupils straight in the eye. But you keep taking yours for a walk all over the room, except where I sit. Do stop ignoring me. It makes me feel as though I'm not worth looking at. I dressed up especially for you; I spent nearly half an hour styling my hair in the hope of impressing you. And what did you do? You gave me a cold shoulder. Now, I've to wait for three whole days before you come again. Before we met, time used to fly. It doesn't anymore. I've already done the homework you gave me. I hope it'll make you happy. I hope you'll look upon me as a model pupil. You're a lucky man, *master saheb!* You've chosen for yourself a job that brings you into contact with lots and lots like me. But I never came across anyone like you. I'm so glad you agreed to teach me. I'm so glad you like my poems. I'll write more, better than ever before, and boast of having at least one fan …'

It went on. By and large, the cheerful and frivolous mood changed into serious self-expression, thoughts well co-ordinated, sentiments streamlined and goals clear:

'What're you doing to me, *master saheb!* I never felt like this before. I can't eat, I can't sleep, I can't relax. I see you wherever I look, I hear your voice whenever I'm alone, I sit on my own talking to you for hours. But there's never a connection between what I ask and what you reply. You're not even aware of my presence. Is this all I mean to you? Just another pupil? Tell me something. Answer me. Be honest. Do you notice how my voice splits when I talk to you? You do, don't you? And when you look deep into my eyes, what do you find in them? Don't you spot your own reflection in them? Twice a week, physical distance between us shrinks down to a few feet. Yet, is it so difficult for you to take notice of me? To hear the throbbing of my heart? To measure the racing of my blood? To sense the speeding of my breath? What more do you want me to do? Hang a *I love you* placard around my neck? Is there someone else in your life? If there is, don't tell me. I can't bear the thought. I happen to be a possessive person and, therefore, rather jealous of competition. I've taken it for granted that you and I belong to each other. True or not, the very notion brings me a great deal of comfort and is enough to see me through one lifetime. That's all I care about, *master saheb*—just one lifetime. So, let me hang on to the hope. Let me carry on dreaming about the days ahead of us. Without you, I'm not particularly looking forward to them. Travel with me for some distance, partner! My paths are lonesome; my journey is long and my goal out of sight! I love you! I love you! I love you! I had heard people say so to each other in the movies, I had read it in *Munshi Premchand*'s novels. I used to laugh at it as well, you know? Until it happened to me too. I know now how it feels to be in love with a stone-idol. A storm has built up in my heart and I'm writhing. O *master saheb!* Deny me anything; take away from me whatever you want to, except the Wednesdays and the Fridays. They're the only two real days in my life. I begin to wait for the sound of your bike from ten o'clock onwards. The moment I hear it, my heart leaps into my throat, matching stroke for stroke. Yes, yes, it goes *dharak! dharak! dharak!* It drives me nuts; it takes me to heights I had never climbed before; it makes me dizzy. I rush to the door, making sure in spite of the hurry that I look good enough to catch attention. I *am* pretty!—if only you pause for a while and take a look. But do you? Ever? No! You talk about mathematics, geography and chemistry, whereas I like history. Know why? Because it would be very interesting to see what you've to say on the subject of the *Taj Mahal.* About *Prince Saleem* and the courtesan *Anarkali.* About *Sultana Razia* and her slave *Altaaf.* They're some of the people who gave immortality to love. Come, my prince! Let's also make history together—you and I. And then let's watch from Paradise what the poets of the next generation make of it. We, too, can feature in their lyrics, like *Laila* and *Majnu,* like *Shireen* and *Farhaad*, like *Heer* and *Ranjha.* What did they have which we don't, eh? They didn't even exist and yet are given a lasting place in folklore. Whereas we are real. Our love is real. Our life is real ...'

About twenty such and similar letters later, she became extremely serious about the whole affair. It reflected in her thoughts as well as in the words she chose to express herself. '*Eid Mubarak*, master saheb!' she wrote on the occasion of the festival, 'Last night, we all went into our backyard to spot the new moon and make our wishes. I have only one wish in my life and Allah knows all about it. Soon after spotting the moon in the sky, I wanted to see the other one that shines for me on earth. But there was darkness around me because my moon was not there. They all shouted greetings at each other with joy, except me. My joy was elsewhere. I only had tears in my eyes. I dug my face in my palms and shed them. I missed you so much, *master saheb*! I wished you were there. I wished you were somewhere near me to come and dry my tears. I hadn't seen you for a whole week, except for that one brief encounter in the market that day, which was beginning to feel like eternity. I suspect Ammijan knows I've lost my heart to you. She noticed my distress, hugged me hard, kissed me and said *AMEEN* to my prayers without even asking me what they were. A mother's heart has no substitutes, has it?

Referring to our meeting in the vineyard on the same day, she wrote, 'What a wonderful moment it always is when two people who love each other like we do come face to face! Thank you, *master saheb!* Thank you for giving me so much joy in life, thank you for bringing all that sunshine in my garden, thank you for lending me your shoulder to lean on, thank you for making me feel like a queen, thank you, thank you, thank you! We are a *true pair*, aren't we? You know what I want and I know where to go looking for it. I stretch my empty bowl in front of you and you fill it up with just the sort of goodies I need. I come to you thirsty and you quench my thirst; I come to you in pain and you assuage my wounds; I come to you in hope and you fulfil each and every one of them. You are my *mentor* and I'm your *ward,* you are my *string* and I am your *tune*, you are my *voice* and I am your *song!'*

The note of optimism continued right through the period of serious preparation and into the examinations.

'How will I ever be able to pay you back for all your kindness and generosity, *master saheb?'* she wrote after the exams, 'Has the seashell ever been able to thank the rain cloud for lodging a pearl in its fold? Does the candle flame ever manage to redeem its debt to the melting wax? Can a pupa ever repay its gratitude to the cocoon for its protection and care? Can a ship ever turn its back on the tide that guided it to shore? No! No! No! Neither can I ever free myself of my lasting indebtedness to you, my *dearest master saheb*! Not in this life, nor in the after life! You have been so patient with me; you never once lost your temper; you never once scorned or scoffed me; you never let go of your calm, or your smile, or your manners, my *duke*! Wherever I am, wherever I go, wherever I stand, you will always be with me. Without you, I will be as incomplete as an unfinished story and as meaningless as an inverted rainbow. Rewrite me as a complete story, *master saheb!* Give me a beginning, a climax and a fitting end! Give me a clear direction. Come here and join me. Bring with you some rain, some sunshine; bring the season of yellow flowers; bring some green shoots for the *Beerbahootis*; bring a few dried twigs for the *Laal Muniya's* nest; bring a cushion for the lotus to lean on; bring some dreams to array in my eyes; bring a huge bunch of tomorrows to share between us; bring a brass band, a red palanquin and a thick cluster of fresh *Chambelis* for my *Sehra*! Then we can sit together and play weddings ...'

Then came the trying times of learning to live without me; without the Wednesdays and the Fridays; without the healing of wounds; without the quenching of thirst; without the seeking of comfort.

'O my *master saheb!*' she wrote in one of the many which she had scribbled in course of those four agonising weeks, 'How many moments are there in an hour? How many hours are there in a lifetime? How many lifetimes are there in this long and endless wait? How often does the sun sink and surface in a day? How many shooting stars do fall off the sky each night? How long does the moon tarry in a month? How .many seasons do change in a cycle of time? The geese flew west and came back but *you* did not come; the mendicant knocked for alms a thousand times but *you* did not knock; the bells of countless rickshaws rang outside my house but *your* motorbike did not pour honey in my ears. When will this wait end? When will my knight in armour knock for me? When will my moon shine and make moonlight in my dark nights? When will the spring come into my garden and change its colours? When will the roses grow again; birds chirp again; squirrels race again; seeds sprout again; life resurrect again; when will this death like hush clamped all around me break? *When? When? When?*'

At that stage, something happened. By assumption at least, it could be the start of that nasty dream, but the letter itself did not contain any clues.

'I was wrong,' she wrote in it, 'I was mistaken. I strayed away from the path of righteousness. From the *Siraatul mustaqeem*. Even if I did not sin, I have erred beyond the scope of forgiveness. I have displeased Allah. He is angry with me, He has withdrawn His light.

That is why there is so much darkness around me. The Master of the Universe has recanted me. There is no place for me to rest. The other side of the moon is too dark; the other side of the sun is too hot; the other side of the stars is too paltry; the other side of the sky is His seat where I am not welcome now. I have fallen out of His grace. He is going to punish me by hurting the person who is the closest to my heart. You are the only one who can push me over the brink and He knows it. I can neither hurt you nor can I watch you get hurt. I love you far too much for that. All I can do is to punish myself before He hurts you. I can walk out of your life, make the gap between us infinite, set you free from these bonds so that you can use your own judgement and sort yourself out. I will stop thinking about you, I will stop waiting for you, I will never bring your name on my lips, and never let you enter my dreams. Find yourself a pretty woman who can replace me without causing you any pain, *master saheb*! Who can give you more than I ever could; who can share your future; who can return your love; but above all, someone whom you can take to your bosom without displeasing Allah; without breaching His Code. Let's part while there is time to part like friends. Tomorrow, the day after, the month after, the year after, things might not be the same. It is different now. I am still yours, I am still alone and I still belong only to you. But for how long … Who knows!'

The retractions and the introspections carried on. For some strange reason, she kept putting more and more distance between herself and me. Why? What went wrong? What was getting in the way? What was forcing her to draw the blind on her golden dream? There were still no clues.

'I see something coming between us,' she wrote in the next, 'casting a frightening shadow, just like an eclipse. My moon is disappearing from sight; it's being swallowed up by the shadow, being obscured. No, *master saheb!* No! I won't let anything happen to you. I won't make you suffer on account of me. I won't plunge you into such grief. There's evil in me, there is danger in me, I represent darkness, I spell disaster. Don't come any closer, don't take the risk, I'm not worth it. What a relief that I never disclosed my feelings to you! It's my secret and I intend to take it to my grave. What you don't know can't hurt you. In due course, I, too, will vanish from your mind like the rest of your pupils and time will erase my memory. What is one more in the midst of so many? But it's not the same with me. My options are different from yours and I have a different set of tests to face, the most painful out of them being the nuptial bed. How can I possibly take that test and get through? How can I surrender myself into the arms of another man? I can't. Anything else, yes; I can endure pain, I can cope with distress, I can face disappointments, I can suffer loneliness, I can bear the agony of repression, I can stagger underneath the weight of all those sweet and unforgettable memories which I've accumulated over the months: you, sitting there in that chair, facing me, smiling at me, talking to me, so desperately trying to make heads and tails out of additions and subtractions. I can remember all that and yet carry on living. I can spend my entire life reading my own letters, going over every path we trod together, reviving a million recollections. Sometime, if I get a little too lonesome and depressed, I can summon my thoughts and order them to produce you at once. They would have to do my bidding whenever I demand it of them. That should do me fine, *master saheb!* Your image, at my beck and call! That should do me fine. But how can I submit myself to some other man? This body, which I've kept neat and clean for your hands only; this shrine in which you alone can be the deity, how can I surrender it to others? How can I say the same words to another man, which I've been saying to you? I can't. I won't. If it ever came to that, I will kill myself. So, if you hear about a suicide in Aghapura, it would be mine. Quite a lot of people will tell you that I died, but they won't be able to say why, because they won't know. My secret will be buried along with me. You must go on living, regardless. Unlike me, you can afford to love the woman you marry. But I can't say the same for myself. I'm not a free person. I happen to be a woman of limited options. I'm your bondmaid. I'm *your property!* I'm an unwanted legacy which you can't decline ...'

Then came the last, with the cold finality of a *swansong,* yet without any explanations, without any forewords, without any footnotes.

'Is this where it is all destined to end?' she wrote in it with a shaky hand, 'Are these the crossroads beyond which the track is too narrow to fit us both, *master saheb?* You must leave me here and be on your way. Don't worry about me. I will grow again like a tendril of wild blooms. I will come into your vineyard and breath a new life in its dead bines. I will slip into your dreams and put a healing swab on your wounds. O, *master saheb!* Leave me here and embark upon your mission to find Peace. Let me rest my aching limbs for a while. This soil is soft enough for me to unwind in slumber. These are friendly surroundings; I can recognise a few of the mounds by touch; I can recognise the others by reading the inscriptions on the oblong slabs. I know all the travellers who have turned this corner; I can clearly see their footprints I can smell them; I can even touch them. So, let me wait here until you disappear from sight. Until time and distance put you beyond my reach. Until gusts of breeze carrying your vestiges change direction and flow away. Until the silken straps binding us together snap and set us free. Then I will sit here by myself and decide what to do, which way to turn, how far to go, how fast to run ...'

Soon the night wore out. Darkness gave way to light and the grey sky began to turn blue. Cocks crowed in the barn and ravens clamoured on the casuarinas. I was still a long way from making decisions. There was nothing I could do without seeing Azra first and without making her realize that, if there was still time to restitute ourselves, we were virtually on its brink. No one gets a second chance in life. And never before was I more determined to make a success out of ours than on that auspicious morning. A new dawn had broken, not only outside the room but also within my inner seclusion. The flames leaping out of her letters had set me afire too. Paradise was on the palm of our hands. All we needed to do was to take those few final steps, cross the last bridge and just reach out...

Before making one move or the other, I decided to do a bit of my own research first. If Mr. Ansari could take the matter to an expert, so could I. After all, interpretation of dreams is mere conjecture and astrology, an inaccurate science. There was no harm in taking a second opinion, as one expert's conclusion did not necessarily have to match another's. If at least some room for ambiguity or uncertainty emerged, I could persuade Mr. Ansari to reconsider the situation. So, I got cracking. A phone call to a distant relative who was quite knowledgeable in matters related to *Saints* and *sages* produced the name and address of another dream specialist. I made an urgent appointment to see him and rushed.

Peer Saheb, the honorary president of the *Nizamiah Dream Interpretation Services,* lent me a patient ear, rolled all the details of Azra's dream over and over in his mind and finally broke into a beaming smile.

"There's nothing extraordinary about white-haired old men in green robes and black blankets, son," he said, "I, too, have white hair and a white beard, I often wear a green robe, wrap around me a black blanket during the winter months, sometimes even carry a hurricane lantern if I'm out and about on a dark and fog-laden night. But that doesn't make me a symbol of fear, does it?"

Not until then did I realise what an uncanny look alike he himself was to Azra's nocturnal persecutor! Then I remembered a dozen others who also dressed and looked like him.

"*Phew!* What do you know!" I exclaimed.

"Wait a minute," he said, giving the sensitive issue some more concentration, "To tell you the truth, I'm not so intrigued by the dream itself as I am by those five tamarind seeds. If we can crack their mystery, rest assured you will go laughing all the way to the nuptial bed! How're you fixed for money?"

"Whatever belongs to the others is in plenty, but not much of my own. Why?"

"Can you afford to purchase a gold ring with a small emerald? You ought to be able to find one for around a couple of hundred rupees from any jeweller near Chaar Minaar, or even from *the lovers arcade*"

"What for?"

"What I've in mind will solve your problems in a jiffy. If you can get hold of the ring and give it to me, I'll consecrate it with special worship at midnight tonight. You can collect it first thing in the morning, then take your sweetheart to the *holy shrine* and put it on her finger."

"What will that do?"

"For as long as she wears the ring, the dream will stop and the spell cast upon the tamarind seeds will break."

"Will it, really?"

"Oh yes, it will. I can stake my honour upon it."

For what it was worth, I bought the ring and gave it to him by lunchtime. As promised, it was consecrated at midnight and returned to me in the morning, along with written instructions on the procedure to follow. 'Go together to the *holy shrine* at daybreak,' wrote Peer Saheb, 'put this ring on your beloved's finger and then address yourself to Allah. A Shrine as holy as that is said to be thronged by Angels at all times. When they hear you pray, they, too, will join in and invoke Allah's mercy. Beseech the Lord to protect your sweetheart against evil and keep her out of harm's way. Allah is always more eager to give than to winch. I have no doubt your prayers will be heard and answered. For as long as she wears the ring, the dream will not recur. Go now and gather His Benedictions with both hands, for they're always in plenitude. May Allah's blessings be upon the both of you. Ameen!'

The writing itself did a lot to hold my spirits and wedge my courage. To be able to go back to Mr. Ansari so soon and put him in the picture, I needed both. However unlikely, there was always the possibility that he had deliberately fabricated the excuse about the dreams just to put me off for a while and came up with the *hoax* of the tamarind seeds merely to strengthen his claim. If so, I could upset him with the rush and, instead of resolving the existing complications, might even end up creating new ones. But I just could not help it. His keeping her away from me like that behind a solid *iron curtain* and beyond my reach was raging no end of havoc upon my nerves. I desperately needed to see her and sort it all out with her alone. Not with Mr. Ansari, not with Mrs. Ansari, not with Vaseem, not even with Mamma and Papa, but with just her. Even though entertaining such wicked suppositions about people to whose daughter I had just proposed marriage was quite unforgivable, but I simply could not afford to take any risks. Such things were known to have happened; if her parents were determined to prevent our marriage, for one reason or another, they could go to any lengths to do it.

So, mumbling the most sincere and fervent *Bismillah* ever, I went ahead and contacted Mr. Ansari on phone at the paper mill for an urgent audience. Without even bothering to find out what it was all about, he said he would be home by five that evening and I was welcome to drop in any time after that. Significantly, the distinct note of hostility that he had displayed earlier on was gone from his voice; I had never known him to be more polite than that even during those early days of our acquaintance when he was at his best behaviour.

After finishing work at the Institute, I saw Shabbu off in a *rickshaw* and made straight for Aghapura on my bike, my heartbeat constantly fluctuating between fast and slow, based entirely upon the drift of my thoughts. The mere fact that Mr. Ansari was polite on the phone did not mean he was not annoyed by my impatience. He might well be. After all, our most recent conversation only a day ago had ended on a fairly optimistic note, in which, rather than rejecting my offer outright or recanting me, he had merely asked me to wait for a while until he could thrash it out with his wife and daughter. In spite of a gentlemanly handshake on it, I had run out of patience, obtained alternative interpretations, rung him up at his workplace and pressed him for an urgent audience. It was enough to upset even the most forgiving of fathers, and in less daunting circumstances, let alone an undecided parent trying to do his best for his daughter's future happiness.

Luckily for me, when I knocked, nothing untoward happened. Mr. Ansari let me in with his usual politeness, seated me in the lounge, asked after my health, fetched the tray of tea and refreshments from inside and laid it on the coffee table. Sufficiently encouraged by his positive attitude so far, even made bolder by it, I waived the hospitality aside for the time being, told him whatever transpired in Peer Saheb's house earlier and put the ring as well as the note in his hand, my eyes hot, my breath held, my limbs contrite.

"I do apologise for jumping the gun like this, Mr. Ansari," I admitted frankly, "but I only wish you could step into my shoes and feel the way I feel!"

"I do, even without stepping into your shoes, Mr. Quraishi," he admitted equally frankly. "Any woman who is loved by a man as much as my daughter is loved by you, must be an exceptionally lucky woman, and I'm not going to commit the sin of getting in the way. Wait here for a while and help yourself to some tea. Let me see what she has to say. I won't be long."

Holding the note and the ring in his hand, he went inside to confer with his family, leaving me out of breath. His attitude had, indeed, changed quite significantly since the last time we sat together in the same room and discussed the same topic, which brought down quite a crippling load off my mind. If only such a feeling of cordiality continued throughout and enabled us to cross the threshold of our married life with blessings from both sides! Hanging on to the pleasant thought, Allah's name on my lips and Azra's face in my eyes, I sat dreaming about things to come—that house packed with guests, the melodious notes of the *Shehnai* echoing in their front yard, the air laden with fragrance of flowers and perfume, bliss and elation in evidence everywhere, a pretty bride attired in the magnificence of traditional bridal wear sitting underneath the red canopy in readiness to take her conjugal vows, and a happy bridegroom on his way to hold her hand, to accept her vows, to make her his pledges, to unite in holy wedlock, to get her on board his red palanquin and take her away to his dreamland!

Long before those blithesome thoughts wore out, he returned from inside with a clear expression of relief on his face and broke the glorious news that Azra had agreed to go to the *shrine*.

"Sooner rather than later, how about tomorrow morning?" he suggested, taking me quite by surprise!

Whether or not a visit to the shrine produced results, the very thought that I would be able to see her in a matter of a few hours drew a noisy gasp out of me. The agony and torment of the past few days had been limitless. All I had wanted was a chance to speak to her alone. Suddenly, the very man who had declined as simple a request as that not long ago, was now doing me a favour I could neither forget nor ever repay. It did seem Allah was so receptive to my cry for help. He was answering me even before I let it out. And by way of yet another token of His generosity, I was rewarded with one more concession in the same run of luck—he offered to send her along with Vaseem instead of himself or his wife, which meant that, if a long and persuasive conversation with her became unavoidable, I could hold it in peace and without embarrassment. One more load came off my mind at once.

Throughout the night I did not have a wink of sleep. Heavily blended with a curious mixture of hopes and expectations, relief and apprehension, triumph and defeat, it was one of those awful nights that paste themselves to the rolling moments and bring even time to a halt. Unwilling to spend the tiresome hours in the silence and solitude of my room, I waited until everybody went off to sleep and then sneaked up the terrace for a breath of fresh air. In sharp contrast to the hot and humid confines of downstairs, the upstairs was much fresher and comfortable. A mild midsummer breeze had started to blow in and driven out the muggy heat of the day. There was no moon in sight but the sky was kept reasonably bright by the countless stars twinkling in its vast expanse. A night like that, bright even without the moon, moving in spite of seeming motionless, tugging behind it a long awaited dawn filled with exciting promises, even the distinct chance of their fulfilment, had come into my life after a long wait. I felt confident that I could start counting down its tarrying moments on my fingers, setting aside the last few for some prayers too, some praises to the Lord, some thanks for coming to my rescue in the moment of my dire need, some quiet preparation for the auspicious moment of an encounter with the woman of my dreams, with the queen of my heart, with the companion of my sojourn, soon to become the captain of my ship and take over the helm!

My going out early in the morning, on most other days to the congregation at the mosque, but that day on a special mission, on a mission of life and death, on a battle for survival that I could not afford to lose, or surrender, or compromise, or draw a truce, was not even noticed by my family. As usual, I went on my bike, locked it up in the cycle stand and, without letting my attention stray away from my main task, without looking around, without heeding the cries for alms from those impervious beggars, I concentrated on the cycle *rickshaws* coming into the street from both directions with their screens drawn, in the fervent hope of spotting my quarry soon.

After only a brief wait, a rickshaw pulled up by the kerb near where I stood. Vaseem got out first, said *Adab arz* to me with due courtesy and then helped Azra step out. Upon seeing her, my heart fell into such loud poundings I thought it was going to come leaping out of my throat. Behaving sensibly, Vaseem lost himself in the crowd and disappeared from sight, presumably to ensure us privacy. It enabled me to concentrate on her and soak in her image in full. Except the gleaming eyes, much of her face was hidden behind a thin veil and the rest of her clad in a black cloak. At that stage, a sweet and much missed *'Adab arz, master saheb'* poured honey into my ears. I had been so desperate to hear the magical cords of that voice for so long; I had been dying to fill my lungs with the evocative fragrance of her breath; I had been pining to see that beautiful face; that honey-soaked smile; those dreamy eyes; those artistic eyebrows; the thick welter of those lashes; the wild tufts of her locks! Without wasting any time on hesitations or on formalities, I bent down and picked up her hand, for the first time ever, and gave it a gentle squeeze. She, too, responded by tightening the clasp of her fingers on mine into a firm grip—a grip that I hoped would last for as long as both of us lasted upon the face of the earth!

Thus hand in hand at long last, we turned round to face the shrine. Never before had I seen a dawn as spectacular as that nor realised that there could be so much difference between one dawn and another! At that early hour of the morning, the sky was dappled with wandering puffs of ashen clouds; The dome of the mausoleum rose in all its splendour and magnificence against the spotless background of the grey sky like a painting taken out of Sheerazi's immortal canvasses. The sun had not yet emerged, but the horizon had just split like a pod and ushered the very first silver streak of day. Pigeons flew around in flocks, free and merry, at peace with one another. Alongside the path, endless columns of cripples and beggars had lined up for alms as usual. The florists were doing brisk trade, and baskets of sweet meats, together with bunch of jossticks and strings of fresh *Chambeli* buds, were being sold on a nonprofit basis. Those who could afford to pay, they paid, and those who could not, they got them free. I could, and I gladly paid.

Leaving our footwear outside the doorway, we entered the shrine. A large crowd of devotees had already gathered inside it. A strangely exhilarating fragrance of fresh flowers, jossticks and incense smoke filled my lungs. The soul-stirring effect such an emotive assembly had on me was so sublime I found it difficult to keep a hold upon myself. After handing in the basket of sweets and jossticks to the high priest for consecration, we laid our clusters of chaste white buds at the two majestic tombs covered by green cerements and heaps of flowers, circled them thrice, kissed the stone at their feet and moved away. It was a formal ritual of homage I had participated in ever since I was a boy, but never in the company of a woman with whom I had fallen so desperately in love. The very thought made me tighten my grip on her hand, to which she responded with a similar symbolic gesture, emphatically confirming her consent to our unbreakable bonds, wordlessly resting my heart assured of her matchless love and of her lifelong companionship!

By the time our homage was paid, our basket of sweets was consecrated by the priest with the *Fateha* and kept ready for us. After collecting it, I took her to a quiet corner where it was not too crowded and both of us sat down on the spotless marble floor. I did not know if Vaseem had stayed outside the shrine or was somewhere inside and keeping an eye on us, but at that time, my mind was fully absorbed by other priorities. Her veil being transparent and lit up by sunrays filtering in through the high arches, I was able to see her salubrious face quite clearly. The smile of contentment and expectation she wore had no substitutes in all the treasures of King Solomon put together. And the hope that it was soon going to be mine overwhelmed me with a sudden upsurge of joy.

"Azra!" I whispered to her, "First of all, please believe me I love you more than I have ever loved anyone in my whole life."

In response, she rested her gleaming eyes upon my face once and then did not move them again.

"I know you're going through a tough emotional crisis," I continued whispering. "Your father told me all about it. I hope I can relieve you of a fraction of your torment at least. I don't know anything about dreams, nor am I certain that this ring is the answer. But I do have a suggestion to offer, and it's this: today, on this bright and breezy morning, underneath the shelter of this *holy shrine*, in such proximity to those two venerable tombs, let's bind ourselves for life with a promise. And to help us keep that promise through thick or thin, let's also address Allah and pray. I'm told Angels who will join in and invoke His mercy always throng this *shrine*. Shall we?"

At that stage, two large tears swelled in her eyes, rolled down her cheeks and soaked in the veil.

"*Master saheb,*" she whispered back to me. "I seem to have caused you a great deal of anguish. I'm sorry. This has taught me a lesson that I, too, will never forget. More than that, it has made me realise how much I love you. There is no sin in us and I am not ashamed to seek Allah's help, His love, and His peace. As of this moment, I am yours for life. *InshAllah*, I will never sway from this decision and I will never belong to anyone else except you."

On that exceedingly optimistic note, we lifted our hands heavenwards and prayed. I did not ask for anything in words. If Allah was there, truly present, then He must know what was going on in our minds; He must be able to interpret our emotions. We had to bank our hopes upon someone, and I could not think of one worthier than Him. My prayer, therefore, contained nothing but praises to His glory.

When it was over, I held her hand once again, put the ring on her finger, pressed it against my lips and then let go as more tears flooded out of her eyes.

"With this ring, I pledge myself and my whole life to you today, Azra, in the presence of Allah, His Angels and His Saints, and I promise never to forsake your side, whether in sickness or in health, in poverty or in affluence, in sorrow or in joy—to live together and to die together!"

It is a vow so often taken by so many, perhaps in different words and languages but always in the same spirit. I took mine that day, full of hope that He who had brought us together would also keep us together for as long as we lived.

With that, the purpose of our visit to the *shrine* was served to our mutual satisfaction. She promised me that she would never let herself be over awed by silly premonitions or anything else for that matter, and I reassured her that nothing was strong enough to get between us anymore.

Giving alms without restraint, blessings showering upon us from all directions, we emerged into the forecourt. At that stage Vaseem caught up with us. Both of them got into a rickshaw, most of her face still hidden from sight but her anxious eyes firmly fixed upon me, no longer tearful, no longer uncertain, no longer afraid.

Brother and sister left. Later that night, in the privacy of my room, and for the first time, I told Shabbu and Rox about Azra and me.

CHAPTER (12)

To say that my sisters were merely delighted by the great news would be a gross understatement; they went mad with joy. It was the best thing that had happened to them so far; they were about to acquire a *bhabi*, or in plain English, a sister-in-law. And since I had chosen her myself, they took it for granted that she must be the best. For once, Shabbu dropped her cool and turned into a child—the child in her who had been surfacing less and less as she grew older. It made a pleasant change. The atmosphere in the room became exceedingly jovial. Keeping the noise to a bare minimum, they played a game which little girls play, something on the lines of *ring a ring of roses*. They had a right to enjoy themselves and I let them.

Once the initial ebullience subsided, we settled down to some serious talking. First things first, they wanted to know everything about the bride to be, her complexion, her face, her features, her height, her weight, her build, the colour of her hair, the number of plaits she wore, her choice in clothes, her academic qualifications, her intellectual pursuits, her family background, the whole lot came under the microscope. In matters of facts, I gave them all the facts, but in matters of opinion, I gave them my own biased version of her, glad that she had not yet been seen, glad that the element of surprise was still in tact.

"Bearing in mind that beauty," I reminded Rox, giving her a taste of her own medicine, "lies in the eye of the beholder ..."

"Yes, indeed!" she conceded readily enough, thus cornered.

"And if you are wondering about other crucial statistics, you might as well know that she is neither a *Fat Cow* nor does she own a *Fat batwa*. She is just an ordinary, simple but very accomplished young lady."

"Accomplished in what way?" Rox commenced her *inquisition.*

"She makes excellent *chapattis* and *daal*, she also makes delicious *Jilebis* and *Laddoos*, and she writes brilliant letters as well as some soul stirring poetry."

"But she *does* make the moon blush?"

"Cut the crap, Rox!" Shabbu screamed from sheer frustration at not being given the chance to ask a question or two of her too. "And do something useful. Go make some Horlicks."

"I beg your pardon, Baji," Rox apologised as a measure of courtesy. "I'm nearly done. You can have him all to yourself while the queen of the kitchen goes to make Horlicks, or coffee, or cocoa, or Ovaltine, or *Qahva*, or *Joshanda*, or whatever!"

"Yes, she does," I told her, picking up where she left off. "Not only does she make the moon blush, she also carries the entire milky way in her eyes, takes spring into gardens, unfurls corollas, paints wings for butterflies, builds nests for the *Laal muniyas*, brings the rainbow into being with her index finger, transports clouds on the palm of her hand and sets them up where she likes. In addition to all that, she also owns a team of four *unicorns* and rides around on her *chariot of dreams*! Enough?"

It was enough to pop her eyes wide open with amazement, so she came at me from a different angle this time.

"Where did you meet her?" she asked me point-blank. "How did you come across her? For how long has *this* been going?"

"What's been going on?"

"This."

"This what?"

"You know ..."

"No, I don't."

"Yes, you do."

"No, I don't. This what?"

"This," she insisted, cheekily winking at me to illustrate her point.

"You're fired!" Shabbu screamed at her once again. "Get off your butt and go make some hot drinks. And when serving, do tell us what they are—be it Horlicks, be it cocoa, be it *Qahva* or be it *Joshanda* or even drainage water."

"Just so we know what's going down our gullets," I added.

"Oi!" Rox instantly objected to the aspersions cast upon her culinary skills, "That's going to cost you dear, *brother!*"

"An arm and a leg, *sister?*" I asked.

"No," Rox ruled out the impractical with a mild shake of her pretty head,

"When I return with the drinks, I want to hear from you just how the dickens did you fall into this ditch filled with love potions. *Like this?* Or, like *this?*"

Needless to say, a tripping over and a falling, once on the bed and once on the floor, demonstrated each of the *like this.*

"So this was what the preoccupation was all about?" Shabbu asked me as soon as her back turned.

"Yes."

"Is anything wrong?"

I gave her a brief account of what had been happening in course of the past few weeks. Understandably, it plunged her into brooding. While she brooded, I began to dream. Peace felt good for as long as it lasted, until my attention was drawn to a few harsher realities. Such as, who was going to break the news to our parents?

Breaking the news to my sisters was the easy part. But it was not the same with the parents. I could not see myself going into their bedroom and saying to them, 'Listen here, folks! Make what you like of it, but I've fallen in love with this dreamy eyed pupil of mine and decided to *wed-'n-bed* her. If this buggers up any of your plans, I'm sorry, I can't help it. Like they say—love *is blind ...*' I did not stand one chance in a million of making it as far as their bedroom door with that kind of a message on my lips, let alone talking things over. It was, however, a different matter with Shabbu; she had all the makings of a dependable propitiator. But as soon as I settled my pleading eyes upon her face, she suddenly went ghastly pale.

"Don't look at me like that!" she said with a shudder, "I ain't cut out for this sort of thing and you know it."

"Yes, you are!"

"No, I'm not!"

"Yes, you are!"

At that moment, Rox reentered the room with three steaming mugs on a tray, saw the expression of dismay on Shabbu 's face and suddenly froze in her tracks.

"What's the matter with you?" she asked Shabbu, once again popping open her eyes with fake shock, "You're looking like an *insurance claim* which has just been *repudiated!*"

"And you like a *toadstool* trying to pass for a *mushroom,*" Shabbu retaliated.

"But not succeeding," I added, rubbing some salt into the wounds of her wounded pride.

As a measure of courtesy, Shabbu explained to her the issue at stake and my suggested solution to tackle it. But my choice of a *propitiator* did not meet with her approval at all.

"Listen here, guys," she said, passing on a steaming mug to each of us and sitting down with hers, "If you want to have your turkey skinned properly, you take it to the *butcher* and not to the *chef.*"

"Which *butcher* are we alluding to?" I asked her, reacting to a tingling sensation in my teeth. "Bearing in mind that what we are talking about is not a *turkey* for you to roast but my entire life. *Yourself?*"

"Pretty obvious, isn't it?" she asked in a most casual tone, "You should learn to trust the hand that holds the knife as well as knows how to use it."

"And what makes you the expert, might we know?" I asked her, keenly watching her animated face.

"Try this for size," she replied instantly. "Whenever Papa speaks, everybody listens. When I speak, Papa listens. Right?"

She was right. Papa had, indeed, demonstrated vulnerability to her built-in charms on more than one occasion. Whether or not she would be able to cope with a mission as crucial as that was another matter.

"And what happens if, when skinning my turkey, you get a bit carried away and dig a shade too deep into its thigh?"

"You will end up with a thigh-less turkey on the table. So what? A turkey is a turkey, regardless of how many drumsticks it comes with!"

"What do you think, Shabbu?" I asked her, unable to make up my mind, "Do you think she'd be able to pull it off?"

"If you wish to trust your *fate* to her *mouth,* then all I can say is, good fate to you ..."

"And what's wrong with my *mouth*?" Rox demanded, flapping her eyelids, the pace of blinks never faster.

Plenty of things were, although neither of us ventured to elaborate upon it for tactical reasons.

"The proof of the pudding," Rox carried on, turning a deaf ear to the aspersion on her mouth in the heat of the moment, "is in the eating. Why don't you ask me to give you a *demo* of my negotiating skills right now?"

"Fair enough," I agreed to it, "Let's have a *demo*. What will you tell him?"

"Here goes," she said, putting away the mug, clearing her throat, wiping her mouth, blinking her eyelids, polishing her pupils, suppressing a smile, patting herself on the chest and a lot more besides, "I'll tell him—'Get ready for this, Papa! Yusuff Bhaijan has found his *Zulayqa* at long last, but doesn't want to marry her because she hasn't got a fat *Batwa!* Can you believe that? Isn't it a pitiful reflection upon the Quraishi stock? Doesn't it go against the very principles by which you have taught us all to live? Money, no doubt, is important, but not important enough to trade away our morals, our principles and our values, is it?' How's that?"

That was absolutely brilliant! If she could really put it over to him in those words and with such passion, not only would he say yes to her, he would even come looking for me with a cane in his hand for a hard spanking!

"You *do* know which side of your bread is buttered, don't you, Rox?" I said with genuine admiration.

"Cheers," she acknowledged.

"When are you thinking of delivering the message to him?"

"Never put off until tomorrow what you can do today," came yet another sagacious remark.

"What, *now?* At this time of night?"

"When you've put your head on the *anvil,* brother, why be afraid of the *hammer strokes,* eh?"

"Don't push your luck, sister! If he has just woken up from a bad dream about the bank manager giving him a nasty chase, your philosophising about his last remaining collateral might not cut any ice with him!"

"Yes, you are quite right," she agreed with yet another sweet smile, "I think I better catch him tomorrow evening, after setting up his *hukka* pipe on the lawn, a long way from bad dreams and bad nightmares."

"Not tomorrow. Do it on Saturday."

"All right, then. Saturday it is," she agreed and the three of us shook hands on it.

The next few days were hectic, to say the least. By then, the contractors with successful bids for the refurbishment and outfitting jobs at the institute had already begun their work and were making swift progress. Letting us get on with our planning and administrative tasks, Mr. Raza visited the building from time to time and personally supervised the progress. Concentrating on the work was an unavoidable necessity as well as a contractual obligation, and I got on with it, but my mind kept wandering. No matter how hard I tried, I could not succeed in getting Azra out of my system even for a brief while. Whenever a *rickshaw* with its screens drawn arrived outside the office, carrying a mum to see Shabbu regarding her daughter's admission next year, my heart fell into nasty palpitations in the hope that it was she come to see me, to show herself to me, to quench some of my thirst and some of her own thirst too, take me back to her tiny living room, sit facing me, bless and beguile me with her cherubic smiles, let me hold her hand, let me squeeze it, squeeze mine back, kiss the emerald on her ring, talk about things to come instead of talking about things bygone, about *our* love life instead of the love life of Akbar or Jehangir, about the arrival of heirs in our kingdom to inherit our own thrones and crowns, instead of the Red Fort in Agra or the *Sheesh Mahal* in Delhi! Whenever the postman dropped some mail through the letter box at the office, I jumped to my feet in the hope that one of them might be hers, written on her perfumed paper; superbly calligraphed in her own hand like the rest of the others; containing an appropriate postscript to her protracted correspondence; superimposing a new text of elation on the old one; enclosing a new set of poems with new themes; some novel vocabulary in which to convey some novel and unfamiliar feelings which she had been experiencing of late! Whenever the phone rang, I rocked in my chair in the stormy expectation that it might be hers, pouring honey in my ears with a sweet *hello!* telling me how she was and asking me how I was; making a secret date for a quick game of hide and seek in our vineyard; or to the cinemas to watch an amorous Hindi movie full of romantic songs; or for a quiet picnic in the rose gardens of *Baagh-e-aam*, or for a stroll hand in hand through the superb Art Galleries of the Saalar Jang Museum. But she neither visited, nor wrote, nor phoned.

Only one day before Rox was timetabled to confront Papa with the gripping front-page story of my being kidnapped by a young rider aboard her *chariot of dreams* and held captive in the secret location of her heart, I decided to make sure that my hiding place was well and truly inaccessible even to the most adroit crime busters Papa might employ in order to retrieve his one and only son from the clutches of his mystical captor, I paid the Ansaris a surprise visit. Being my lady's permanent abode, it was, no doubt, laden to the brim with that profoundly stupefying fragrance of her body and her breath; her clothes and her locks; her Henna and her Kajal, but she herself was nowhere to be seen. The obvious reason for her going underground again was, Muslims being Muslims, once a formal proposal of marriage is made by one side and accepted by the other side, tradition demands that the would-be bride and her groom are tabooed on each other and held apart with steel clamps until the very night of the nuptials when a tiny reflection of *HER* is conceded to *HIM* in a mirror, literally held at an arm's length! Resorting to it, she was locked up again behind the *iron curtain*, out of my sight and my reach, filling up the vacuum with her ambience, indeed, but doing very little to appease the irreconcilable demands of the eyes. Mr. Ansari looked pleased to see me, rewarded me with an affectionate hug, sat me in the lounge, but instead of asking Azra to come and say hello to her dearest *master saheb,* fetch the *Jilebis* and the *Laddoos*; put some in his mouth with her own hand; look after him and take care of him; he quickly reached for the curtain on the door that gave access to the kitchen and readjusted the frills on it, making sure even the vaguest silhouettes of the bride were not stolen by the bridegroom! Then, whilst my immediate interest centred around the ninth, the rest of his eight children rushed into the lounge and mobbed me as usual, seemingly well aware of the rapid progress which their sister and I had made in matters of the heart, addressed me as *Bhaijan* instead of the conventional *master saheb* and talked to me just about everything else under the sun except their Azra Baji. Giving them precisely ten minutes in which to indulge with me in whatever frivolities they liked, Mr. Ansari excused himself briefly and went inside, presumably to have a tray of refreshments set up for his future son-in-law, while the rest of them plunged into avid conversation. Contrary to habit, Vaseem also entertained us with his charming company, although much of his time was spent in *crowd control* rather than in *conversation.* His favours to Azra and me were beginning to pile up; were it not for his diploma, she and I would not have come across each other; were it not for his generous decision to give it up, she would not have been relieved of her mission and freed for marriage so soon; and were it not for his sense of understanding and gentlemanly behaviour at the *shrine,* we would not have managed the time or the chance to sort things out between us. Quiet, patient and tolerant, he was one of the finest lads I had had the pleasure of coming across lately, and I made up my mind to help him accomplish his goal, whatever the costs.

Exactly fifteen minutes later, Mr. Ansari returned with the tray of refreshments, set it up on the coffee table, watched the competition going on around me with an indulgent smile and soon dispersed the crowd. From the familiar aroma of the hot *Pakoras,* the fresh sweetmeats and the *Orange Peco* tea brewing in the pot, I could tell precisely whose hand was behind all that generous hospitality; no doubt, she was not there herself to entertain and to look after me, but her spirit was, staring at me through the walls, hovering above me underneath the ceiling, coming towards me with her arms outstretched, from the left and from the right, from the front and from the back; enveloping me from all sides; drowning me in her entelechy; absorbing me in her pith; breathing me in and breathing me out! On that day, I had no problems with helping myself to the delicious tokens of her affection—hers, or her mother's, or her father's, which no longer mattered; by reason of our bonds, they, too, had become as dear to me as my own parents. Giving me as much of his attention and love as he would have given to his own son, Vaseem, Mr. Ansari gorged me until I was bursting to the seams.

"Let's stop being formal," he said in excellent spirits, "It's about time you called me *Uncle* Saleh and I called you *Yusuff* ..."

How about that! Not only had I become *Bhaijan* to the rest of her brothers and sisters, I also became Yusuff to her father and he Uncle Saleh to me in the same breath!

"Have you told your parents?" he asked, without seeming to crowd me.

"I'm going to—tomorrow. Do I have your permission?"

"Of course, you do. No need to waste any time. And if you're wondering about your bride, then don't. She's never been better."

"I'm so glad."

"Don't worry about a thing. No one can rob you of what you have been given by Allah Himself. Oh, yes, I almost forgot. Take a look at this miracle!"

So saying, he produced the five tamarind seeds from his pocket once again. Although the hair on my nape stood up at their sight, I looked. After rolling them in his fist precisely as he had done before, he cast them on the floor. The pattern had changed. Each time he tried, the combination differed. How? Why? Who knew! Who cared! As far as I was concerned, the real miracle was something else; before visiting the *shrine*, my fate had looked dismal. But after the visit, it did transform: we were lost for a while and had found each other. Period!

I returned to the office a completely different man. My concentration came back to me, and my enthusiasm revived. From then onwards, I did everything right; talked to those who came to talk to me; transacted business and knew precisely what I was doing; answered the phone without my heart sitting in my throat; read through the mail without my eyes getting moist; turned a deaf ear to the bells of cycle *rickshaws*. An uneasy uncertainty about the strength of Azra's resolve which had been nagging me oft and on was also gone; there were no more impervious problems in Aghapura; she seemed at the top of her form; her father was at peace; her mother was at ease; her sisters and her brothers had broken past the barriers of formal respect and replaced it with love. All that remained to be seen was the reaction from my side. But with such a lot going for us and in our favour; with Allah protecting us both; with His angels escorting us through the paths of our life; with His saints guarding our progress and our future; with the resolute backing of two sisters like Shabbu and Rox; with an emotionally governed father like Papa and a devout mother like Mamma; what could possibly go wrong! We were crossing that final furlong towards our cherished goal; we were walking on the last bridge; the end of the first leg of our journey was in sight; the glare of dawn was on the horizon; all the twinkling stars were disappearing one by one; the entire canvass ahead of us was changing over!

On Saturday morning instead of Saturday evening as planned, inside Papa's room instead of on the lawns as thought, shortly after he shook off whatever nightmares he had been having through the night, it fell into Shabana's share of the luck to break the headline news about my captivity to Papa because, apparently, in spite of all those courageous words and mind-boggling idioms, Rox freaked out at the last moment and passed the parcel on to poor Shabbu. It caused such a stir in our house, I could feel the tremors pass underneath my feet from one end to the other. Within ten minutes of that sensational press release, Mamma breezed into my room, her cheeks still flushed from kitchen heat, from summer heat, from excitement heat, from emotional heat.

"Is this true?" she asked me, "Or has Shabana taken leave of her senses? What's all this rumour I hear about you falling in *love*?"

Going down on my knees, I confessed to her.

"So, this is what you've been doing all along, eh?" she asked, suppressing a smile and touching her nose with her index finger, "Peeping at girls through net curtains?"

I told her I had done no such thing, but she insisted that I must have. How else could I know what Azra looked like?

In less than a minute after she left, Papa barged into my room for the first time in living memory. Startled, I shot to attention, fairly certain that his interrogation would centre around my sanity, finally recommending me a psychiatrist's coach in preference to the nuptial bed. But I was wrong.

"Is this true?" he too asked, peering at me through his thick convex lenses, "Or has Shabana sent her brain to the *Dhobi-ghaat*?"

Which, by the way, is a place on the banks of the Gandipet Lake where washer men and washerwomen congregate twice a day to wash clothes! Going down on my knees once again, I confessed to him too.

In less than a minute after he left, naughty Rox rushed in, giggling.

"Is this true?" she asked, mimicking all the others, "Or has Shabana left her brain at the pawn-broker's stall?

Before I could lay my hands on her pigtails, she ran away.

The worst behind me, I thought Papa would make arrangements to meet Uncle Saleh and talk things over. After that, I thought Mamma and my sisters would go to their house and see the bride. After that, I thought they would organise our formal engagement. After that, I thought a tentative date would be fixed for the wedding. And after that, I thought—But that was not how things progressed in our house.

On the following day, which was a Sunday, during a brief lull in activity between our blithesome get together on the lawns, mostly dominated by illuminating anecdotes from the family life of our beloved Prophet, and Rox's summons for supper, always dominated by her vociferous exhortations that those who keep food waiting on the table shall be kept waiting for food by Allah, I went into my room, latched the door from inside for the sake of safety, fetched a few of Azra's letters from their secret hiding place, relaxed on the bed and became engrossed in what had by then become my obsession, to read and to reread her passionate love letters. The time was getting close to seven, and on account of the twilight of dusk as well as a thin layer of an early mist, visibility outside the house had become impaired. Worry gone from my system for the time being at least, thoroughly reassured by the positive attitude of all members of my family, big and small, I too was in a buoyant mood; the radio tuned in to 'Binaca Geet Mala' from Shri Lanka, a superb 'Ghazal' by Rafi on air and me accompanying him. The night was pleasant; news was great; life was smooth; the music was appropriate; the story of my life was running on track; someone was thinking about me; someone was dreaming about me; I was in her heart; I was in her thoughts; her Aghapura was not too far from my Asifnagar; currents of air coming from there were fetching her sweet perfume wrapped up in their gusts; homing pigeons from here were going there carrying my messages of love to her; the twilight around my house was the same as the twilight around her house; we were far apart and yet somehow connected to each other; we were inseparably linked; we were inextricably harnessed!

At some stage of my blissful ruminations, the chain of my endless thoughts was shattered by the unexpected emergence of a dim glow in the distance, cutting through the layers of darkness, swinging like a pendulum and heading towards the house. Drawn by curiosity, I put away the letters I was reading, walked up to the window and stood staring at the strange glow with puzzled eyes. Soon it came within range of visibility, identified itself as an hurricane lantern, being carried by a ghost-like figure. Worried more than puzzled, I rubbed my eyes and focussed full attention upon it. In due course, the vague silhouette became less vague and transformed into a very fat man. To my utter incredulity, he had white hair and a white beard, both long, wore a large turban on his head, was clad in a green robe and had a black blanket wrapped around his shoulders. Except for the *beckoning* bit, the rest of him was so unbelievably similar to Azra's nocturnal persecutor, it made me gape.

Some mild pressure on the brain eventually resolved the mystery of his identity. He was Moulana Akbar Ali Saheb, to whom several references have already been made, a reputable marriage broker in Hyderabad with access to most Muslim families, held in high esteem by all alike, so much that no self respecting parents ever gave their children away in marriage without including him as a *go-between*. Some referred to him as *the fat man*, some as *Kaddoo*, and some even *Kaana Dajjal* because of his squint. Just like Peer Saheb of the 'Nizamiah Dreams Interpretation Bureau', he too ran his own *International Heart to Heart Bonding Service*, but unlike Peer Saheb, he did not believe in honorary work. He charged a solid commission to his clients, usually around 5 percent of the dowry. In most cases, he made the match himself and conducted all the negotiations from start to finish; in some cases he just acted as icing on the cake; but in all cases, he grabbed his pound of flesh!'

His entry into the picture in connection with my fairly straightforward marriage proposal understandably puzzled me. For one thing, my match was not in need of making but it was already made. Both of us, though growing under the protective wings of our parents and living in the sacrosanct seclusion of our nests, had somehow met; somehow braved; somehow progressed; made plans for the morrow; bred our aspirations first and only then brought our parents into the picture. In our case, the services of people like Moulana Saheb were superfluous to requirements. Long before he could make our match on earth, Allah had already made ours in Paradise, and we were sent on earth with each other's ribs in our spines. So, we did not need the matchmaking skills of a mediator. And as far as the issue of the dowry was concerned, that too was inapplicable to us because all the give and take between us had already been completed; she had given me her heart and I had given her mine; I had pledged myself to her for life and so had she; we had taken our vows in truth and were merely waiting to conform to the formality of repeating them again in the presence of a *quazi*. I had told Papa about Uncle Saleh's financial limitations as well as the true extent of his liabilities, and consequently, the issue of dowry had been taken out of the proposition.

However, if Papa had, for the sake of prestige, decided to recruit him into his camp as *icing on the cake,* quite prepared to pay him a fees out of his own pocket, it was entirely a matter of his and Mamma's choice. I was not going to tell them how to run their show; how to organize the first wedding in their house which had come to them after a very long wait, albeit without the *dosh.* But the real fear which took the wind out of my flute was something else: if Papa gave that venerable man a general power of attorney and appointed him as his *Harbinger of Good Tidings* for the Ansari household, it meant he would begin to frequent their house regularly for the wedding preparations. In Hyderabad, summer had nearly drawn to a close and monsoon rains were heading our way from the Western Ghats. At our altitude, it meant longer, darker, colder and wetter nights, beleaguered all the more by low lying clouds. Suppose, on one such cold, dark and hauntingly crepuscular night, as Azra sat in her room knitting a jumper for me, her attention was attracted by a passing motorbike and she looked through her window to see if it was me; then suppose, just *suppose,* at that particular moment, Moulana Saheb happened to go visiting her house on some errand or the other and emerged out of the darkness with a hurricane lantern in his hand; suppose, just *suppose*, upon sighting his spooky figure, clad in a green robe and wrapped in a black blanket, her heart went *'dharak! dharak! dharak!'* from fear and blood in her veins curdled; and finally, suppose, just *suppose,* she tried to scream for help but her voice remained trapped in her vocal chords; the swirling cloud carried on advancing towards her; the hostile night became even more hostile; the surroundings plunged into a curious hush and time seemed to come to a halt, what would she do? How would she cope with the crisis? How would she summon help? What would happen to her?

By and large, the suppositions became so impetuous, the ground underneath my feet suddenly felt shaky. Without further ado, I jumped to my feet, put on my slippers and rushed out of the room in a desperate bid to intervene and talk my old man out of it. But by the time I made it to the front veranda,it was already too late; not only had Papa hijacked his spooky visitor but also disappeared somewhere upstairs along with him.

The upper floor of our house, although fully furnished and regularly dusted, was put to use only on very special occasions. A tête-à-tête between *him* and *him* over a known topic hardly fell into the category of special occasions, but I could clearly guess why their confabulation was taking place upstairs rather than downstairs. In his kind of a reverberating voice, Papa never stood the chance of doing anything in private, with Rox giving him hot pursuit all the time. I have known him run from room to room in order to shake her off his tail. But if privacy was what he had had in mind when taking Moulana Saheb upstairs, he hardly seemed to be getting much of it. For, while the rest of us stood at the bottom of the stairs, Rox was already up on the landing, no more than two feet away from them, listening intently to every word uttered. And poor Papa, unaware of being thus *shadowed* by the *media,* was roaring away like a tiger.

"Get off your *butt* and be on your way," I heard him command Moulana Saheb like a sergeant major in the British Army, "deliver my greetings to Ansari and tell him my son has *decided* to marry his daughter. What did you say? *Which* daughter? How the hell am I supposed to tell you that? I don't even know how many *daughters* there are ..."

On that somewhat precarious note, Moulana Saheb came tumbling down the stairs like an oversized pumpkin and made for the door in one heck of a hurry. I did not realise at the time that the main reason for his rush was to put as much distance as possible between his own neck and Papa's hands!

"Heaven help Azra!" I said to myself with a shudder and went back into my room.

CHAPTER (13)

When Moulana Saheb agreed to be recruited into Papa's camp as a *Harbinger of good tidings* for the Ansari household, put forward a proposal of marriage between Azra and me on our behalf and then finalise a convenient date for our side to go to their house to see the bride, I wonder if he had any idea at all as to the sort of trouble he was getting himself into, despite the pair of them being childhood mates. Delaying matters by a few days was his first mistake. A professional matchmaker with a healthy list of clients, he organised his daily appointments according to the alphabetic order of his clients' names, and obviously could not go to 'Q' without tackling 'A' to 'P' first, but Papa would not have any of it. His argument was, if Moulana saheb was going by their first names, then his 'A' for *'Abbas'* should come first; and if he was going by their surnames, then the 'A' for *'Ansari'* should. In either case, there was no justification in his being kept waiting for so long. In his view, hopping from surnames to first names *willy-nilly* was amateurish and a sad reflection on his credentials as a professional. And in order to teach him a lesson in *customer relations*, he kept on phoning him every two hours and filling up his answering machine with all sorts of angry messages. He also wrote him three nasty letters, and as though all that was not enough, even paid a few surprise visits to at least four out of the poor man's five wives in a bid to track him down!

During those seven days of utter anguish for the rest of us, he did very little other than talk at length about the profession of marriage broking; its significance in a theocratic society; how sanctimonious a broker should be; conscious more of his duties to his customers than of the money he was going to make; deal with them swiftly and equitably; show some concern for their feelings; get himself a suitable *Naib* if he was too busy or too overworked;

deputize, delegate, create job opportunities, make things happen, keep his promises, live up to his expectations, show some signs of life, take the initiative! Apparently, in spite of his many other preoccupations, our beloved Prophet too sometimes engaged in matchmaking, especially for young ladies of his own household, or of his outer family, or for those who were having difficulties in finding suitable matches, or anyone else who approached him for help. Matchmaking, therefore, was an honourable profession, and people who were unfit to cope with it should find themselves alternative avocations, he argued. If it was taking Moulana Saheb seven whole days just to make one visit and set the ball into motion, he failed to see how he could rely upon the services of such a *slow coach* to organise an entire wedding from start to finish without his blood pressure shooting up and culminating into a coronary thrombosis, or worse still, a cardiovascular accident, i.e., a stroke!

Regardless of the academics of right and wrong, the abrupt lull in activity resulting from Moulana Saheb's preoccupations was having adverse effects upon quite a lot of us. Papa felt frustrated because his progress was held up, but my case was even worse than his. During my most recent meeting with Uncle Saleh, I had assured him that I was going to talk to my parents about Azra and me on the following day; since then, no more news from me had reached him; he did not know what exactly was happening at our end; whether I managed to apprise them of the situation or still having cold feet; how did they react to it; did they agree to the alliance or turn it down. I could not bear to think of how much distress our strange and inexplicable silence was causing Azra; how bruised were her feelings; what was going on in her mind; where did it leave her ego, her pride, her confidence. Thinking about that alone pushed me over the brink, especially when I knew that the delay was not due to any insurmountable problems at my side. It was, therefore, of the utmost importance that I got in touch with Uncle Saleh and brought him up-to-date. Hence, after waiting for Moulana saheb to break the ice until the middle of the week, I phoned him up at the paper mill and explained to him what was happening. To my immense relief, he did not seem too bothered about it and took the pragmatic view that a week or two's delay in matters as protracted as a marriage was only to be expected. He was not particularly worried, and neither was Azra, he said. In fact, his advice to me was to quit worrying and let my parents take it from there at their own pace. Once again, he stressed that no one could snatch away from me what I had been given by Allah Himself, which put all my concerns at ease.

Now, the trauma being endured by poor old Rox was completely different from mine. I came to know from Shabbu that, unable to withstand the tension resulting from the delay, or to put it more precisely, from her inability to find out exactly what her future *Bhabi* looked like; whether she really drove around in a chariot drawn by unicorns; whether a Milky Way was truly clustered up in her eyes; whether she did unfurl corollas, carry the clouds on the palm of her hand, draw the rainbow on the sky with the tip of her index finger and etcetera, she was getting dangerously close to a nervous breakdown and had begun to display acute withdrawal symptoms as well as suicidal tendencies. Apart from that, I came to know from the same incontrovertible source that she was also sustaining heavy financial losses towards the costs of transport between our house and the bride's. Apparently, having obtained Azra's address from Papa in a moment of his indiscretion, she had been going around her house at least thrice every day in the desperate hope of cracking the mind-boggling mystery. Succeed she did not, but it seemed she did end up with one heck of a lot of rickshaw fares on one hand and an equal amount of shouts from Mamma on the other for her prolonged and inexplicable absences from home. As a result, she had lost her sleep, her appetite, her poise, her bearing, even her sense of humour. The pallor on her face so telling, it seemed the maid suspected she was being haunted by ghosts and suggested Mamma to consider taking her to an exorcist at once!

At around ten on Sunday night, the irksome stalemate was eventually resolved when there was a knock on the front door. Four afflicted people rushed to answer it: I, more or less sure as to who it could be; Shabbu, in a spirit of concomitance with me; Rox, in a spirit of competition with her; and Papa, in order to assert himself over the others. I did not realise at the time that, in view of the late hour, the dark night, the rain, the fog and all the rest, he had also brought along with him his loaded Winchester, just in case. When he opened the door by a fraction and we all took a peek outside, his caution about the inclement weather and the nasty conditions associated with it did turn out to be quite justifiable; it was, indeed, an horrendous night; the fog swirled listlessly; crickets squeaked in the grass; toads hid in potholes and croaked; a host of moths flew in attracted by the light; a wayfaring bat also tried to follow suit but changed its mind at the last moment and turned away. All that was there for us to see and ponder over, but it still did not give away any clues as to who our visitor was; there were no signs of human presence anywhere for as far as the eye could travel.

"Oi!" said Papa in a gruff voice for starters and added only two more words to it saying "Show yourself!"

No one did. The fog continued to purl; toads carried on croaking; crickets kept up the pandemonium; moths became bolder and began to crash into our faces; the bat also came accompanied by its mate this time but still could not decide whether to get in or to stay out.

"Oi!" Rox repeated after Papa in an absurdly thin voice, taking heart from him, "I'll have you know that, when Papa shoots, he can pick the sting off the backside of a drone in flight!"

If it was really Moulana Saheb come to deliver some news of Aghapura, the deadly barrel of the Winchester, as well as Rox's highly exaggerated description of his shooting skills must have put the fear of hell into his heart, for he took shelter in the shadows and stopped even breathing.

"Papa ..." I said, making a courageous bid to intervene and go to our visitor's rescue.

"Who spoke?" Papa asked, looking over his shoulder and indicating for the first time that he was beginning to have some trouble with his hearing too, in addition to his sight.

"Ahm ..." I said and left it at that.

Moulana Saheb remained concealed. I had a feeling he was shying away from us more out of fear than out of modesty. An encounter with my old man when he was flanked by his daughters *plus* armed was fraught with perils. He could abruptly develop homicidal tendencies without giving any advance warning.

"Must be the clowns from the slum," he murmured to himself, returned his attention back upon the darkness and shouted one more 'Oi!' into it.

"It's me," Moulana Saheb responded at that stage in a meek voice, barely louder than a whisper.

Realising what exactly must be preventing him from entering the house, my sisters quickly dispersed. Only then did our worthy visitor make himself visible, partially at least. But it did not satisfy Papa.

"Show yourself fully or be damned!" he shouted, this time pointing the gun straight at him.

When the stakes went up so high, Moulana Saheb braved and rushed into the light like a moth rapaciously heading towards the candle flame.

Withdrawing the barrel of his Winchester from its intended target, Papa spent the next several moments taking stock of his visitor from head to foot with cold contempt. Frankly, looking at the poor man's dismal plight, any other compassionate host would have said: *'you nearly got yourself shot to death*, did you know that?' But not Papa! "You very nearly got *me* packed off to the *Andamans* on a charge of murder in the first degree, did you know that?" he asked instead, "Haven't you got any regard at all for the feelings of others? Their safety? Their freedom?"

In response to that rather hostile reception, all Moulana Saheb could say was a very muffled *Assalamu alaikum.*

"*Walaikum assalam,*" Papa replied without much enthusiasm, "Fine time to pick on door knocking! Where the hell have you been loafing around for the past four days? Why didn't you phone? Why didn't you write? Why didn't you make at least some effort to get in touch with me? To respond to my messages? My troubles? My visits? Why? Why? Why?"

Without offering any explanations on the spur of the moment, Moulana Saheb entered the hall, his hair and beard swept by the wind, the turban barely held in place by his two arched eyebrows, his yellow teeth revealed in a gesture of appeasement, his large eyes bulging out, looking very much like a reluctant billy goat on its way to the slaughter house.

"At the end of the day," said Papa, grinding his teeth and playing the butcher without mercy, "you do expect to milk me for a little something, don't you? Do you, or don't you? Eh? Eh?"

No answer came from the billy goat. Once again, he was taken upstairs. There was no longer any need for confidentiality and there was no electricity upstairs, yet Papa dumped him in one of the rooms plunged in the dark and shut the door behind him. Quite relieved to realise that, once a two-way communication link was set up between the two patriarchs, the initiative would be back in Papa's safe hands, I returned to my room. While I decided to let them thrash it all out between themselves, Rox decided to do something else. Eavesdropping was in her blood. Her ear pasted to the door of the room in which they were having a chat, she became engrossed in listening.

Ten minutes later, Moulana Saheb emerged from the dark room in a big rush and made yet another swift departure, once again in a hurry to put some distance between his neck and Papa's hands. As soon as his back turned, I was quite surprised to hear Papa shouting for me in the room next to mine. To the extent to which I knew, no one lived in it. Wondering why he was looking for me there, I went to find out.

"Are you looking for me, Papa?" I asked him.

"Yes," he replied, "Where were you?"

"In my room."

"Where is it?"

"Next door."

"When did you change rooms?"

"I didn't change rooms, Papa. You're looking for me in the wrong room."

"Am I? No wonder I couldn't find you."

Then he gave me the brilliant news that Uncle Saleh had invited our family to go to their house on Friday to break bread with them as well as to see the bride. A huge load taken off my mind at long last, all that remained for me to do was to spread the mat and say thanks to Allah for His generosity and compassion right through the trying times. But before I could do it, both the girls came rushing into my room to find out what happened. I told them, at the same time noticing with a surge of concern that something had gone drastically wrong with poor old Rox's pretty face: the bottom half of it was concealed from view behind an ice bag.

"What happened to you?" I asked her first, and then I asked the other, "Isn't she looking like a *hope* that has just been *crushed*, Baji?"

"*Khun…khun…khun…khun…khun…*" mumbled the first one inaudibly, while the second one looked aside to mask a smile.

"Pardon?" I said.

"Eavesdropping, as usual," Shabbu explained. "But before she could settle down, Moulana Saheb came barging out of the room and rammed the door into her face."

Both of us burst into laughter.

"It isn't funny, you know," Rox complained bitterly, taking the ice bag aside, "I also lost a tooth in the process. One of these days, I'm going to shove a sugarcane stick up *Kaana Dajjal's* hairy nose and straighten out his squint. How on earth does he think I am going to go around making arrangements for the wedding with a toothless jaw, eh? Anyone considered that?"

What a mess she was! In sympathy with the wounded jaw, the bottom lip had also swelled up.

"Don't worry, Rox," I said quite sympathetically, "A jaw is a jaw, whether it has sixteen teeth or fifteen!"

Meanwhile, at the institute, everything progressed according to schedule with pinpoint precision. Once the builders finished their tasks, the outfitters took over from them. After all the classrooms were furnished with tables, chairs, blackboards and cupboards; the labs with necessary equipment; dining halls with optimum furniture and amenities; assembly halls with impressive podiums and both the offices with all their requirements, the end result was better than expected. Mr. Raza asked me to organize an inaugural ceremony on a grand scale and invite several important people, such as the minister for education, the governor of Andhra Pradesh, the mayor of Hyderabad and the princess of Birar, all of whom had a good reputation for community service. It could be a nice way of making influential friends and enlisting their support for the future of the Institute, he said. A ceremony on such a scale was bound to be expensive, but he did not mind the expense.

Soon, the crucial Friday night caught up when my family was scheduled to take their first step towards finalising a lasting union between Azra and me. My sense of relief was infinitesimal. So was Rox's. The problems she had been experiencing lately with the state of her nerves, her withdrawal symptoms and the suicidal tendencies over which Shabbu had shed some light, not to mention the crippling financial losses resulting from them, were about to be nipped in the bud. She was, at long last, going to find out the truth about her *Bhabi*; about my superb taste in women even without my having any experience in that field; about the meaning and connotation of the metaphors I had used for describing my bride; about the chariots of dreams and the unicorns of bliss; about rainbows and milky ways; about springs and about corollas. She would soon discover the true extent to which her brother had been smitten by her divine charms; what sort of magic was mixed in her smiles; how intoxicating was the fragrance of her breath; how captivating was the elegance of her limbs; how stilted were the phrases of her body language—in short, what was it about her that could steal a man's heart with so little to spare; that could dominate a man's dreams with no more room for anything else; envelop a man's entelechy to such an overwhelming extent!

For me too, it was a great day of triumphs and rejoicing. I could easily shut my eyes and recall to mind that moment in our derelict vineyard when I saw her for the first time playing hide and seek with her cousin Sakina and their friends. Her enigmatic charisma, her irresistible charm and exuberance, her unspoilt beauty and her unrestrained youth, her provocative figure and her vivacious personality, they had all combined together and taken me prisoner at the very first skirmish. I had laid down my arms without a fight and surrendered myself to her. Just like a dream entrapping the awareness of a somnambulist, she had tied me up with a silken thread and taken me away to unfamiliar territories. Being severely restrained by my tricky circumstances, my duties and my responsibilities, pledged up to my eyes in all sorts of irredeemable debts of gratitude, I had never thought it possible for me to fall in love with a total stranger, face such tests and trials as I did, and win her hand. Letting out countless sighs of despair without anyone hearing their hiss; shedding silent tears of anguish without anyone spotting their trickles;

breeding hopes without anyone catching their scent; seeking Allah's favours and His blessings without anyone picking up the signals; I had come a long way in my daunting affair with her. And so had she—twice as hard for a young woman from a traditional and orthodox Muslim family to cross the line and brave all those storms. But we did, and eventually made it to the shore with the help, cooperation and devotion of our parents.

In our house, the arduous task of getting ready began soon after lunch. Their visit to the bride's house being an event arranged at the behest of her parents, tradition demanded that they were given a royal treatment. Hence, dressing up well, being nicely groomed and titivated, soaking up in perfume, knocking heels, talking posh, keeping their chins up, not too lightly treated, not too easily impressed, waited upon, hosted, cared, looked after, was all part and parcel of standard protocol. Whereas to Mamma and Shabbu, going to see a bride who had been already seen and sought by the one to whom she mattered the most made a welcome change, in the case of dear old Rox, it was just the opposite. Suddenly deprived of the right to express her opinions, to pass comments, to select and reject, to balance the books, she had been unceremoniously *sidelined*. Hence, she spent much of the afternoon nagging me. *'There ought to be a law against love marriages in one brother families,'* she kept saying. 'And, whilst being pampered in the bride's house,' I cautioned her, 'should you find it necessary to open your mouth uninvited and utter some of your pet gibberish, do bear in mind that it is a house in which the walls have ears, the doors have tongues and the ceilings have eyes!' That warning dealt yet another grievous blow to her ego. 'And that, by Jove!' she said despairingly, *'is a blatant infringement of the right to free speech,* coming as it does on top of the infringement of the right to *self expression*! A sister's birthright, if I might be allowed to add ...'

As soon as dusk fell and cocks began to crow in the barn, it was time for them to go. Eyes gleaming, gold glittering, heels knocking, lips bathed in smiles, cheeks flushed from excitement, chewing *betel-rolls,* causing ripples, fingers crossed, hopes risen, they left. Papa also went along for his first formal handshake with Uncle Saleh out of many more to come, even though, on that night, the ladies' section in which the bride normally sat was going to be out of access to him. Whenever else he got his chance to see the bride, it would not be on that occasion. The daughter deprived of her right of *veto* by dint of circumstances and the father of his right to *inspect* by tradition, they went consoling each other. I did not go, as I was not expected to. The occasion was formal, seeing the bride for the first time by the bridegroom's family in itself a ceremony. I had nothing to worry about anymore and I was not worried. But I did have quite a lot of thinking and visualising to do with which I got on. I wondered what sort of magical effect the first note of the *Shehnai* in her front yard had on Azra; how fast and how loud her heart throbbed; how many sparkles of ecstasy lit up in her eyes; how many bashful smiles played touch and go on her lips, how deep did her cheeks flush, how many dreams did she gather from the kind hands of her generous Guardian Angels and tuck them up behind her eyelids! I also pictured her clad in a red *sari* as most brides to be usually are, her head covered by the *Ghoongat*, the middle parting arrayed with glitter; the large eyes sunk in the euphoria of dreams; lips relaxed in a divine smile; submitting herself to a rather lengthy assessment by several prying looks; at least one pair out of them excessively demanding and critical!

When they came back, their mood was boisterous, their minds made up, their hearts content, their comments unrestrained. Azra, they said, was just the girl for me, so beautiful, so elegant, so feminine, so refreshing, so shy, so well behaved. They were full of praises, ladies impressed by ladies and the gentleman by the gentleman. The food was good, the behaviour of their hosts was good, the discipline of the children was good, the vocabulary of their parrot was good, and so was the bride. Mamma's description of her began to resemble more and more like the description of Princess Bilquis from the Arabian Nights. Even though Papa was quite satisfied with the overall picture, he did look somewhat frustrated at not being allowed to see the bride; oral sketches annoyed him.

"And why is Rox looking like a *Thumri* sung by Ustad Ghulam Ali Khan?" I asked Shabbu, but looking at Rox, at which everyone burst into laughter.

"Because it's a great *Raga*, sung by a *great* master, I had a *great* day, I feel *great*, and I think this house will be a blessed house when someone as salubrious as Azra crosses its threshold!" she said, addressing one and all alike, and wearing an animated expression on her face.

"Coming from you," I said, my eyes wide from surprise, "I think it's just about the greatest compliment I ever heard you pay to anyone so far. Do you really mean it?"

"Yes, I do," she replied, for once readily agreeing to be impressed, "But I also have a small criticism."

"And what might that be?"

"Well," came the guarded reply, "she could've been a shade taller …"

As if I cared! With the exception of that one telltale flaw on the height hinted at, the unanimous vote went in favour of the bride.

The show carried on well into the night. In anticipation of a possible aftermath, Mamma had armed herself with an adequate stock of bread pudding for afters. That, together with some hot drinks, was brought in and served by Shabbu. Just as I expected, Papa discovered a distant link between the two families from yesteryear, binding us together even more as a wider family. He also discovered the link between Mrs Ansari and Mrs. Khan, but brushed it aside as totally irrelevant. After listening to all those glorious tributes paid to the bride by his family, notably by Rox, a new zeal entered in his feelings and swept him off his feet. A great believer in destiny, it seemed he passionately ascribed to the notion that true marriages are made in Heaven, and conceded that ours was one of them. Neither money, nor worries about it, nor the future prospects of his daughters featured in his conversation at all. He seemed ecstatically happy to realise that another one of his and Mamma's dreams was well on its way to being fulfilled.

"I wonder what would have happened if," Rox reflected aloud with an imperceptible shudder, "I hadn't liked the bride ..."

"Mine and not thine the eye that spotted the beauty, Rox," I reminded her, "and hence, mine and not thine the eye that matters the most.

"Well, spotted, *Bhayyaji!*"

"Shukriya, *Behenji!*"

"I think I had better get myself a couple of hoary unicorns and a second hand buggy from *Chore bazaar,* hadn't I?" she quietly whispered in my ear, surreptitiously winking at me.

"For whom, my precious?" I whispered back, "You just blew your chances of getting yourself a fancy husband!"

"I did, didn't I!" she said with one of her sweetest smiles, "But if marriages are really made in Heaven, I'm sure Allah will bless me with a Yusuff of my own whom I, too, can drive around in my secondhand buggy, if not in a 'Chariot of dreams!' ..."

"Good luck," I said, affectionately squeezing her hand.

It felt so nice for all of us to sit together like that and freely talk about a subject that, a few years ago, would have been considered too immodest to be discussed by children in front of their parents. But attitudes had changed and our peers had accepted the change quite magnanimously. Were it not for their sense of understanding and sacrifice, probably that night would not have even arrived in our lives. Azra would have stayed shackled to her responsibilities, sat her exams again next year, started the job, matured from a bashful teenager into an austere adult; her views on life tainted by the nature of circumstances in which she grew up; her smiles turned into grimaces; her eyes devoid of lustre; the *Shalwar* and *Khamis* relinquished in favour of *khadi saris,* her twin plaits amalgamated into one, or wound into a working woman's bun; the fun gone; the sentiments dead; the poetry muffled; the romance driven out. And if Papa had treated my affair with her as a storm in the tea cup; a mere distraction; an indefensible departure from the main stem of my duties; a pointless exercise; a trivial crush; a minor irritation that needed to be nipped in the bud at once, my course of life would also have changed. I would have probably married some *fat cow* with a *fat batwa,* gone off to the Middle East, fathered half a dozen children and simply got burnt up in the embers of bygone memories. But it did not happen; they did not let it happen; they responded to us positively; they put our feelings in honey-tinted chandeliers and gave them longevity; they treated our love with respect; they blessed it with sincerity; they put our happiness above everyone else's; rearranged their portfolio of priorities without putting it into conflict with ours. To that extent, and even to a much greater extent than that, both she and I owed them a great debt of gratitude; we owed them an equal share in all our dreams come true; we owed them the worth of a lifetime of joy and happiness.

Deep down in my heart, those were the true feelings that beggared expression. Even so, they had to be put into some sort of words; the debt acknowledged; our thoughts coordinated; our bonds strengthened; our perspectives synchronised; our sentiments streamlined. To do just that, I waited until they said good night and retired to bed, continuing my pleasant natter with the girls. It reached its climax when, overwhelmed by their emotions, both of them rushed into my arms and broke down into sobs out of joy for Azra and me. Giving them a kiss and warm hug each, I flicked their tears, thanked them for their dedication, their solidarity, their backing, their prayers, their love, their concern, their share in that something exclusive which bound us together, which gave us a strong sense of belonging and of identity, which made us a family unlike certain others: a wild tamarind tree with so many branches but just one root!

Before calling it a day, I knocked on Papa's bedroom door and went in. Mamma was also there, rubbing Amritanjan on his head, probably to relieve an ache he must have picked up from strain. I thanked them both for making that day such a magnificent day of triumphs and rejoicing for everyone.

"You're welcome, son," Mamma replied, speaking for the both of them, "If you're happy, so are we. Besides, we couldn't have wished for a better match for you than that. She is, indeed, a twenty-two-carat diamond, and we hope she will shine in your crown like the *Koh-e-noor!*"

"I've invited Mr. and Mrs. Ansari to visit us next Sunday," Papa said, "It's a matter of tradition that they, too, are given an equal opportunity to see the bridegroom—regardless."

"Whether or not there's a dowry involved," Mamma observed, "marriages still tend to be pretty expensive affairs. We are thinking in terms of Rajjab for the wedding, which's considered to be a very auspicious month for marriages. Your Papa needs a bit of time to find the capital, and so do we, for preparations."

"For several other reasons, besides," Papa elaborated upon it. "You're our only son, this is the first wedding in both the households and we're all eager to do things in style."

It was the least to concede. I did know the month of Rajjab was considered to be good for weddings, and there were five more months in between, but I agreed. Papa did not have access to lump sum capital, which was true. And neither did Uncle Saleh. Short of seeking help from Sal, I myself had no other recourse; but then, I at least had one, whereas he did not have even that, to the best of my knowledge. I had no idea how he was planning to cope. Marriages are the sort of irksome occasions when tradition becomes unavoidable as well as painful. Religion itself does not stipulate rituals but society expects to see them. If we could, Azra and I would have gladly gone over to a Quazi and taken our nuptial vows in the presence of two witnesses, thus sparing both the families a great deal of expense and hardship. But they had their own feelings, their own ideas, and their own expectations.

A fortnight later, preparations began in our house to welcome the bride's side. Mamma and the girls deliberately organised the event on a modest scale, as it was not the time to impress but to make friends. They were the only guests, which created a pleasant and congenial atmosphere. Ladies entertained ladies while Papa and I took care of Uncle Saleh. Vaseem sat with us in the lounge, wearing perfume and a smile just as refreshing. Probably because of their father's indifference to *'purdah'*, the rest of the kids also moved around freely. A man for all seasons and of impeccable manners, Papa maintained a steady flow of engaging conversation. He did not seem to have any difficulty coping with the youngsters either, one moment a child himself and another moment a sage!

"I'm starting work at the paper mill tomorrow," Vaseem said, talking to me in a low voice.

"Are you? Doing what?" I asked him.

"Sorting out their mail. I've already met the boss and he showed me what to do."

He was another one like me in the making. To ask him if he was looking forward to the job felt like an insult. He had given up a career for it!

"By the way, Azra Baji sent you her *Adab arz,*" he said.

The pleasant greetings, conveyed through an equally pleasant messenger, touched the cockles of my heart.

A few days after that blithesome get together, Azra and I were formally engaged, to be married on the 14th of Rajjab. That inevitably meant yet another prolonged period of separation for us, as engaged couples are not expected to socialise with each other, or even be seen together until after the wedding. We were no exceptions. We might have had an unconventional romance, but that was as far as the matter was allowed to stretch. Expecting such an eventuality, clever Rox had cleverly managed to obtain a photograph of Azra and *bartered* it to me in exchange for three *Kashmiri* silk saris at least. A close up in colour, it was quite good, but nowhere as enchanting as the *real thing*. In addition to the pack of her love letters, I now had something to look at and beguile myself with.

At work, the inaugural ceremony went ahead as planned, grand and spectacular. Before the proceedings began, we made a point of giving our distinguished guests a conducted tour of the premises. After that, as part of the agenda, two well-motivated teachers went on the podium, addressed the packed audience and outlined the ultimate aim of the institute. The chief guests took it from there, paid warm compliments to the foundation and expressed the hope that the community would put those facilities to better use. Uncle Zama, Mr. Raza and several other patrons looked pleased with the results. So was I, especially by the enthusiasm displayed by members of our recently recruited staff.

Seeing Sal that night reminded me of an important favour I had to ask. Without some help from him, Papa did not stand any chance of making preparations for the wedding. It was the first time I had touched him for money, but there was no other choice; the need was never greater. And he, pleased to hear that I had broken my staunch principles at long last and decided to wed a *pupil* of mine, lent me twice the amount I asked. It enabled my folks to begin preparations with a great sense of relief from tension.

As though all that was not enough, my one remaining wish was also fulfilled in the same run of luck. Even if I could not hold my future bride's hand and gaze into her big black eyes, I had been desperately hoping to hear her voice on the most basic of modern technologies—the telephone. One gorgeous morning, as I sat daydreaming about the golden era that was going to unfold in my life very soon, that one wish also came true. The telephone rang, and when I picked it up, her cherished voice fell into my ears and raised goose pimples all over my skin.

"O *master saheb!*" she said in an emotion ridden husky voice, "my sweet *master saheb!* My precious *master saheb!*"

"Azra! Where are you? Where are you calling from?" I asked, choked up.

"Not from too far away, *master saheb!*" she replied, teasing and tantalising me as ever. "Just bend your head and look. I am where you always keep me, where you have locked me up, where you hide me and look after me! In your heart, in your eyes, in your thoughts! And how are you keeping?"

"Don't ask. What about you?"

"Happy and expectant. Cool and at peace. Calm and tranquil. Just like the lucky *Heer* in the arms of her beloved *Ranjha!*"

"And who told you that I'm still alive?"

"Well, if you must know, this is how it happened. The mist told the dewdrop, the dewdrop told the rosebud, the rosebud told the butterfly, the butterfly told the cuckoo, the cuckoo sat on the branches of the pomegranate tree in our backyard and sang it to me."

"Why is it that I can't see you? We aren't a courting couple anymore, you know? We are about to get married and move on to bigger and greater things."

"Because *separation*, they tell me, *intensifies* love."

"Poppycock!"

"Oh, *master saheb!*" she said, becoming sober. "When are you going to come to my house riding on the white stallion? And what is happening about my red palanquin?"

"One's in the pastures and the other is at the carpenter's. All I have to do is to go and get them. Are you ready?"

"Ready, waiting and counting! Hurry up, please …"

The delightful invitation choked me and I ran out of breath again. After talking about this and that for a while, she left. 'Look after yourself, *master saheb,*' she said before going. 'Do be punctual on the fourteenth of Rajjab,' she admonished. 'If I get the chance, I'll call you again,' she promised. After saying all those nice things, she dumped me in the blues and went away.

Time began to pass. Wedding preparations in both the houses gathered momentum and progressed at breakneck speed. Shabbu could not lend a hand as she was constantly tied down to work, but Rox more than made up for it. She and Mamma got together, recruited a small army of experienced volunteers from out of our own wider family as well as some of the latter's close friends to lend a hand, obtained all of Azra's vital statistics, beginning with the size of her little toe right up to the length of her middle parting, finished the entire shopping, followed by the sowing, the dyeing and the decorating with professional care and competence. Every evening, after Shabbu and I returned from work, we were taken upstairs and treated to a spectacular display of ready-made as well as homemade garments, all neatly pressed and hung in the wardrobes. Luckily for me, I did not have to approve or to disapprove of anything; I had already approved and endorsed the one thing that mattered the most.

Enrolment at AIM lasted for less than a week before all the places were taken. As scheduled, we threw open the doors on the thirrd of September. All together, there were over a thousand pupils coming from deprived homes, happy at being given the chance to start all over again, making full use of the facilities provided by the foundation and blessing the great names behind it.

The weeks that followed were the best in our lives so far. We had a solid income, our jobs were rewarding, our status was quite prestigious and I waiting to be united in holy wedlock with the woman I loved the most in the world. It multiplied my faith in Allah, His love, His kindness, His compassion, and His concern. If it is true that every human being is assigned two Guardian Angels by Him for protection and guidance, I certainly seemed to have mine in place, taking care of me every moment of my life. At work, I was loved by my pupils and respected by my colleagues; at home, I was pampered by my parents and mollycoddled by my sisters. During the nights, I was rewarded with endearing dreams about my ladylove; during the days, I was blessed with guarantees of their fulfilment. Downstairs, the house reeked of hypnotic aromas of pure silks, raw cottons, herbal shampoos, bath oils, henna and sandalwood, incense and scents, flowers and pot purees; upstairs, the glamorous display of carefully hung dresses reproduced her images galore. There was not a single spot in the house that was neutral, was free of her imprints, bore no allegiance to her! The day began with her name, the night ended with her thoughts; the sun rose by her command, the moon tarried around her being. That was the true extent to which she dominated us all. Papa talked only about her, Mamma revolved only around her, Rox propelled only towards her—Azra will sleep there, Azra will sit here, Azra will use that dressing table, Azra will eat in this plate, Azra will get that chair at the dining table ... .

Before long, the new moon of Rajjab also appeared on the horizon. We all went up the terraces and watched it. The sight of the thin crescent reminded me of that prior occasion on which we had gone there to see the new moon of EID not long ago and the wishes I had made that night. They were all on their way to being fulfilled, each and every one of them; somewhere beyond those tree tops, my queen was getting ready to wear her crown and make a spectacular debut into her new kingdom. Lasting happiness was almost around the corner for both of us. Hence, raising my hands heavenwards, I shut my eyes and thanked Allah for guiding our raft to the safety of the shore through all those storms.

In the morning, I went to work as usual. Anver, a colleague of mine whom I had appointed to act as my Deputy, was already busy attending to correspondence. We worked together until break. By then, the rains had come to an end and the humid monsoon days were gradually turning quite pleasant. Engaged in lively conversation, both of us sat looking back upon the progress we had made so far as well as sipping the Espresso coffee supplied by the catering department. At around eleven o'clock, the telephone rang. Anver answered it and then passed it on to me.

"Yusuff?" said Uncle Saleh, taking me by surprise.

"Yes, Uncle?"

"Listen. Azra's running a high fever. She hasn't uttered a word in the past three days except mumbling your name. Do you think you can come here for a while?"

"Of course, I can. I'm on my way."

All of a sudden, butterflies began to flutter inside my stomach. The only times when engaged couples are allowed to see each other are in extreme emergencies; no one neglects tradition without due cause. How bad was she? Did they call the doctor? Did they have money for her medicines? Why wasn't I informed sooner?

Leaving behind me a brief note for Shabbu, I rushed.

CHAPTER (14)

I had absolutely no idea how I managed to drive through the chaotic mess of cars, scooters, cycles, *rickshaws* and jaywalkers without any crashes, but I reached Uncle Saleh' s house in less than half an hour. All along the way, the only name upon my lips was Allah's. I did not know if there was any real cause for such immense concern, but I felt as though my small world was thrown inside some sort of a gadget and was being churned upside down. Azra was my whole world, to the exclusion of all else. I felt so possessive about her even a mosquito landing upon her skin and sucking her blood without my knowledge was not acceptable to me. To that extent, I made no exceptions; I made no concessions; I made no compromises; I agreed to no stipulations. Every inch of her, including the invisible down on her body were sacrosanct, irreplaceable, priceless, inviolable and non negotiable. In a place like Hyderabad, with its massive turnover of floating population, catching a bug was probably a most trivial matter, next to nothing, but it had such a devastating impact upon me, I felt routed.

As soon as I knocked on the door, Uncle Saleh answered it and let me in. Upon getting a whiff of the inside atmosphere, my heartbeat dramatically soared up. Everything in it represented Azra—the sound of the latch, the squeak of the hinges, the framed picture of the *Ka'bah* on the wall, the choir mattress on the living room floor, the thick volumes neatly arranged inside the bookshelf, the purple curtains fluttering on the window, the empty vase, the jossticks stand, even the non stop soliloquy of Jehangir. With her around, visible to sight, audible to the ear, coherent to sensors, they all made sense, they seemed in place, in order, in arrangement. But without her, everything looked a mess, in disarray, meaningless, out of place. It was her house, she was the most celebrated occupant in it, she pervaded over everything, she gave all those objects a definition, and she made them real by putting her stamp upon them. Tiny puffs of breeze came from inside laden with the fragrance of her body and her hair, of her clothes and her breath; sound waves emerged out of nowhere and scattered the sound of her voice around the house, her laughter, the rustle of her *Dopatta* and *Shalwar*, the chink of her bangles, the jingle of bells in her anklets, the knock of her clogs; a myriad recollections came out of hiding, reproducing her contours and her silhouettes; her images and her reflections; the walls paid homage to her, the doors opened and closed at her command, the parrot sang his eulogies to her, the sunrays came in through the windows to touch her feet, the beams of their light took pride in hallowing her personality. Or, so it seemed, to me at least. My eyes roving everywhere for a tiny glimpse of her, my heart beating away in the hope of an encounter with her, my ears strained to pick up the sound of her voice in the background, I followed Uncle Saleh.

To be able to get to her room, we had to go through an open veranda around which the house was built. Much of the space was taken up by wedding preparations and reeked of cotton fabrics, of pure silks and camphor. I had no idea how he managed the money, but seemed to be doing all he could to make the first major event in his household a grand success, with the help of his family and his relatives. The sound of sewing machines thumping away behind some of the closed doors could be distinctly heard; a brand-new wardrobe for the bride appeared to be in the process of being put together by her own folks as well, a whole new future being cast for her to revel in, to enjoy, to show off; elegantly styled and cleverly coordinated suits intended to enhance her beauty, to accentuate her glamour, to multiply her charisma. How would her comely body look in the imbroglios of those Banarasi saris; how would the frills of those illusive taffetas define its magical contours? What would the ecstatic moments of a wedding do to her being; how would she transcend from a shy bride concealed in the folds of the silks and the voils into a bashful wife held in the adoring arms of her husband?

As all those evocative thoughts kept passing through my mind in an endless chain, we arrived at her room. It was quite large and looked more like a dormitory than a bedroom, containing five single beds in a row, presumably shared by all five girls in the family. The one on which she lay was positioned to the farthest and was also the largest. Her head was supported by two pillows and the rest of her covered by a white bed sheet. The very sight dealt me a nasty blow. Somehow, I had always associated her with liveliness, with vivacity and exuberance, a throbbing source of energy, a gushing fountainhead of dynamism, a pivot around which everything revolved. Seeing her brought down to a sudden halt like that by an ailment had never even remotely occurred to me as a possibility. That alone pushed me to the brink of tears, though I held them back with an enormous effort.

"Azra!" Uncle Saleh whispered to her, "Look who's here. You have been asking for him all day, haven't you? Wake up and say hello."

She did not respond. The lids remained firmly drawn on her eyes, my entire universe remained sunk in the twilight of sorrow, my heart went deeper down the quick sands of blighted hope, my sun rescinded into anonymity, my moon sheltered behind a veil of distress, my stars buried themselves in the ashes of darkness. For the first time ever, she did not extend to me her radiant smile of welcome; did not lay down for me the gleaming carpet of her looks; did not drown me in a whiff of her perfume; did not bewitch me with a flash of her plaits; did not allow her cheeks to betray the secrets of her heart.

"No need to rush her, Uncle. Let her sleep. I'll wait," I said.

Thoughtful as always, he pulled a chair closer to the bed and forced me into it. He seemed to know what was going on inside my heart; he seemed to know that a mammoth tidal wave of grief had risen somewhere in the distance and was heading towards the balustrade of my resistance; that, with my partner flat on her back, I had suddenly become as helpless as a pupa outside its cocoon; and also that, at that particular moment, and all of a sudden, I was not too far from reaching the end of my tether.

"If I were you, I wouldn't lose my head over this," he said, obviously to calm me down, "Just a freak fever, that's all."

I simply nodded. Leaving me with her, he went inside for a while. I looked at her again. Like a tender rosebud removed from frost but exposed to the hot winds, she had shrivelled up. Only three days of *just a freak fever* had taken such a toll on her. I could not bear to see her crumpled like that. A sour lump rose in my throat and got stuck there until I forced it back. Unaware of my presence or of her surroundings, she carried on sleeping. If only I could gather her up in my arms and take her away with me to a remote corner of the earth not yet conquered by illness and disease; where I could sit her on the pedestal of eternity and prostrate at her feet; where I could keep her out of harm's way and protected from the whirl blasts of ill wind for as long as we both lived; at least, for as long as I lived, moved around, ate, slept, remained a part of the living world.

After keeping me waiting for an unendurably long time, she finally woke up. The lids slowly parted and revealed the eyes—as aglow as live cinders.

"*Master saheb!*" she exclaimed in a weak voice, taken by complete surprise.

"Hello, Azra!" I said, forcing myself into a pretentious smile, if only to keep her spirits propped up, "How are you feeling?"

To be able to answer me back, she seemed to need quite a bit of preparation. First, she wet her parched throat by gulping down some saliva. Next, she pressed her dishevelled hair back in place to get a clear view of me. Then she tried to smile but could not quite manage it. However, the eyes did respond to her effort and lit up with a random gleam.

"Oh, *master saheb!*" she said once again as soon as she could deliver some words, "Seeing you here in my room and this close to my bed reminds me of what *Mirza Ghalib* had once written in one of his poems."

"What did he write?"

"*This must be a rather special blessing from God that you've come to my house, my love! One moment I stare at you bewildered, and another moment I stare at my humble abode, bewildered!*"

"Then it must be even a greater blessing of His that you reside in it, *my love!* Your presence makes this *humble abode* a thousand times more glamorous than the *Sheesh Mahal!*

The compliment cheered her up a bit. "I hope no one can hear me," she said, lowering her voice, "They'd think I'm being immodest. But I'll say it nonetheless. *I love you!* I fell in love with you on the very day we met."

"So did I. Only, I was too scared to tell you about it."

"You? Scared of me? My *mentor,* scared of his insignificant *pupil?*"

"Well—of being thrown out of the house. If your *Abbajan* had thrown me out, I'd have died on your doorsteps."

"Which would've made me a widow even before I got wed."

"I'm glad I didn't."

"Are you sure this is okay? I mean, our being together in the same room without even a chaperon present? We aren't supposed to see each other until we're married, you know?"

"If memory serves me right, we are *already* married. In the presence of Allah and two of His holiest saints, which is more than what I can say for a Quazi."

While the smile remained on her lips, for some reason the look froze. "There is something I must tell you, master saheb," she said, lowering her voice further, "A strange thing happened that day at the *shrine* that I haven't told anyone. I did not expect I'd have to, but I think I better—just in case."

"What happened?"

"Soon after you put the ring on my finger, I saw both the saints emerge from their tombs and look at us. Then, suddenly, tears filled in their eyes and rolled down their cheeks. Why did they weep instead of being happy for us, *master saheb?* What do you think they were grieving over? "

"I don't know. Are you still seeing that old man in your dreams?"

"Not since I started to wear this ring," she said, kissing the tiny emerald on it. "Absolutely *miraculous,* isn't it?"

"If you say so."

"I do. And so is this, which Mamma put on my finger on the day of our engagement, to make me yours for ever," she added, kissing the ruby on it and then fondly staring at both the rings with her glittering eyes.

"You *are* mine forever, aren't you?"

"Of course, I am. Yours alone and no one else's. Take a look at this, for proof," she said, waving her *Henna*-soaked palms in front of my eyes and showing off the deep colour with pride.

"What does that prove?"

"Didn't you know? According to common belief, for those on whose palms the colour of Henna lasts longer than twenty-one days, they say their love lasts longer than their lives!"

"Good. And according to Allah's promise in the Qur'aan, for those whose love lasts longer than their *lives*, it will also last into the *after-life.* "

"Ours *will*!"

"Ours *must!* "

"Yes, *master saheb*, it must *and it will!* "

"When are you going to stop calling me *'master saheb'?* "

"Probably never. I love calling you *'master saheb'*. That's because you're my dearest master saheb, my sweetest master saheb and my very own master saheb!"

"Thank you. I'll make sure the change of name enters next year's register of voters."

"Oh, master saheb … I feel so tired," she said, suppressing a yawn and rolling her eyes around in their sockets, "Would you terribly mind if I took a quick nap? And promise you won't go away? Promise? Promise?"

I promised her by crossing my heart. After shutting her eyes only for a brief moment, she shot them open again.

"What? Finished already?" I asked.

"Just *checking,* that's all," she said.

Then she fell asleep. On account of the blocked nose, her breath became noisy. Quietly pulling the chair a bit closer to the bed, I put my elbow on its wooden frame, rested my chin on my fist and sat gazing at her. Her eyes were half shut, her mouth was puckered and the brow had gathered a mild frown. One of her hands lie across her gently heaving chest and the other rested on the pillow near her head. The temptation to hold them in mine for a while, press them against my lips and my eyes and then give them a gentle squeeze of reassurance became irresistible but I managed to overcome it with a great deal of effort. Content with just looking, I quietly sat there, my eyes going over every minute feature of the pretty face again and again, the sharp eyebrows as if drawn on it with a pencil, the slanting eyes drowned in the stupor of sleep, the slim nose moulded to sheer perfection, the small nostrils responding to the intake of breath, the rounded cheeks wallowed in pink, the tender lips still looking like a dew-soaked rosebud at dawn waiting to be tickled and woken up by the first ray of the sun. There were only two more weeks to go before the woolpacks of rain clouds descended from the sky and washed her silken hair; before the young night gathered stardust in its veil and sprinkled it on her wavy curls; before the butterflies came from far-off hills and titivated her face with their own magical colours; before the spring sneaked into her room and painted her cheeks with the pink of the carnations; before our dreams turned into realities and filled our hearts to the brim! Meanwhile, I hoped that nothing untoward happened to delay the moments of our bliss, to shatter our hopes, to hold up our *chariot of dreams* somewhere along the Highway to Heaven by any unforeseen mishaps, any unpredictable hurdles, any unexpected contingencies … .

An hour or so later she woke up, looked at me and widened her eyes with surprise. She did not seem to remember having seen me in the room already. "Oh, *master saheb!*" she exclaimed, "I was beginning to give up hope. Where had you been?"

"To the pastures for the *stallion* and to the carpenters for the *palanquin,*" I replied, if only to cheer her up.

The timely mention of those two indispensable ingredients for any traditional wedding put an extra tint on her cheeks. Making a resolute effort by herself, she turned on her side and faced me. A myriad sparkles lit up in her eyes and the smile played touch and go on the lips. Her look unwaveringly dug into my face as she stretched her hand for mine, firmly held it regardless of all the restrictions upon physical contact between us and pressed her lips on it.

"Did you know that Ammijan and a couple of my aunts are busy sewing all sorts of dresses for me so that I can show myself off to you?" she said with an animated expression on her face, "My favourite is the red B*anarasi sari* with golden borders. They're making stars in the fabric with silver thread. It has also got a matching blouse. I wish I could wear them now!"

"Do you want to? Just say the word. I can get you another sari for the wedding. Ten, twenty, thirty, fifty, I don't care. I'll weigh you in Banarasi saris and heap them up at your feet!"

"I can't, with this pain in my stomach. Ouch! It's hurting again."

"Let me bear some of it for you, my angel! I'm bigger than you and I'm stronger than you. Please?"

"No!" she said emphatically, "I'm glad it's me and not you. How long is it before the wedding?"

"Not too long. Only last night, we all went up the terraces and watched the new moon of *Rajjab*. Papa had been itching for days to sight it."

I told her about it, hoping it would please her and get rid of some of the gloom that was dragging her down into the doldrums. But instead of bringing her relief, my words seemed to set her mind adrift. She looked lost, the face abruptly shed much of its colour, the rosy cheeks took on a distressing pallor, the smile forsook her lips, two large tears appeared in her eyes, quietly quavered on the lashes for a while and rolled down her cheeks like pearls rolling out of sea shells. I also felt her grip on my hand tighten as she bit upon her lower lip to restrain her grief.

"Azra! There is no need to despair, " I whispered in her ear, "Just concentrate on getting well quick. With my fervent prayers added on to your mute determination, we can still make it to the chosen date smack on the dot."

Whether or not my brave words and exhortations had any real impact upon her, our confidential whispers had to be brought to an end. The arrival of Uncle Saleh into the room, accompanied by an old woman, presumably either a relative or a maid he had hired to fill in for his absent daughter in the kitchen, together with all the paraphernalia for a sponge bath, caused an unavoidable diversion. As there was need for privacy, I left Azra's side for a moment or two, assuring her that I would be right back.

He took me into an adjoining room. There was a plate of food on a small table and some coffee in the mug. The very sight made me sick. I sat in the chair for a while, just brooding. When he pressed me to eat, I declined. My head began to spin. Keeping as firm a hold upon myself as I could, I asked him what happened. He said it all began about a week ago when she visited her aunt in Asifnagar along with her mum. While the grownups were engaged in conversation, she teamed up with Sakina and her mates for a chat. They all knew about the wedding and kept teasing her with teenage talk, until a large party of gypsies barged into the yard and mobbed the girls. They were nomads from Poppy Hills who often visited the city in a big bunch in order to raise alms. One of them, presumably carrying a bug of some sort, went sick in the grass near Azra who accidentally stepped on it. Mrs Khan quickly got rid of the unruly intruders and washed her sandals as well as her feet with lukewarm water at once, adding some phenyl to it as a precaution against contagion. The incident was over and was forgotten, but Azra woke up in the morning with a severe cold and mild fever. Vaseem immediately took her to their GP who thought it was just a bout of flu and prescribed her some antibiotics. She took them and the cold did disappear soon, but the fever had persisted since.

"And now I've got a different doctor looking after her," he said, concluding.

"She's complaining of pain in her stomach. What's pain got to do with flu?"

"I've no idea."

As soon as the maid finished with her task and left, I went back into Azra's room. Her face freshened up with a wipe and some perfumed powder, hair brushed, pillows rearranged, bed sheets and blankets sorted out, an ice bag placed on her head presumably to combat the excessive body heat, I found her in a much better shape than she was when I left her. On account of sheer fatigue, she had fallen asleep once again, and the bag seemed poised to slide on to her shoulder. Gently putting it back on her head, I sat in the chair. After a little while, she woke up. I smiled and she reciprocated.

"Feeling better?"

"Yes—in heaps. I was afraid to open my eyes in case you'd gone."

"I won't go. Not until I'm thrown out."

"No one's going to throw you out, *master saheb!* My parents happen to like you a lot, in case you didn't notice. Besides, this is still my house—and you're my …"

"Yes? Go on—say it. I'm your what?"

"My—guest'. Guess what I'd like to do soon after the fever is gone? Go for a stroll with you in the public gardens and sit on the lawns, picking daisies and teasing the *touch-me-nots*."

"And after you come to my house, we'll do the same every day. We've got a large garden at our place. I'll walk you down the amaranthus glades; I'll entreat the morning breeze to gently blow the veil off your face; then I'll cajole the young blooms to welcome you with their bashful smiles; then I'll persuade the spring to beguile you with melodies never heard before!" I said.

That seemed to strike a note with her. The large eyes opened wide, the black pupils latched on to my face, the life-bearing fluids in them gleamed, the pallor which had tainted her cheeks earlier gave way to a new flush, the parted lips joined together and eased into a lilting smile, a whiff of breeze blew in from the half open window and ruffled up her hair.

"And?" she said, wanting to hear more of my romanticising our future, decorating it with dreams, elevating it with plans, colouring it with promises.

"When the night falls and the moon comes out, I will wash your feet in the cascades of moonlight; I will turn the milky way into glitter and sprinkle it on your hair; I will string together the young buds of night queens into a garland and hang it around your neck; I will put the *Chakore* in a cage made of gold and ask her to sing new lullabies for you ..."

"And then?"

"And then I'll fetch the best artist in the world to paint your portrait for me; I'll ask him to give your hair a hue rich enough to make the rain clouds roll with envy; I'll ask him to give your lips a pink deep enough to inspire passion in every rose; I'll ask him to give your eyes a lustre dazzling enough to throw the sun into a panic ..."

My wild promises tickled her to such an extent she burst into laughter. Getting carried away in an avalanche of emotions, my open arms involuntarily stretched towards her and she almost threw herself into them, but modesty overcame self-surrender at the last moment.

"And I had thought I was the poet between the two of us!" she said, resorting to speech.

At that moment, her sister Mehjabeen arrived in the room, balancing a tray on one hand and using the other for an *Adab arz* in my direction. I quickly got to my feet and relieved her of it. In response, she covered her head with her *Dopaita,* touched the centre of her brow with the middle finger of her right hand in the traditional way, finished the greetings and then broke into a dazzling smile.

"Thank you, *miss*," I said.

"Glad to be of service, *sir, "* she replied, elaborated the smile into a shy chuckle and ran away.

"Isn't she gorgeous?" Azra asked, looking so proud.

"Absolutely adorable. As is the *queen,* so is her *kingdom!"* I complimented.

There were two bowls on the tray, one containing hot soup and the other some boiled vegetables. As soon as I got ready to feed her, she eyed me apprehensively just like she used to do at the mention of mathematics. The brow creased a bit and the nose wrinkled as usual.

"What's the matter? Don't you want to eat?"

"Do I have to?"

"As far as I'm concerned, angel, you don't ever have to do anything you don't want to. But seeing that the fourteenth of Rajjab isn't too far away, it all depends upon how keen are you to keep that crucial appointment with me."

"Will you come riding the white *stallion,* wearing the *sehra,* accompanied by a brass band and trillions of guests?"

"Yes."

"Will you also fetch for me a red *palanquin,* accompanied by the *Shehnai* Party and trillions of more guests?"

"Yes, I will."

"In that case, feed me. With your hands and with your love, adding a little passion in the soup for taste and sprinkling a little dazzle on the veggies for appetite!"

I fed her. She ate as much as she could in small mouthfuls without making any more fuss, the large eyes focussed upon my face, smile pasted on the lips, hair ruffled once again, blood drawn to the cheeks, her consummate beauty still in tact and as triumphant as ever, enjoying herself thoroughly at being thus served by the man of her dreams, planting a secret kiss on my hand whenever it got within her range, at the same time making sure the stolen pecking was not being watched from discreet corners. It was my utmost joy to be of service to her, to look after her, to take care of her, to love and to cherish her, to sit her on lotus petals and wash her feet with dew, to sleep her on ostrich feathers and cover her up with dreams, to walk her on velvet cushions and roll her up in silks. If only the fever was gone, things got back to normal, days immersed into nights and nights unfurled into days, the thin crescent of Rajjab quickly augmented into a full moon, the brass band arrived, the Shehnai echoed, the Quazi pronounced us man and wife in the presence of a large crowd of jubilant guests and launched us off on the first leg of our journey to our dreamland!

Shortly after she finished eating, wiped her mouth with a napkin, lay back on the bed and the tray was taken away, Uncle Saleh ushered the doctor into the room. Quickly doing away with the greetings, he got busy checking her pulse and her temperature as well as talking to her.

"Well done, young lady," he complimented her upon inspecting the thermometer. "You've thrown away at least two degrees of heat off your system. That's what I call *real* progress. How's the pain in the stomach?"

"It still hurts. I mean, oft and on."

"Don't worry. It'll soon go away."

"How soon?"

"Can't say, but you certainly seem to be getting on top of it. Keep up the good work."

She simply nodded. Writing out one more prescription, he wished her luck and left.

Soon the day wore out, the rest of the children too returned from school, came into the room first, said *Adaab arz to* me with customary zeal, smothered Azra's face with kisses, asked how she was, held her hand, kissed it turn by turn, told her how much they loved her and how much she was being missed, wished Allah in all solemnity and sincerity to bless their beloved sister with a speedy recovery, recited the *Durood-e sharif* below their breath and blew it on her chest. In response, she too hugged and kissed them one by one, asked them how nice or how miserable their day at school was, listened to the anecdotes they had to tell her with patience, cracked a joke or two to make them laugh, told them to wash up, eat, go to bed and have sweet dreams. Watching that picture of family bliss brought back many fond memories from my own childhood days and touched the cockles of my heart.

A few moments later, after dealing with their supper, doing the dishes and putting them away, I got the impression that their mother was getting a bit restless to spend some time with Azra, but my presence in the room was preventing her. As we had not yet been formally introduced, *Purdah* was still prevailing between us. Even though the very thought of leaving her behind and going away for the night was unacceptable to me, I did not have much of a choice. Surrendering to the painful inevitability with a heavy heart, I prepared to leave.

"I think I better go now, Azra," I whispered to her, "Your mum still has a lion's share in your life and is getting pretty desperate to claim it. I'll be back in the morning and stay all day. I won't go to work until my queen is up on her feet and on her throne. Okay?"

She answered me with a mere nod, while the pleading look had something else to say. Giving her hand a gentle squeeze to prop up her spirits, I pressed her ruffled hair back in place, looked deep into her moist eyes, straightened the blankets and forced myself into a pretentious smile.

"There's a good girl!" I said, feeling rotten inside, "Now, don't neglect the food and remember to take all your medicines on time. We've both got a deadline to meet. Okay? *Shab bakhayr?*"

"*Shab bakhayr!*" she mumbled almost inaudibly.

The situation in my house was more or less as I had expected to find, the air fraught with tension, Papa restlessly pacing in the veranda and Rox keeping him company. As soon as I parked the bike in the shed, they rushed to me for news of Azra. I gave them all the information I could and assured them there was no cause for alarm. Uncle Saleh knew our telephone number and would ring us up if there were an emergency.

For the next seven days, Azra did not make even an iota of progress or show any signs of recovery. Her temperature fluctuated like a yo-yo, sometimes going alarmingly up and sometimes coming deceptively down. The doctor visited her twice a day instead of once and filled her with all sorts of medicines. Yet, neither the cause for the fever became clear nor was there any explanation to the pain. She kept suffering, most of the time her agony hidden behind an outer facade of courage.

Towards the end of the week I, too, began to panic. No doubt, the doctor had been doing his best to cope with the crisis, and Uncle Saleh did assure me that if she was in any kind of serious danger, we would be alerted at once, but such palliating words were no longer enough to console and comfort me. At that stage, I needed guarantees. Thus far, I had been hanging on to Allah by the strong and indestructible thread of my firm faith in Him; whether I was offering *Namaaz* or was looking after her, I had been constantly praying to Him; I had been calling upon Him with all His great names and begging for His intervention and help; I had been reciting below my breath only those passages in the Qur'aan that contain His glory, His love, His compassion, the promises He has made to us and the hopes He has given us. He is said to be the best Healer of all and I firmly believed that He really is and sought Him alone. It was about time He stepped in and took charge.

"*Master saheb!*" Azra said to me one evening just as I was preparing to leave, "When you're here, time flies. But after you go, nights don't seem to budge. What do I do?"

How could I break her heart? I told Uncle Saleh whatever she said and he responded to it swiftly.

"By all means, stay the nights too, son!" he said without another thought.

"I don't give a damn about the neighbours any more or anyone else for that matter. You know something? Ever since the two of you got engaged, we've been looking upon her as *your property*. We're merely her *caretakers*."

My property! When did I ever have anything in my pockets to match her price, to pay for the richness of her divine smile, for the treasures contained in her golden heart, for the affluence concealed in her bountiful arms, for the paradise she carried on the palm of her hand, for the luminance she generated with her lustrous eyes, for the benedictions that sprouted wherever her feet fell, for the joy that always accompanied her? The most I could give her was my love, my loyalty, my service, some care, some attention, and some dedication. If that were enough to make her my property, then indeed, she would stand paid in full to that extent. I had dealt with gossip and tradition; I had dealt with nightmares and haunting; I had dealt with tamarind seeds and superstition. By the same token, if I could deal with that awful fever too and put her back upon her feet, I would cross any sea or scale any mountain to accomplish that miracle. But how? Each time she let out a gasp of pain, something inside me kept dying!

Uncle got over the situation by simply introducing me to his wife. From then onwards, I stopped going home. It made her very happy, strengthened her resolve, exacerbated her determination, and gave her the impetus to try even more. I fed her thrice a day with my own hand, kept careful track of her medicines, oft and on spoke to her doctor too, let her lean on my shoulder and take small walks in the room, talked to her, encouraged her, consoled her, helped her relax and sleep on time, laughed when she joked, elevated her spirits if she became broody, narrated interesting stories if she got bored. In course of those few trying days, she became a million times more precious to me, I drew even closer to her, I loved her more, and my admiration for her touched its peak.

Ever since I stopped going home, day-to-day news about her also stopped reaching my folks, even though Uncle Saleh did try his utmost to stay in touch on a regular basis. But to my family, it was not enough; where Azra was concerned, nothing was enough. In order to make up for it, my sisters began to visit us daily and as often as possible. After coming home from their schools, Vaseem and the other children also joined hands in keeping her entertained. On those occasions when they sat together engrossed in lively conversation, I, too, felt very much at ease. But peace seldom lasted long enough. Pain struck her again and again quite mercilessly, dashing our hopes. Sometimes she broke into sobs, sometimes she convulsed, and sometimes she screamed. There were times when she also passed out for long periods, throwing us all into a panic. Like a catalyst, she kept changing our relief into fear, our hopes into despair, our smiles into tears, without giving us time, without telling us why.

Matters finally reached a stage when the date of the wedding had to be postponed indefinitely. The news plunged her in such a state of shock she turned into shale. That was the one thing with which she simply could not come to terms. Once the goal was withdrawn, she went completely adrift. There was no need for her to panic; I was not running away; nothing had changed; nothing was going to change; the fever would subside one day; the pain would disappear; *Rajjab* would come again; the *Shehnai* would be back; the white stallion was sure to knock his hooves underneath her marquee; the red palanquin would halt at her doorstep one more time for her; the spring would return; flowers would bloom; the *Laal muniyas* would make many a nest; Jehangir would carry on shouting her name; my world would never be complete without her being a part of it; but she sank into oblivion and withdrew into herself hours on end, without speaking, without weeping, without getting the weight off her chest.

Three days later, she woke up with something on her mind and quietly waited until her mum finished with the morning routines.

"Come on, *master saheb!*" she whispered to me as soon as her back turned, "let's play weddings today. You be my bridegroom and I be your bride. It'll make a big crowd when Shabbu Baji and Rox also join in. *Please?*"

She was in such a delirious state of mind it was impossible to reason with her. Whatever efforts I made at discouraging her, it only strengthened her resolve some more. She became obstinate and insisted upon being dressed in the red *Banarasi sari*. As her mum commenced the incredible task of *preparing the bride*, Uncle Saleh stood lock-jawed and watched. My sisters arrived in time to lend a hand, their faces white, their eyes startled, their lips sealed, their hands trembling. But her sisters, still too young to grasp what was going on, broke into a festive mood. Thrilled to bits by the absurd razzmatazz, she patiently sat through the laborious preparations. Her palms and feet were adorned with a fresh application of Henna, her face was titivated with makeup, her eyebrows and eyelashes were lined with *Kajal*. Rox brushed and styled her hair, Shabbu slipped a new set of bangles around her wrists, and her mother got on with the jewellery. Silent tears kept dribbling down their eyes but she was not even conscious of their grief. Clad in those glamorous clothes, smiles dancing on rosy lips, sparkles gleaming in the lustrous eyes, gemstones on the choker chain around her slender neck glittering, bangles on her wrists jingling, adorned and dolled up, flushed and excited, what a breath-knocking bride she made! Despite physical weakness, mental delirium and emotional stress, she still emerged on top, the best, the inimitable, and the unparalleled! Barely seven days from the real thing, the fantasy she staged and the performance she gave was no less enchanting.

I did not know what to do or what to say. The trail of tears trickling down my sisters' cheeks, the ghastly pallor on the sad faces of both her parents, their vacuous looks and their silent sighs, the innocent chuckles of glee let out by the little girls in the room and her own incredible resolve to stay on top of her grief became suddenly too much for me to cope. I could neither defy despair nor succumb to it; no matter how hard I tried, I could not team up with her to *play* the role of her bridegroom, whether to amuse her or even merely to subside her delirium; I could not persuade myself to take any part at all in those tragic proceedings; I could not accede to her wish on that occasion. If it was her way of getting at the inaccessible, I did not feel any motivation whatsoever to walk alongside her on that uneasy path. I would sooner wait than reconcile with any substitutes; I would rather bank my hopes upon fate than renounce it altogether. But she, once again, insisted with uncharacteristic bluntness that I did.

Sadly, her resistance broke down completely before she could finish what she had started. Pain struck her again, this time far more unbearably than ever before. She broke into piercing screams and began to writhe like a fish out of water. In spite of making a combined effort, we could not subdue her. The girls realised at once that all was not well with their sister, came to attention, restrained themselves, stood in different corners of the room and began to cry. Unable to watch her torment, Vaseem dug his face in his palms and broke down into loud sobs. No one seemed to know how to console or comfort the others.

Uncle rushed out and fetched the doctor. His arrival brought some order into the room, the snivels and the sobs subsided, the children moved away from the bed, we all stood hushed and turned our anxious eyes upon him. He became engrossed with his patient, somehow managed to check her temperature and her stomach with the help of the ladies, checked her pulse, her tongue, her eyes, his brow dented and his lips pursed, while the rest of us carried on staring at him, his verdict awaited with bated breaths. 'Allah' was the only name on every lip. The cry for help, which rose from that room at that moment, must have rocked the very throne upon which He sat.

After his examination came to an end, the doctor let out a cold sigh of despair and confronted uncle with a grim expression on his face.

"I'm afraid matters are beginning to get out of hand," he told him without mincing his words, "If she doesn't show at least some signs of recovery by tomorrow morning, I will have to admit her to the hospital. It's no longer possible for me to treat her at home."

"What exactly is the matter with her, Doctor?" I asked him, making myself bold somehow.

"If I knew the answer to that question, " he replied in a sympathetic tone, "I wouldn't be standing here groping in the dark and raking my brains."

Before going away, he checked her once again, gave her one more jab of some sort using his own stock of medicines, then some tablets and a new prescription. Right through the examination, she neither made a sound nor moved. Oft and on, a finger or two just twitched as she continued to draw a heavy breath. Those of us with the strength to be up on our feet stood surrounding the bed, hushed and frozen; we were with her but she was not with us. The *Banarasi sari* crumpled, the makeup wore off, mouth flexed, eyes rolled aimlessly in their sockets. The smile was gone, the thick lashes did not lift, the flush in the cheeks gave way to a pallor, people came into the room and left, her mother went away somewhere, Shabbu became busy putting the children to bed. Rox, Vaseem and Mehjabeen did not so much as move a muscle. I, too, turned into a rock,

Towards evening, she picked herself up a bit. Relieved by the encouraging signs, my sisters left for the night. The doctor made two more visits without having to be sent for. Soon, with the exception of Vaseem, all the other children fell asleep. He stuck to her side, refusing to go, refusing to eat, refusing to rest. His tears did not dry even once. 'Azra Baji slaved away for a whole year with her books just to help me through college,' he had once told me, so grateful to her and so proud of her. It was not easy for him to stand there and watch that person suffer so much. But he bravely managed, in no mood to forsake her side for crowns or for kingdoms.

Round about midnight, it was time for her medicines. The doctor had left clear instructions as to what to give and when. I knew them all; I had memorised everything. Circling the bed on tiptoes, I reached the small cupboard on which the medicines were kept. As the glow of the bed lamp was not enough, I also switched on a brighter light. Then, according to instructions, I gathered several tablets and capsules in a plastic container. Water was kept in a jug close by. Pouring some in a glass, I turned round.

That was the moment when my horrified eyes came into contact with a sight so bizarre it hit me like a thunderbolt. In the brighter light, her face was clearly visible. There was a tiny blister on her lower lip, a few on the cheeks and some on the forehead. As soon as I saw them, the plastic container slipped from my hand, the glass dropped on the floor and shattered, the sound of crash exploded in my ears like the blast of dynamite. I became aware of an insane urge to scream but my voice muffled inside my throat; I became aware of a desperate urge to run but my legs refused to move. My vision blurred, my head spun and my blood curdled. I remained where I stood, neither alive nor dead, neither moving nor motionless, neither speaking nor struck dumb.

Probably woken up by the same noise, Vaseem also saw what I did and went berserk; the screams that I could not let out, he did. After that, it was like a stampede. A large crowd of people rushed into the room from all directions. Nothing registered in my mind, nothing made sense, and nothing seemed real. I felt someone hold my hand and bring me out of the room. I did not protest, I did not resist, I did not know who, I did not know why, I did not know to where. When the wall touched my back and it was no longer possible for me to retreat any more, I slumped on the floor. That was just about all the movement left in me.

At some stage I heard someone mention a name that confirmed my worst fears; a messenger was being despatched to fetch Hakeem Dastgeer Khan, the local quack. Everyone knew who he was and what he specialised in. There was only one reason why people sent for him: *SMALL POX* ... .

CHAPTER (15)

Why did my hearing come back to me all of a sudden? Only to hear those grievous words? Why was my vision restored? Just to see that pitiful spectacle? If I had found my voice instead, it would have done me a lot of good; I would have screamed as loud as I wanted to and for as long as it helped. I would have raised such a hue and cry for Divine Clemency as to rock the very throne upon which *Allah* sits. I would have approached His Angels one by one, poured out my heart to them, shed tears of blood, appealed to their compassion, to their sense of justice, to their pity, enlisted their support, gathered them all behind me and organized a revolt in Paradise. I would have called upon every *Mo'azzan* in the world to climb the minarets of mosques five times a day and invoke His mercy instead of giving Him praises all the while. I would have negotiated a truce with *Allah* to spare Azra in return for whatever was mine; reminded Him of the promises He has made in the Qur'aan to all good Muslims who had faith in Him, His Kindness, His Munificence, His Omnipotence, His Omnipresence; who followed the path of Righteousness; who never strayed away from the *Siraatul mustaqeem;* who established worship, who gave alms to the poor, who kept their end of His Covenant. I would have demanded Him to keep His end, I would have held Him to His word, and I would have dared Him to stand by it. I would have stopped the earth from moving, reversed the course of nature, plunged the universe into chaos, plucked the stars from the sky, caused the sun and the moon to collide and to explode and made a complete hash of His Creation until He either gave in to me or declared that day the *Day of Judgement!* If my voice had returned, I would have delivered a plea stirring enough to melt the mountains, for the clouds to shower blood instead of rain, for the wind to gasp instead of gust, for the birds to stop singing and mourn along with me, for the flowers to fold up their petals and sink in grief. If my voice had returned, I would have entered into a dialogue with Him, made out a special case for Azra and myself, brought back from Heaven a message of goodwill and joy for all the young people in the world who loved each other. There was so much I could have done with my voice; there was such a lot to say; there was all that to give and all that to gain. If only I could speak! If only I could speak! If only I could speak!

But I could not so much as wince. See I did, a spectacle so frightening I could not believe my eyes, a rush too maddening to be real, and an activity too confounding to be comprehended. There were people all around me, coming here and going there, throwing this and grabbing that, holding him or pulling her, taking one or giving up the other, none of which made any sense to me. I saw brass buckets filled with steaming water and loads of towels all being rushed into Azra's room, which had become the nucleus of everyone's attention. Some were going in, some were coming out, some stood frozen, and some sat hushed. Their combined voices sounded like some sort of a discordant caterwaul in the distance, their moving figures looked like shapeless forms, my surroundings wore the outlook of a grim battlefield, the action shifting from inch to inch without any signs of abating. What was the purpose of all those endless exertions; what were they aiming to accomplish; what were they hoping to gain? What was there to wait for; what was still on its way; what was still outstanding? How long did they have before the curtain dropped for good; how much could they do within those rapidly disappearing moments; how far could they go; how much scope was there for retrieval; what were the odds; how high had the stakes risen?

And what was my recourse? Send for Shabana and Roxana; ask Mamma and Papa to help me out; cling to them for support in the moment of my direst need; on the brink of annihilation; at the edge of the precipice? Borrow their shoulders to shed my tears upon? Only, there were no tears in my eyes. They had dried up, they had frozen, they had evaporated without any trace, they were blocked behind a huge balustrade of repression. I was not in a position to budge that obstacle and set them back aflow. I was so stunned, I could not even tremble. How many hopes had I banked on her; how many dreams had I gathered in my eyes; how many plans had I made for the morrow; how many expectations had I associated with her; how hard had I farmed on the field of my hopes; how many seeds of bliss had I sown in it; how well had I kept it weeded and watered from dawn to dusk; for how long had I been waiting for the crop to bear fruit! Everything stood on the verge of being wiped out, hanging by the tail, almost gone … .

Soon the doctor arrived. I could not see him but I heard his voice. Understandably, his recommendation was to rush Azra to the hospital and give her the best and the only chance she had. But insurmountable obstacles were being put in his way. What sort of obstacles? Her mother, in spite of being overwhelmed with grief, had put her foot down; it seemed Azra made her swear upon Allah that she would not be sent to the hospital under any circumstances. *'But why?'* I heard someone ask. Apparently, the oversensitive young lady, in a bid to maintain her *notional rectitude*, had refused her body to be touched by other men! Can you believe that? So pure and chaste even at a time like that! She would sooner die a horrific death than live thus *disgraced,* she would rather be destroyed by a cruel affliction than agree to one crucial inevitability, make one small concession, and give up so little for such a lot! And if the daughter was as fussy as that about protecting her *honour,* the mother was just as fussy about *honouring* her pledge. One would not agree to go and the other would not allow her to be sent, neither of them prepared to face up to the harsh realities that the options had narrowed down to either the hospital or the graveyard; it would have to be either an ambulance or a coffin; either the doctors or the undertakers; either the nurses or the mourners!

Then the quack Hakeem Dastgeer Khan arrived, wearing the airs of a Divine Healer. There was nothing new about the methods of treatment he employed; he was known to have done the same thing every time and he was known to have failed in every case. Small Pox, the deadly disease that seldom spares its victims, has no dependable cure, despite whatever claims are made to the contrary. His only recourse was a tree called the *Neem,* which grows here abundantly and is often found in most houses. Its sap is so pungent, germs cannot survive it. Or, so they say. One stood right in the middle of their front yard underneath which I had parked my bike so many times. At Mr. Khan's request, someone rushed out, chopped several branches of the tree and dragged them in. Behaving more like an accomplished surgeon than a bungling quack, he snipped a large quantity of its tender shoots, tied them up into bunches and took them inside Azra's room.

I had no idea at the time what was done with them or how long it took, but at some stage, the Hakeem finished his task and left. So did the doctor, his advice ignored, his recommendations turned down, his prescriptions discontinued straight away. Then the great multitude of people who had gathered in the house also began to disperse in ones and twos. The frenetic rush came to an end; the tumult subsided; silence returned. My heart kept going in a weak flutter, my eyes moved from one oblivion to another, my head felt empty, my body felt heavy, my breath stifled. As the painful moment of seeing Azra in her tragic condition approached, I writhed in agony. How was I to watch that sight? How was I to cast my eyes upon that carnage of hopes, that debris of dreams, those piteous remains of all my long cherished expectations? How was I to confront the woman I loved so much forsaken alone in the narrow confines of that room to fend for herself, surrendered to the icy neutrality of destiny, abandoned in the lap of death? How was I to witness the perpetration of such a terrible catastrophe, how was I to stand aloof and watch my helpless *gazelle* trapped inescapably in the midst of a pack of bloodthirsty lions, being ruthlessly torn apart and consumed bit by bit? From where could I possibly get the courage to see the smile taken away from those untouched lips, the never-ending glitters in those magical eyes put out for good, the Henna-soaked hands covered by unsightly blisters, the dainty fingers twitching from unbearable pain? What did we ever do to deserve such a pitiful fate, such a morbid end, and such an awesome plight? She was the partner I had chosen to walk alongside me on the troubled paths of my life; she was the mate I had found to help me build my nest and share it with me; she was the beacon that was going to guide my raft to shore; she was the fountainhead that was going to keep my valley for ever green; she was the deity that was going to occupy the shrine I had built by the sweat of my brow; she was my love, she was my dream, she was my goal, she was my reward, she was my oasis in the midst of sand dunes, she was my joy, she was my inspiration, she was my vision, she was all things to me, she was everything to me, she was the only thing that mattered to me, that I wanted to have all to myself. She was the one whose *chapattis and daal* I wanted to live on, in whose arms I was hoping to fall sleep, on whose lap I was planning to wake up. With she near me, I was the king of the castle; I was the knight in armour; I was the emblem of glory. Without her, I was a hapless pauper, I was a worthless entity, I was an inconsequential mite!

In due course, Uncle Saleh arrived from somewhere and stood in front of me, his eyes still streaming and bloodshot, his voice muffled, his limbs shivering, his courage gone, his hopes dead, forsaken by the daughter he loved so much, staggering under a burden he was not equipped to carry, facing a plight he had not bargained for, confused by a test he had not expected to face, sunk in grief, speechless from shock, refusing to reconcile with the truth, unwilling to confront reality, unable to control the course of events. When he stretched his hand towards me, I simply panicked and backed off. I felt so scared of being taken into her room and shown what was going on inside, I tried to hide, I tried to vanish into thin air, I tried to turn into a fistful of ash and disperse in the wind. The balustrade behind which my tears were trapped did not budge; watching his grief did not mobilize my grief, hearing his voice did not activate my frozen limbs. If I could, I would have screamed; I would have refused; I would have asked him to go away; somehow delayed the painful moment of reckoning for as long as possible, given her image a lasting protection in my mind, the way she was, the way she ought to be, the way she was entitled to be. The face that had made the moon blush, the eyes that had taken light into darkness, the smile that had brought so much joy into my life, the unblemished skin as opulent as marble, the soft hair as ashen as dusk, the tender lips as pink as young roses. I could not bear to see her mangled, to watch her suffer, to let her go. She was too much to lose so soon, she was too precious to be given up, and she was too close to me for parting.

That night, a lot of unpleasant tasks seemed to have fallen upon poor Uncle Saleh's shoulders. Taking me into his daughter's room under those circumstances must be terribly painful for him. Only, having already gone through a level of grief that could never again be surpassed, he was able to handle me with relative ease. What I had not yet seen, he already had; what I was yet to confront, he had already confronted. He had come past the storms that still awaited me; he knew precisely what lie on her bed; he knew what to expect; the worst was behind him; his strength of endurance had been tried and tested. I felt his hand grab hold of my elbow; I felt a gentle pressure upon it; I felt a shooting pain in my chest; I felt as though I was walking on live cinders with naked feet. The distance between her room and me protracted disproportionately; the floor ahead of me suddenly seemed to rise and touch the ceiling; my eyes failed to transmit what they saw; my mind refused to absorb what they did. Coordination was gone from my senses. I was looking but it felt as though I was sunk; I was moving but it felt as though I was tied; I was walking but it felt as though I was floating.

After we entered the room, he left me there and went away as he would have done if it were her bridal suite; it was her nuptial night; and if she sat on the bed clad in red, waiting to surrender herself into the arms of her loving bridegroom. But that was not how things had transpired. There was no sound of the *Shehnai* in the background, there was no fragrance of the sensuous *Chambeli* or the euphoric rose mingled in the air; there was no rustle of silks and taffetas to hear; there were no expectations rampant in the room; there were no shy smiles or coy restraints on offer. Only a death like silence; only a dreadful calm; only the noxious fumes. My blank looks travelled in every direction except where she was. All I could see was bunches of the *Neem* shoots that the Hakeem had hung from the ceiling here and there. The hush around me was utterly chilling. The light I had turned on earlier was still on. Together with the breeze, a lot of tiny moths had also travelled in through the open windows and were fluttering around the bulb. That was about all the movement I could see and all the noise I could hear.

Summoning what little courage there was inside me, I forced my attention upon the bed. She lay on it, eyes glued to the ceiling, limbs absolutely contrite, mouth sealed, breath held. The Banarasi sari was replaced by a nightgown, all the items of her jewellery were removed and her hands tied to the bed probably to prevent her from scratching the blisters. Traces of makeup were gone from the face; her hair looked dishevelled; scales had emerged on the lips. But the patterns of Henna on the palms were still visible and so was the ring I had put on her finger at the *shrine* that day. There were more blisters, on the cheeks, on the chin, on the neck and on the arms. The rest of the body was concealed underneath her blanket but I could guess what must be its state. Like a tree besieged by a swarm of termites, like a flower taken over by green flies, she was being consumed, bit-by-bit, and inch-by-inch. The queen had fallen in the battleground, the enemy too fierce and formidable to be overcome, too many against one, too cruel for compassion.

If she was aware of my presence in the room, she showed no signs of it, made no attempt to address me, did not move an inch. I had no idea what was going on in her mind, how frightened she was, how much pain she was suffering, what was the extent of her distress, her agony, her hopelessness. In a moment or two, her eyes filled, tears spilled, the teardrops rolled down like pearls and soaked in the pillow. I wished she said something, either bade me farewell or gave me new hopes, either agreed to stay or prepared to leave, either chose to live or elected to die. I wished I could read her thoughts, share her torment, alleviate her pain, and prop up her courage. I wished I could do something to help her, anything, and everything. I wished I could pick up those dreadful blisters with my fingers, collect them in a dustbin and chuck them out the window. I wished I could take her backwards into time with me and live all over again, or take her forwards into time and never once look back. I wished there was some way in which a happy past could mingle with a happy future without necessarily travelling through the painful present.

Suddenly, a fit of near insanity overcame me. Rushing to the bed, I held her face in my hands, looked into her dazed eyes and kissed her on the lips in spite of the horrendous blisters. That was the closest I had ever come to her body apart from the ritual of holding hands once or twice; that was the only time I kissed her; that was the only liberty I had taken with her. But she broke away from me at once, her strength feeble, her movements badly impaired by the straps with which she was tied to the bed.

"*Master saheb!*" she almost screamed, frightened, distraught, choking up, "Don't … Please don't!"

"Remember the oath we took in the *shrine,* Azra?" I asked her in a rasping voice, "To *live* together and to *die* together?"

"I was … looking forward to our … living together more than … dying …" she said, delivering the words one at a time. "You said nothing can come between us … Nothing can tear us … apart … Nothing can take one away from the other … You said … you said …" she began to stammer, her voice choked by grief.

"Looks like I was wrong, doesn't it?"

"Please don't touch me again, *master saheb! …* Keep away from me … This disease is contagious …"

A bitter lump stuck in my throat. If only I was there on that bed instead of her; if only I could change places; if only I could trade my life for hers!

"Tell me the truth, *master saheb!* I'm going to … d…d…die, aren't I?"

How could I say *yes* to that question? How could I admit to it? How could I accept the unacceptable, endorse such a damning finality? How could I bang the door in her face? How could I turn my back upon her?

"Isn't this … a little … too soon, *master saheb?*" She asked me in a sad voice, "I haven't yet found out … what it means to be … married … to be loved … to be shared … to be caressed … I don't know how it feels … to have a … man's arms around me … To be whispered sweet words intended for … my ears only … To be told that paradise is … where my feet are … Everything seems so unfinished … so incomplete … so utterly insufficient …"

It was. She was being struck down in the prime of her life, which was not fair, which was not becoming, not necessary.

"Why make only to b…break … Why create only to…to…to destroy … Why all the fuss over … n…nothing? Ouch! I'm feeling itchy all over … Could you please … untie my hands? "

Instead of untying her hands, I picked up a bunch of those *Neem* shoots that was left on the bed for that purpose and gently ran it over the blisters.

"What am I going to do without you, Azra?" I mumbled in a hoarse whisper. "Surely, you aren't going to leave me alone and go away like this, are you?"

"You must ... forget ... m...me ... *master saheb*. You're a good man ... and ... deserve the best ... . I'm ... no longer ... good enough for you. I know what ... this affliction ... does to people ... I've seen it ... with my ... own eyes ..."

"Let's take you to the hospital, angel? Please? Who knows—there might still be a chance? At least a little bit of extra time in which to invoke Allah's mercy? I'll beg Him as no one has ever begged Him before."

"No ... *master* ... *saheb* ... No ... First of all ... there's ... no...no ... chance ... . Secondly ... I'd .... rather ... die ... than ... live ... like ... a ... c...c...cadaver ... . But above all ... I don't want ... anyone ... to see my ... .nakedness ... I happen ... to ... be a ... woman of ... severe limitations ... I'm ... not ... my ... own ... mistress ... I belong ... to you ... I'm *your* *p...p...property* ..."

There it was again—*my property!* She said the same thing in her letters too. *'I'm not a free person. I belong to you. I'm your property.* I'm an unwanted legacy which you can't decline'—she wrote in one; 'This body which I've kept neat and clean for your hands only, this shrine in which you alone can be the deity, how can I surrender it to others?' she wrote in another. There was a big difference between letting herself be treated by the doctors and 'submitting herself to another man,' but she was too finicky to recognize it.

"Well," she said, following a quiet sigh, "to be honest ... with you, I'm not entirely ... dissatisfied with my lot so ... far. I got the best ... attention and love ... from my parents, I enjoyed the ... smashing company ... of my brothers ... and sisters. ... And what's more ... I was also lucky enough ... to have come across ... a man like you. It felt ... so nice to be loved ... and wanted ... You and your fancy thoughts! ... You turned an ordinary girl like me ... into a celebrity ... You flattered me ... to the skies ... You made me feel as though I was one up on Princess ... N...N ...*Nilofer!* Thank you so much ... Thank you ... so much!"

At that point her eyes filled once again and a whole stream of tears trickled down. If the blisters were still itching, she made no effort to free her hands; if she was in pain, there was no sign of impatience in her mien; if she was frightened, there was no trace of fear in her expression. The tears had nothing to do with physical pain. I could see it was just grief.

"So ... my dearest *master saheb!*" she said, finally closing the book, "Time's come for me to say ... *AL VIDA* .... at long last! Let's p...p...part here and now ... You're the only man ... who knocked on ... the door of my heart ... I let you in ... and then never once ... let you out ... I know ... parting is painful and ... you're entitled to ... grieve over me ... But don't...don't let yourself ... be destroyed by it ... There are ... many ... more b...b...blossoms ... in the garden where ... I come from. Find another soon ... and march on ... Nothing will stop ... after I'm gone ... and nothing must. ...Whenever you ... think back ... think of me ... as I was ... yesterday ... and not ... as I'll be tomorrow ... AL VIDA ... *master saheb* ... AL ... VIDA!"

With those words she turned her eyes back upon the ceiling and stopped crying. Digging my face in my palms, I burst into loud sobs. The balustrade of repression finally gave way and released a spate of tears. I felt as though my back was broken. Nothing made sense. I could not believe I was about to be dealt a blow as crippling as that. What did we do to deserve it? What was happening and why? I had always thought *ALLAH* was on our side and not against us. It was still within His means and in His hands to intervene and rescue. There was no way in which I could let go of Him, I would not take a *no* for an answer, I would not relinquish hope. Hakeem Dastgeer Khan and Neem leaves was another story; one was a mortal and the other just an instrument at playing God. But it is different with Him. He has the power to take as well as the ability to give. He has the right to break as well as the skill to make. He can offer as well as deny; He can deprive as well as restitute. How could I possibly reconcile with fate without His final word? How could I accept destiny without His say so? That was the whole reason why we always abided by His commandments; why we so firmly remained within the boundaries He has set out for us; why we acknowledged His presence in Heaven and why we submitted to His will on earth; why we believed in His abounding love; in His limitless kindness. Until that moment, my need of Him had never been greater and my faith in His response never firmer. I must try Him! I must move Him! I must melt Him!

Probably hearing my loud sobs, both Uncle Saleh and his wife rushed into the room.

"Is there some place where I can sit and pray, Uncle?" I asked him, somehow squeezing my grief back inside me; somehow getting a hold upon myself; somehow making a desperate bid at speech.

"Of course, there is," he replied courageously, "*Every* place is a place where you can sit and communicate with Allah. Here, there, anywhere. Don't waste time looking for Him. He'll come looking for you. Beg, ask, beseech, exhort, demand, do what you like, but don't give up on Him ... don't give up hope .... don't give up ... don't give up ... d...d...d..."

His words too muffled in grief. But he managed to escort me into a room in which there was a mat, a copy of the Qur'aan and some jossticks burning. The process of begging and beseeching for Divine clemency appeared to have already been begun in that room by someone else. Kneeling on the floor, I raised my hands towards the sky and shut my eyes. It plunged me into pitch darkness—a darkness that could lift only if and when His light appeared in it.

"*YA ILAAHI!*" I said, addressing Him below my breath, "I've come to you for a favour. I need you, I need your attention, I desperately need a minimum measure of your sympathy, your mercy. Ever since I grew old enough to be able to watch, to hear, to read and to understand, all I ever watched, heard and read were praises to you, the promises which you have made, the guarantees which you've given. I was so impressed by all that, I loved you, I respected you, I believed in you. So far, there has never been any reason for me to seek evidence of your kindness, to verify your claims, to test your sincerity. I do accept even now that you're the greatest just as I always have. I will not go to anyone else for what I want. I've no place else to go other than where you are. Please spare Azra. In the name of all your Holy Prophets from Ibrahim to Mustafa, in the name of all your saints and your sages, in the name of your glory and by your authority, please spare her. It was by your will that we came across each other; it was by your consent that we fell in love; it was with your name that we got married too. Take away from me anything you wish, if you must, my voice; my vision, my movement, but give her back her life. Please help her to endure the suffering, give her the strength with which to cope, speed her recovery. She's so young, she's so frail, and she's so unprepared. Don't put on our shoulders any more burden than we can carry; don't subject us to tests that are beyond our scope; don't ask us to render what we ill afford. I beg you! I beg you! I beg you!"

Did He hear? Did He respond? Did His heart melt, His pity stir, His eyes stream? Did He make even one single gesture of goodwill, of compassion, of pity? If He could not get rid of the blisters that had already grown on her body, did He stop more from growing? If she was half destroyed already, did He at least end the damage there and begin the task of rebuilding her? If she must die, did He at least give her a less painful way of dying? If He must strike one amongst us, could He not have picked me for a target instead? If His hands were tied, if He was helpless, if He, too, had His own limitations like everyone else, then why go around making all those big promises? Why raise our expectations and then trample upon them? Why cheat us powerless mortals who cannot match His superior skills? Why draw those into a duel who cannot fight back? Why assert Himself over those who had been created for servitude? Why make and then break? Why create only to destroy? Why all the bloody fuss?

He did not give a damn. He could not be bothered. He was not even there where He ought to be. His throne was empty. Apes had taken over His seat. Darwin was running His big show. Freud was writing the next set of Scriptures!

Her torment lasted for seven whole days, during which time her condition deteriorated rapidly. The horrific pustules spread all over her body. In spite of being a mortal, in spite of his track record of failures, in spite of the futility of *Neem* leafs, Khan never slackened his tireless efforts. Having given up on men and their ineffective means, her entire family turned to *Allah* and became engrossed in sad supplications, offering nonstop rounds of *NAMAAZ* and reciting aloud all those sections of the Qur'aan that contain praises to *Allah*, which give hope to the hopeless, inspire confidence in His love, build faith in His compassion. My parents and my sisters too made as many visits every day as they could, watched the dismal state of our plight with tearful eyes and joined hands with the others in those never-ending prayers. But nothing worked.

'*Those whom God loves die young,*' say the sagacious. *Allah* probably loved her much more than any of us did. He is also the stronger between us. He can take away whatever pleases Him and spare whatever beguiles Him. After all, this happens to be *His* universe, which *He* created out of nothing; this is a dollhouse, which *He* set up for *His* own amusement. All these toys that lay scattered on its floor are *His* toys, *His* 'action men' and *His* 'Cindy dolls.' He can break them if *He* gets fed up, *He* can wring their necks if it catches *His* fancy, *He* can pull their limbs if it tickles *His* whim, He can pluck out their eyes if it gives Him pleasure, He can crush them underneath His feet, He can change them around, He can trade them away, He can dump them in the rubbish skip. Although it is a silly thing to do, no one has the guts to tell Him so because He is God and God cannot be silly! If anyone was silly, it was I and it was Azra. Like a couple of ignorant imbeciles we believed in Him, we trusted Him, we put our faith in His generosity, we staked our lives upon His

Word. What was worse, I had taken the liberty of picking for myself one tiny bud out of His abounding arboretum. He begrudged me that. He was so annoyed by my trespass into *His* sacred domain He rose up in all His Mighty Wrath to punish me for it. Out of sheer malice, out of sheer spite, out of sheer hatred. And there I was, the invincible clown, still believing that God is merciful. Merciful, my foot!

As her final moments began to draw, they gathered together to bid her farewell. What a way to send her off! In His name, with His word, by His will, would you believe! They kept chanting *'Inna lillahi wa inna alaihi raja' on!'* Know what that means? 'We are all Allah's *property* and we must eventually return to Him.' *Property!* Sounds familiar, does it not? 'Ever since the two of you got engaged, we have been looking upon Azra as your *property,* son; we are merely her caretakers,' Uncle Saleh had once told me. Now, suddenly, he, too, was uttering the same slogan with his own mouth. She was no longer *my* 'property' but *His*; she was no longer coming to me but going to Him. The ownership had changed hands without the courtesy of my knowledge or my consent. Why did they not tell me? I would have refused to give her up or I would have matched any price. I had a right to be told first. I loved her. I needed her more than He did. I was banking on her; I was relying on her. She was my partner, she was my companion, she was the captain of my ship; she was my stalwart and my guide. I needed her so much, I needed her so much, I needed her so much! But He robbed me. Damn Him! He robbed me in broad daylight. And yet, not only were they letting Him get away with it, but also glorifying His crime with slogans of praise, with hymns and with canticles.

I did not lend my voice to that assiduous recital. By then I had come to hate Him bitterly. In my view, He was no longer fit for worship. Not for me, anyway, even if I was branded an ingrate by His standards. I had always been given to understand that God is love, God is kindness, God is justice, God is generosity, God is clemency. 'Allah is always more eager to give than to winch,' Peer Saheb had written in his note, 'Go and gather His bounties with both hands for they are always in plenitude.' But He proved Himself to be otherwise. I made up my mind never again to bow to Him. Or cry for His help. Or seek His mercy. He had nothing to give. He was bogus. He was humbug. He was a sham. Even rocks would have bled at my grief, but He did not. He could not. He never so much as bothered even to pause for a while and listen.

In the early hours of one morning she passed away, without taking another look at the world she had finally renounced or at those whom she had left behind. I remained frozen in my corner, my limbs contrite, my breath held, absurdly azoic. My dream was shattered at long last; my whole future disappeared in that one instant. An entire harvest of hopes and dreams lie in ruins, destroyed, annihilated, and dissipated. Over nothing! We had been doing fine, working our way through the troubled paths of life, minding our business, loving one another, looking forward to being with each other. But then He struck. Like an eagle, like a vulture, like a buzzard. He suddenly pounced upon us from out of the blue, picked her up in His vicious claws and flew away. I was rendered alone. I had no one to comfort me. I had no place to go to. The phone on my desk would ring a million times but it would never again bring me her voice; the postman would deliver many a letter but none would be from her; Aghapura might survive the tragedy of her death but was no longer worth setting foot upon!

And thus the prophesy of the dreadful tamarind seeds was fulfilled to the hilt. Only, she was not bad for me—I was bad for her. That was where all the pundits had gone wrong!

CHAPTER (16)

Islam, a product of the desert, requires all Muslims to bury their dead swiftly. Accordingly, preparations were made for Azra to be laid to rest in a nearby cemetery at dusk on the same day. How all those preparations were managed by the family, who came to their house and did what, how long it took them to do it, I have absolutely no idea, I do not have any recollections of the grim proceedings, I took no part in them. I could only guess that those who would have come to prepare a bride for the auspicious occasion of her wedding and seen her off on board a palanquin, clad in red, prepared her to be seen off on board a coffin, clad in white. Utterly overwhelmed by grief, my tongue lost, my vision blurred, my ears cupped, my limbs contrite, I simply sat huddled in some dark corner of the house where there were no noises to be heard, no people to be seen, no one to talk to, no one to answer back. Even if there were, I was not accessible to anything or to anyone. Unable to cope with the enormity of my distress, my mind just packed up on me and withdrew into the voids. The farther I was from human company, the better it seemed; the greater the distance between me and the world, the safer it felt. I forgot completely that I had a family of my own, two ageing parents and two young and extremely sensitive sisters, not to mention close friends like Sal, who must have come there with some bold words of solidarity for me. If they had; if they were there and were watching my tragic plight from somewhere around; if their love for a wretched son, for an ill-fated brother and for a miserable friend was churning them upside down, was dragging them towards me with heavy chains, they did not seem to succeed in bridging the gap that had opened up between them and me, probably at its widest then than ever before. Neither did I bother to go to them, soliciting their support, in search of peace, in need of relief, on the lookout for comfort. Before the body was wrapped up in cerements and transferred from the bed to the coffin, when someone told me that it was my last chance to see her face, I refused to take advantage of it. As far as I was concerned, no cerecloth in the world was thick enough to obscure that radiant face from my view; no coffin in the world was fast enough to take that comely body away from my reach; no grave in the world was deep enough to keep it beyond my grasp.

Time and tide wait for no man. Soon, the moment of her final departure from that beloved abode in Aghapura, and from the arms of those who loved her caught up, suddenly escalating the muted sobs of her mourners into piercing screams, the loudest and the most poignant of all being her mother's, redeeming the *debt of breast milk* which her daughter owed her. I could hear everything but could not respond to anything; my body was with her body and my soul was with her soul. When the burial procession set off and the chanting of *Inna lillahi wa inna alaihi Raja'oon* began once again, I did not lend my voice to it, I did not lend my shoulder to her coffin, I did not do anything to participate in her *final rites.* Where the burial party came to a halt, I, too, came to a halt; I joined the congregation for the *Namaaz-e-janaza* along with the rest of the others; did whatever they did, I prostrated when they prostrated, I said Salaam when they said Salaam and sat through the painful service without absorbing a word. After they finished, I accompanied them as close to the freshly dug grave as I could, then staggered and stopped underneath a huge tree. The last few steps between her resting place and the water margin of my inner courage became totally insurmountable, so I did not even try to bridge them. Taking refuge behind the trunk of that tree, I stood aloof, my eyes dry, my look lost, my throat parched, my knees wobbling, my heart sunk, my mind obtuse.

After it was all over; after her frail body was committed to the womb of mother earth and the curtain on the tragic story of her life was dropped for ever; those who braved to do the job lifted their hands heavenwards and said a few parting prayers for the eternal salvation of her soul. Then they dispersed together, leaving her behind, sunk in everlasting sleep underneath a mound of damp soil, now guarded by the wild shrubs, sung by the wayward birds, caressed by the passing breeze, protected by the rolling clouds, looked after by the invisible angels, Allah's *property* in Allah's domain, dust mingled unto dust, her friends forsaken, her family plunged in grief, her memories rampant everywhere. Still unable and unwilling to get any closer to the grave, I slumped underneath the tree, leaning my back against its trunk, and shut my eyes. The grave disappeared, the cemetery disappeared, the mosque disappeared, the world disappeared. Only a shooting pain in my heart remained; an overwhelming sense of loss remained; a frightening awareness of loneliness remained; a bitter taste of defeat in my mouth remained. Time passed; I did not open my eyes; I did not attempt to reestablish contact with my surroundings; I saw no point in feeling alive; I carried on floating; I carried on chasing her *empty chariot* across an interminable stretch of silvery clouds; I carried on searching for a lost treasure in the expanse of eternity; in the pits of infinity. At some stage of my grievous ruminations, the wind picked up speed, became waterlogged, turned cold, rain came pelting down; there were flares of lightning and there was roar of thunder; the storm trapped me; the rain soaked me; my grief pinned me down. Yet I refused to open my eyes, to look, to think, to run. I could not possibly leave her alone there in the midst of such a nasty night, such a nasty storm; I could not let the muddy streams of rain water creep inside the grave and soak her too; I could not abandon her on her own and go away. She was the undisputed queen of my heart; she had always lived inside that palace in luxury; she had always had me near her at her beck and call; she had never been thrown out in the cold to spend an entire night all alone, wrapped up in a white cloth and covered by palm leaf mats; she was not accustomed to such rough treatment; she was too young and fragile to be dumped like that. So I, too, stayed on along with her, near enough to hear her if she called for help, to respond to her if she sought company, to comfort her if she felt scared.

At some stage of the dark and fearsome night, after the storm subsided and calm returned, I suddenly saw a dim glow in the distance swinging like a pendulum and heading towards me. In the confusion which the spectacle raised in my frenetic mind, I had a strange premonition that it was either the Angel of Death who had been persecuting poor Azra in her dreams, come to take my soul too and set it free along with hers, or my Guardian Angel whom I had once seen in my own dream, come with the golden key to lock me up in the golden cage along with her. Both the destinies equally acceptable to me, so long as they kept us together, just like Allah had kept Adam and Eve together, whether in Paradise, whether on earth, whether in reward or in chastisement, I held my breath and waited. Slicing through the dense folds of darkness, the glow got closer and closer still, until the figure of the person holding it emerged out of obscurity and materialised into a young man of about the same age as me. After a polite exchange of Salaams, he introduced himself as the *imam* of the mosque near the cemetery where Azra's service was held. Whether or not he was aware of my connection with her and the tragedy I had endured, he made no attempt to pry into it, but merely offered the hospitality of his house at least for one night, if I felt up to it. He said his wife and children had gone to Khammam visiting her parents; there was plenty of room to spare; his kettle was still hot and I was welcome to a drink of tea or coffee. He seemed like such a kind person and spoke to me so softly I could not refuse him. Besides, having just had a taste of cruelty meted out to me by the Kindest of All, *The arham ar Rahimin,* I felt I could do with a measure of kindness being offered by a mortal like him, a man, just a man, a mere man, a man of God, a man who had taken a vow to spend his entire life spreading His word, providing guidance to the stray, inspiring the confidence of the *Qaliq* in His *Maqlooq!*

Accepting his kind invitation with gratitude, I went with him to his house not too far away. After lending me a palm leaf mat, a clean bed sheet and a pillow, he brewed some coffee and sat up with me for a while. It was only inevitable that Azra and her tragic death featured in our conversation in course of which I told him the whole sordid story, if only to get the weight off my chest, including my bitter grievance against Allah for the raw deal I received at His hands. He felt sorry for me and for her, sympathised with my plight, understood my grief, and instead of preaching me sermons in spiritual retrieval, asked me to spill it all out. He assured me that Allah, too, was there to listen, to give comfort to the bereaved soul, to lighten the load, to help cope, to build strength, to support the unsteady, to teach man how to be strong in moments of stress, how to be bold in the face of adversity, how to be content, how to be at peace. He also said that I was welcome to stay with him for as long as I wanted to and for as long as it helped, share with him his maze Chapattis and tamarind chutney, look after the grave sometimes, or sit in the mosque and meditate, until I could get to grips with myself, until I could learn to let go of what was gone and be content with what was left.

So I stayed on, without even sending word to my family. I woke up every day at dawn to the cry of the *Mo'azzan*, went back to her grave, swept all the wilted leaves that had been shed by the trees in the vicinity or been blown around by the wind, and never allowed any grass or weeds to grow on the soil. Somehow, its external tidiness gave me a sense of relief. What sort of a mess lie inside was another matter; it was not visual and I did not even think about it. Gathering fresh flowers from wild shrubs dotted around the cemetery, I laid them at her. I knew she loved flowers; I used to buy her a bunch of either the *Chambeli* or the *Juhi* every time I visited her for her lessons. Whilst living in the imam's house, I could not afford to buy some of those as I did not have any money on me, but what was the use, anyway? She was hardly likely to distinguish between the wild clusters and the garden blooms. The fault was entirely mine—recollecting so well a past that would never recur. But I could not help it. My mind refused to believe that she had left me alone to cope with life and gone away forever. Wherever I looked, I always saw her, sometimes hiding behind the tall trees and signalling me to seek her out; sometimes bewitching me with the flash of her thick plaits; sometimes laying down for me a feast of her smiles. Quite often, I sat close to the grave and spoke to her as if she was listening to me as well as replying. I just made up her side of the conversation which stimulated my overwrought emotions. The monologue I enacted always resembled a confidential chat between two newlyweds. I deliberately addressed myself as *'master saheb'* because it conjured up her images in front of my eyes as though we were both sitting in our kitchen in Asifnagar, she rolling chapattis for me and I helping her out. Only, I could not touch her; she was beyond my reach.

Forty days thus passed away. In course of those first forty days since the burial, the entire text of the Qur'aan is recited as often as possible and by as many people as volunteer to do it. Being closest to her, I, too, should have done the same thing, but I did not. As a priest and as a man of God, my host did admonish me several times to do it, explaining to me how important it was for the journey of a soul from *here* to the *hereafter* to be blessed with the benedictions of such recitals, and even lent me his own copy of the Qur'aan, but it had no effect upon me. As I could not refuse him to his face, I cheated him. Whenever I was not attending to her grave, I sat inside the mosque, the volume open in front of my eyes but without reading a word. As far as I was concerned, honesty had lost its significance. If God could cheat, so could I; if He could lay false claims to mercy, I, too, could lay false claims to devotion. To my way of thinking and by my standards, they reciprocated each other. Once upon a time I used to be a good Muslim and proud to be one. But it brought me nothing. When it came to the crunch, no one made any concessions. If He could not prevent her death, He could have at least spared her the torment; there is more than one way of dying. But He gave her the worst. No doubt, death destroys everything, but she was destroyed before she died. So much for my being a good Muslim; a devout Muslim; a subservient Muslim.

On the fortieth day after burial, Muslims pay their first ceremonial visit to the grave for laying wreaths and for offering benedictions. Realising that I was broke, the imam had bought a basket of flowers along with a bunch of jossticks for me with his own money and left it on the mat. As usual, I woke up to the cry of the *Mo'azzan*, borrowed a matchbox from the kitchen and came out of the house. The mid winter dawn, overlain by a blanket of thick fog, looked hauntingly crepuscular. It was also bitterly cold. My teeth chattering, shivers crawling up my back, silent tears dribbling down my cheeks from a fresh upsurge of grief, I walked to my lonesome destination in slow strides. Her forlorn grave lie without a headstone, without an identity, without any borders. Random gusts of wind gathered up fallen leaves from here and there and scattered them around. By then, the mound of soil had turned quite hard. That day, I swept it with my hands instead of with the broom. The basket contained a thick lattice of fresh roses that I laid at her and then lit the jossticks. Other than those, I had nothing else to offer her by way of homage, except my love, of course, and that love was still hers for the asking.

As I sat there shedding more silent tears, a whiff of breeze containing a familiar fragrance entered my lungs and shook me up. My heart fluttered noisily, shivers ran down my back, the tears froze and goose pimples rose all over my skin. I could feel her presence near me; I could feel her fingers run through my tousled hair; I could feel the smother of her warm breath on my cheeks; I could hear the chink of her bangles, the thump of her footfalls, the knock of her clogs, as if she was there; as if she had come herself to accept my blessings; to reduce my torment, to offer me solace; to drag me out of doldrums. The thoughts, the feelings, the recollections and the images it stirred up joined hands and pushed me over the brink. I sat rooted to the ground, searching the shadows around me, unfurling secret layers of fog, chasing invisible gusts of breeze, concentrating on vague silhouettes, startled by the rustle of leaves, by the racing squirrels, by the flapping of birds, by wafting butterflies, drowned in forlorn hopes, sunk in unlikely expectations, swept by endless anxieties.

After a little while, Uncle Saleh appeared in the distance, flanked by several men, come there to lay their wreaths and offer their benedictions. I had no wish to be found by him sitting by the grave, still in mourning. If he saw me, I was sure he would drag me away from her, whereas I was not yet ready to go. Outside the cemetery, an unkind world was lying in wait for me. Getting lost on its tangled paths was quite easy; being devoured by its insatiable demands was easy; extending the distance between Azra and me was easy; but closing the gap afterwards would not be so easy. Hence I made a quiet departure from there, went back to the mosque and sat down on the mat, eyes shut, lips sealed, sunk in oblivion. The street was beginning to come alive—people, going about their business; life, getting back to normal again; bells of rickshaws, hoot of horns, roar of engines, cows mewing, dogs barking, crows clamouring. All my wounds opened up and began to hurt; my heart pined for my lost mate and my mind fell victim to all sorts of persecuting thoughts. What was I to do? How was I to get to grips with myself? How was I to reestablish contact with a bygone existence? How was I to pick up the threads? Where was the beginning? Where was the end? Where was peace? Where was Azra? Why did things go wrong? Would they ever be the same again?

Uncle Saleh seemed to know where I was and came into the mosque for me. Probably the roses on the grave gave me away. Seeing him for the first time since her burial exacerbated my grief; he was her father and therefore one more vestige of her past existence. He reminded me of all those things which I had been struggling so hard to forget.

"What the heck do you think you're doing here, Yusuff?" he asked me in a soft but firm voice. "As though losing a daughter wasn't bad enough, are you now determined to make sure that we lose a son too?"

There they were, the demands, the tangles, and the cul-de-sacs. Azra was no longer important, but I was; she did not matter anymore, but I did; she was dead, but I was still alive, which made me belong to the living. Forty days were long enough to forget, to dry the tears, to heal the wounds, to balance the books, to even out losses with gains!

Papa, he informed me in a while, suffered a massive heart attack three days after Azra's death. No doubt, he had recovered since, but was still bedridden. The first piece of news from the outer world and yet it had to be as poignant as that! One love, encroaching upon another; one painful tragedy, making room for a different tragedy; a new phantom, rising out of the ashes of an older one; concern for the living, asserting itself over concern for the dead. My head bent, my lips quivering, my eyes streaming, my tongue lost, my ears cupped, I sat like a stone statue without venturing even to look at him.

"Is it so hard for you to face the facts and accept them?" he exhorted me. Seeing that I was making no attempt to reply, "Azra doesn't need you anymore, Yusuff! But your parents do. Your sisters do. We do, dammit! Do you know something? In the past forty days, I've aged forty years! How much more do you think I can take?"

I did not so much as lift my head, let alone answer back. His job done, he got to his feet. He knew my recourse, he had pointed out the way; it was now up to me to crawl.

"Come and see us some time, son," he added before leaving. "Children have been asking to see you."

That was one promise I simply could not make or keep. "Uncle Saleh," I said, addressing him for the first time, "You are quite right. It's about time I arranged my priorities in the proper order. I *will* go home. You and Auntie have been very kind to me all along. I respect you both and I do love your children dearly. But I don't think I'll ever be able to set foot in your house again. Simply too much of me has been lost in it."

"Well, I understand," he said in a heavy voice after some thought. "Goodbye, Yusuff. May Allah bless you."

Allah bless me! With what? He was forty days too late to do anything.

For a long time after he was gone, I sat there debating with myself. I wondered how Papa was. I wondered how my mother and my sisters coped with the crisis. Money must also be a major issue; the medical bill for his aftercare by itself must have been quite phenomenal. Whether or not my salary was still being paid by the foundation was uncertain. What a mess! I should have gone home after Azra's burial and we should have mourned her death together. But I did not. I let them down just when they needed me the most. I was not where my duty lay, all in Azra's name, thus bringing her memory into disrepute, which was wrong. In my house, she must always be remembered without reproach. Perhaps that was the reason why I never once saw her in my dreams. Perhaps she was angry with me. I had been ignoring my responsibilities, holding back my share of the contribution towards discharging my dues. So much was still outstanding, so many tangles yet to be sorted out, many other hurdles to be crossed, a lot of goals to be set and reached, so much more to be done and not a lot of time to do it all in.

My mind fully made up to return home, I mentioned it to my host first, who had, by then, become like a blood brother to me, a brother that I never had. 'I think you must. And don't worry about the grave, I'll keep an eye on it,' he said, endorsing my decision wholeheartedly. I shook his hand as well as thanked him for his kindness and his hospitality. Offering to repay the out-of-pocket expenses he must have incurred towards my upkeep felt like an insult to his generosity. My gratitude covered it all.

I could not go away without taking Azra's leave. So I went back to the grave for the last time. "Azra!" I whispered to her, "Forty days ago, you went away where I couldn't come looking for you. Now, I'm going away where you can't come looking for me. To the world outside this cemetery you renounced. I can't do the same. I've a role cut out for me in it. The show must go on, regardless, like they say. Life must go on. My journey must progress, whether or not you travel with me. Peace to you, my angel! *Al vida* ..."

With those words I turned round and walked away, taking my first step in a direction which could only increase the distance between us.

Back to square one, I commenced the arduous task of picking up the threads. My house was plunged in a curious hush, bearing the scars of the grievous wounds its occupants had sustained recently. It somehow looked crushed and crippled. The shrubs were stripped of blooms, the birds no longer sang, the roses were gone, the lawns were overgrown, even the peacock stood aloof on the parapet wall with his head cocked up, his eyes rolling and lost in gloom. There were no 'Hi, Bhaijans' from Shabbu nor any cheeky remarks from Rox. They were not even around. Mamma was in the kitchen and Papa in his room. The heart attack had left him in ruins. Lustre was gone from his eyes and charisma from his face. He looked sort of wilted. His appearance crushed my heart. Would my presence by his side in the moment of need have made any difference? The question became purely academic. Harm was done; apportionment of blames no longer a redress.

Making amends with my sisters was equally important. Roxana, more possessive between the two, and therefore, considerably rigid, rendered our reconciliation very hard. Rolling up her sleeves, she drew swords on me. 'If we were as easily expendable as that, why did you say that you loved us, that you cared, that you were there for us too?' she demanded in a sharp voice. Unmindful of the grievous lacerations her harsh reproach was inflicting upon me, she kept adding one blame to another. 'First, Azra died. Then, Papa very nearly did. Three women, up against crisis after crisis. If Shabbu Baji hadn't had the courage to hold us together, we would've gone to pieces. And where were you? You were so wrapped up in yourself, you couldn't even spare us some thought, could you?' she demanded. When the stakes went soaring so high, apologies and exculpations became unavoidable. I begged her to forgive me. 'Don't be so final and irreversible in your judgements, Rox,' I beseeched her, 'leave some room for errors too. After all, I am only a human. I never laid any claims to perfection, did I?' She finally forgave me. My words must have moved her heart, for she also broke down and cried. Not for me but for Azra. She said she had recited the Qur'aan twice already and offered its benedictions to her soul. 'May she rest in peace and enter Paradise,' she said and resolutely waited until I added a solemn *Ameen* to it.

Then there was Shabana. Suddenly straddled with a weight she was ill-equipped to carry, she seemed to have done astonishingly well. Taking charge of the helm, she steered the sinking ship away from the doldrums, got Papa admitted to the nursing home, paid off the doctor's bills, coped with the costs of medicines, comforted Mamma and held Rox's spirits. All that, without using the money Sal had lent me for the wedding, without letting it interfere with her professional obligations, without allowing anyone to grumble over my prolonged absence from work and without interrupting me in my mourning. She, too, had quite a few things to say to me and she did; she knocked down my hangovers, threw away the blindfold, crushed the cocoon in which I had sheltered myself and committed me to the rough winds.

Falling in line was not half as difficult as I had feared it to be. My job was waiting, my colleagues relieved to have me back and students pleased to see me again. They seemed to know all about Azra's death; their solidarity was demonstrated on the very first day at work with a service dedicated to her memory. By then, Mr. Raza had managed to get loudspeakers installed in every classroom in order to speed up communications and to enhance discipline. One of the teachers wrote a few touching lines of dedication, which were read out on the microphone by a young student and followed by two minutes' silence. The gesture was so kind it moved me to tears. Obviously, no one could heal my wounds, but everybody was doing whatever possible to reduce the pain.

Thus, I began to live all over again. Work offered me the most effective relief out of all my repressions and hence I clung to it. Papa made a gradual recovery, Mamma outlived her shocks, Shabbu stuck to the job and Rox passed her exams. By and large, Azra's memory receded into the background. Out of fear of being sucked back into the tragic saga again, I deliberately avoided visiting the cemetery, even for laying a random wreath. Our paths had parted; our worlds had changed; we were both trapped in two different stints of time, each completely inaccessible to the other. Keeping pace with the living does not compliment coming to a halt with the dead; they have their own separate stipulations. Resigned to one, I gave up the other. Even if Papa was no longer the key protagonist in our lives, he was still the pivot around whom we all revolved. Getting my sisters married during his lifetime became my topmost priority. He deserved the honour as well as the reward.

One day, I received an unexpected letter from Vaseem. He wrote to say that he and Uncle Saleh had both resigned their jobs at the paper mill and the whole family moved out of Hyderabad to Warrangal. After discharging their debts from the severance pay Uncle received from his employers, enough was left over to purchase some farming land and a small cottage there.

'Abbajan has admitted me to the Warrangal Polytechnic,' he wrote, 'which is approximately fifteen miles from where we live. I ride there on the bike every day. I'm glad I can work for my Diploma now.

'Our new house is quite good. We grow paddy and pulses on our land. We don't know how to farm, but we are learning fast. People around here are good and very helpful. Two men from the village work for us and take care of the crops. We haven't reaped a harvest yet, but we hear this year's yield is going to be quite good.

'Except Mahjabeen, the rest of my brothers and sisters go to the local school. She stays home, helping Ammijan with the housework just like Azra Baji used to. There is always plenty to do. Cattle need looking after every day and the vegetable patch needs regular watering. Ammijan is quite keen on her poultry and Abbajan has started keeping honeybees. It's necessary for our parents to be constantly involved in something. Otherwise, they become broody, which makes us depressed.

'We often talk about you but never in their presence because whenever your name is mentioned, they begin to cry. From time to time, Mahjabeen and I go to the lake for fishing and talk there. She is beginning to look more and more like Azra Baji. That's why she has become very special to me. If you see her, you, too, will like her. She packs my lunch every day just like Baji used to. She is also a good cook. Why don't you visit us one day? Our new house isn't as close to yours as the old one was, but not too far either. About four hours journey by train, I guess.

'I've seen Azra Baji many times in my dreams. She said she is glad that I'm going to the college again. I think she is quite happy where she is because she talks a lot. She keeps saying to me *'don't do this, don't do that,'* as if she cares. One night I told her off for leaving us behind like that and going away. She broke into tears. So far, she hasn't mentioned you, though. I thought of asking her several times if she was upset with you for any reason, but forgot. Next time she comes to see me, I will. Do you want to send her a message? If you do, write to me and say what it is. I'll be glad to pass it on.

'We miss you very much, *master saheb!* If things had gone well, we wouldn't have left Hyderabad. Your house wasn't too far from ours. I would've come every day to see Baji and you. We had made so many plans together. Whenever I remember them, it pushes me into tears. She loved me very much. One day, I might become an engineer, but she won't be around to see it.

'Well, I must stop now. If you don't come to Warrangal, it's all right. We understand. But I'll look forward to your reply, though. My parents have asked me to send you their best regards. Meanwhile, a big *Adaab arz* from all of us to all of you.'

The letter moved me but I did not reply. Neither did I go to Warrangal. Azra was dead; her house was vacated; her family had gone away; the imam was looking after her grave. There was no need to stir up the hornet's nest again. At one time, I had thought I would never be able to survive the tragedy of her death. But all that was finished. I had learnt to live without her; I had made peace with myself.

By the beginning of summer, everything got back to normal. Papa made a total recovery. Lustre returned to his eyes and charisma to his face. In spite of all our ceaseless efforts and recommendations at ministerial level, decision from the education board to grant A.I.M. the status of a recognised high school did not come through yet. When the academic session came to an end, the responsibility of running the institute for one more year was given back to me, which I accepted with utmost pleasure. Work was rewarding and at the same time kept us financially well-off. But acting upon my advice, Shabbu resigned. She had gathered enough honey for our *hive* and deserved to be left out of the rat race. I had made other plans for her.

The new season brought a fresh stock of pleasant evenings. The trials and tribulations of the painful past had driven us closer as a family. Watching Papa in his favourite cane chair on the lawns smoking his hukka pipe and Mamma sitting near him with her knitting filled me with contentment. I hoped things remained as they were and decided to make sure that they did.

One evening, as all five of us sat chatting, I broached upon the topic of Shabbu and Rox's weddings, which had become my top priority.

"Don't you think it's about time?" I asked Papa.

"Yes, it is," he agreed, a shade worried by the reminder, "But how? Where's the money?"

"You're looking at it," I said with an encouraging smile, "This is the best time to flog me, whilst I still have a job. Go on, Papa. Do it. It shouldn't be too difficult for you to find a *fat cow* with a *fat batwa* for the principal of an institute owned and run by the *Jamayyat Ul Ulema Foundation,* should it?"

"No. But are you sure?"

"If I wasn't, I wouldn't have brought it up. You know me."

"While I am, no doubt, quite anxious to get the girls wed," he said with a deep frown on his brow, "I've no wish to ruin some other girl's life for the sake of my own. Are you really sure you're ready for a new beginning?

"Yes, Papa, I am. You've my sworn word on it." I confirmed with my hand upon my head.

PART II

MR. GODFREY

CHAPTER (17)

At the end of a prolonged search with the help and guidance of his old friend, Moulana saheb, Papa found what he was looking for all along, a perfect match for me in every respect that was just waiting to be made! *Rehana Abdallah*, my chosen bride-to-be, was a novelty to all of us. Born and brought up in Bradford, UK, she was not a familiar figure to any of the Muslim households of Hyderabad. She was an *unknown factor* except for two things: unlike Uncle Saleh, her father was an extremely rich man, and unlike Azra, she was his *one and only*. I can safely add one more point to it: whilst Azra was my own choice, Rehana was not. The proposal was put forward by a professional matchmaker and accepted by Papa for reasons best known to him alone. I was not consulted and neither was my consent sought.

As Brides are seen by ladies only, Mamma and my sisters went to see her, knocking heels, talking posh, chewing *betel-rolls*, wearing gold, hopes raised, fingers crossed. I had no objections to their making a decision on my behalf; like Shabbu had once pointed out, they loved me and had good taste, which guaranteed satisfactory results. Even if talking Mamma into an unlikely pact was easy, it was not so in the case of my sisters. Especially in the case of Rox, who had already demonstrated an inflexible level of rigidity when it came to putting her finger upon a bride for her *one and only* brother. Besides, all those *birthrights* of a sister in matters of vetoing and comments that had been so rudely taken away from her on the prior occasion were back in her hands and she was firmly determined to exploit them to the fullest extent.

The bride, as I gathered from them after they returned, was a knock out, a sensation, a dream! The initial *survey report* was incredibly mouthwatering! 'Is she really that good?' 'Yep, yep' 'Build?' 'Slender and petit.' 'Height?'

'Five-foot-three.' Tall enough even by Rox's standards?' 'Oh Yep.' 'Description of hair?' 'Dark, Silken and lustrous'. 'Eyes?' 'Almond shaped'. 'Nose?' 'Slim'. 'Teeth?' 'Pearly; Colgate would gladly pay her a small fortune in return for just one smile'.' In their TV commercials?' 'Yep.' 'As the one wearing the ring on confidence?' 'Yep.' 'You sure?' 'Yep! Yep! Yep!

"Have you brought any photographs?" I asked Rox.

Even if she had, Shabbu would not let her show them to me. 'No,' she said quite bluntly, putting her foot down, 'suspense enhances expectation and expectation breeds contentment,' she argued. Besides, a review of their choice amounted to casting aspersions upon their taste. They rejected the suggestion point blank. Giving up on them, when I turned to Papa for help, he just shrugged, wearing a *don't-ask-me-I-haven't-seen-her-either* expression.

Next, it was my turn to be seen and approved by Her Father & Company Unlimited. When they came, they did not just come but *descended* upon us like the locust. Our forecourt was packed to capacity with gleaming cars, and our *haveli* choc-a-block with so many smartly dressed ladies it seemed more like the wedding itself than just a *viewing*. Mr. Abdallah, in conjunction with a large number of his experienced *quality controllers,* carried it out. At the end of a close and prolonged scrutiny, I was unanimously pronounced *fit for breeding.* He himself declared I was worth every *penny*; it seemed he was paying a lot of them for my *genes!*

Satisfaction on both sides resulted in Rehana Abdallah and Yusuff Quraishi getting formally engaged. On that occasion, no one seemed inclined to await the return of Rajjab, and for a good reason too. In spite of that minute search for the right needle in the right haystack, the girls' weddings continued to remain precariously linked with mine; for them to be able to get on with theirs, I needed to get on with mine first so that my dowry was released into Papa's hands for making the preparations! While we were already in the last lap of March, they settled for the nineteenth of April.

Proximity of the date suddenly turned the heat upon Papa who landed straight into cash flow problems. Unfortunately for him, Sal's help was no longer available as he had gone away to the US visiting friends and relatives. Clothes and jewellery became his main hurdles. There was, no doubt, a convenient 'buy now and pay later' scheme available in most shops, but like all transactions involving credit, it, too, was subject to status. With his only collateral stuck in the clutches of the bank, Papa was hardly a creditworthy customer for them—a rather nasty ordeal for one who had just recovered from coronary thrombosis! He was also very disillusioned with the business community of Hyderabad. The word of an honest man was no longer good enough for them, he complained bitterly. 'My son,' I gathered he explained to the jewellers and clothiers of *meena bazaar* 'is in the process of receiving a very lavish *baksheesh* in return for his hide', but it did not cut any ice with them. 'Aha!'—the uncompromising merchants were said to have unanimously cried, 'There's many a slip between the cup and the lip, like they say. What happens if either your son or his bride fell victim to, shall we say, *AIDS* in the meantime?' A somewhat unfortunate choice of excuses, it is also said to have drowned Papa in an ocean of fury.

However, being a man who knew how to get his eggs boiled, he somehow overcame his teething problems. The next thing I knew was, all those superb clothes bought and made for Azra were sent off to different orphanages, the jewellery part exchanged and the entire upper floor converted into warehouses for bespoke tailors and ready-made garment manufacturers once again. As I have already mentioned before, when it comes to spending money, Papa seldom looks back. Neither does Rox, who had always played a significant role in stimulating his flair for the spectacular.

While she rushed around here and there doing just that, poor Shabbu got stuck with the mundane, such as choosing the style and contents of invitation cards, preparing lengthy lists of friends and relatives, updating addresses, writing them out on envelops, sealing them, stamping them and mailing them. Our outer family being wide and the circle of our friends from all sides even wider, the scale of the task was phenomenal. But she managed to cope somehow, though without quite realising the consequences of her well-intentioned actions: as we all know, sending invitations attracts guests just like honey attracts the bees and all sorts of people began to arrive from far and near. That, in turn, gave rise to severe accommodation problems. But quite unperturbed by the sudden explosion in population, Papa resorted to setting up *refugee camps* on our lawns. It worked nicely, thanks mainly to the predictable climate of Hyderabad. Leaving sheltered premises for the ladies, men slept out of doors.

Celebrations in our house were launched with the ritual of *haldi*. The word simply stands for *Turmeric*. If you asked me what on earth has Turmeric got to do with weddings, I would stare at you with blank eyes. Frankly, I do not have the foggiest notion. But it must have some bearing because the colour of clothes given to me that day was yellow; the canopy underneath which I was made to sit was yellow; the strings of marigolds hanging from the top were yellow as was the general colour scheme of dresses worn by the ladies who dominated the event. A bunch of them sat in one corner playing the drum and singing passionate love songs about lovers separated in *autumn* and reunited in *spring*. Another bunch stood surrounding the canopy underneath which I sat, holding a large brass container filled with Turmeric paste and waiting for some sort of a signal from somewhere. When it came, there was a stampede. Within the blinking of an eyelid, I was covered from head to foot in the paste. So were the performers, each at the other's throat with a vengeance, laughing, screaming, chasing, the room in a mess, the canopy in a shambles, the whole thing aimed at triggering off the festive mood.

After it was all over and the rush subsided, I returned to my room to recover my breath. But as I lay wiping the paste off my face and hands, the very first acid test of my strength of endurance rang in the distance, shattering my respite. I heard the shrill notes of the *Shehnai*, heading towards our house, and reeled under its utterly devastating impact. It underpinned the beginning of the end between Azra and me forever and sent tremors of grief rocking through my body. Suddenly, I could not cope. In spite of my iron resolve to follow the course of my destiny, I reached the end of my tether at once. Rushing into the bathroom, I muffled my ears with cotton wool, shut my eyes, crouched on the floor and broke down into sobs. Months of repressed grief gushed out like a flood. I realised how little time had done to heal my wounds. Were it not for our wretched fate, that *Shehnai* would have come from her house. But such was not the case. The real bride for whom my heart still pined was no longer the star of the show. She had been bypassed, overtaken and forgotten. Her name had been taken out of all the footnotes in the story of my life; it had been crossed out of the fate lines on my palm; it had been nipped in the bud. Yet, there was a part of me dug in and buried underneath the hardened mound of sad recollections still refusing to let go, clinging on to a grievous past, lighting candles in its darkest recesses, groping around for the exit.

At that moment, Shabbu came looking for me. I was still in the bathroom, crouched on my knees and crying. She saw me and rushed to my side. The appearance of a friendly face that knew what I must be going through and could share and sympathise with my hidden grief exacerbated it some more. Holding her hand, I dug my face in her palms and broke into more noisy sobs.

"Isn't this where we change tracks, Shabbu?" I asked her, looking at her flushed face with tearful eyes, "Isn't this the real end between Azra and me?"

"Yes, Bhaijan, I'm afraid it is," she replied, herself getting close to tears, "but your tracks changed a long time ago. You must forget Azra because she is dead, whereas Rehana is alive and has agreed to join you at your own invitation. If you feel you can't walk alongside her, there's still time to say so. Say it and free her. But for God's sake, don't drag her into the flames in which you're smouldering. That isn't what we promised her."

"I know that," I agreed with her, "I thought my wounds have healed. I thought I was free. But I'm not, Shabbu. She's still out there, clad in a peach-coloured dress, looking at me through that window, partly concealed by a purple curtain, laughing and waving at me. How can I rub that image off my memory, Shabbu? What do people do to forget the unforgettable? How do they cope in similar situations?"

"Listen, Bhaijan," she said, hurriedly drying my face with a handkerchief. "I will not let you use Rehana as a touchstone to test your feelings. You made a deal with her, you entered into a pact of honour, and you made her some inviolable signals. Now, it's time you abided by them. You either keep your end of the bargain or you don't. What's it going to be? Will you or won't you?"

"Good grief!" I shouted at her, hurt by the inflexibility of her attitude. "You won't ever give an inch, do you? Either this or that. Yes or no. Do or die. I agree there's nothing in the middle, but can't you at least have a heart? Can't you?"

For a few moments she fell into a grim silence. Outside the room the *Shehnai* was screaming away, the pitch at its peak. There was not much time left either to seek comfort or to give it.

"Your *dowry* is awaiting you, Bhaijan," she said, firmly and finally, "A lot of money. More than we ever saw in our entire life. Wasn't that what you'd had in mind when you asked Papa to find you a bride? Wasn't it? Well, you've got it. Only, there're a few strings attached. Such as a *wife,* her whole *future,* her *happiness.* You made big plans as to how you'll spend that money: on me and on Rox. What plans did you make for Rehana?"

I shot to attention and gaped at her, stunned by the line of her argument.

"Any day, I'd rather marry a cobbler and be happy with him than buy myself a fancy husband with that kind of money!" she said and stormed out of the room.

It took me quite a while to get over that. The blow she dealt was extremely severe. It had never been my intention to marry for money only. I needed a wife too; I needed a friend. I had so much love to give, I needed someone to give it to. I was in pain and I needed someone who could assuage my wounds.

I knew Azra was dead. I knew nothing could bring her back. I had tried hard to forget her and had almost succeeded. I did not reply to Vaseem's letter. I did not go to Warrangal to look them up. I never once went back to the cemetery. It was difficult to lock her out of my mind but I managed. The moment of my surrender to her memory was a moment of my *weakness*. How could I help it? So many things had been reminding me of her. The *Rita shells* with which I shampooed my hair in the morning had reminded me of her; henna reminded me of her; the fragrance of jossticks, the sight of roses, the songs of the *laal muniyas*, the restless butterflies in the garden, the blazing sun in the azure sky, everything had been reminding me of her. All I had in my hand were a few moments in which to bid her my farewells and then lock up the doors. They too were disappearing fast. My factual bonds with her had already snapped and my notional bonds were also beginning to. Every road in front of me was a road that went *away* from her and not *towards* her. I was on one, dragging my heels, no doubt, but nonetheless progressing. Why was everyone in such a big hurry to wipe out the memory of one who had already been wiped out of existence? She had a right to be remembered, all through the next seven days, if not beyond. There, at the end of that time, on the threshold of a new beginning, we were going to part, anyway. No one would talk about her, least of all me. Except in passing, perhaps; a random reflection, a mention here or a mention there, an ode now or some poems next, that was about all. She had become superfluous to our requirements. Once a fountainhead of all my joy, she was now an unfrequented side stream; once a golden shrine, she was now mere debris. With barely seven days before the trumpets of finalities blew, it was my last chance to remember her as my love, and for her to be remembered with such love. Even that was getting to be too much … .

I came out of the room, my face dried, my tears held back, wearing a smile that had no business being on my lips. But then, there was nothing else I could do other than smile; there was no direction to take other than face forward. I had already kept the guests waiting for long enough. I seemed to have caused even a few eyebrows to rise. Where is the bridegroom? Why is he taking so long? What is holding him up? Nothing big. Nothing important. Nothing of any real consequence. Just a minor hiccup. A bit of a nuisance. A wayward stone … .

My dowry was brought by a servant amidst tight security and accompanied by the music party. Upon my emergence, the *Shehnai* stopped playing. A chair had been made ready for me in which I sat. The servant put a silver tray near my feet, covered by red muslin. I was asked to lift the cloth, which I did. For the sake of appearances, a small quantity of gold sovereigns was sent, together with a sealed envelope addressed to Papa. It could only be a bank draft towards the balance, from the bride's father to the bridegroom's. I wished Shabbu could see that. Money was not my concern either, but Rehana was. We were about to set out on a long journey together, our paths unfamiliar, our goals out of sight, committed to a lifetime and armed with hopes alone. Love was our only recourse. Without it, both of us would be doomed. I was not looking forward to such a doom and I had a firm feeling neither was she.

After delivering the money along with his employer's merry greetings, the servant went away. So did the *Shehnai* party. I, too, came back to my room. From then onwards, whenever I wanted to cry or sigh, I cried without spilling any tears and I sighed without making any sound. My faithful Azra, though, did keep me constant company. 'Don't waste yourself over me, *master saheb*,' she kept whispering in my ear repeatedly, 'you're a good man and deserve the *best*.' From what I could see, it seemed I was also getting the *best*. My bride appeared to have the *best* of both the worlds; she was rich as well as good looking. And if rumour had anything to go by, she was also a very kind and compassionate person. Just my type. I could do with her kindness and compassion. I could do with her love. I had received such a crooked deal from *Allah*; I could do with any mortal who was able to square it!

Noticing my somewhat aloof and withdrawn attitude, Shabbu became very sad. There was no need for her to, really; I did not bear her any ill feelings. Besides, she was right in whatever she said. Money was not important to her, either, and neither was a fancy husband. Nothing in life is worth ruining another life.

"You're cross with me, aren't you?" she asked me, rushing to my side at the very first opportunity, eager to put out the spark that had come between us for the first time.

"No, Shabbu, I'm not," I assured her.

"Thank you," she said kissing my hand, "The human heart has no substitutes, Bhaijan. *Sow* in it only what you wish to *reap*. Love begets love."

"Indeed!" I agreed, full of respect for her noble sentiment.

She cheered up. Our tiny misunderstanding nipped in the bud, we were friends again.

The days that followed were absolutely hectic. The endless visits of messengers from the bride's side continued, invariably accompanied by the music party, sometimes the melodious *Shehnai* and sometimes the merry *Nawbat*, depending largely upon the nature of the occasion and purpose of the visit, outwardly aimed at obtaining the bridegroom's approval of the bride's wardrobe, but in reality intended to impress our side by her affluence as well as the high esteem and affection in which she was held by her parents. If so, the glossy razzmatazz certainly had its desired effect; it did knock the breath off most of our guests. My mind made up; I, too, cooperated fully; I joked, I laughed, I sang and fell into line. It would have made life a lot easier if Rehana and I were allowed to go to the *holy shrine* and get married there, in the presence of all those invisible Angels and holy saints, but the show was important, to our families if not to us, and it went on.

On the day of the wedding I woke up to face the ultimate. A couple of men took me into the bathroom and gave me another ritual *ablution*. The towels with which I was dried were new and so were the clothes I was given to wear. As I was starting a new life, it was symbolic that I did not have any association with the past. Whatever things I had used so far were thrown away; the *sheets* on my *accounts ledgers* were wiped clean. After the 'ablution', Shabbu and Rox took over from the men folk and did an immaculate job of grooming me. When they finished, someone else came, put a turban on my head and then tied a *Sehra* to it, which consisted of long strings of fresh roses.

Based upon our horoscopes and worked out by the *Ulemas*, the time of *Nikah* was fixed at ten past eleven precisely, but in view of the distance between the two houses and the progress of a slow moving procession, we were scheduled to leave a lot sooner. One of the guests held my hand and brought me out of the house. The sound of the brass band blasting away in the distance had the same effect on me as the first note of the *Shehnai* did a few days ago. I felt my knees shiver and threaten to topple me; I felt a tingling sensation in my teeth; I felt my heart getting ready to explode; I felt the stiff collar of my *Sherwani* turn into a noose around my neck and choke me. At the end of each and every heavy step I took, the thick strings of roses swayed, letting in tiny reflections of my surroundings, the most poignant of all being the majestic *white stallion* especially decorated for the happy occasion and eagerly awaiting the arrival of his distinguished rider that day. The very sight devastated me. How many times had we not talked about the white stallion, the brass band, the red palanquin, the *Sehra*, the guests, the songs, the merry music, the bliss, the spate of joy, the currents of excitement. Thinking about all that, a bitter lump of grief stuck in my throat and I felt an insane urge to refuse to mount the horse unless I was guaranteed that its destination had been diverted from Saifabad to Aghapura, but somehow managed to dispel it. Instead, taking advantage of the cover afforded by the Sehra, I began to cry. Then I summoned Azra for the last time. She came, clad in her peach and sandalwood suit, both plaits held with yellow ribbons and hung to the front, one end of the Dopatta tied around the waist like a cummerbund, the other covering her head, wearing her favourite perfume and a smile just as refreshing, looking like an ivory doll once again, the way she was, the way she was entitled to be, the way she wanted to be remembered. Then, standing close to me, closer than ever before, she circled her arms around my shoulders, blessed me with a warm kiss on the mouth, our only kiss, her parting gift, her most precious memento, whispered a soft *al Vida, master saheb* in my ear, helped me climb the saddle, turned round and walked away on staggering steps into the dark obscurity of oblivion.

Rehana took over from there; my tributes to the dead ended and my duties to the living took over. Just as Shabbu had said, it was either do or do not, either yes or no, either go or let go. There was nothing in the middle. The gap closed forever and my thoughts centred on the woman with whom I had agreed to share my life.

We reached the bride's house in time for the auspicious moment. The proceedings began at ten past eleven sharp. First of all, surrounded by a hushed audience and addressing himself to Allah, *the Quazi* recited several appropriate passages from the Qur'aan. Then I was asked to confirm under oath that I had agreed to accept Rehana's hand in holy wedlock by my own free will. When I did, he chose three men from amongst the guests, one to act on his behalf and the other two as witnesses, instructed them to go into the ladies' wing, ask the bride the same questions asked of me and not to return without her reply either way. The men went inside, soon came back and conveyed her consent to him. After some more recitals, I was asked to repeat the conjugal vows, which I did. He then pronounced us man and wife, entered our full details in a register and obtained our signatures on it one after the other. With that the simple *Nikah* ceremony came to a satisfactory end.

Thus I came to marry Rehana, in the name of a God in whom I did not believe; by the hand of a priest for whom I had lost all respect and in accordance with a book that I no longer trusted. I believed more in myself than in Him. I did not believe in fate but I believed in the law of averages, according to which, after enduring so much grief and so many bitter disappointments, some joy was bound to come my way.

Time for blessings and greetings arrived. Overwhelmed with joy, Papa embraced me and wept; the second of his dreams had been realised at long last. Until then, Mr. Abdallah but now *Uncle Haroon*, my father-in-law, came next. His blessings were aimed at both of us, wishing us a long and happy married life, to which the *Quazi* added his own message of greetings, followed by the rest of the guests. I was welcomed in Rehana's household and she in mine with open arms and with unrestrained bliss. There was no room in it for doubts and uncertainties, for retrospections and regrets, not even for past memories. Every bit of it was swept away in the wake of such jubilations.

According to standard protocol, Uncle Haroon laid a grand feast for guests from both sides, giving us the first taste of his hospitality. Before we got up to partake in the lavish meal, I was allowed to remove the *Sehra*, which I did and looked around me. Surrounded by the close circle of his own friends, chewing *betel-rolls* and wearing *surma* in his eyes, shaking the hands extended towards him for greetings, Papa was beaming. It was his moment of triumph. No power on earth could have tempted me into denying him that. I was glad I could give him back at least something in return during his lifetime for all those hardships he had endured for us.

After the feast was over, all the men and many of the older women came home for a breather, leaving behind the younger girls to get on with preparing the bride for the most important night of her life. In sharp contrast to the copious *Falak Numa Palace* where Uncle Haroon had arranged the wedding as well as the feast, our house felt oppressively hot, crammed with so many guests. I being the star of one show that had just ended, and also of the other, which was about to begin, I was given priority treatment in the bathroom for a cool shower before taking lessons in *conjugal relations* from cousin Ifthequaar, a senior cousin who invariably performed that delightful task. He did it, with a great deal of relish too, teasing me at every opportunity he got, until I could no longer carry on with the instruction from sheer embarrassment. But the candid lesson did fill my head with all sorts of exciting ideas. I had never been in that kind of a situation before; I had never spent an entire night in the company of a woman; locked up in a room with barriers on self restraint legitimately removed; I had never had sex; never read any covert books on the subject nor looked at any pictures of nudes flaunting their private parts. To be perfectly honest about it, I did not know what a naked woman outside her apparel looked like. But upon being suddenly equipped with *carnal knowledge* as well as an active imagination to go with it, the night that was yet to begin filled with rosy expectations!

While we were busy in our house with our preoccupations, the girls left behind in the bride's house had their work cut out for them. Starting with nail varnishing her little toe, right up to and including the sprinkling of glitter in her middle parting, their laborious task of dolling up the bride carried on well into the twilight hours until we, too, got there. When we finally did, the palace filled up choc a block once again with guests from both sides, The *Shehnai*, the *Nawbat* and the band playing together in one breath, giving the memorable occasion a truly befitting grand finale. Such was the pitch of the noise, I felt my ears plugged, making it impossible for me to hear my own heartbeat, let alone the last-minute instructions on protocol being given to me from every direction.

When the moment for bidding farewells arrived, the music as well as guests were politely hushed up for the *badhai* ceremony. Being a *valediction* to the bride, it was inevitably marred by a touch of grief. Lovingly brought up since birth by her parents, Rehana no longer belonged to them. Marriage is a gamble that most Muslims take, its outcome often unpredictable. Uncle Haroon and his wife were no exceptions. They might well have spent the best part of their lives in the West, but having elected to marry their daughter in the Eastern style, they, too, had gambled away a lot. The endless rituals in their house lasted for approximately an hour or so, after which we prepared to bring the bride home. A superbly decorated red palanquin, arranged by Papa, was already waiting in their front yard to fetch her. A few moments before our departure, Uncle Haroon held me in a tight embrace and whispered an emotive admonition in my ear.

"Take care of her, Yusuff," he mumbled in a voice choking with a mixture of joy and grief, "She's a good girl and we hope the two of you will be happy together."

As far as I was concerned, there was no question of doubt about it. I had had my emotional turbulence at the start of the day but it was all gone. We were both on the threshold of a new life; making a success out of it depended entirely upon us. For once, our future was in our own hands and the key to happiness tucked away in our fists. Shabbu was so right when she said that waiting in suspense has its own thrills. In all that time, I had only heard about Rehana and heard little else other than Rehana. The knowledge that, while we drove home in a car, she, too, was on her way to join me harboured many an expectation. It filled me with a curious sense of belonging as well as of possession. I felt as though half of me was left behind—something mine out there somewhere, the distance between us already unacceptable, the delay intolerable!

In sharp contrast to the *badhai*, the *jalwa* ceremony held at our place was a mirthful affair. Being a reception given to the bride, it was enriched with joy and therefore assumed an air of exuberance. As soon as she arrived, both of us ended up in somewhat unkind hands, the final event dominated by the ladies just like the first one was. To begin with, both of us were made to sit side by side on the padded floor. All I could see next to me was just a bundle wrapped in red. Then our feet were washed in a container filled with fresh milk. Getting a bit carried away, I deliberately edged mine close enough to touch hers. The first skin-to-skin contact sent vibrations through my body. So did my first glimpse of her; I was conceded one tiny reflection of her face in a mirror, literally held at an arm's length for no more than a split second. After that, Rox put a piece of sugar candy on her shoulder and asked me to pick it up with my lips. As soon as I did it, all the ladies got together and demanded me to tell them which one of the two was sweeter—the sugar candy or the bride! How could I tell? I had tasted only one whereas the other was still outstanding. On the strength of a measly reflection in the mirror? And why not! 'My bride,' I declared proudly, which had its desired effect; the entire house suddenly came alive with deafening screams of laughter.

By the time we were left in the bridal room, the night had already risen high. The bed was festooned with rose garlands and Rehana sat on it, still hidden in her veils and still an *unknown factor*. I did not know what to expect. Sitting close to her, I slowly lifted the *ghoongat*. For the first time her face emerged from hiding. I noticed her eyes were shut; her soft cheeks were wet with tears and lips trembling. She was scared and had every reason to be. Born and brought up in England and yet out of sheer loyalty to her parents, she, too, had played herself with very high stakes.

"Don't be afraid, Rehana!" I whispered in her ear, "I hope I, too, can measure up to your expectations …"

CHAPTER (18)

That night, that wonderful, ecstatic and epoch-making night, that the most crucial night of our entire lives, when Rehana and I met for the first time, we did meet like strangers, but in less than two hours, we became the best of friends. And who would not be after so many of those intimacies and so much excitement!

Once it was all over, the raging storms subsided and peace returned, she spent quite some time cuddled in my arms, her face flushed, her mouth bathed in smiles, her dreamy eyes dwelling on mine quite avidly. Neither of us spoke; the occasion did not demand or depend upon speech. We were both submerged. Then, after a brief while, seemingly inspired by a bright idea, she began to run her fingers through my hair, giving it a new style each time.

"Sorry, sweetheart," I commented dryly, "it won't work. I already tried the exercise before and abandoned it. As the saying goes, he who's born ugly dies ugly ..."

She smiled. The large and gleaming eyes lit up. Watching the multiple expressions in them was a sheer delight. I kissed both the lids one after the other.

"Is there a bathroom attached?" she asked me.

"Yes, there is. But why?"

The smile accentuated and the eyes glittered like gemstones.

"Dirty man!" she whispered shyly. "I must wash myself ..."

"Is this really necessary?"

"Well, I was asked to."

"Oh? By whom? Not by Cousin Ifthequaar, I hope?"

"Who's he?"

"He's Cousin Zulfequaar's brother."

"And who're they?"

"Uncle Shehryaar and Auntie Jannisaar's sons."

"Pardon?"

"A senior cousin of mine who's is an expert on sex. In fact, it was he who told me what to do tonight, where to plant my seed. 'There's a general misconception amidst the untaught youth,' he said, 'that babies come from belly buttons. Well, they don't. It's only a false door. In fact, it's a human *cul-de-sac* that you can't crash through, negotiate or argue with. So, do yourself a favour and leave hers alone because women do react violently to men who take anything below their waistline for granted. *'Sow only where you wish to reap from!'* And that is precisely what I did; I sowed where we can reap from one day in the future! How does my knowledge of *Human Agronomy* grab you, eh?"

She burst into laughter first, then quickly bit her tongue and checked herself.

"When Daddy hired some private eyes to investigate you and report back to him," she whispered conspiratorially in my ear, "they paid you all sorts of glowing tributes and told us what a nice bimbo you are. What they didn't tell us was, you're also the funny guy.

"Well, you know now.

"Yes, I do. But I've got some news for you too."

"Oh? What might that be?"

"I suffer from three bad habits: I cry easy, I laugh easy, and if I can't do either of them, I faint."

"You do, eh? The funny thing is, when my daddy hired some private eyes to investigate you and report back to him, they paid you all sorts of glowing tributes and told us what a nice bambina you are. What they didn't tell us was, you also suffer from these three highly contagious diseases."

"Ha! Ha! Ha! Well, you know now. Where's the loo?"

I showed her. She went in, had a quick shower and came out. Rox had thoughtfully stocked up the dressing table with all sorts of cosmetics. While she sat in front of the mirror brushing her dishevelled hair and touching up her worn out makeup, I took my turn in the bathroom. By the time I finished, she had started to sort out the bed.

"What do you think you're doing?" I asked her.

"What does it look like?" she asked me.

"Meddling with vital evidence," I declared.

"Pardon?" she demanded.

"That was another thing Cousin Ifthequaar asked me to make sure. 'Whatever else you do, for God's sake don't change the bed sheets on the nuptial bed,' he instructed me, 'as they happen to be the only incontrovertible proof that your wife was a *virgin* until you *interfered* with her.' Comprehende?"

She broke into laughter again. A physically exacting night, following on the heels of an equally exacting day, wore us out and we fell asleep.

When the day broke, we were woken up by the maid's knock. I got out of bed and let her in. She barged into the room and threw me out. I landed straight into Papa's lap.

"Well?" he asked me, polishing his lenses with a clean handkerchief. "Isn't she good?"

"Papa, please ..." I protested.

"Generation gap!" he muttered disapprovingly, "In this day and age, children simply don't want to confide in their parents and their peers. When I got married and my uncle asked me the same question, I told him everything."

"Papa, please ..."

In our households, the routine that follows the nuptials is a sound public relations exercise aimed at promoting goodwill and harmony between two entirely unconnected families who had been brought together by virtue of a marriage arranged by an equally unconnected professional broker. Frankly, until both sides accepted the proposal, we did not know anything about them and they did not know anything about us, apart from some information gathered by word of mouth. Hence, social intercourse between the two families positively began on day one of the marriage with a formal invitation to me to spend the next three days in Rehana's house, and a similar invitation extended to her to do the same in mine, all culminating in the *Walima* feast, which was hosted by my family but organised by the new mistress of the house. So, whilst the ladies became worriedly engrossed in trying to undo the harm I had done to Rehana, I quickly helped myself to breakfast and got into a waiting car. Pretty soon she, too, joined me, once again transformed into a red bundle.

They lived in a very large, ultra modern house situated in Saifabad, built for them to their own design and specifications. It contained every conceivable comfort and luxury, including air conditioning in all the bedrooms and air-cooling in the rest. As soon as stepping into it, I felt as though I had just emerged out of baking desert sands and walked straight into paradise. Quickly introducing me to her mother, Rehana excused herself for a while, got the maid to take our bags upstairs into the bedroom earmarked for us, freshened up a bit, changed and came back. Very much a *sari* and a *single plait* person, she had the elegance and the figure to go with both. Though their only child, and consequently well taken care of, she was neither spoilt nor mollycoddled. On the contrary, she seemed to be the pivot around which the entire household revolved. The maid took orders from her alone; her mum let her do all the running around and her dad, too, seemed to rely upon her for most of his own needs. Without wasting too much time on transforming from a new bride into a seasoned housewife, she got cracking with the domestic chores with amazing alacrity and competence. Having anticipated that the next three days were going to be rather hectic, with loads of her relatives already lined up to see her bridegroom, not to mention visits from my family in order to get to know them, she politely urged me not to stand on formalities but to shout for attention if I needed some. Reassuring her that I would, I left her to get on with her duties and concentrated upon familiarising myself with her parents.

Uncle Haroon, in his mid-fifties, slim, tall, alert, agile, health conscious, at the same time, quite chatty and pompous too, mostly dominated the conversation. I came to know from him that he was a major exporter of mica to the West and did a roaring trade. Even though he worked from an office situated in an outer Borough of London called Corydon and mostly spent all five days of the working week in a separate house in Bromley, which he had bought for himself for that purpose, his choice of Bradford for setting up the family home was deliberate. An attractive West Yorkshire city in the Midlands, it had a large concentration of Asian Muslims, many of them quite affluent and successful people. They had mosques in prime locations, single sex schools for girls only with Islamic and Arabic studies as part of their curriculum, shopping precincts that mostly catered to the specific needs of their Asian customers, good cinema halls, which showed Indian and Pakistani movies only and many other facilities. The result was, in spite of living in the West for so long, they were able to remain practising Muslims, conserving time-honoured traditions as well as retaining cultural identity in matters of food, apparel and language. That, he pointed out to me, accounted for Rehana's preference towards wearing saris, speaking fluent Urdu, offering regular *namaaz*, fasting without fail during the month of Ramadan and observing all the other Islamic festivals. But above all, it also explained how she had consented to an *arranged marriage*.

In sharp contrast to her husband's incredible capacity to hold the reigns of conversation in his hands, Auntie Zeenath was a different kettle of fish altogether. Quiet, composed, reticent and yet affable, she was a woman with a smiling face who struck a cord with me at once. There was something quite impelling about her that exuded confidence and inspired trust. Right through my lengthy chat with Uncle Haroon, she sat alternating her attention between me and the nutcracker with which she was crushing *supari* nuts for making *paans* after the guests arrived. Looking at her, as at Rehana, it was impossible to believe that they had spent the best part of their lives in a country with which they had so little in common. Frankly, I could not be more at home if I had married the grand daughter of *Nawaab Mukarram Jah* and was being entertained in the Morning Room of the *Gulshanara Palace* by *Begum Mukarram Jah* herself! Both mother as well as daughter looked so refreshingly indigenous to the country of their origin, they had not let themselves be diluted in any way into a foreign culture by which they were constantly surrounded.

As far as Rehana herself was concerned, she exceeded even my wildest expectations. Our temperaments were well suited; we were on the same wavelengths; we experienced no difficulty whatsoever in establishing a rapport, in understanding each other, in sizing up our requirements, in reading each others thoughts, in being good partners. Probably accustomed to taking care of others more than being taken care of, she was an amazingly ongoing person, cool as a cucumber even in the hottest of moments. Inclined to listen first and talk later, to negotiate before arguing, to sit before running, to give before taking, she made an enterprising companion, a dependable friend and an astute supporter. I fell in love with her head over heels. Not the sort of mercurial passion that either quavers or shatters, but something stable, something solid, something steady, something longer lasting. For a person like me—the tender pupa that had traded away its cocoon to the ill winds of misfortune—she was just the sort of an outer layer I desperately needed to wrap around me for protection. Having so accidentally found someone like her for a life partner, an year or so ago I would have probably spread the mat and gone down on my knees to thank the Divine Croupier for dealing me a good hand at long last and transforming my fortunes at the gambling table, but I did not. For understandable reasons, my heart went out more to the matchmaking skills of Moulana Saheb for setting up such an ideal target, and to the shooting skills of Papa for scoring the bull's-eye!

In the course of those three days, my own folks too made several visits to their house. In our households, we look upon marriages not only as the coming together of two different individuals but also of two entire families. That was precisely what happened in our case too; the Quraishis joined hands with the Abdallahs in a big way. On several occasions all the *purdah* restrictions were waived, which gave Uncle Haroon the opportunity to meet my mother and sisters and Auntie Zeenath to say hello to my father. For the first time since setting the ball into motion, he came face to face with Rehana too. An invincible conqueror of hearts, she won his without much effort and became his instant favourite. And why not! After all, having breezed into our lives from over the other side of the Himalayas and the Alps, she was destined to replace his daughters pretty soon and give him, by herself, the same amount of love that he had been receiving from two.

On the fourth day, both of us returned to our house, all set for the main *Walima* feast, to be organised entirely by the bride. It was as big a feast as the one that had been laid out by Uncle Haroon in the *Falaknuma Palace* on the day of the wedding. Only, on that occasion, *we* were the hosts, entertaining guests from both sides, but masterminded by Rehana with a helping hand from Mamma and the girls. Being her first major responsibility in her new home, the significance of the event could not be stressed enough. She was in the hot seat with the spotlight turned straight upon her. It was not only a test of her competence as a hostess but also an open acknowledgement of her primacy over my sisters. Enter Rehana, exit Shabbu and Rox! If a little harsh, that is how things are done. But then again, they, too, would similarly preempt their sisters-in-laws in the homes of their husbands after they got married. All a matter of simple tradition, it is accepted in a spirit of give and take.

Even though no one ever doubted the outcome, the feast was a grand success. Keeping things under firm control, making as much use of the casual maids as of the professional chefs, attention to detail meticulous at all times, without once given either to oversight or to negligence, without dropping her cool, without causing anyone any offence, she slaved away all day, almost as if she had spent her entire life behind wood-fired ovens, and managed to emerge on top. She seemed to have an inborn flair for running things with a positive attitude, for motivating crowds, obtaining results, making friends, inspiring fans, combining lenience with firmness, taking the rough with the smooth. Yet there was nothing in her behaviour or her attitude that even remotely suggested inexperience, indecision, spite, vanity or self-approbation. If at all, there was any pride on display, it reflected only on the animated faces of her own parents watching their young daughter succinctly discharge not only the first major responsibility of her married life but inarguably of her entire life!

By the time we finished, it had already gone well past the hour of midnight. Every joint in my body virtually dislocated, I helped myself to a cool shower, changed and waited for her in our bedroom. Soon she, too, arrived, clad in a delightful sari, adorned with jewellery, fresh and fragrant, hair neatly styled, face done up, wearing some pleasant perfume and an equally pleasant smile, making it all look more like the beginning of an exciting night than the end of an exacting day. There was not even a hint of impatience in her mien or a crease of fatigue on the face. When I stretched my arms towards her, she walked into them; when I kissed her, she kissed me back; when I thanked her, she thanked me back.

"Tired, Mrs. Quraishi?" I asked her.

"Yes, Mr. Quraishi," she replied, messing up my hair and restyling it as usual. "But why? What've we got on mind?"

"Quite a lot," I replied, carefully rearranging her hair to my own fancy. "We took the cake out of you, didn't we?"

"Hmmm," she agreed, the smile emphatic, the looks meaningful and inviting. "So far, I've rendered unto Caesar whatever belongs to Caesar. But that which belongs to God, it is set aside for God alone ..."

A delightful invitation, extended in an astonishingly subtle manner, the message came through with impeccable grace. But that night, it was my turn to serve her. She had done enough. Much more than making a success out of the *Walima* feast, she was well on her way to making a success out of our marriage. She changed my thinking; she reerected my goals; she literally gave me a new lease on life. All that, in four wonderful days of togetherness, an entire future ahead of us filled with similar ones.

"*Begum Saheba*!" I quietly whispered in her ear. "If that was a proposition, I was never made one better."

"*Janaab-e walla*!" she whispered back, matching word for word and look for look. "If that was a compliment, I was never paid one richer."

Brains too, as though beauty was not enough! Helping her rest her back against the pile of pillows I had already arranged for her on the bed, I gently massaged her shoulders. Her eyes did not leave my face and neither did the smile fade.

"Tell me something, Rehana," I said somewhat broodily. "You have raised my hopes so high, sometimes I feel terribly scared. You won't dash them, will you?"

"Perish the thought! Don't you have faith in me?"

"Faith did not get me too far. I tried it once before," I replied, dropping the first hint of my past misfortunes.

"Then you must try again," she stressed. "And again and then again! Was it not what the tiny *spider* told the mighty *Caliph* as he lay hiding from his enemies inside a ditch?"

Upon a sudden impulse, I decided to tell her all about my tragic love affair with Azra. She had a right to be told, by me first before she came to know from others. Women are known to be somewhat touchy about such matters. Hurting her feelings was the last thing I wanted to do. I had found someone like her by sheer chance. Just as I was beginning to relinquish all hopes of being happy ever, she had stepped into my life like a rare blessing. I learnt from her how to love and laugh all over again; gathering precious moments of bliss scattered by her, I was amassing a new wealth of joy. If I was not cautious, the conspiracy of inopportune circumstances, could hit me once again, by the connivance of evil stars, by the assertions of cruel fate, by the unsparing dictates of my own unpredictable destiny. That was the one thing I dared not risk. Without meaning to, without wanting to, without having to, Azra could so easily cast a shadow between us. I could not afford that, either. Her memory was equally precious and just as sacrosanct. Letting my present to be destroyed by my past—one love by another—seemed wrong. So, rolling all those thoughts in my mind, I went ahead and told her everything. She listened to my sad narrative with sympathy, calm and quiet, eager and attentive, without any interruptions, without any impatience, sometimes stirred, sometimes moved, sometime sad, but never once hurt.

"Thanks for telling me," she said when I finished. "I feel honoured. But I knew all about it. Your parents told my parents and they told me."

"Oh? Really?"

"Un hunh," she said effortlessly. "I'm not a greedy person. I'll gladly settle for half of that love. Giving it away?"

"All that and much more! Sure you can handle it?"

"Try me," she said and returned to my arms.

In the course of the weeks that followed, our house turned into Paradise. Soon after the long distance and short distance guests departed, everything returned to normal. Uncle Haroon went away on a business tour of the country, meeting his mica suppliers and Auntie Zeenath got busy with her own socialising. Rehana, as she should, became a part and parcel of my family. Her rich parents had left a big car at her disposal. She took us out on one shopping spree after another, sometimes dragged us to picnics in the public gardens, or over to the movies. Her friendship with my sisters flourished; she loved them; she took care of them; and as the spouse of their older brother, she also felt responsible for them. To me, she was not the island in the midst of nowhere that I searched, but a traveller who shared the ship in which I sailed; she was not the beacon that guided me to safety but a life jacket that protected me from drowning; she was not the oasis concealed in the camouflage of treacherous mirages but the grove of date palms underneath which I reposed; she was not just the rider of a *chariot of dreams* but the owner of a piece of paradise towards which her *unicorns of bliss* were heading! She was the reward of my toils; she was the goal of my race; she was my finishing line; she was the only one next to Azra whose *chapattis* I could relish with equal zeal; she was the one on whose shoulders I could rest my head; in whose arms I could fall asleep; on whose lap I could rise awake.

In the midst of such peace and tranquillity, a vague hint of trouble appeared on the distant horizon soon after Uncle Haroon returned from his tour. First of all, his chauffeur came to our house and took away the car. A few hours later, he and Auntie Zeenath dropped in to break bread with us. We were delighted to have him back. Rehana more than the others; after all, he was her father. A thoughtful man, he brought many attractive gifts for everyone, all in good taste. Initially, the conversation dwelled upon matters of universal interest. His tour featured in it from time to time, so did his suppliers, the pitfalls and tripwires of his business, the appalling road conditions in South India, the deteriorating standards of hotels, the sharp contrast in weather between one place and another. We listened to him as well as made random contributions to the chat. They had supper with us and left.

Three days later, we came to know that a tentative date had been finalised for their departure to London. Rehana took the news in her stride, without demonstrating any signs of stress. It was, she assured me, an inevitable outcome of marriage and had been expected, so I gave her the benefit of doubt and kept quiet.

On Thursday night, Papa asked me to take a day off work on the following Monday. "Any special reason?" I enquired, at that stage out of mere curiosity.

"You and I have an appointment to see Haroon's solicitor. Someone called Mr. Rao."

"Oh? What about?"

"God knows," he replied with a big shrug.

I, too, said no more. Asking Rehana about it seemed pointless. If she knew, she would have already told me; we did not keep any secrets from each other. Besides, there had been nothing about her attitude that suggested worry. No doubt, on account of non-availability of transport since her father's return, all shopping sprees had been temporarily suspended, but inside the house the fun and frolic were still going strong.

On Monday morning, Uncle Haroon's chauffeur brought the car to pick us up. We were told that his boss was already with the solicitor and was waiting for us. The unexpected change in my routine did not miss Rehana's attention but no attempt was made by her to pry. She never pried.

Mr. Rao's office was situated on Abid Road—a haven for the rich. When we got there, the receptionist escorted us into his large office at once. In his early fifties and somewhat on the flabby side, he sat behind an impressive desk, in the company of his client. First of all, we were introduced. I kept my mouth shut and let Papa do all the talking, whatever it be. Speaking for myself, I was already quite aspersed by the whole affair. If Uncle Haroon had anything important to convey to us, I failed to see the need for a mediator.

A plain-speaking man, Mr. Rao finally explained what it was all about. It seemed Rehana and I were required to be remarried by a civil registrar of marriages. The suggestion itself sounded quite preposterous but I did not say a word. When it came to such things, Papa himself was a rather hard nut to crack. I was sure he would deal with the situation in his own way.

"Why?" he asked Mr. Rao, looking just as outraged.

"To enable your son to go to UK," Mr. Rao replied.

That was the first time I had heard about it. When Papa negotiated my marriage without my involvement in the decision-making, I had let him. But for the same reason, if Uncle Haroon had decided to run my life, he was in for a big disappointment. I had no intentions of going anywhere away from Hyderabad, be it to Bradford, or be it to Timbuktu.

"What has his going to UK got to do with a civil marriage? As it is, they are legally and quite legitimately married to each other, aren't they?" Papa asked him pointedly, showing signs of impatience.

The question brought the whole thing out into the open. It seemed, in order to be able to enter UK on matrimonial grounds, I needed an entry permit issued by the British High Commission in Bombay. Whilst marriages performed by Quazi were not necessarily deemed invalid, they were often viewed with plenty of suspicion, and applicants without proper marriage certificates issued by the civil registrars were seldom given the permit without they being thoroughly flushed out. Besides, the new Immigration Act in Britain had imposed further restrictions upon issuing permits on grounds of matrimony alone, except where there were legitimate extenuating circumstances. Why complicate matters, if they could be resolved by submitting a simple marriage certificate, Mr. Rao argued.

"Is there anything else?" Papa asked him soon after he finished.

"I'm afraid there is," Mr. Rao replied, restlessly shifting his weight from lap to lap, "The Entry Clearance Officer normally requires proof that your son and his wife were reasonably well acquainted with each other before they got married."

"In other words," Papa snapped without any hesitation, "he requires proof of *pre-marital courtship*. Am I right?"

"Broadly speaking, yes."

"And how on earth are you planning to overcome that?"

"By manufacturing evidence. What else can we do? Rules are rules."

"I see," said Papa, swallowing a sour lump of disapproval. "And have you considered the implications of an overriding civil marriage upon the existing religious marriage as well as all its broader ramifications?"

"Yes. But do we have to go into that now?"

"You may not, but I do," Papa said. "Unless, of course, my son and his wife don't mind living in sin for the rest of their lives, and bringing up illegitimate children. Why don't you ask them? It's their life, not mine."

Suddenly, objections raised by Papa towards the suggestion put him straight on a collision course with Uncle Haroon. The very thought stifled my breath ... .

CHAPTER (19)

In desperate need of time to concentrate on the issues that emerged in course of our meeting with Mr. Rao and to coordinate my thoughts before confronting Rehana, I asked the chauffeur to drop me off at the institute, which he did. There was plenty of work to do and I got on with it, but my mind was not on anything except her. Suddenly, I felt terribly scared. What Uncle Haroon had extended to me was not a casual invitation to go to my wife's country on a sightseeing tour, but by bringing into it a solicitor, even if he was a family friend, he had given the matter a more serious tone. Was Rehana aware of it? Was the idea his own brainchild or was it a joint decision taken by the entire family? More than all that, was it an afterthought to the marriage or was it an expectation upon which the marriage itself was based? Why was I not consulted on a matter of such magnitude and proportions until the very last moment? Was it merely because they assumed that I, too, would welcome the heavensent opportunity of settling in the more prosperous West just like umpteen other young men in my plight who had excellent academic qualifications but no prospects of career advancement? Did they make a genuine mistake of blindly taking it for granted that whatever was good for *Zakr* must also be good for *Bakr*? Or was there something more to it than what met the eye?

The very thought blew the lid off the Pandora's box and let loose a whole series of other equally unsettling thoughts. Was my wife aware of what was going on? Was she, too, expecting me to move to England and pitch my tent there? No doubt, for a budding young woman like her, born and brought up in the West, her agreeing to an arranged marriage by itself was a challenging accomplishment. But did she agree to it entirely out of loyalty to her parents and respect for her tradition, or was it because the proposition was offered to her with a few strings attached that made it seem interesting and persuaded her to take the plunge? Even though she had done such a marvellous job of adopting herself to our way of life in a very short time, did she do it because of her spirit of enterprise or was she only compromising with a bad situation out of sheer expedience? Was she really as happy in her new home and in the midst of people with whom she had come to share her life as she was pretending to be? Or was it merely a public relations exercise? Given a choice, what would she herself prefer to do? Would she agree to spend the rest of her life making *chapattis* on wood-fired ovens, being bitten by mosquitoes, being festered by cockroaches, harassed by flies, chased by bats, frightened by geckos racing around on ceilings, vexed by rats having the run of the kitchen after nightfall? Was that the sort of life she had bargained for? Were those the sort of humid nights and oppressive days for which she had traded away the comforts of a luxurious house provided for her by her rich father? What was so special about me for whom she had made those sacrifices; put the Alps and the Himalayas between herself and her beloved parents; given up her friends; relinquished her lifestyle; turned her back on all those flashy cars and motorways; the glamorous shopping centres; the cologne sprays that kept her body refreshed; the blow driers and curlers that lent magic to her hairdo; the shower gels and foam baths that protected her delicate skin; all those umpteen little things that added quality to life and enhanced its simple joys? Frankly, she had not even seen me until the night of our nuptials; she was not in love with me like Azra was; she did not have to talk herself into giving up so much for so little. So, why did she upset the applecart, for herself as well as for me?

I needed to find that out, from her more than from anyone else. I needed to be aware of her feelings, be in tune with her thinking, keep the records straight between us, mend the breaches as soon as they occurred, bridge the gaps if some had opened up in order to avoid heartbreaks later on. Even though I did at one time contemplate on going abroad in pursuit of livelihood, I had changed my mind about it. In spite of the progress we made as a family, I still pretty strongly felt that my duties towards my parents and my sisters were far from over. Getting the girls married was not an end in itself; if anything, it was only the beginning. Mamma and Papa were at such a ripe old age they had to be relieved of family pressures and set free to concentrate upon their other priorities. Every arranged marriage being a gamble, the girls desperately needed a pillar of strength to lean on in moments of their need. To them, I was that pillar, and I wanted my availability to them in such moments guaranteed and not left to chance. But what about Rehana? What about her rights as a wife as opposed to my duties as a son and a brother? What about the rights of a wife to shape the course of her married life? To plan ahead for the family which would soon come into being as a result of marriage? To think about our children, her children, her plans for them, her hopes and her aspirations? What about her right to determine the venue in which we would pitch our tent together? What if, soon after coming to know all about the small print of my job, about the real long-term prospects of the principal of a tutorial institute being run on an *ad hoc* basis by the *Jamayyatul Ulema Foundation*, she had become disillusioned, perhaps even got worried, and herself suggested it to her father to arrange for my emigration to her own country? What if, by reason of her Western upbringing, she did not consider the mechanics of her marriage as important as its spirit or its essence? What if, on the portfolio of a modern girl's priorities, religious beliefs did not feature as prominently as facts of life did? What if she was prepared to bend the rules a little bit for the sake of common sense? What if she did not see eye to eye with Papa that getting remarried by a civil registrar really amounted to living in sin and bringing forth illegitimate offspring?

I needed to sort out that too with her. I knew precisely why Papa objected to an overriding civil marriage. In a country like mine, Secular in constitution and yet crammed with a large multi religious population, making concessions to different communities in matters governing their private relations becomes unavoidable. Since Islam does not recognise any form of marriage other than a *Nikah* performed by a *Quazi* and in the prescribed way, Muslims are allowed to follow the Mohammedan Law. By the same token, Hindus are permitted to conform to the *Bhagawath Geeta* and Christians to the Holy Bible. But enshrined within the framework of legislation, there is also the marriage performed by the civil registrar, which overrides all the others. Wherever a religious marriage has been subsequently superseded by a civil marriage, it is thenceforth governed by entirely different set of rules that are quite often in clash with religious stipulations. In the case of Muslims, such an overriding civil marriage does seriously interfere with the preaching of the *Qur'aan* and therefore renders the *Nikah* void for many reasons. For instance, whilst a marriage performed by a *Quazi* can also be annulled by the *Quazi* on grounds prescribed in the *Qur'aan,* a civil marriage can only be annulled by a judge and upon entirely different grounds that do not have much in common with most of the Qur'aanic recommendations. Again, whilst Islam permits Muslim men to have more than one wife, provided there are extenuating circumstances, courts deem bigamy a crime. Whereas children born of wedlock performed by civil registrars are lawful and legitimate in the eyes of the law, Islam unequivocally considers children born of any union other than the *Nikah* illegitimate. The entire issue is so complex there is no such thing as *two plus two makes four* about it. Himself a practising Muslim, Uncle Haroon must be well aware of the situation and had yet come up with the contentious suggestion. I needed to explain it all to Rehana in full and with my own mouth, so that there was no room for misunderstanding, and a decision as crucial as that was taken by both of us in the full knowledge of all its ramifications.

Soon it was five and the bell rang. The institute plunged into its habitual tumult of rearranging the furniture, of noisy footfalls, of conversation and laughter, of *khuda hafizes* and *Fi amaanAllahs*, marking the end of one more tiring day. Anver and the other admin staff also wished me good night and left. Once they were all gone, the *Ghurkha* commenced his rounds, noticed I had not touched the coffee brought by the *chaprasi* earlier on, asked me if I would care for another hot drink and then carried on with his business. Within a matter of moments, the building plunged into a poignant hush, broken only by the squeak of his leather shoes. The wall clock kept ticking; loose sheets of note paper underneath the paper weights rustled rapaciously to the incoming gusts of evening breeze; a wandering fly trapped in the spider's web on the wall kept buzzing and making futile attempts to free itself while its captor accelerated its pace to bind the victim with ruthless tenacity, reminding me very much of my own piteous plight. My mind focussed on it alone and lost to the rest of the world, even to the rapidly advancing hands of the clock eating up the time. I simply sat sinking and surfacing in a cloud of confusion. The more I thought about it, the more convinced I became that Rehana could not have made any long-term plans for us, or even remotely involved herself in making them without the courtesy of a consultation with me first. Though those were still early days to suss her out beyond doubt, I was sure of that much. To ask her views on the matter was not difficult; to expect her support and her loyalty was not improbable; to hope for a quick resolution of the issue was not farfetched. But it was the fear of coming into an implacable conflict with her so soon after our marriage was what really raged an endless havoc upon my nerves. I could not afford its staggering price; I could not survive a second fatal blow so soon; I could not visualise my life without her as my partner; I could not let anything come between us. If Uncle Haroon had asked me to refund the dowry he had given me in return for letting my wife and me make up our own minds over such crucial matters, I would have gladly done it.I had rich friends, and I knew how to beg. But he was aiming at some other direction, the only direction to which I could not afford him access.

The long hours of the evening passed away in silent debate, in total confusion, in endless fear. Before I realised it, it was already ten. No one at home knew of my whereabouts since 5 p.m. when the working day came to an end, and I had not phoned to tell them that I was safe. Barely a few weeks from bridehood, Rehana panicked quickly. And if Papa had told her whatever transpired at Mr. Rao's office, she was likely to worry even more. Nobody had done anything to hurt us yet and we were already under the toll of punishment. Only, the physical distance between us at that moment was something I could easily bridge. A short ride in the rickshaw was enough to unite us; a simple apology to placate my conscience and an affectionate hug to restitute her torment; all of which was within my means. But what Uncle Haroon and his solicitor friend had proposed was entirely different. A crippling blow, it could kill.

When I got home, the situation was worse than I had expected. Dressed and dolled up as usual to welcome me home from work, Rehana was pacing the outside veranda along with Rox, her face drawn, her smile gone, her eyes moist, and her body tense. The extent of relief my emergence brought to her face was so infinite, mere explanations and apologies seemed too simple an option to redress her torment. Feeling quite ashamed of myself, I did not even attempt to offer them. But Papa, seldom blowing his top from anger, came down on me like a ton of bricks. He was so furious at me for not phoning home to say I was safe, he did not even bother to ask me where I had been for so long and what had held me up. He only talked about *her*, how much grief I had caused *her*, how insensitive I was towards *her* feelings, how wrong it was of me to have made *her* suffer like that.

"She doesn't deserve to be treated like this," he shouted at me for the first time since I was a little child, "and don't you ever do it again, not in this house, not whilst I'm still around. Is that clear?"

As we sat around the dining table, Rox served us food in the usual way. Conversation was sparse; the mood still heavy; the air fraught with tension and everyone completely ill at ease. On any other day, under different circumstances, such a laudable demonstration of mutual solidarity and concern would have made me really proud. But that night was an exception. My wife and I had suddenly come at an unexpected crossroad that did not display any signposts and it was uncertain in which direction we would turn; together or alone; towards a common destination or towards separate goals.

When we retired to our room, the ponderous mood carried on. Instead of changing and preparing for bed, I dropped in the easy chair without speaking while she stood by the door leaning her back on it. Silence in the room became disturbingly profound; the distance between us seemed deceptively unbridgeable; the straps that held us apart felt threatfully strong. She had a grievance and I had a worry, both justifiable, both cancerous, both in need of eviction and yet stuck in our throats. Ironically enough, her distress and my fears were the outcome of the same crisis and yet we were trying to resolve it from different platforms. For the first time since getting married, it seemed as if we had lost our common ground.

Breaking the stalemate at long last, she took the first step and rushed towards me. Even though I locked her in my arms, my worried eyes remained pinned to the door behind her, afraid that Uncle Haroon might walk in any moment and take her away from me.

"I know what this is all about," she whispered to me softly, taking hold of my hand and tightening her clasp on it. "Mum told me everything."

"If you knew, why didn't you talk it through with me first?" I asked her, because I had to.

"Nobody talked it through with me, either," she replied in a passive tone, "I phoned Mum and asked her where you and Papa had gone off to in Dad's car *after* you left, when she told me for the first time what's happening."

"Whose idea was it then?"

"Not mine. Presumably Dad's, even though he hasn't discussed it with Mum either."

"Well?" I asked her, looking deep into her moist, gleaming, opulent, eloquent eyes. "What about you, Rehana? On which side of the Himalayas and the Alps is it going to be?"

"It makes no difference to me which side, so long as we're together."

"And what about your daddy?"

"I can't obey two masters at one and the same time. It would have to be either you or him. You tell me whom I must."

"You'll back me? Against your own father?"

"That's what he had asked me to swear to, when I was a bride."

I said no more. She had made herself absolutely clear. Her love, richer than her father's wealth, abounded. She not only took her conjugal vows but was also honouring them. She was a wife first and only then a daughter. I locked her even tighter in my arms, no longer looking at the door, no longer uncertain, no longer afraid. We were united in our crises and working things out between ourselves, which was great!

To the best of my knowledge, she did not even bother to talk it over with her dad. They visited us on the very next day but no mention was made about the unsavoury incident at Mr. Rao's office. Papa talked to them as if nothing had happened. The conversation around the dining table was pleasant and effortless. On account of one thing or another, the date of their departure had not been changed, which was a great relief, at least to me. The less the chances of our loyalties being put on trial, the better off we were.

When it was time for them to go, we all went to the airport to see them off. Their departure, understandably, was marred by a touch of grief. While Rehana was quite accustomed to her father's absences from home, it was the first separation between mother and daughter. Both of them kept bursting into sobs.

Before the final farewells, Uncle Haroon took me aside and whispered a quiet word in my ear. "Don't take any note of what happened at Mr. Rao's office, Yusuff," he said. "Just call it an old man's whim, if you like. Your happiness is what counts more than anything else. And of that, there are plenty of signs in evidence. May Allah bless you both."

I thought it was nice of him to say so. My clever wife seemed to have beaten her daddy without even moving a finger or uttering a word. I could see in her a resolute sentry tenaciously guarding the frontiers of my life. I had a feeling she would not allow anyone to intrude upon its sacrosanct borders. If a little modest and egregious, it was ours together.

The grief of their parting did not last longer than the sound of their aircraft. The car was back in Rehana's exclusive use and she drove us home herself. Perhaps one of the plus points of Western lifestyle, she was very bold. I could not visualise my sisters driving such a big car through the chaotic traffic of our old fashioned city. I did, however, notice a curious glint in Rox's eyes clearly indicating that her head was beginning to fill with new ideas; but if she ever got 'round to trying her hand at driving, I hoped Papa would put his foot down. With that sort of a crazy *child* behind the steering, the very lives of all the other road users could be in serious jeopardy!

As of that day, a noticeable change came over Rehana. All those tireless outings and extravagances suddenly stopped. Apart from taking Papa to the *Mo'azzam Jahi Market* or Shabbu and Rox to the superstore for groceries, she pretty much stuck to the house and fell into a routine. We did go to watch the movies now and then, as well as had picnics over weekends on clear days in order to break the monotony, but that was about all. I went to work regularly while she concentrated upon household matters. Most of the knitting and sewing gadgets she had brought along with her from England came out of hiding and were put to use. Mamma and the girls learnt many new things from her and she from them in turn. Apart from that, on account of her western upbringing, she spotted the intrinsic value of all those umpteen antiques and artefacts gathering dust upstairs, and their upkeep became her passionate pastime. The three of them spent no end of time cleaning and conserving them. Our home became an example of family bliss, and Rehana everyone's darling. I, too, flourished in her loving arms and in her companionship.

Once everything settled down, Papa shifted his attention on finding suitable matches for the girls. Even though I was neither told nor did I attempt to pry into the details of how much dowry pas paid by Uncle Haroon for my hand and what other stuff Rehana came with apart from her winsome looks and golden heart, it was only obvious that, after taking away all the wedding expenses as well as the money we owed Sal towards the *other* wedding, which never took place, enough was left in his hand to contemplate on getting the girls married. Apart from availability of funds, he also had a brilliant organiser of major events in the shape and form of Rehana. With pressure gone from all sides, fully aware of his balance sheets and his limitations, he discussed the matter with her first and only then sent for his influential *teammate,* Moulana saheb, to find suitable *bidders* for the *merchandise* going under the *hammer* underneath his own roof, secretly relieved to realise that Roxana's potshots at *Kana Dajjal's* fatal squint had not reached *Kana Dajjal's* sensitive ears.

Out of the several proposals put forward by Moulana Saheb, his choice for Shabbu was Riaz Ghaznavi, a well-established architect with a thriving practice, catering in the main to the needs of an affluent clientele from right across the state of Andhra Pradesh. Though not quite a Prince Charming on the lookout for a dreamy-eyed Cinderella, he was a mature man acquainted with the ups and downs of life. A few years ago, while returning home from Bombay, his parents died in a dreadful car crash on the Khandala Ghats. Since then, the responsibility of looking after eight brothers and sisters fell upon his shoulders. He was desperately in need of help with raising the young family. If governesses and *aayas* could do the job, he would have hired a dozen of them already. But at thirty-eight, he needed a wife too. No doubt, for a man of his financial standing, there was no shortage of brides, but he wanted someone with a heart big enough to feed nine lives with love. Apart from that one honour-bound stipulation, he did not seek anything else; he did not need anything else. It seemed like a tailor-made setup for Shabbu. One fine evening, his family and friends came to our house, looked at the bride and accepted the proposal without any hesitations.

For Roxana, Papa chose Dr. Khaleel Ahmad, a real-life Prince Charming, who belonged to the stuff that dreams are made of. Still quite young, incredibly handsome, as chatty and fun-loving as the girl he was going to marry, he was the only son of a very wealthy doctor whose reputation spread like the fragrance of musk. Those who talked about him did not talk about the money he made but the money he gave away; at the end of each working day, his secretary arranged for one charity or the other to stand by; half of what the thriving practice fetched went to the poor, leaving him rich nonetheless, both in terms of money as well as blessings. Another glorious evening when his family was invited to come and inspect the *merchandise*, Rox passed the *assessment* with flying colours. A true connoisseur of good looks and an ardent admirer of excellence, she got what she always wanted—a *Yusuff* of her own whom she could drive around in her *chariot of dreams*, be it the secondhand *buggy* drawn by two *hoary unicorns* which she was planning to purchase from Hyderabad's notorious *Chore Bazaar*!

Soon after all the other negotiations were concluded and a date for the twin weddings also finalised, Papa entrusted the responsibility of organising the event in the competent hands of Mamma and Rehana, putting every remaining Paisa out of my dowry at the disposal of the very person who was instrumental in his acquiring it. When I came to know from her that the remainder by itself was as much as one hundred and eighty thousand rupees, I could not believe my ears. Uncle Haroon appeared to have been truly more than generous in his evaluation of me. I was not worth such a priceless treasure like Rehana as well as so much *dosh*, which, incidentally, made me wonder why he chose me as her partner. For a young lady of her social and financial standing, not to mention her other wonderful qualities, there must have been quite a wide choice of suitors available to her. Yet, regardless of my utterly abysmal pecuniary background, his eye had fallen upon me.

"Why did he pick me up from the gutter, dearest?" I could not help asking her, digressing a little from the main issues and pointing out the bewildering anomaly.

"Well," she replied, dismissing the question rather casually, "marriages, say the *Ulemas,* are made in heaven. Maybe, I was born with your rib in my spine …"

"Maybe," I agreed somewhat dubiously, "although a more down-to-earth explanation would have satisfied me better."

"Stop worrying about money, *dearest,*" she said, changing the subject. "Apart from what Papa has set aside, I, too, have built up some of my own savings. Mum sent me quite a bit from Bradford and I've stopped spending, in case you haven't noticed."

Which was true. But it had never even remotely occurred to me that the purpose behind the frugality was as auspicious as that. Frankly, not only did the savings belong to her, the rest of my dowry also belonged to her. I belonged to her, my parents were her parents, my sisters her sisters. Asking her how much was there in her piggy bank seemed like an insult to her generosity, and I did not even broach upon the issue.

"And since there are no *dowries* to shell down for either of them," she said with an animated expression on her pretty face, "let's blow all of it on their clothes and their jewellery, and a wedding ceremony so spectacular. May the honest people of Asifnagar remember it for a long time to come."

Opening up the pages of a thick ledger, she first entered in it the capital to which access was available. To the one hundred and eighty thousand rupees, which came out of my dowry, she added all her savings—a sum I prefer not to disclose. The total was divided equally between the two brides. Then began the laborious task of drawing up the comprehensive shopping lists. She was so keyed up, she would not let me sleep. I sat with her for as long as she wanted me to, her joy mine, her company welcome, her voice music to my ears, her smile a feast to my eyes, her companionship a boon, her proximity a blessing, putting at her disposal all the big and small ideas that crept into my head too. She worked hard and relished every moment of it. Sometimes the brow creased with consternation, sometimes the glossy eyes lit up with excitement, sometimes the welter of lashes flapped incessantly, the slender nostrils flared, the perfect teeth dazzled. With those cheeks flushed, those tender lips hardly ever shedding their smile, so elegant even in simple clothes, so vivified and exuberant, she was a feast to my worshipful eyes! No wonder she had become the darling of everyone amidst whom she had come to live. Organizing two simultaneous weddings was not a joke by anyone's standards. But having set to work, she never once paused or looked back.

CHAPTER (20)

'When the rose buds bloom each dawn, one of them will be me; when the birds chirp at noon, you will hear the sound of my voice too; when the rains come, every cloud will scatter a few of my tears on this soil. Like the wild tamarind tree, I might grow all over again in someone else's yard, but here's where my seeds are sown and here is where I shall always return ...'

Those were Shabana's words to me, uttered man a moon ago. When phrased in Urdu, they had sounded as sweet as any of Azra's poems and touched the cockles of my heart. And on the twenty-seventh day of Rajjab, with those very words echoing in my ears, both my sisters prepared to take leave of us.

Whenever I look back on the glorious day of their weddings, more than one thing springs to my mind; it was a strange day; it was a day when the tide of joy reached its peak in our house; it was a day when the sun and the moon seemed to have appeared together in the sky and enriched the earth with twice its share of light; it was a day when nursing mothers forgot to suckle their babies and their babies forgave them for it; it was a day when florists trading in *Mo'azzam Jahi Market* ran out of stocks; when date palms produced their utmost yield and the price of almonds shot up! It was a day when everyone wore new clothes; when unbreakable promises were made; when inviolable vows were taken; when hearts were pledged to hearts; hands were clasped in hands and lives were bonded with lives! It was a day of music and merriment; of *Shehnai* and *brass band*; of white stallions and red palanquins; of flowers and perfume; of *surma* and betel rolls; of gemstones and real pearls! It was a day of greetings and good wishes; a day of welcomes and farewells! In short, it was a day never meant to be forgotten and it has not been.

It was also a day when doom and disaster stood closest to me than ever before and stared me straight in the eye; when a storm of preponderant proportions suddenly gathered on the horizon and threatened to drown us in mid-ocean; when the pride and honour of Quraishi family hung by a brittle thread; when my father would have died in disgrace; when my sisters would have cast off their bridal garments and gone into hiding; when a happy household thus swinging in a tide of bliss would have plunged into immeasurable grief and shame. It was, therefore, a day the memory of which has seldom stops haunting me.

Reverting back a little bit in time, let me begin where I had left off. For ten whole weeks Rehana worked around the clock along with my parents without a moment's rest. Even though my job prevented me from lending them a free hand, I gave them every minute I could spare. Careful planning was absolutely crucial to her mission and so was keeping track of finances. By and large, the pages in her ledger filled up one by one. As items purchased were crossed out of the list, the blanks were filled with errors of omission that came to light on second thoughts. While Mamma and a team of professional stream stresses concentrated upon sewing, she discreetly took the girls to the shops with her in her car, so that their choice featured in her selections, finished all the shopping, stored expensive jewellery and clothes with due care, and adding a touch of Western foresight to it, got them insured against fire and theft. She booked *shamianas*, the *Shehnai party,* the brass bands, the stallions, the caterers to organize the main wedding feast, got some extra furniture for the guests, built up adequate food stocks in order to cope with the ever increasing flow of long distance relatives who poured in day by day, hired professional cooks and chefs and managed the entire show almost single handed with exemplary patience and competence. In spite of it being quite large, there was not enough room in our house to hold two simultaneous wedding ceremonies. So, she booked a civic hall that is usually available on rent for such occasions. Her cautious mind never once given to oversight, her nerves of steel never before put to such a gruelling test, her physical strength never more under stress, she really went to town. Whoever opened their mouth, they only talked about *Bahu Begum,* or *Munni Begum,* or *Shahzadi Begum.* The little lady wants this; the little lady wants that. Her wish was their command. At ease with those whom she knew well, as well as those with whom she had only recently come into contact, *Shahzadi* always kept marching onwards like a non-stopping train.

As the crucial date began to approach, the house once again turned into a choultry. At that stage, I, too, took leave from work and became fully involved in the preparations. Sal, who was back from the States, also joined hands. And then there were our two famous Cousins Ifthequaar and Zulfequaar without whose presence and participation no marriages are known to have been performed in our wider family. Our combined efforts made it possible for the guests to spend time in comfort.

In course of my marriage, I had had my fill of rituals. Now, it was my sisters' turn. We could not see what was going on in the ladies' wing, but the frequent outbursts of laughter indicated that the show was in full swing. Unlike me, they had made many friends at college, most of whom attended every function. As a result of it, youth dominated in all the events that not only added glamour to the surroundings but also enhanced the festive mood. The seven days leading up to the weddings were packed with fun and frolic.

Everything progressed on schedule and according to our plan. Under the careful supervision of Cousin Ifthequaar, the civic hall was turned spectacular. By the time we got there, the *Quazi* had already arrived. When the invitees from the bridegrooms' side also joined in, it bore the outlook of a busy beehive. Surrounded by dignitaries and prominent personalities, Papa looked thrilled to bits; the third of his cherished dreams was also on its way to being fulfilled. The arrival of the bridegrooms, lead by a brass band, was the greatest moment of all. Swept by a sudden surge of joy, the guests gave them a standing ovation. Their faces were hidden behind the *Sehra*, but I had a feeling they, too, were just as thrilled as the rest of us. After all, they were about to wed two of the best girls that ever lived on earth! Frankly. I never thought my sisters would get married in such style and quietly saluted all those kind people who had helped. The knowledge that the foremost amongst them was my own wife made me even more proud of her.

In an atmosphere charged with immense excitement, the *Quazi* performed both the *Nikahs*. Right through the long recitals, the guests sat hushed, except when praises to Allah were given. And whenever they were, they paid Him tribute in one voice, from time to time the chorus of their chants sending vibrations through the walls. I could not rob Him of those moments of glory; at least on that one occasion, His devotees outnumbered me.

The feast that followed the weddings was held at our house. Food prepared by professionals was absolutely sumptuous and mouth-watering. Papa had made a laudable gesture of charity by inviting one hundred cripples and beggars to come and share the meal with us. While the well-off received plenty of attention from paid hands, Sal and I looked after those who were not so well off. Batch after batch they ate to their hearts' content, blessing the brides and the bridegrooms with a long and happy married life.

By the time we finished the feast, it was nearly three in the afternoon. Except for those living with us, most of the local guests had gone. Inside the ladies' wing, women became busy preparing the brides for the *badhai* ceremony. After a while, Sal also excused himself briefly and went home for a breather. Papa occupied elsewhere along with Cousins Ifthequaar and Zulfequaar; I, too, stole a brief respite in order to recover from the endless exertions and stretched my aching limbs on a comfortable armchair nearby, my thoughts centred on my sisters. As a family, we had been very close to each other. We grew up together, we cried together, we laughed together, sometimes we had fun, sometimes we quarrelled, sometimes we fell out, sometimes we made up, we faced shocks, we shared pain, we endured hardships, withstood all sorts of trials and tribulations. I could not figure out how on earth I was going to bid them farewell. Their hands were already pledged and it was only a matter of hours before they, too, became someone else's *property!*

It was while I thus sat mulling over those sweet and sour thoughts when three men at the gate, engrossed in conversation but also looking at the house from time to time, caught my attention. And since they were wearing khaki uniforms instead of plain clothes, which clearly indicated that they could not be our guests come to attend the wedding, it also seemed somewhat odd. So, just to find out who they were and what they wanted, I got to my feet and strolled over to the gate.

As I approached them, they discontinued their conversation and eyed me with furtive glances that somehow made me feel quite uncomfortable. Then, for the first time, I noticed a large truck parked not too far from the gate containing a dozen or so armed guards belonging to the Reserve Police Force, whose conspicuous presence near our house had already attracted the attention of a group of idle onlookers from here and there, notably Mr. Khan and some of the squatters whom he had once encouraged to set up their shacks on our site. It was my first encounter with him since that unsavoury incident in the vineyard a long time ago, but his very presence there set off alarm bells ringing in my head.

"Is there something I can do for you, gentlemen?" I asked the men in uniform, ignoring the rest.

Instead of answering the question, one of them handed me an impressive-looking document. From what little sank into my head, I realised that the State Bank had obtained an *ex parte* decree against Papa towards the recovery of the loan. The document in my hand was an attachment order issued by the district court and the man who served it on me appeared to be a bailiff empowered to seize possession of the house. The very sight of it sent shivers of panic running up and down my back. I was not even remotely aware that the bank had taken such a drastic action; we had neither received any notice of intent from them nor had the court issued us with summons to attend the hearing. To the extent to which I was aware, an *ex parte* decree is given to plaintiffs only when the court has issued summons to the respondent and the respondent has failed to respond. In that particular context, I knew it for a fact that no such thing had happened. Unless, of course, the summons did arrive but were mistakenly overlooked by Papa due to his multifarious preoccupations with the weddings. Or, alternatively, some corrupt bureaucrat working at the court swallowed a large bribe from the bank and dressed up the whole thing to make it look quite in order.

"But why now?" I asked them, making no effort to conceal my panic. "Why at this particularly awkward moment in time?"

They did not say anything. Obviously, as bailiffs, they were merely authorised by the court to take physical possession of the house without putting them under any obligation to answer for the court's actions. I could see the message written on their faces as well as in their reluctance to press ahead with the job.

"Are they too with you?" I asked them next, pointing at the guards.

"Yes. I'm afraid they are," one of them replied.

"What for?"

"It's standard practice for court bailiffs to be supported by due authority in the event of—*resistance*. We do come across all sorts of riffraff in this game and the courts make sure that the bailiffs are adequately protected while they are discharging their duties."

"What exactly are you planning to do?"

"We're empowered by the district judge to take possession of the house."

"And how would you do that?"

He took some time answering the question, the expression on his face soft and the pitch of his voice at its lowest. "We would have to evict anyone and everyone occupying the property, lock it up and then put the court's seal on all the locks," he explained, deliberately making it sound more like a statement than a threat.

"And if we resist?"

"You could get arrested, Mr. Quraishi," he replied, still without any hostility in his mien, "Whoever obstructs due process of law is liable to be. I'm afraid this is a serious situation, sir. I hope you …"

"Are you saying that you'll storm into the building, throw us all out of our own house and lock it up?"

"That's more or less what an attachment order implies, sir."

"And if we resist, you will set your armed guards on us? Is that what you're saying?"

"In the event of an extremity, we might have to resort to it. But let's hope things won't have to go that far."

By then, a few more passers-by paused to see what was going on and needlessly augmented the audience. Some deliberately stood close enough to overhear the conversation while the others formed into small groups, talking to each other in whispers and breaking into muted heckles every now and then.

"There's a wedding feast in progress, for God's sake! How on earth am I supposed to cope with this on the spot?" I mumbled incoherently.

In answer to it, they merely exchanged quiet looks between themselves and stood with their heads bowed. There was still no trace of hostility or impatience in their attitude. Inside the truck, the guards sat wearing neutral airs, as willing to leave, as they seemed prepared to strike. Sudden tremors ran through my body. It was not just a serious crisis but also a blow strong enough to destroy us. Such a disgrace in the presence of all those guests and at a time like that could easily kill Papa. No doubt, it was extremely foolish of him to have let matters reach that stage, but too late for regrets. Doom seemed almost upon us. There was no way of predicting what the girls would do to themselves out of shame. Although it was not their fault, they were too sensitive to swallow their pride and pretend as though nothing happened. Their friends were still present in the house, not to mention so many of our relatives. Dr. Ahmed was a man of such high social status, I could see gossip columnists having a field day at the expense of his good name in the local newspaper. Riaz Ghaznavi, a successful architect with prominent clients also faced a similar disgrace. Perhaps, being lofty and compassionate, they might turn a blind eye to the ugly situation; perhaps, being wealthy, they might even come forward and throw the money in the bank manager's face. But what would happen to the honour and self-respect of our family? It would no longer be worth a penny. That night, instead of two pretty brides leaving the house travelling in red palanquins, it could easily be their cold bodies carried in white coffins. Shivering like a leaf, I stared at the bailiffs with dazed eyes.

"I'm sorry, Mr. Quraishi," said one of them in a soft voice., "We're merely doing our duty."

"The two brides in the house are my sisters, Mr. Bailiff. They re my flesh and blood, they're my dream, they're all I've got, they mean everything to me. Do you have to execute the order today? This very moment? Can't it wait until tomorrow?" I asked him beseechingly.

At that stage, probably reacting to the overwhelming grief squeeze in my trembling voice, the heckles from the crowd ceased at once as everybody came to attention. In the ensuing silence, all I could hear was the loud thumping of my heart. A crisp sun blazed in the orb of the clear sky above me; a lone kite quietly glided on the span of its wings; a butterfly gathering honey from a fresh marigold flapped its wings noiselessly; something rustled in the grass; drops of sweat trickled down my face and drenched my clothes; the sounds of human activity going on around the house gradually receded into distance and muffled. I became so tense; I had a job keeping myself up on my feet. The Bailiffs looked once again at the house surrounded by the *shamianas* and packed with guests. At that stage, something seemed to snap inside them—a seam which burst open and let in some pity.

"All right, Mr. Quraishi," he said, making up his mind and shaking his head disapprovingly at the whole affair. "I won't execute the order today. I, too, have daughters, and I know how it feels."

His generous words stopped the shivers rocking my knees and steadied the ground underneath my feet. Digging my hands into my pockets, I grabbed hold of whatever money there was on me and offered it to them. One by one they looked at it and then shook their heads.

"You keep it, Mr. Quraishi," said the man who was leading the conversation. "Today at least, your need is much greater than ours."

I felt ashamed of myself for having thus insulted their generosity. They might be poorer than us, but they were in the same class of people whom money cannot buy. Not because they had plenty of it, but because they had something else more valuable than money: they had compassion; they had feelings; they had due regard for their fellow humans.

"I'm sorry, I wasn't thinking straight," I apologized.

"It's all right," he said with an indulgent smile. "Tell you what. We'll go away along with this attachment order as if we never came here. If you see the bank manager first thing in the morning and sort it all out with him, we won't even have to come here again tomorrow. Do you think you can manage that?"

He spoke as though he was talking to a child who had broken a priceless family heirloom: 'sort it all out with Mum and Dad.' But how? There was no more money left in the house and Rehana's piggy bank had been drained to the bottom. But then again, I had rich friends and I knew how to beg … .

"Okay, I will. And thanks for the cooperation," I said.

"You're welcome, sir."

"Won't you have some sweets, at least? It's a double wedding and there's plenty to spare?"

"Thank you very much, Mr. Quraishi, but please don't bother. We're in uniforms. Frankly, the less people see us, the better for everybody."

So saying, they got into the truck and left. Only then did the tremors rocking my whole body subside. I did not really give a damn what happened in the morning. That night, moments before their husbands came to take them away, the honour of my sisters was saved; my father's life was saved; his name was saved; his dream was saved. Rehana's endless toils were saved, and together with all that, a little bit of me was also saved.

Returning to the room, I threw myself back in the armchair and shut my eyes. The world disappeared. It felt good to get out. I had had too much of it all at once. My limbs stopped shivering and all the contrite muscles loosened. Fragrance of flowers and jossticks, often in plenitude on those occasions, filled my lungs. With my mind trapped in a state of limbo from severity of tension, concentration was impossible. I just let my thoughts drift as far away from the weary chaos around me as I could.

Perhaps the pallor upon my face was so telling, someone informed Rehana that I was taken ill. Yet another unpremeditated act of kindness towards me, it brought her rushing upon her feet. To her, I was precious; of her world, I was the sole occupant; in her mind, I was all that mattered. News of my being taken ill was so unbearable to her, she came running into the men's wing without any regard to *purdah*, kneeled close to me and held my hand, hers already gone a little cold.

"What's the matter?" she asked me, looking at my pallid face with immense concern. "Are you all right?"

I could not tell her anything in front of all those people. Not far from where I sat there was a bathroom. I quietly escorted her into it. Realising at once that the news I bore must be quite dismal, she shut the door behind her and faced me with a nervous look. I had quite a job finding my tongue but somehow managed the words and told her about the bailiffs and the attachment order. It knocked off her breath too. She stood leaning against the door for several chilling moments, unable to talk.

"What've you decided to do?" she finally asked.

"I haven't got a clue," I replied.

"I haven't got a penny left. Are they asking for the whole of the loan?"

I remembered having seen a schedule appended to the order, giving details of the amounts involved, but in my highly stung state of nerves, I had not had the courage to note the details.

"I don't know," I replied.

She began to think, which was more than what I could say for myself. My mind was a total blank.

"Do one thing," she suggested, recovering from her shock in due course. "Go to the bank in the morning, see the manager and find out how much money is required."

"And then what?"

"What else? We'll have to sort it out somehow. Let's first see how much is involved."

"I can ask Sal to help out."

"Tomorrow, if necessary; but not tonight, please."

"All right."

"And stop worrying. This is a very special night. We've two brides to see off. Let's do it in style."

She had courage, enough for herself as well as for me. Were it not for her proximity and availability, I would have been all alone that evening, staggering under the impact of such a severe blow. She shared half of it without flinching.

"And one more thing," she whispered in my ear, "when you go to the bank in the morning, promise me you won't go riding on the motor bike?"

"Why?"

"Saleem Bhaijan can give us the money, if we asked him to," she said, managing a brave smile even at a time like that, "but if anything happened to you, who'll give me another *you?*"

I promised. After making sure I was sufficiently composed, she went back into the ladies' wing. Shahzadi's resourcefulness was on trial again; but I had a feeling she would come riding the crest!

When Sal returned from home, I did not breath a word to him. He was not running away and neither was the bank. One more night was not going to change our fortunes. Like Rehana said, it was a very special night that had arrived in our lives after so many tests and after such a long wait; we had two brides to see off on the most auspicious journey of their lives. There was no need to taint its grandeur with the inauspicious. Masking my feelings well, I busied myself with work.

The bridegrooms arrived on time, riding on their stallions, accompanied by the band and along with the palanquins. It was a great relief to see that the unexpected crisis did not claim any casualties. My sisters were leaving home in the right spirit, in the right transport and in the right company.

Shortly before their departure, the ladies' wing was cleared for us. Papa and I went inside to say our piece. Unaware of the devastating storm that swept behind his back, he looked absorbed in other thoughts. Before he made a start, Mamma and Rehana also joined us. Immaculately dressed for the crucial *jalwa* ceremony, the brides stood with their heads bowed. Their cheeks were wet, tears still streaming down their eyes. Until that night, we were partners in the same enterprise, beset with all sorts of hazards and challenges, but ours together. I hoped they would see better times in the homes of their husbands. We had done our best to make sure of it; the rest was left to chance.

When they touched Papa's feet with trembling hands, he was moved to tears. Then he solemnly admonished them to love and to obey their husbands; to give them their utmost support towards discharging their commitments and responsibilities; to be loyal and trustworthy; to be candid and honest; to model their homes in the spirit of Islam; to bring up their offspring as good Muslims; to give them the right guidance; to lead them on to the path of righteousness and urge them to stay on that course right through their lives; but above all, never to fall short of expectations. He knew his daughters well; such virtues were ingrained in them. But being an indispensable formality, it had to be spoken and he spoke in excellent style, well suited to play the role of wisdom and sagacity.

My turn next, I held them both in my arms simultaneously. It was an extremely emotional as well as poignant moment for me. Bidding them farewell was not easy. There were plenty of people in the house to make Horlicks, but none who could make it worse than dear old Rox! I would miss that, and a great deal besides. Her unrestrained laughter, her loud singing without much talent, her wisecracks, the hilarious metaphors aimed at describing how I looked, our surreptitious challenges and counter challenges, the fierce competitions in jokes from *beerbal*, the firm resolve with which she stuck to her duties, her charismatic personality, her vivacious exuberance, her magnetic charm, the richness of her love. Rehana had pampered her a little, but so what! The *doctor* could take over from there and spoil her some more. He was rich enough to afford her compulsive extravagance.

For me, parting Shabana's company was a severe blow. Were it not for the timely arrival of Rehana in my life to subsidize her loss, I would have gone completely astray without her. She had been my guide and my support; an anchor that prevented me from drifting afar; a glare that flooded my lonesome paths with light; a source of inspiration and a marvellous friend. She cried with me and laughed with me; she was always around to put me back upon my feet whenever I slipped and fell; she dried my tears in times of grief; she assuaged my wounds in moments of pain; she wedged my courage in the midst of despair. Behind the sober exterior, she was also a turbulent strait of emotions. We were lucky to have had so many good years of her life; the rest going to a man that richly deserved them.

They said goodbye and left. Most of the guests also went away and some peace returned to the house. For the first time in weeks, we all sat together in the lounge, recalling to mind many an unforgettable memory from the past few days. My parents looked exhausted but contented, which was fine by us. There was no need to spoil their mood with bad tidings; they had done their bit and deserved to be left out of the rest of our problems. We laughed and talked as if we had seen the last of our troubles. There was not a crease of worry on Rehana's brow or a trace of physical fatigue. Shahzadi seemed to know so well the tact of taking the *rough* with the *smooth!*

First thing in the morning, I set out on my uneasy mission, travelling by rickshaw as promised. Along the way my mind fell a victim to all sorts of disconsolate thoughts. Even though I could not question the bank's right to proceed in court against us, the timing was unforgivable. Being behind in a few payments did not have to be visited with such a severe punishment. After all, it was just a monetary transaction and the value of the house was in no danger of depreciating. A month or two would not have made any difference. If nothing else, at least an adequate warning should have been given to us. It was lucky that the bailiffs were decent and considerate men; it was lucky that I noticed them in time; it was lucky that I had a wife like Rehana and a friend like Saleem. Without all those advantages I would have been sunk.

Although there was no prior appointment made, the manager spared the time to see me and also treated me with due courtesy. Apologies were neither expected nor offered. I asked him to name the smallest figure acceptable to him. If I managed thirty-eight thousand rupees towards the accumulated arrears of interest, he said the court order would be withdrawn. I had five clear days in which to meet the deadline. That was the best he could do. It was also the most I could cope with. At least on one prior occasion, Sal had come up with a similar sum by himself. If he could do it then, he could do it again. The need was never greater.

By the time I returned home, my sisters had arrived. So had Riaz and Khaleel, to spend the next three days with us. Papa looked beside himself with joy; Mamma already fussing over her son-in-laws and Shahzadi a busy hostess again. We spent what was left of the morning in pleasant conversation. Seeing me relaxed, she relaxed. The maids had relieved their darling *Munni Begum* of all culinary responsibilities and forced her to sit with us. She sat close to me, feasting my eyes, stimulating my love, rewarding my heart.

Later in the afternoon we stole a quiet moment to ourselves and withdrew to our room. The topic of foremost importance being the bank, I gave her the details. I also assured her that I would be able to cope. But she did not agree to my borrowing money from Sal; she had her own ideas.

Before disclosing them, she first took a *blank cheque* from me that I would do her bidding whether or not I agreed with her suggestion. How could I refuse her? After the past few months, her standing in the family had sharply skyrocketed. If I dared go against her wishes or displease her in any way, I stood the risk of making powerful enemies within the family perimeters. So I promised.

Without uttering another word, she fetched an ivory casket from her chest of drawers and put it in my hands. Somewhat puzzled by the unexpected gesture, I opened the lid and looked inside. It contained every item of her personal jewellery that was given to her by us as well as her parents during our wedding.

"What's this?" I asked her, completely taken aback.

"Sell it and pay off the bank whatever money you can get."

"Rehana!" I protested with dismay. "Have you gone mad?"

"No, I haven't," she replied without the slightest change in her expression, "If I make one phone call to Daddy, he will catch the first available flight, come here in person and pay off the whole of the loan without batting an eyelid. But is that what we want?"

"No, we don't. Sal's different. He's my friend."

"So am I. Besides being your wife—that is."

"Listen to me, Rehana. There's no real need for this."

"Yes, there's. These are *our* problems and *we* must learn to solve them by ourselves."

"I can, without selling the jewellery."

"How? By borrowing from *Paul* to pay off *Peter?* Or, are you going to ask for *charity?"*

"If I accepted these, I'd be doing the same, won't I?"

"Is that what you think? *MY* money, spent towards *MY* family's needs, you look upon it either as a loan or as a charity? Is that all I'm worth?"

"No!"

"Then stop arguing. This is the safest way, I assure you."

"In less than a week, you're going to have to attend two *Walima* feats. What will you wear?"

"This!" she said, showing off her black beads necklace with great pride, which happens to be a symbolic ornament worn by all married women in our families. "With this around my neck, I'm as rich as I can ever be."

What could I say! In terms of money, forty thousand rupees is not a lot even by our standards. Around fifteen hundred pounds sterling, probably peanuts to a rich Mica merchant like her dad. But the sentiment behind it was so priceless. She was also right. Even if I borrowed the money from Sal, I would have to give him back sooner or later. How would I do that? My salary was the only source of income for the whole family. That too was uncertain, depending very much upon the decision of the education board. My future had very limited scope, whereas my commitments more than likely to increase. A moral obligation to a close friend by way of an un-repayable loan was the last thing I wanted. Overwhelmed with gratitude as well as with love, I gathered her in my arms, but before I could lift her up, she stopped me.

"Wait!" she said, wearing the sweetest smile I had ever seen on her cute face. "Handle the package with care. *Contents are fragile …"*

A bit confused by the warning, I stared at her. That was the moment when she broke the most thrilling news of my life. What a pleasant surprise and what a choice of time to give it to me in! I was going to be a father!

Out of sheer habit, I almost shouted *al-hamd o lillah* but checked myself in time. '*He*' had nothing to do with it. At least not as far as I was concerned … .

CHAPTER (21)

Rehana's jewellery fetched enough money to pay the bank the required amount in order to get the court order withdrawn. I was not sure whether paying off the accumulated arrears of interest was resolving the crisis or merely putting it off until another day, but the size of the loan was too large for me to do anything else. I made sure of one thing though; I took a promise from the manager that if ever he were going to take us to court again, he would not do it without sending me a prior intimation at least. Any day, I would sooner persuade Papa to sell the house and move into smaller accommodation than live with that sort of a sharp knife held against my throat all the time, especially now that most of his outstanding commitments had been discharged in full. Thanks to his own tireless efforts, I got a caring partner in life and the girls had been married well. What more could he want?

The three days that followed the weddings were packed with fun. After the guests left, there was no longer any need for the brides to stand on formalities. Neither they tried to, nor did their husbands allow them to. A time to know each other and make friends, we did just that. Riaz was Shabbu's ideal partner and Khaleel fitted on Rox like a glove. Each partner seemed as happy with the other as could be expected, which made us happy too. For all the problems of *squints* and *cataracts* they suffered from, Moulana saheb did seem to have fixed his targets well and Papa taken his potshots equally well, both with uncanny perfection!

Choosing an appropriate moment, I broke the good news that Rehana had given me. Mamma and Papa's joy knew no bounds and the girls went over the moon. Even Riaz and Khaleel, by then having grown quite fond of my resourceful and hardworking wife, warmly congratulated us both. *Munni Begum's* latest accomplishment went quite well with the maids too. The ladies in the household began to treat her like a glass poppet. Some blessed her, some praised her, some hailed her and some thanked her, completely ignoring me as though I had no share in it!

Shortly after the *Walima* feasts life in our house returned to normal. I went back to work. Rehana took charge of the house, relieved Mamma of most of her domestic preoccupations without seeming to be pushy and set her free to manage her time according to her own preferences, be it worship, be it gardening, or be it looking after Papa. She did all three in sensible measures, for once putting her feet up and taking life easy. So did Papa, no longer running around in circles in order to cope with conflicting priorities. Whenever Khaleel was at the clinic, Rox spent most of her free time with us. Shabbu was not so free on account of her husband's brothers and sisters, but she, too, visited us regularly. Even if we were no longer living together, it hardly seemed to matter. Whenever time permitted, we saw each other; if not, we spoke on the phone.

Time passed. Rehana's tummy began to show. Under the careful supervision of Dr. Julia Fernandez, a reputable gynaecologist in the city arranged by Papa through his doctor friend, she did all the recommended physical exercises and kept herself fit. On account of the extra drain put on her normal nourishment by the baby in her womb, her eating habits significantly changed. She consumed a lot and started to put on extra weight. It suited her though; somehow, she looked even prettier. I had quite a job keeping my hands off her. The more I hungered for her, the more she teased and tantalized me. Sometimes, I pressed my ear on her stomach and listened to the activity going on inside; sometimes I made her sit in the chair and simply feasted my eyes; sometimes, I just smothered her with kisses. In the privacy of our bedroom, I served her, I tended to her, I nursed her, I groomed her. She was my whole world, she was my golden dream, she was my ardent heaven, and she was the only thing I had all to myself.

One day, shortly after I returned home from work, she told me Uncle Haroon was back. Apparently, he phoned her from Santa Cruz Airport in between flights, on his way to Madras and then farther South, meeting his suppliers as usual.

"Just business?" I asked her casually.

"Yes," she replied.

"Auntie Zeenath isn't with him?"

"No."

"Is he coming here as well? I mean, to Hyderabad?"

"Of course, he will be. You don't expect him to go back without seeing us, do you?"

"Did he say when?"

"In about a couple of weeks or so, I guess."

I kept quiet but the news did worry me quite a bit. I had not been expecting him to come back so soon. Rehana's jewellery became my major concern. Going around our family circles with a bare neck and bare hands was one thing; but his finding out what happened to his daughter's property was quite a different matter. From what little I knew of him, he often tended to measure life in terms of money only. Such people scared me.

First thing in the morning, I phoned Shabbu and asked her to expect me for lunch as I had something important to discuss with her. Without asking me what it was, she extended the hospitality of her home with her customary enthusiasm. I went to work but my mind was not on anything. I needed quite a lot of money in order to purchase a similar quantity and quality of ornaments as I had sold away. Not that I expected Shabbu to come up with it, but she was the only person to whom I could take my troubles. Marriage had not changed things between us; I continued to receive the benefit of her sound advice and guidance.

It being a Saturday, the institute closed at one. I drove over to her house with due haste where she sat up waiting for me. Riaz was at work and the children had not yet returned from their schools, which enabled us to talk in confidence. Without beating around the bush, I told her everything that happened on the day of their weddings. The bombshell left her totally aghast and out of breath.

"What do you know!" she exclaimed soon after recovering from her shock, "I did notice Bhabi's bare hands and neck and asked her several times. Guess what sort of tripe *mem saheb* fed me! *Allergy,* she replied without batting an eyelid. Contact with gold was giving her skin rash, she said. Some allergy, eh?"

The thought of how convincing an excuse my enterprising wife came up with forced a smile out of me, regardless. And I had been under the impression that she never *lied!*

"Got any ideas?" I asked Shabbu rather nervously.

"A bit too late for ideas, isn't it?" she said, looking into my eyes. "This is time for action. We can't let her daddy come to know about this. No way!"

"You aren't thinking of tapping your old man for the money, are you?"

"If necessary, I might. But I've something else in my mind."

"Such as?"

"When the bailiffs came to seize the house, we should have paid off the bank, you, me and Rox. It doesn't mean I'm looking upon Bhabi as an *outsider;* she's a marvellous person and I never more admired her sincerity. But it isn't fair to take advantage of her kindness and generosity. Let me handle it, Bhaijan. I'll sort it out personally. Besides, if Riaz came to know that I was neutral towards our combined responsibilities, he'd be furious."

There was a great deal of sense in what she said. That day, when Rehana came to our rescue, I had accepted her generous offer without too much fuss because it was one time when I could not possibly have deprived the brides of their jewellery. But things had changed since then; the circle of our family and friends had widened considerably. Small wonder that Riaz would be furious if Shabbu turned a *deaf ear* to the situation. So would Khaleel be. Considerably relieved by her undertaking, I left the matter in her capable hands. I knew whatever she offered to do, she always did it in the best way possible.

She kept her promise a lot quicker than I had expected her to. Only three nights later, as I lay idling in bed, Rehana put in an absolutely spectacular appearance. Fresh and fragrant from a recent shower, elegantly dressed in spite of the awkward tummy, wearing an exquisite set of glittering ornaments, the beauty of the flawless face enhanced by a subtle application of her Western makeup aids, chewing an occasional *paan* that lent the cute lips an incarnadine tinge, she stood near the door keenly watching my reaction.

"*Well! Well! Well!*" I exclaimed, taking stock of her from head to foot. "Looks like your *allergy* has vanished! Not by the healing touch of Dr. Julia Fernandez, I guess?"

"No. By courtesy of Shabbu Baji and Rox. How do I look?"

"Absolutely sensational!"

"You owe me an explanation. I thought this was going to be *our* secret?"

"It still is. Only, one or two extra people are sharing it. Are you cross?"

"Well, I can afford to forgive you this once."

"Eternally grateful. Won't you join me?"

Assuming an air of regality, she stretched her hand. Quickly piling up some pillows on the bed to make a backrest for her, I helped her up. She sat, legs crossed and head held upright, her sparkling eyes fixed upon my face. The diamond on her nose stud glittered; the string of garnets around her slim neck twinkled; the gold bangles on her dainty wrists brushed against each other and made music; the tiny earrings swung whenever she shook her head; thick strands of dark hair surrounded the angelic face, a vivacious smile played hide and seek on her blessed mouth.

"Are you going to say something or are you planning to spend the rest of the night merely *inspecting* the *merchandize?"* she asked.

I sat on the bed close to her. Resting her head on my chest, she gave me her hand first. I held it. Then she offered me her lips. I kissed them. Her warm breath gently brushed my skin, the glow of the ceiling lamp reflected in her eyes, a sweet perfume of honeysuckle emanating from her clothes and body refreshed my inner seclusion, her nearness filled me with contentment.

"Daddy has begun to bother you again, hasn't he?" she asked.

"The truth is, I love you so much, I'm scared even of the wind touching you. Don't let yourself be blown away."

"I won't."

"I feel jealous of the moon. Don't look at it."

"I won't."

"I begrudge the ground your feet."

"I'll stop walking."

"I begrudge the air your breath."

"I'll stop breathing."

"I love you."

"How much?"

"More than there're stars in the sky. More than there's sand in the desert. More than there are waves in the ocean ..."

"There isn't enough room in my heart to store so much."

"Add your eyes to your heart and then try it."

We sat chatting for a long time, recollecting the past and making plans for the future. A baby featured in them; a hope awaited its arrival; a love prepared to welcome it in our laps. 'Are you expecting a son or a daughter, Mr. Quraishi?' she asked. 'One's as welcome as the other, Mrs. Quraishi,' I told her. Then we thought up some names; chose the best places in town for our evening walks; finalized which lullabies to sing and when. Hand in hand, snuggled together, submerged in bliss, we visited a notional toyshop and filled up a large shopping basket with all sorts of bargains. 'Cheque or cash?' asked the girl at the checkout. 'Charge it to Uncle Haroon's American Express,' I told her. Rehana laughed. I shrugged. Somewhere in the background, a baby chuckled. It was fun! It was loads and loads of fun!

"Why did you tell Shabbu Baji about the jewellery?" she asked me, once both of us were back on earth from the dreamland.

"I had to. My pride was at stake. Are you angry?"

"No, I'm not. *Your* pride is *my* pride."

"Thank you. And how did Shabbu manage?"

"Simple. These belong to her and Rox. I'll return them as soon as Daddy's gone. Clever, isn't it?"

"Brilliant! Next season, I'll buy you a new set."

"From Tiffany's?"

"From *Gulbahar* Florists in the *Mo'azzam Jahi Market*."

We both laughed. If I could, she knew I would weigh her in gold and give it all away to the cripples and beggars outside the *holy shrine*. After one more round of blithesome conversation, I switched off the lights, she snuggled closer to me, and sleep put us back on *dreamland*.

Two weeks later Uncle Haroon arrived in Hyderabad. To begin with, his chauffer came and took the car away. Pace of activity in our house accelerated at once. The maid tidied up the lounge, she and Rehana cooked a nice meal to entertain him over supper, Papa trimmed his beard and smartened himself, and Mamma wore a new sari. Rehana also dressed up nicely, showing off the jewellery. As it looked like a suitable occasion for introductions, Riaz and Khaleel joined us along with Shabbu and Rox at our request. I came home a bit early from work. All set and girdles tied up, we waited for our honoured guest.

He came on time, punctual to the minute, supper in our house treated no different from an interview with the director of trade and industries. The reunion between the father and the daughter was quite emotional, to say the least. He could see that she was pregnant and seemed pleased. Papa and Mamma extended him a warm welcome. Before he could switch his attention upon me, Riaz and Khaleel were introduced. Then he moved on to Shabbu and Rox and blessed them. Finally, I, too, was rewarded with a hug.

Conversation around the table was pleasant and cordial. He did most of the talking, which began with news of London and of Bradford. Next, he took the customs lads at Santa Cruz Airport to the launderers, criticised the appalling road conditions in South India and then shuddered at the thought of hotel food. For Riaz, the architect, he had a lot of mean things to say about Barrett's and Wimpy; for Khaleel, the doctor, he had a scathing assault on the National Health Service; for Shabana and Roxana, he had American Georgette and Japanese Nylon. He joked and laughed, gave his compliments to the chef, gave Allah his thanks for a tasty meal and apologized for his manners following a mild burp.

"Frankly," he carried on, dwelling at length upon the food, "this is the first decent meal I've had in two whole weeks."

"Why didn't you bring Zeenath along?" Mamma asked him.

"Yes, why didn't you?" Papa also added his own voice to it.

"I should've, shouldn't I?" he answered their question with a question, neither offering an explanation nor accepting blame.

"How about one more helping, Uncle?" asked Rox, waving the ladle in his face.

Before the poor man could open his mouth, Mamma interrupted him again. "Is there someone in your house to cook food for you?" she asked.

"Why don't you stay here?" Shabbu extended an uncalled for invitation, if only to keep Rehana's heart.

"That's a thought!" Papa said, "Why don't you?"

"Thank you, my dear," Uncle Haroon replied, addressing himself to Rox first and settling the issue of a second helping once and for all. "I wish I could but there just isn't any room inside me. How nice of you."

Rox withdrew the ladle. Before he could deal with Shabana's invitation, conversation reverted once again to the controversial topics that had already been discussed. Himself an inveterate chatterbox, Khaleel opened up new venues in the National Health Service, made a pass at the B.M.A. and cast a few aspersions upon the Ministry of Health and Social Security. Which, in turn, lead to a full-scale debate on the Welfare State itself. At least on three separate occasions, I noticed Rehana open her mouth to say something but shut if off as no one seemed prepared to give her the chance. I consoled her by squeezing her hand underneath the table.

Around half past ten Riaz became broody; seven big problems sat staring him in the eye, their only solution in the form of Shabbu a good six miles away from them. Husband and wife excused themselves and left. An hour or so after their departure, Rox and Khaleel also followed suit. Only then did our honoured guest shift his attention upon Rehana and me. He told us how glad he was to know about the rapid progress we had made as a husband and wife team. Next came her health and appearance, both declared satisfactory. Which, incidentally, reminded him of Papa's heart. His polite enquiry was received with thanks and answered with brevity. Towards the end, after making a casual reference to how things were with me at work, he took his leave, promising to drop in again on the following day.

Some peace and calm returned. Somewhat worn out by the extra activity, Papa and Mamma retired to bed earlier than normal. But there was no question of *Munni Begum* also doing the same, without giving the maid a hand in the kitchen. For a good half an hour or so, I could hear the tap running. 'They're washing the dishes,' I told myself. Then I heard the clangs of crockery and of utensils. 'Good. They're putting them away,' I told myself. Then suddenly, I heard the sound of laughter. 'Good grief! They've started to chat!' I told myself with dismay. Finally, I heard the kettle blow. 'Coffee is on its way!' I told myself and ran upstairs.

Rehana joined me soon. She did bring coffee as well as an extra helping of the delicious bread pudding that Mamma had specially made for our famished guest. She looked pleased to have seen her father after a long gap. He dominated her conversation. She recalled to mind many an anecdote from yesteryear, from her childhood days, her schooling, how much her parents loved her, how much they had done for her. I did not attempt to change the topic. Anyone who had taken care of her at any time in her life was entitled to my unlimited gratitude.

Over the next several days, we all had an absolutely hectic time. Accustomed to leading an active life, Uncle Haroon moved around with the speed of lightning. Whatever spare time he had, he spent it in our company, and whenever he was not eating with friends or relatives, he broke bread with us. Oft and on he also treated us to lavish feasts in expensive restaurants. His manners flawless, his attitude beyond reproach, his behaviour exceedingly pleasant, he made a much better impact upon us than he had done in the past.

However, towards the end of the two weeks of uninterrupted pleasantries, his tune abruptly changed. One miserable morning he rang me up at work and, after dispensing with the initial how do you dos, announced right out of the blue that he was taking Rehana back to Bradford with him.

A piece of news crippling enough to break my backbone, yet delivered with astonishing ease and in the most casual vein! We had been meeting practically every day since his arrival, but talking to me face to face was not his style, not even when the matter was as important as that—hardly a topic that could be thrashed out at work over the phone.

"Why?" I asked him, if only because nothing else sprang to mind.

"Pretty obvious, isn't it?" He said, miles and miles away from the tremors in which I rocked, "Her first childbirth must take place in her parents' house, under their supervision and at their expense. All a matter of *tradition.*"

Full stop. If so, I had never heard of that one before. And even if so, I failed to see how it could apply to us. Had I been married to Azra instead of Rehana, it would be a different matter altogether; unlike one, the other would have gone away from this street to that. But Bradford was not the same as Aghapura; the distance by itself being phenomenal. So were the major hurdles in between, such as the Himalayas, the Great Desert, and the Alps. Not to mention all those little restrictions on travel, i.e., visas, entry permits, laws, regulations. Tradition was too inadequate an excuse for imposing them between us. The baby in Rehana's womb belonged to the both of us equally; we had ensured the services of a gynaecologist whose reputation was above board and she had been doing pretty well so far. Taking her back to Bradford was utterly preposterous, neither necessary nor tolerable. What would happen to me without her? How would I go back to the house each evening if she was not going to be at the other end to welcome me with a couple of biscuits and a cup of tea? How could I breath, sleep, survive? But all that was not Uncle Haroon's concern. He simply stuck to *tradition.*

"I see," I said without seeing the slightest bit of sense in the proposition that he had offered me, "Have you talked it through with Rehana?"

"Not yet," came his reply, hurtfully laconic just when some detail was desperately needed.

"Well, what can I say!" I mumbled quite inaudibly, "If you want to take her back and she's willing to go, I guess there is not a lot I can do to stop either one of you, is there?"

"No need to get worked up, Yusuff," he snapped, getting rather vexed. "Just a matter of few months before your wife and your child are back in your arms."

A matter of few months! Was it really as simple as that? Between now and then, there were so many nights and so many days, each day and night filled with long hours, each hour filled with unendurably dreary minutes, and each minute filled with immensely acrid moments, every one of them to be carefully counted and then painfully spent. In such sensitive matters of the heart and the passions that govern its tempo, duration by itself never has any relevance. While an entire lifetime is often not enough for love, one night of grief without it could so easily kill. To him, a few months were a few months; but to me, they were as insurmountable as eternity.

"Anything else?" I asked him.

"All being well, we'd be flying on Thursday," he replied.

Three measly days before parting of ways; before the start of a new trial for me! Dropping the phone back on the cradle, I gulped a bitter lump down my throat. My face too expressive to hide anything and my colleague Anver too sharp to miss attention, he probably read trouble written all over it.

"Bad news?" he remarked, presumably feeling sorry for me.

"I seem to have a knack of attracting them," I replied with a profoundly arctic sigh of despair.

I went home as soon as the office closed, my nerves wrecked, my mind afire. Unaware of her father's plans, Rehana was waiting in the veranda to greet me as usual, smartly dressed. The sweet smile with which she extended the welcome raised goose pimples upon my skin. Three days later, it would be a different story: Papa locked up in his room, Mamma locked up in her worship chamber, Shabbu busy with Riaz and Rox busy with Khaleel, and I convulsing alone in the poignant silence of my deserted room. It seemed the little nest, I had built for us on a tiny branch was caught up in unexpected storm, our shelter too inadequate to ignore it; our strategies too imperfect to cope with it; our defences too insufficient to take it in our stride.

Rolling those painful thoughts in my mind I went upstairs. A few minutes later she joined me with a tray of steaming tea and some *J.B. Mangharam* biscuits in a plate.

"Go on and tell me all about it," she said, pouring my cup of tea for me. "How was your day at work?"

At work, it was just like any other day; but outside work, it was a day to which I wished I had not woken up. I answered her question without mentioning anything about her daddy's unsettling phone call. Before breaking her heart too, I wanted to check with Papa about the existence of such an absurd traditions. He must know how hard it would be for me to send her away so far and for such a long time. He had helped me out with Uncle Haroon's big ideas once before and with such firmness too. He had the status as well as the ability to deal with people like that.

After the tea, I went into his room. He, too, looked extremely ill at ease, probably for the same reason, and asked me to sit in the chair first. I did and brought up the topic without beating around the bush.

"I know," he said in a somewhat subdued tone. "Haroon has already told me about it. What can we do?"

"Is there really such a tradition in existence?"

"Yes, there is."

"Even if Rehana doesn't want to go?"

"Has she told you that she doesn't want to go?"

"I don't think she knows yet."

"What she wants or what you want makes no difference to the situation. A *tradition is a tradition.*"

"Are you saying that Uncle Haroon can force her against her will?"

"It's his prerogative."

"If Shabana and Roxana decide not to come here for their deliveries, would you, too, do the same? I mean, force them against their wishes?"

"No, I won't. But imagine how I'd feel."

"Does this mean you aren't going to intervene?"

"I will. But first of all, tell *Shahzadi* what I've told you just now. If she still doesn't want to go, then let me know."

Which was as good as turning me down. Considering his own respect for tradition, he was hardly likely to stand up for us against it. And without his intervention, neither could Uncle Haroon be expected to give a toss. Regardless of how we felt or what we thought, I could see the pair of them come to an amicable understanding behind our backs. They had already done something similar once before; when they finalised our marriage, they had taken that decision too behind our backs. If they could make such irreversible decisions without consulting us, the issue at stake was utterly trivial.

"Supper is served," Rehana announced as I sat on my own in the lounge, given to sudden pangs of depression and brooding.

I went into the dining room. Noticing the intensely grim expression upon my face, she asked me if anything was the matter. At that stage I told her everything. I had to. Not only what her father had said but also what mine did. She sat hushed for quite a long time, seemingly struck by the inexpectency of the tidings more than their nature.

"Are you leaving the decision to me?" she asked me towards the end of the uncomfortably prolonged silence.

"The decision," I told her without mincing my words, "has already been taken by both sides. What remains to be seen is, whether we're going to abide by it or not."

"If you ask me to go, I'll go. If you don't want me to go, I won't. You tell me what to do." she said.

Just as I feared, the ball came bouncing back into my side of the court. Frankly, we were all taking shelter behind each other; Uncle Haroon behind *tradition*, I behind Papa and Rehana behind me. How could I expect her to rebel against her parents? If she, in spite of her Western upbringing, could agree to an arranged marriage if only because her parents had asked her to, she would never defy them over anything else regardless of what was at stake.

A civil war within family perimeters was something neither of us could even remotely contemplate. The beaten track of subservience upon which we walked was a path we had chosen to tread by our own free will. There was no question of turning away from it now; the cause was not big enough.

"I think you better go, Rehana," I told her, left with no other viable option. "It's your parents' right. Don't disappoint them."

"Okay, I will," she agreed, if reluctantly, "Papa's quite right. Imagine how he'd feel if Shabbu Baji and Rox refused to come home for their first deliveries."

That was that. I informed Papa that she was going. It was painful for him too, but he received the news with considerable relief.

That night, we retired to our room earlier than usual. The mood was pensive, the air fraught with tension, both of us ill at ease. Instead of talking about her *departure*, we talked about her *returning* home together with the baby. We also searched for and discovered quite a lot to draw comfort from. 'The same moon which shines on you will shine on me too,' she said. 'When the geese go West, I'll ask one of them to whisper an *'I love you'* in your ear from me,' I said. 'If I find a stream long enough to connect the East with the West, I will set sail on it in a *dream boat* for you loaded with my *cargo of love*,' she said. 'When a woolpack of dark clouds gather on the distant horizon to usher in the monsoon, I will slide down the rainbow track and make it all the way to your fairy castle somehow,' I said. Resigned and reconciled, we stayed awake until midnight, sometimes listening to the sad hoot of the nocturnal *Chakore*, sometimes watching the moths flutter around the bed lamp, sometimes lost in thoughts.

More or less as I had expected, Uncle Haroon went ahead and booked her passage without even bothering to talk things through with her. He knew that she knew, which was good enough for him. As soon as my sisters heard about it, they dropped everything and came home to spend the next few days with their precious *Bhabi*. For Rehana's sake, I asked them not to make a big thing out of it. They agreed and occupied themselves with helping her out with the packing. But hiding behind doors of empty rooms from time to time, they also did an awful lot of weeping. It showed on their faces. Papa kept pretty much to himself, getting ready to face life without *Shahzadi*. Mamma, less emotional amongst us, adapted a more philosophic view and took the matter in her stride. *Munni Begum's* decision to deliver her first child on foreign soil did not go well with the maid and the gardener. How I felt about it was better guessed than expressed.

Then came the final night before her departure. By then, I had made so many compromises, it no longer hurt. Without giving me a chance even to open my mouth, Rehana kept extracting from me one promise after another. 'Don't ride the bike when you're not in a fit frame of mind; don't work too hard; don't delay writing to me or answering my letters. Don't worry about money; as long as I'm alive, and wherever I'm, that's one worry I can afford to spare you. Make regular payments to the bank; whatever happened that day must never happen again, especially when I'm not around to take care of it. Look after Papa; he really isn't as well as he pretends to be. Mamma, too, isn't a particularly strong person. You mustn't bare them any grudges. They don't like my going away like this, but they've no choice in the matter. Neither must you think ill of my parents. They're using *tradition* merely as a pretext. The fact is they love me; I'm their only child. How can I refuse them? How can *you* refuse them? All said and done, when it came to the crunch, they did give me up for you, didn't they? I know separation is painful. I know waiting is painful. I know being so far away from you is painful; lying in bed without your arms around me is painful. But it'll pass. If we have to suffer a little in order to give others a lot, why not? That's what life's all about, isn't it? Making a few concessions, seeking a few rewards, shedding a few tears, spreading a few smiles, facing a few droughts, gathering a few harvests, giving a little, taking a little ...'

"And what do you want for yourself, my precious?" I asked her in the end.

"Keep fit," she replied with her typical smile. "Know why? Because, after I come back with our first baby, we're going to plan on another—the one who'll be born in *our* house!"

In the morning we all went to the airport to send her off, including the maid and the gardener. When we reached there, my feelings were the same as they were on the day they lifted the coffin on the shoulders of Azra's pallbearers; borne down by the heavy weight of loss; struck by an intolerable sense of grief; immersed in a bottomless sea of despair. But then again, on the brighter side, her mode of transport was an aircraft made with several tons of solid steel and carrying living beings instead of dead bodies. Even though her eyes were filled with tears, she waved to us from the departures enclosure; her escort was visible to the eye and her destination was known to us. If a little hard to get at, it was not altogether beyond reach. We could write to each other; we could talk on the phone; the Himalayas could be crossed and so could the Alps. All that was possible. Rehana had promised me that she would be back soon after the baby was born, which too was equally possible.'

See you soon,' she whispered in my ear before leaving, which I knew she would. That was why some said to her: *'have a safe journey'*, some said to her: *'we'll really really miss you'* and some said: *'we'll wait for you'*. But no one was saying *'Inna Lillahi Wa Inna Ilaihi Raja'oon!'* Rehana was not *Allah's* property. She was *mine* alone and therefore must return to *me*. Parting with her on such an optimistic note did not feel half as bad as I had feared it to be!

CHAPTER (22)

Rehana's abrupt departure left Papa in a shambles and he took to bed straight away. Rox, who was never required to cook a meal or wash a dish by her wealthy husband, returned to his side once again. Her presence filled at least some of the vacuum in his life left behind by Rehana. Running around all day as before, she slaved away, refuelling his *hukka* pipe, stocking up his snuff and *paan* boxes from time to time, sewing buttons on his shirts, pressing his clothes, darning his socks, polishing his shoes, as if he needed them. Hardly ever getting out of bed, he spent most of his time lost in thoughts.

Precisely ten days after she left, I received Rehana's first letter. It was so long I had to read it like a book. Not content with favours already done, she added one more to them; enclosed with the letter was a bank draft in the sum of £15,000. 'This is my own money and has nothing to do with Daddy,' she wrote in it, 'my life's savings. I really can't think of a better use for them. At the current rate of sterling exchange, you ought to get enough Indian rupees to level the score with the bank for good. Redeem the debt and give Papa the title deeds of the house. This is the least I can do for him in return for such a lot that he has done for me. You *will* do it, won't you? For my sake? Don't disappoint me, please ... I miss you so much. I miss your arms around me at night, your constant care and attention; I miss Rox's hilarious conversation; Shabbu Baji's illuminating wisdom; her affection and guidance; I miss Mamma and Papa; I miss my kitchen and my maid; I miss my kingdom and my coronets ... I do roll the chapattis for Mum here too, but it doesn't feel the same; the rice here has a different flavour; yougart is rich but tasteless; chickens are huge but full of fat ... . I feel so cast off and marooned ... A year or so ago, if anyone had told me that I might feel like a stranger in my own house one day, I would not have believed it. But I do. Marriage has changed everything for me. You, your rich love, your gentle folks and their love, they have combined together and turned me into a stranger to the very streets in which I grew up as a child. But it will all be over pretty soon. Meanwhile, do please finalise two names out of the big list of names we had compiled that night and send them on to me, for a son as well as for a daughter, to be on the safe side ...'

I did her bidding without any qualms. Sal handled the whole transaction on our behalf; exchanged her draft for Indian rupees; paid off the debt in full; recovered the title deeds of the house from the bank manager and gave them to me, together with whatever was left of the cash. I told Papa about it the same night and handed him the documents according to her wishes. Clutching them in his unsteady hands, he remained silent for a long while. To him, they represented things that had nothing to do with banks and loans. It was her concern towards his feelings, her loyalty, her efforts to make him happy even from across such a distance that touched the chords of his heart. The documents transformed into something much more than paper and print; they became a part of her being. He kept stroking them as though it was her head on his chest. Just like she expected, he was happy, very happy to realise that his memory had not been dusted out of her mind; she was still aware of his worries and still at pains to reduce them. From then onwards I never saw him without those papers, sometimes clutched in his hands, sometimes pressed against his chest and sometimes hidden underneath his pillows, but never farther away than his reach.

Time passed. By and large, I, too, became accustomed to the idea of life without her. During the day, work kept me occupied. Riaz and Khaleel took care of the evenings. I spent the nights either reading her letters or writing to her. It made me feel as though we were having a conversation. My versatile ability to conjure up fascinating images came in handy; her place in my bed never once looked empty.

Soon it was summer. We received the long awaited decision of the education board on the future of the institute: permission was granted to run a full-time recognised secondary school in the premises. It inevitably meant my resignation from the principal's post, as I did not have the necessary teaching qualifications to remain in office. So I bowed out. Staff and students got together and held a modest valediction. Mr. Raza made a point of attending the function. After a brief speech, he thanked me for all that I had done to make such a thumping success out of what had started out like an experimental idea and eventually grown into a major project benefiting so many budding lives to such a great extent. Frankly, it was all a team effort and one of the very few success stories of my life. I cherish the memory to this day.

Approximately a fortnight later, I received an unexpected phone call from Mr. Rao's secretary for an urgent appointment to see her boss over a matter of considerable importance. I knew it could only have something or the other to do with Uncle Haroon, but dared not trifle with the invitation. Whatever it be, I had to suss out his strategies and be in readiness to confront them. My time being completely free, I left it to her.

On the following Monday, I went to see him as arranged by her. Receiving me in his luxuriously air conditioned office with customary warmth, he offered me a seat and engaged in some casual conversation while waiting for snacks and drinks to be served. My job at the institute did feature in it, but only in passing, and as a matter of mere courtesy, I brought him up-to-date.

"There's a somewhat awkward matter I've to discuss with you, Mr. Quraishi," he began, helping himself to a cigarette. "At times it might seem as though I'm prying into your private affairs, but if you come across anything you don't wish to talk about, just say so. I won't take offence."

Considerably intrigued by the ominous prelude, I waited for him to proceed.

"Since the last time we met, has anything happened to change your mind about emigrating to U.K.?" he asked.

"No," I replied, deliberately choosing to be reticent in the amount of information I was prepared to release.

"Do you really stand a better chance of getting employment in that country?"

"Probably. But why?"

"Well," he said, pulling upon the cigarette and blowing out the smoke, "I recently received a letter from Mr. Abdallah to find out your views on the subject. Does it bother you in any way, my talking these things over?"

"No, it doesn't. But there isn't much to talk about. I'm not interested."

"Why not?"

"Because I was born here, everything I cherish and value is here—my parents, my sisters, my friends, my whole life."

"Don't you think the same applies to your wife too?"

"Of course, it does. But I don't recall our having had any conflict of opinion on this subject. Why do you ask? She hasn't been complaining, has she?"

"Heavens, no. She isn't even aware of this meeting between us."

"I see. Whose idea is it, then? My father-in-law's?"

"Yes."

"What's he up to this time?"

"He wants the two of you to live somewhere near him."

"He *wants!* And what if *we* don't want what *he* wants?" I retorted quite sharply, on one hand infuriated by yet another attempt by Uncle Haroon to run my life for me, and on the other hand firmly determined to stay in control of the situation.

"It could get you into a lot of *trouble,*" he replied in a mild tone, deliberately making it sound more like a warning than a threat.

"I beg your pardon?" I snapped quite impatiently, feeling hot under the collar.

"Don't scream at me, Mr. Quraishi," he said, trying to put the lid on the explosive conversation. "I'm only telling you what he's asked me to, as well as what little I know myself."

"Can you tell me what sort of *trouble?*"

He took some time answering the question, his hawk like eyes penetrating the outer mask on my face without any difficulty. "Do you know why exactly has Mr. Abdallah taken his daughter back to Bradford with him?" he asked at the end of that rather prolonged inspection.

"For *delivery,*" I replied, sticking to the facts as I knew them. "I gather it's a matter of family *tradition* that her first childbirth should take place in her parents' house."

"That wasn't the real reason," he informed me, though not too surprisingly. "Tradition was merely a convenient *excuse* for taking her back. Your father-in-law has made other plans for the two of you."

"Oh? Such as?"

"He has no intentions of sending her back here. If you want to see your wife again, or see your child, you'll have to go to Bradford for it."

The shattering piece of information took away my breath. I knew it was not past Uncle Haroon's nature to have things his way all the time, but I had never expected him to go to such limits. It meant he cheated me as well as my entire family, including Rehana. I became so furious I wanted to scream, but what was the use? With *her* in *his* clutches, my anger did not amount to a lot. Even the man talking to me belonged to the opposite camp. Holding back my breath, I simply fell into silence.

"All along, it's been his wish to keep you both near him," Mr. Rao elaborated. "That's why the suggestion of a civil marriage was made in the first place, but noticing your father's temper as well as your own resentment, the idea was dropped for the time being."

"And now he reckons he can force me into it?"

"Yes."

"What makes him think I'd give in?"

"Common sense," he replied, wearing a ghost of a smile. "He knows you love your wife enough to do anything for her sake."

Uncle Haroon, using my love for my wife against me! It was true; I would do anything for her. The very realisation rendered me speechless.

"Don't get into a panic," Mr. Rao said, probably noticing the intense pallor on my face. "Although, at the moment, I'm merely following my client's instructions, it doesn't necessarily mean that I agree with what he's doing. Or, to be more precise, with the tactics he is employing in order to accomplish his goal. To be perfectly honest with you, I find them rather reprehensible."

His censure of his client's actions, if not his intentions, was neither of any consequence to me nor of any comfort. Frankly, his views in the matter could hardly change anything.

"What difference does it make whether you *approve* of them or not, Mr. Rao?" I went ahead and asked him.

"It could *win* you a valuable *friend*," he replied after some thought.

"Win *me* a friend? How?"

"I'm so revolted by this whole affair, I'd rather help you than act against you."

"In spite of being retained by Mr. Abdallah?"

"I accept only such work as I like doing. I have no doubt you'll agree with me that, in my position, I can afford to be choosy?"

"Does my wife know what's going on?"

"No, she doesn't."

"What do you think she'd do upon coming to know?"

"As things stand, precious little, I'm afraid."

"Why?"

"I'll tell you why. To begin with, when she left here, she travelled on her previous pssport."

"So what? Anything wrong with that?"

"Plenty. Her surname, for one thing. She's now Mrs. Quraishi and not Miss Abdallah. But when she went home from here, she went using the old passport which is no longer valid."

"Why did she?"

"The simple answer to the question is, she didn't know. Her father made all travel arrangements and she had no reason to mistrust him. She still doesn't have any idea of what he has done and why."

"Wasn't it risky? Something for which she could get thrown into jail by the authorities?"

"Yes, it was. It is one of the reasons why I am unhappy with my client's tactics. But he took a chance and got away with it. How often do you get addressed by your surname taken from your passport whilst you're in transit?"

"If she could go back to England travelling on her out-of-date passport, what's stopping her from using it again to come here?"

"It's no longer in her possession. He's kept it locked away in his bank vault."

"Can't she ask him for it?"

"She can, but he has no intentions of returning it to her."

"She ought to be able to apply for a duplicate?"

"The chances of her being issued with a duplicate passport under a different surname and including the baby look pretty slim to me. She hasn't even got a proper marriage certificate to show for it."

"Why can't she complain to the authorities?"

"Would you, in her place? I mean, complain against your own father to the authorities, whether he's right or wrong?"

"Well," I said and simply shrugged.

"Being born abroad by itself doesn't make any difference to a person's profile. Don't forget that her upbringing is in no way dissimilar to your own."

Which was true. Rehana and I were birds of the same feather, slaves of habit, prisoners of principles, victims of loyalty.

"In the circumstances, what's your recourse?" he asked me, as though I had instant solutions to such daunting problems.

"I don't know," I said, beginning to get drenched by sweat that poured down my forehead in spite of the air conditioning.

"Now do you see how much of a *trouble* you're in?" he pointed out.

"What do you think I ought to do, Mr. Rao?" I asked him out of sheer desperation.

"In my opinion, your *first* step in the right direction would be to go ahead with the application for an entry permit."

"What's the use, Mr. Rao, when I don't want to settle in that country?"

"Listen to me, Mr. Quraishi, and pay good attention to what I am saying," he said in a soft voice, "For all the tea in China, your father-in-law might decide to let your wife come back after all. Or, as soon as she found out what's going on, she might take the whip in her own fist. So can her mother, come to think of it. But if matters really get out of hand, it might become necessary for you to go there yourself and fetch your family with you. In such an event, that permit could be your only means of entering the country."

"Will you help me get it?" I asked him, virtually going down on my knees.

"I'll be glad to," he agreed, and then added as an immediate after thought. "Provided you sign an authorisation for me to act on your behalf and let me have your passport."

Keeping my fingers crossed, I signed the authorization where he pointed out and promised to hand in the passport at the reception later in the day.

"Is there any chance of my getting the permit in time for the delivery, Mr. Rao?" I asked him before leaving, if only to satisfy my curiosity.

"Can't say," he replied, "One or two things do stand out in your favour. Your wife isn't just a resident of Britain but a bona fide citizen by birth. She's also separated from you, both of whom seem good enough reasons to exert some moral pressure upon the British Embassy, at least to expedite matters. Let's see what happens."

I shook hands with him and came out. While driving to his office was easy, coming back turned into quite a feat. My legs felt numb and the handle bar of the bike kept slipping away from my grip on account of nerves. Uncle Haroon's shadow had started to fall between my wife and me once again; sheer disaster masquerading in the guise of paternal love; an extreme form of madness on the verge of destroying us. I hoped Mr. Rao would succeed in his mission of mercy; I hoped the British bureaucrats at the embassy would bend the rules a little bit for us; I hoped someone would be charitable enough to pay for my fares; I hoped I would soon be able to see Rehana's face, see the baby too, give it a name out of the long list we had compiled that night, sing those lullabies we finalized, rock the cradle, change the nappies, listen to the prattle of tiny feet; I hoped we would eventually succeed in finding a place of our own under the sun, here, there, somewhere, anywhere, and put the past behind us.

By the time I got home, Shabbu and Rox had also arrived to see us. Out of caution, I decided not to tell anyone whatever transpired at Mr. Rao's office. Papa's health at its worst, his strength dwindling and his grief repressed, he was in no condition to sustain nasty shocks. Probably reading the grim expression on my face, Shabbu did suspect something was up and tried to probe, but I evaded her. Short of dealing her a painful blow too, the tidings I bore had no redeeming features. I just forced myself into silence, into routine, into indifference, talking when they talked and laughing when they laughed.

Judging from her most recent letters, it became clear to me that Rehana really had no idea of whatever was going on. She was still talking in terms of a few months, whereas according to Mr. Rao, her father had made much longer lasting plans for us. And since they were obviously made without her knowledge, it seemed possible that her mail was being intercepted. The fear took away my courage even to put her in the picture. I could neither seek information nor give her any. Keeping such a big crisis to myself soon began to take its toll. My lips sealed, my mind constantly beleaguered by fearsome thoughts, my heart crushed and my wits addled, I kept sinking deeper and deeper into quicksand again. Now there was no question of parting company with Rehana, even if it meant going away. Somewhere with her was better than anywhere without her. There was a love inside me gasping for fulfilment; there was a husband inside me convulsing for his wife; there was a dreamer inside me searching for his stolen dream; there was a father inside me screaming for his child.

Not long after that illuminating conversation with Mr. Rao, I came face-to-face with a catastrophe of phenomenal proportions. Rox came into my room, wearing a ghastly pallor on her face and said Papa was asking to see me. More than the message itself, her grim expression shook the ground underneath my feet. He had taken Rehana's departure too seriously. For as long as she was there, she had gone out of her way to make sure that he did not feel forsaken by his daughters and filled in for them in a much grater measure. She was his *mini bank* for the safekeeping of his money; she was his accountant, his adviser, his escort, his bastion, and his source of inspiration. She kept all his affairs up-to-date; washed and pressed his clothes; crushed his paan' into a pulp for easy chewing; maintained his *hukka pipe*; drove him to the market every day; made sure the maid cooked only those dishes to which he was partial and thus spent more of her daylight hours with him than with anyone else. Because of her dedication and her sincerity, he loved her so much, he set aside ten minutes after each *namaaz* to pray for her good health and well being. Once she was gone, his entire existence came tumbling down like a house of cards. No doubt, ever since her departure, Rox did her utmost to hold his spirits and pull him out of the doldrums, but things were never the same with him. His general health deteriorated quite rapidly to such an extent, it raised serious concerns in the minds of his doctor friend, Uncle Mohsin and Khaleel, both of whom suspected he could be heading for another coronary thrombosis. Hence, when Rox delivered his message with such an immensely distressing expression on her face, I got into a panic and went to see him. After greetings, he signalled me to pull a chair close to the bed and sit down. Mamma was not present in the room, which meant our conversation was intended to be confidential.

"Have you heard from *Shahzadi* lately?" he asked me first.

"Yes, Papa. She's fine and has sent you lots of love as usual."

Letting out a deep sigh, which was a clear indication of the extent of his distress, he reached for his glasses, put them on and settled his eyes upon me. "Time's come for me to take leave, Yusuff," he said softly. "Let me begin with thanking you for all your help. You've been a good son."

Those words were enough to take me over the brink. I could distinctly read a message of farewell in his eyes. "We still have long ways to travel, Papa. Please don't leave me alone just when I need you the most?" I urged in a voice choking with grief.

"I'm afraid this is where I get off," he replied without any trace of doubt or uncertainty.

Listening to it, a sour lump stuck in my throat. He was very special to me. We had had great times together; we had taken the good with the bad in our stride; we had had a lot of fun as well as done an equal lot of head bashing against the walls in moments of stress. As father and son, we had been very close to each other. His confinement to bed by itself had deprived me of a great stalwart.

"Tell *Shahzadi* I'm grateful to her for all her love, for caring and for giving so much in so short a time," he said.

"Yes, Papa. I will."

"I'd hoped I would be able to see the baby, but never mind. *A good tree can only bear good fruit.*"

"Is there anything in particular you wish me to do for you?"

"No, there's nothing outstanding. Shabana and Roxana are happily married; you've a matchless partner; your mother's got three sons and three daughters now. What more could I want?"

"Papa? Are you really going to leave us and go away?"

"Yes. Don't let anyone overdo in his or her mourning. I've led a full life and am going in peace. There're no regrets, except one. I wish I could've seen *Shahzadi* one more time. *SHAHZADI ...* "

He could not finish what he started to say and shut his eyes, her name the last word upon his lips. I rang up Khaleel at his clinic and told him. He and the ambulance arrived one after the other. It was all more or less over, but we took him to the Nizamia Hospital just the same where Mamma and my sisters joined us. Grief at a time like that was inevitable. We cried between ourselves and consoled each other. Rehana was the only person missing but her name was on every lip, just like it had been on Papa's.

After three quiet days in the Intensive Care Unit, he passed away. While his death was not altogether unexpected, it could not have come at a worse time. Torn apart from my companion, forsaken by those who should have cared, facing trials I was not equipped to cope, set adrift on a dwindling boat too far away from shore, I was as vulnerable as a pupa outside its cocoon. Burying him was not so difficult as coming back to a house in which his time had run out. His stamp was upon everything; his voice echoed in every nook and corner; his belongings sat idle hither and thither; his *hukka pipe* lay cold and abandoned, his memories scattered all around. There was not a single room in the whole house which was neutral, which did not have a profile, did not have a history, some association or the other with an unforgettable past. It was not easy to forget him; to put him behind; to accept life without his presence in it after such a lot of living together; extricate his name from the lines on our palms and assign it to the past!

A week after the burial, putting an end to the mourning and surrendering to the inevitable demands of life, my sisters left. In her immensely distraught state of mind, Mamma needed constant attention and nursing for a while. I was not capable of giving it to her. I was not capable of giving anything to anyone anymore. I felt so completely drained and evaporated. Shabana and Riaz took her with them. I, too, was offered accommodation in their house but I did not go. I could not go. I could not rush into new preludes without reaching the end of old epilogues. It was too soon for me to lock up the doors and forget everything. It was too soon for the wounds to heal. It was too soon for the scales to level, thus tilted by the abrupt removal of one amongst.

That night, all of a sudden, I found myself completely alone in such a large house. It was like being immured alive in the icy obscurity of a desolate cyst. The death like hush surrounding me felt utterly awesome. In order to combat darkness and establish some form of link with the living world, I switched on all the lights in the house. The dim bulbs glowed with cold neutrality, attracting a host of wayfaring moths and burning up their wings; geckoes crawled on ceilings in silent pursuit of their prey; mice ran amok in locked rooms; crickets squeaked in the grass outside; random gusts of breeze went rustling through the sleepy shrubs; oft and on some ravens roosting in their nests woke up and let out startled coos for no apparent reason. Beleaguered by such a hostile night, overwhelmed by solitude and borne down by grief, I decided to sort out the house in order to keep myself diverted and occupied. It turned out to be a fatal choice when I came face-to-face with Azra's photograph which Shabbu had hidden away in her own chest of drawers and forgotten to destroy or take away with her.

Suddenly, memories that I had put out of my mind with such a lot of difficulty revived with a bang and surrounded me. She was still wearing her serene smile as if nothing had changed; as if all the landmarks she had left behind were still fluttering along the path on which she once passed; as if its soil was still clinging on to the footprints she made; as if the air around it was still laden with her exhilarating perfume; as if her *chariot* was still filled with her cargo of *dreams;* as if her *unicorns* were still flying around on their wings of bliss; as if her *master saheb,* her *dearest master saheb,* her *very own master saheb* was still waiting outside her door holding a cluster of fresh *Chambeli*; as if her love was immortal, her life was eternal, her death was unreal, everything hers had been preserved by time in pouches filled with the elixir of infinity! A tiny spark emerged from the darkness and lit up the sparkles in her eyes; a mysterious whiff of breeze woke up from its sleep and sent her curls bouncing; the smile accentuated as usual; teeth gleamed like pearls; the cheeks flushed like roses; the welter of lashes flapped incessantly; the tiny earrings swung; the ruby on the nose stud glittered; the bangles stirred up many a forgotten melody; the gentle arms came crashing out of the picture frame; put the crown of her undying love upon my head; circled around my neck, pulled me closer, and closer still, until the gap between us was bridged.

Overwhelmed by a fresh surge of grief, I took the picture into my room and sat staring at the salubrious face for a while as tears came flooding out of my eyes. The words *master saheb*! echoing in her blessed voice in the profound silence of the house lent me more than the minimum measure of comfort I needed to get to grips with myself. Then, reacting to a sudden impulse, I took it over to the mantelpiece on which Papa and Rehana's pictures were already present. Putting hers next to him, I gazed at all of them. He, thus flanked by the two graceful young ladies, looked absolutely spectacular. Three pieces of my heart, torn away from me, two by death and one by distance. Together, they not only represented most of what I loved, but also everything I had lost. Nearly everything.

From that night onwards, I began to live in the house like a hermit, more or less cut off from the outside world. I did not have a job; I had no hobbies or interests; no preoccupations of any sort; no one to keep me company except silent photographs and transient recollections. If I wanted to, I could have obtained a fresh list of potential pupils from Sal and resumed the tuitions, but I did not. I was no longer competent to coach anyone, or to do anything else for that matter. My brain felt damaged; my heart felt crushed; my enthusiasm for life felt dead; all roads ahead of me were roads that led into non-negotiable cul de sacs; all goals yonder were goals I had already crossed and come past; all that remained for me to do was to look out and wait, look out and wait, look out and wait!

Letters from Rehana did not pause. The one she wrote upon hearing about Papa's death was the most painful of all. Other than that, her pet topic continued to be the baby. Not even a hint was dropped about her father's misguided plans.

Although Mr. Rao filed an application for the entry permit soon after we spoke, there was no response from the British High Commission. In spite of being represented by counsel, I kept bombarding them with letters, some beseeching, some angry, some conveying the full details of my wretched plight, some containing a description of the pangs of separation I was enduring due to no fault of mine, some brief reminders. But they did not extend even the courtesy of an acknowledgement. To them, I was just another serial number, just another index card, one more folder gathering dust on their shelves. Why should they evaluate my agony and come forward to console me, anyway? My grief was not theirs.

Soon, I lost track of time. My sisters and their husbands carried on visiting me regularly. While Khaleel mainly concerned himself with the state of my health, Rox often begged me to lock up the house and go live with her where she could look after me. Riaz urged me to abandon my self-imposed isolation and become a normal man. Mamma, having somehow come to terms with her grief, sent for me again and again but I did not respond. Frankly, I did not dare show myself to her in such an awful condition from fear of shocking her. Owing to inadequate nourishment and insufficient sleep, dark patches had surrounded my baggy eyes, giving me the grotesque appearance of a man haunted by ghosts. I also felt like one. The maid, scared that I might have gone mad, refused to live under the same roof with me. One day, Shabbu came and took her away.

Then, suddenly, on a bright and cheerful morning I received an unexpected phone call from Mr. Rao.

"Your interview with the Entry Clearance Officer in Bombay has come up on the twenty-seventh of this month," he informed me. "Can you make it?"

"Make it!" I screamed with joy, "Just try and stop me!"

"In that case, better come and see me for a briefing before you go," he suggested.

I agreed and rushed.

CHAPTER (23)

"Mr. Quraishi?" said the man in Room 608, looking at me from behind a large desk.

Peter Godfrey, the Entry Clearance Officer at the British High Commission in Bombay, had auburn hair, a face as neutral as a piece of rock, granite hard features which made him look sinister, completely devoid of emotions or feelings, not even extending to me the courtesy of a smile.

"Yes," I replied and waited.

"Take your seat," he offered.

That was about as far as he went by way of cordiality. I sat down, my heart going in a weak flutter. Somehow, my prospects in his hands looked pretty bleak to me.

"Well," he began, without bothering to take another look at me. "I presume you know what this interview is all about?"

"Yes, I do," I replied and waited for him to proceed.

"Would you mind if I switch on the tape recorder?" he asked, his index finger already hovering around the controls. Then added as an afterthought, "Just routine, that's all."

"Please go ahead," I said.

He did. From then onwards, whatever conversation took place between us was on record. Without wasting any breath, he plunged straight into the business in hand, browsed through the file that lie on the desk in front of him and fired his first question.

"I notice from your details that you've a Master's Degree in Oil Technology. Are you currently employed?

"No."

"Any special reasons?"

"Only the obvious ones. Scarcity of jobs, keen competition, nepotism, favouritism, corruption, graft, etc."

"Have you any source of livelihood?"

Anticipating such an enquiry, Mr. Rao had already given me clear instructions in course of his briefing not to convey the impression that I was desperate for livelihood.

"I do," I bluffed.

"Such as?"

"I've a house in Hyderabad most of which is rented out. It fetches a reasonable income by our standards."

"How much?"

"Around two thousand rupees per month."

"Where do you live?"

"I occupy a self-contained portion in the same house."

"How did you acquire this property?"

"I inherited it from my father. He died recently, leaving us the house."

"*Us?* Who *else* besides you?"

"Two sisters and a mother. According to the Shariyyah we all share the property in proportions laid down by it."

"What is Shariyyah?"

"Islamic Law, which Muslims in this country are permitted to follow by prevalent state legislation."

"In other words, the whole of the rent doesn't really belong to you, does it?"

"Strictly speaking, no. But my sisters are married well and don't need extra funds. They let me keep the whole of the rent as I don't have any other source of income."

"For only as long as it *pleases* them?

How was I to explain to him the nature of our family ties? He was hardly likely to understand them, even if I tried. Hence, I just kept quiet.

"Have you any other independent source of income you do not share with your siblings?"

"No."

"Looking at your passport," he observed, shifting his focus on my passport that was submitted to him by Mr. Rao along with my application for the entry permit, "I notice that you had applied for and were given a visitor's visa to enter the United Kingdom sometime ago?"

"Yes, I was."

"What for?"

"I was short listed for a few job interviews there."

"But you didn't proceed?"

"No, I didn't. I couldn't afford the fares at the time."

"Since then, have you had any job in your speciality?"

"No."

"Have you had any kind of job at all, paid or unpaid?"

I told him briefly about the tuitions as well as the job at the onstitute.

"What a tragic waste of first class university education!" he commented dryly.

I kept quiet. He paused there for a few moments in order to jot down some notes in the file.

"Did you, at any time since coming out of the university, contemplate employment abroad, besides United Kingdom?" he began again.

"Yes, I did. The United States, the Middle East and a few other South American countries who have oil resources."

"But you couldn't pursue those ideas either, on account of costs involved?"

"No, I couldn't."

"In other words, potential opportunities were *available* to you but you couldn't explore them almost entirely on account of *financial limitations?*"

"Yes, you're quite right."

"And now that you're married to a British Citizen, it isn't the case anymore?"

"No doubt, I'm married to a British Citizen, but I'm not yet on British soil. They're two entirely different things," I said rather bravely.

"But your application for entry permit, however, is designed to accomplish precisely that. I mean—to set you up on British soil."

"My application is merely to enable me to join my wife."

"As well as settle down in the country of her birth, work, earn, flourish and prosper …"

"Perhaps. Only, my trying to compete with your Cambridge and Oxford Graduates would be like holding a candle to the sun."

"We do have lots of graduates from Indian Universities who are employed in well-paid jobs."

"You also have lots of graduates from Indian Universities driving buses and running trains for British Rail. It's all just a matter of chance, being at the

328

right place at the right time," I said and then bit my tongue so hard, I could taste blood.

It was an extremely indiscreet remark to pass, which I did regret instantly, but a trifle too late for retraction. I could clearly see Mr. Godfrey's attitude hardening.

"Let me ask you again," he said pretty firmly. "Isn't it true that marriage alone has made it possible for you to enter United Kingdom and, *provided you are in the right place at the right time*, get yourself a decent job and put your hard-earned degree to proper use towards the making of a sound and successful career?"

"Well, yes."

"At the moment, you happen to be quite satisfied with the way things are for you. You're satisfied with the rents for as long as your siblings let you keep them, you're happy with your work for as long as the tuitions are there, you're happy with the rain, the sunshine, the *Roghun Joshes* and the *Biryanis!* But if at any time in the future, you either get fed up or disillusioned, you can wave your magic wand, and *hey presto!* the gates of Paradise would stand open for you. Only your marriage with a British citizen has presented you with this magic wand, or to put it in a realistic phrase, this golden opportunity. Isn't that the case?"

"I guess it is."

"Having established this point," he said after jotting down more notes in the file, "let's proceed to the next point and talk for a while about your marriage and your wife. Have things worked out for the both of you?"

"We're quite happy, thank you."

"Can you *prove* it?"

"Prove *what*?" I asked him, genuinely surprised by the silly question.

"That you and your wife are *happy?*"

"We're about to have our first child," I told him after a great deal of hesitation. "Isn't it proof enough?"

"Not necessarily," he snapped impatiently, dismissing my contention with a mere wave of his hand, "Being *happy* has nothing to do with being *pregnant*. Conception can simply be a biological outcome of sexual intercourse."

"No, Mr. Godfrey," I protested in a slightly raised pitch. "I'm sorry I can't agree with you. We're going to have a child because we want to. Our child happens to be a product of love and not mere copulation—love begotten by love."

"I see," he said without much enthusiasm. "Is your *loving* wife now *living* with you?"

"No, she isn't."

"Why not?"

"Because her father took her back to England for childbirth. There's a tradition in our families that the first delivery must take place in her parents' house."

"Do you write to each other?"

"Yes, regularly."

"Have you brought along any of her correspondence with you?"

"Pardon?"

"Have you brought any of her letters?"

"No, sir," I replied, staring him straight in the eye, "but even if I had, I don't think I'd let anyone else to read them. They happen to be letters written by a *wife* intended for her *husband's* eyes only and not some sort of *artefacts* to be put on display."

"Well, it's up to you. If you'd brought some and showed them to me, it would've helped your own cause."

"Well, I haven't."

"Which means, apart from your own word, there is no material evidence to support the claim that your child's a product of love. What was it you said? *'Love begotten by Love?'* ..."

"No, there isn't."

"All right, Mr. Quraishi," he continued with the savage line of questioning after jotting down more points in the file. "Let's now turn our attention upon your wife. How did you come across her?"

"As a result of marriage."

"How long had you known her before you got married?"

"The first time I saw her was on our nuptials night."

"Was yours an *arranged* marriage?"

"Yes."

"Who arranged it?"

"My father, through a professional matchmaker."

"Do you know if he had—ahm—a wide range of brides to choose from?"

"He must've shopped around. I happen to be his only son, so I doubt very much if he ever considered *underselling* me."

His nostrils flared and a twinkle appeared in the cold eyes. The stupid phrase was just a mindless slip of the tongue on my part, but he pounced upon it like a panther going for its kill.

"*Underselling!*" he exclaimed in a gruff voice. "What an extraordinary choice of words! Is this what your marriage means to you? Just a *sale?*"

"No, sir. It means a lot to both of us."

"Both of you?"

"Yes, indeed. To both of us."

"And you expect me to accept that merely on your say so?"

"Are you accusing me of lying, Mr. Godfrey?"

"You've all the reason in the world to lie, Mr. Quraishi," he observed, relaxing in the chair. "According to what you've told me just now, you never saw your wife until after you got married. You haven't produced a scrap of evidence in support of the claim that you love her and she loves you back. Sometime prior to your marriage, you did contemplate employment abroad, but couldn't pursue the idea on account of financial limitations. You've excellent academic qualifications but you haven't got a job nor any prospects of finding one here. Is there any reason why I shouldn't suspect your marriage as a *marriage of convenience?* Can you give me one good reason? Just one?"

"Yes, I can," I snapped impatiently, "I'm telling the *truth* whereas you're merely *speculating.*"

Frustration must have shown on my face as well as reflected in the level of my voice, for he sat staring at me for the next few moments without uttering another word. The blank expression on his face did not give away a thing as to the real state of his mind. There was neither a shadow of a smile on the puckered mouth nor a hint of fatigue on the wooden face. It was impossible to say whether he was enjoying the conversation or just getting bored. A fly that had somehow managed to creep into the room hovered at the tip of his nose quite tenaciously but failed to distract his attention. The air conditioning motor hummed without a pause; two fans mounted on the wall circulated the humid air; loose sheets of paper lying on the desk in front of him rustled from time to time. My heart fell into a loud pounding; my blood gushed through my veins from sheer anxiety; my legs went to sleep as a result of nerves. I had absolutely no idea what was going on in his mind, but something was.

"You said your father must've *shopped* around quite a bit," he continued, reverting to the same acrid conversation again. "Do you know why he settled for this particular match in preference to the others?"

"No, I don't."

"Could it be because …"

"She happens to be a British Citizen?" I intercepted him. "Marrying her would enable me to enter the United Kingdom on matrimonial grounds? Help myself to a *khushi* job? To a sound and successful career? To utilise my hard-earned qualifications? To flourish and to prosper? No, sir, I don't think so."

"Why don't you think so, Mr. Quraishi?"

"Because, at the time he arranged the match, he had *other* things on his mind."

"What other things?"

"My sisters."

"What've *they* got to do with *your* marriage?"

"He was in desperate need of money to get them married too and my dowry was the only source available to him for raising the capital needed."

"In other words, he settled for this match entirely out of financial considerations?"

"To the best of my knowledge, yes."

"And you too?"

"My reasons were different."

"What were they?"

"To help my father give the girls a decent break in life."

"How much dowry did you get?"

"Two hundred and fifty thousand rupees."

"Was that why you referred to your marriage as a 'sale,' Mr. Quraishi? Because it entailed transfer of capital from one party to the other?"

"Frankly, it hadn't amounted to much else at the time. But afterwards …"

"Yes? What happened afterwards?"

"Nothing that matters, Mr. Godfrey," I said with a shrug.

He, too, shrugged and scanned through the file on yet another fishing expedition. I waited with a bated breath, more or less certain that I was fighting a losing battle.

"I notice from submissions made by your solicitors that your marriage was performed by a priest and not by a civil registrar of marriages. Any special reasons for it?"

There were several, and I told him, as I knew them. After spending a good half an hour or so cross examining me minutely on the subject, he finally zoomed in on the *Shariyyah* Law concerning *divorces* and harped upon it alone.

"Let me get this straight," he said, riveting his attention back upon my face. "What you're saying is, had you been married by the *registrar* instead of the *Quazi,* the procedure for divorce would be different. If you decided to *call off the deal,* you'd have to apply to a judge, appoint solicitors, go through all the motions, bear the costs, and waste a lot of time. But in the case of a *religious* marriage, there're no such stipulations involved. All you need to do is to pronounce the words *'I divorce you'* thrice in the presence of two witnesses and you're *home and dry.* Not only does the divorce become valid but also irrevocable. Am I right?"

"More or less."

"While one is an expensive and time-consuming affair, the other isn't."

"Yes."

"Should you decide to finish the marriage, you can do so *just like that, "* he said, illustrating the 'just like that' bit by snapping his fingers thrice.

"Theoretically yes. But then, so can she."

"Indeed! So can she!"

"What's that supposed to mean?"

"Once you enter U.K. on the strength of this permit, there's nothing to stop you from calling off the whole thing and making a fresh start. Or she, from setting you as well as herself free with those three magic words. Isn't that so?"

What could I say! When the proposal of a civil marriage was discussed in Mr. Rao's office, nobody had *divorce* in mind, neither Uncle Haroon nor Papa. But Mr. Godfrey singled it out nicely, the way he wanted to, the way it suited him, the way it served his purpose.

"You said you agreed to this marriage merely to help your father raise the capital for getting your sisters married," he pointed out, coming at me from a different direction. "In other words, when you accepted this match, all you had in your mind was *loyalty* to your *family.* Am I right?"

"Yes."

"In what way would this loyalty have come under fire, if you had asked to *see* your fiancée *once,* and to get to know her just a little bit before marrying her? After all, a marriage happens to be a lifelong commitment and not a picnic on the seaside. Or, doesn't it?

"It had nothing to do with *loyalty* to my *family.* In case you aren't aware of this, Islam explicitly prohibits men and women from indulging in any form of *premarital courtship,* on any scale, big or small. We being practicing Muslims, we follow these rules to the letter."

"Pre-marital courtship!" he exclaimed, widening his eyes with utter incredulity.

"The reference is to *love before wedlock* . In traditional Muslim families, brides and bridegrooms aren't allowed to even see each other prior to the wedding, let alone have enamoured outings for familiarisation." I elaborated upon it for what it was worth.

"And you call that *pre-marital courtship?"*

"In a manner of speaking, yes," I confirmed.

"You mean, taking one teeny weenie *peek* at your bride-to-be amounts to premarital courtship?"

At that stage, I stopped answering his questions. He stopped pressing me for answers, but did spend yet another uneasy spell reading my face as if they were all written on it. I felt scorched under his piercing gaze. The room once again plunged into a precarious silence; my heart kept beating so loud I could distinctly hear its incessant thumps. Like a blind man locked inside a dark dungeon with an angry bull, I knew I was going to be assaulted, but could not anticipate from which direction it was coming. My mind alert, limbs stiff, persecuted by a vague sense of prognosis and suddenly scared out of my wits, I simply waited.

"Was this the *first* matrimonial proposal you had considered, Mr. Quraishi? Or, have there been others before?" he asked.

The question hit me hard like a thunderbolt. Knowingly or unknowingly, he was getting dangerously close to a side of my life to which I could not afford him access. "Yes. I was engaged to be married once before," I mumbled nonetheless, it being the truth.

"Where was she from? United States? Canada? Australia?"

She was a very simple girl, born and brought up in the depressing neighbourhood of Aghapura, until I turned her into a deity with my love, in my world, in my heart … .

"She was from Hyderabad, sir," I told him.

"Did your father arrange that marriage too?"

In a way he had, except that we were already in love. She was my pupil and yet I had fallen to her divine charm without any regard for traditions, religion, morality, principles, and ethics. Together with Arithmetic, I had also thought her how two hearts add together and then multiply into love!

"Yes, he did," I said aloud.

"Why did it fall through?"

"Horoscopes," I replied without getting into the details. "Something to do with conflicting stars. We tried to defy the prophesy of five *tamarind seeds* but miserably flopped."

"Never set eyes upon her, either?"

We had not only seen each other but also indulged in a brief spell of *premarital courtship*, much of it wasted in fears and uncertainties, etiquette and modesty, appearances and pretences, being the teacher and the taught, writing letters without mailing them, communicating in the language of the eyes, taking shelter in hearts, in thoughts, in fantasies, in dreams, in nightmares. I did court her and she reciprocated, through the medium of our bated breaths, silent looks, suppressed heartbeats, inner emotions, animated faces. Only, if I was asked to submit proof of the storms that raged in our minds, the joy we experienced in each other's company, the hopes we bred and the expectations we harboured, I would never be able to do it.

"She was my pupil, Mr. Godfrey, and yet we fell in love," I told him that much, desperately fighting back my tears.

"*Love before wedlock?*" he deliberately emphasised the words, almost laughing in my face.

The question forced me out of that room. My body was there but I was not. I saw myself in the vast forecourt of the *holy shrine*. The horizon had just split like a pod and ushered in the first silver streak of day. The magnificent dome of the mausoleum rose against the background of the spotless blue sky in all its splendour; scores of beggars and cripples were lined up alongside the path; stall keepers were doing brisk trade and florists were selling fresh *Chambeli buds* on a non-profit basis. I bought a few strings and then gave them to a little lady next to me, clad in a black cloak, her pretty face hidden behind the veil. I could only see her eyes, large, moist, lustrous, gleaming, dazzling, pinned to my face, asking questions, making promises. Hand-in-hand, we walked past a large tree upon which noisy flocks of ravens had gathered, clamouring, hovering, tending to their nests, building new ones. We had a nest of our own to build but a silly old man in green robes was challenging us. That was why I had taken her to the *shrine*, to get rid of her of fears, to wedge her courage, to reassure her that our love could never be destroyed by discarnate phantoms and bogeymen ... .

After that, I saw us both enter the *shrine*. It was spacious, breathtaking and awe inspiring. The mosaic floor was polished to a gleaming lustre and looked like sheen of water in which our images reflected. A packed crowd of devotees sat engrossed in prayers, moved by veneration, eyes shut, minds in communion with Allah, laying bear their troubled hearts, seeking His help,

His mercy, His peace. There were Angels too, invisible to the eye but in attendance upon those who believed in them. Roses heaped upon the tombs; fragrance of incense and jossticks filled the air; the whole atmosphere was strangely charged, silence broken only by the rustle of clothes, by the motion of bodies, by the sound of footfalls, of gasps of breath, of muffled whispers, flapping of wings, cooing of pigeons … .

Then I saw both of us sit in a quiet corner, eyes filled with tears but hearts with hopes. I put a ring on her finger and then we took our vows, our union witnessed by the holy aints; our love consecrated by the invisible Angels; our bonds tied by Allah Himself whom I believed to be the most Merciful and the most Munificent of all; the Scribe of Destinies and Master of Fate, one greater than all the Quazi s and registrars of this world. We made each other a lot of promises that day; made so many plans for the future; exchanged so many pledges. It was love before wedlock; it was our success story; it was our fairy tale. Our goals were in sight, within our reach, without any hurdles. But did it suffice? Was that enough? Could we make it to the finishing line? No, we could not … .

'Love before wedlock ... Love before wedlock ... Love before wedlock!' the echo of Mr. Godfrey's voice poured into my ears and put me back on earth.

"Yes, it was," I mumbled.

"But I thought you said you don't subscribe to the notion of 'premarital courtship'?"

"It was all a big mistake, Mr. Godfrey. I learnt my lesson the hard way."

"What was the big mistake? Falling in love before marriage? Or wanting to marry the person you fell in love with?"

Telling him that she died of Small Pox felt like an insult to her memory. "Falling in love," I said instead. "Someone much stronger than me got in the way and messed up all our plans. That is why I don't subscribe to the silly notion, Mr. Godfrey. Not anymore."

"I see," he said and returned his attention back on the file.

At that stage I realised there was not much point in extending that interview. Our backs had already touched the walls of the narrow room in which we were both trapped and were simply groping around.

"Listen, Mr. Godfrey," I said, somehow subsiding my run away emotions. "Some people fall in love and then get married, others get married and then fall in love. In my case, the latter has happened. I love my wife, I cherish her and I want to be with her because she's my stalwart, my champion, my backbone and my best friend. Jobs and careers are not even at the back of my mind. I don't care whether we live in the *affluence* of your country or in the *squalor* of mine. Here, there, anywhere, but together. That is all I want. So please don't make a mountain out of this molehill. One stroke of your pen can either give me so much or take it all away from me. Have a heart, please?"

"If that's all you really want, Mr. Quraishi," he remarked after carefully weighing my plea in his mind. "Why's it that she can't come here to live with you instead of you going there to live with her? If you had married someone from your own country, wouldn't she have come to live with you in *your* house? Isn't it a time-honoured custom in your families that husbands keep their wives where their home is and not the other way round?"

I would have liked nothing better. If others much worse off than me were managing, there was no reason why I could not. The idea of going to England was not mine. But how could I tell him that? How could I expose to him whose hand was behind it? Who was running the show and calling all the shots? How could I wash our own dirty linen in front of other people's doors? I could not. I just could not and kept quiet.

"Frankly speaking," Mr. Godfrey began to sum up, "I'm not at all convinced that your motives are as honest as you claim them to be. If they were, I see no reason why you can't send for her instead of she sending for you, in keeping with our rules, with prevalent legislation, and above all, with your own traditions."

"And if she isn't in a position to come to live with me here for reasons beyond her control?"

"You're, indeed, entitled to present those reasons to me for evaluation and consideration. So is she, to the Home Office over there in London. Are there any such reasons that you would like me to take into account?"

There were plenty of them, but none that I could put forward without a sense of betrayal.

"Just tell me what's the bottom line, Mr. Godfrey?" I asked him, finally laying down my arms.

Before answering the question, he switched off the tape recorder and then spent some time studying me.

"Off the record," he mused dispassionately, "there're two recommendations that spring to mind out of which I can make a choice. Let's look at both of them one after the other:

"Firstly, I can say that an year or so ago, a respectable Asian businessman settled in the United Kingdom arrived in this country in search of a decent match for his daughter. Obviously, he looked around in his native city of Hyderabad and spotted an upcoming young man of excellent academic qualifications and sound social background with the help of a professional matchmaker. In keeping with prevalent traditions, both the families got together and agreed to the alliance. As a result, the marriage took place. Sometime later, the wife returned home to Bradford and sent for her husband. In course of my interrogation of him in connection with his application for an entry permit, I came across nothing suspicious. This is a straightforward case and I am aware of no reason why his application should be turned down.

"On the other hand, I can choose to say that I found you to be a man of dubious character, questionable ethics and suspicious intent. Although well qualified, you neither have a substantial job nor any prospects of finding one in this country. There is ample documentary evidence to suggest that you already tried to go abroad in pursuit of livelihood but failed. However, now that you're married to a …"

"Depending upon which way you are inclined to?" I asked him, interrupting the lengthy explanation.

"In the absence of evidence to the contrary, what else can one do?"

"I don't suppose appealing to your sense of fairplay would do me much good, would it?"

"My being fair to you or my not being fair isn't the issue, Mr. Quraishi. Laws are passed to be followed, by your wife, by you, by me, and I'm doing just that."

"But you have a choice—you said so yourself. Why don't you choose the former instead of the latter?"

"Because, as a senior executive officer in Her Majesty's Government, I'm being paid to implement the laws passed by Her Majesty's Parliament. It's as simple as that!" he snapped.

Without uttering another word or even bothering to take his leave, I got to my feet and came out of the crepuscular room. In sharp contrast to the pleasant temperature inside it, the long and seemingly interminable corridor leading to the exit door was baking. Dragging myself on heavy feet resulting from nerves, from humiliation and from disappointment, I carried on walking like a somnambulist sunk in a trance. The main foyer was crammed with visitors to the embassy of every colour, age and sex. Somewhere around there, while gazing at those sweat soaked hopefuls who had come to sort out their wrecked lives just like me, I accidentally bumped into someone going past me in a big rush.

"I'm sorry," I said, politely apologizing to him.

"My fault," replied the man in a pleasant tone. "Are you all right?"

"Yes, thank you."

"Going to England?"

"I was hoping to, but I don't think I can."

"Keep my card," he said, forcing one in my hand. "We're travel agents of worldwide reputation in accomplishing all sorts of impossible missions. Whether the task is to *take the Mountain to Mohamed, or to bring Mohamed to the Mountain,* no job is too small or too big for us. Try us sometime, when you need to."

So saying, he grinned, winked at me in a curious way and disappeared in the crowd. *'NEW ERA TRAVELS'* said the card, naming its holder as Shanti Vadkar and listing two telephone numbers, one for the office and the other for his residence. Without realising its significance at the time, I tucked the card inside my wallet and came out.

CHAPTER (24)

A day after that disastrous interview with Mr. Godfrey, all of us gathered at Riaz's place to talk things over. By then, I had already locked up *Kalim Manzil* and moved into a spare room in his house, taking weekly turns with Rox and Khaleel in order to keep them happy too. I had also told them everything about Uncle Haroon's devious plans concerning my future. The news had, quite understandably, shocked everyone, and in the circumstances, the idea of obtaining an Entry Permit to go to Bradford in time for the delivery had seemed like light at the bottom of the tunnel, until those hopes too were ruthlessly dashed by the intransigent stance taken by Mr. Godfrey.

"What the hell is it?" Riaz asked wearing a baffled expression on his otherwise intelligent face, "Is it *good* news or is it *bad* news?"

"Frankly," I replied, "I don't know it myself. At least, not until I've talked things over with Mr. Rao. This was his idea."

"Are you going to write to Rehana and tell her what's going on?" he asked next.

"I don't think you should," Shabbu said, for once putting forward an unsolicited comment, with Rehana's best interests at heart. "Not until later and only after the delivery."

"Wait a minute," Khaleel entered into the conversation, himself as confused as the rest of us. "I don't understand this. If you aren't given the entry permit by the embassy, how can your father-in-law expect you to go there?"

"It's another thing I intend to check with Mr. Rao. He ought to know," I replied.

"Perhaps this is a blessing in disguise?" Rox mused, looking at me with anxious eyes.

"Perhaps," I agreed with her, "only, I would have preferred to be by Rehana's side until this matter is finally resolved. Her being left entirely at the mercy of her father looks like a risky proposition to me."

Everybody endorsed the same view. However, as I had already made an appointment to see Mr. Rao on the next day, the topic was postponed until then.

First thing in the morning I went to his office and gave him the details. I could see that the news I conveyed did not match his expectations. His otherwise cheerful mien undermined by a touch of disappointment, he sat tight-lipped for a while, rolling things over in his mind.

"What next?" I asked him.

A chain smoker, especially when under stress, he went for his cigarettes first, lit one and pulled upon it, his active mind fully focussed upon the awkward situation.

"Let's wait until we hear from the Embassy," he suggested in a while, "Sooner or later, this Mr. Godfrey would have to make his opinions official."

"Are you still hopeful?"

"Miracles can always happen."

One miracle in a lifetime is more than what anyone could expect, and I was already given mine in the form of Rehana.

"Suppose his decision does go against me, as it more or less seems to. What then?" I pressed.

"We can always appeal to an independent tribunal," he said, "The man appears to have built up a notional case against you. We know that the real facts don't bear him out. We'll simply have to convincingly present those facts to the tribunal."

"You reckon I still stand a chance?"

"Evidence is evidence as opposed to opinions. Five different minds seldom think alike. There's plenty of scope."

"How long would that take?"

"I don't have a precise idea, but probably between eight to ten months. Or even more. We'll just have to wait and see."

"But what's the use, Mr. Rao? Rehana would've given birth to the baby long before that."

"So?"

"After the delivery, she'd expect to be sent back. Unless, of course, her father told her the truth."

"He might do just that. What's to stop him?"

"The possibility of a confrontation with her. She might not like the idea of him coercing me like this."

"Fair enough. It would then be a matter between the father and the daughter, wouldn't it?"

"Yes, it would. And that's precisely what scares me."

"Why?"

"Because she's no match for him. Besides, whether she elects to give in to him or take a stance against his wishes, it would happen soon after the delivery and long before the tribunal. If she opts for the latter, she'd come back herself somehow. But if she succumbs to the former, she wouldn't be worth my fighting over, would she?"

"What did you say?" he demanded angrily, drawn to full attention, breathing fire, as if by passing such a comment I had slighted my marriage, I had insulted Rehana, I had treated their entire family with contempt unworthy of them.

His hostile mien threw such a scare into me I dared not repeat myself. He was a big shot, a successful barrister, quite knowledgeable even in our private affairs, but much more than all that, he belonged to the opposite camp. The mere fact that he was being sympathetic towards me did not mean I could take him or his client for granted. So I hushed up.

"Listen, my friend," he said, his piercing eyes glued to my face, "and tell me if you ever asked yourself this question. A man of Abdallah's social and financial status must've had a very wide choice of suitors for his daughter's hand. Yet he settled for you. Why?"

It was a mystery that I had myself been trying to unravel for a long time. Rehana's pet theory aside, his revelations were welcome. Perhaps he could offer me a more convincing explanation.

"You tell me, Mr. Rao," I ventured somehow. "According to my wife, it's because marriages are made in Heaven. But that isn't the real case, is it?"

"No, it certainly isn't," he snapped. "And since you seem to be labouring under a lot of misconceptions, let me give you some food for thought."

When he came down upon me with so much weight, I shot to attention. I could see that I had asked for trouble and judging from his belligerent attitude, I had a feeling I was going to get it in big doses.

"The first time I came across your father-in-law," he said, building upon the same theme, "it was way back in Madras when we were both at law college. Apart from being class fellows, we were also very close friends.

After graduation, I came here and set up this practice. But he decided to try his luck on a venture that he had had in mind for a long time. When he set out for England to fulfil his cherished ambitions, all he had on him were three pounds sterling and a one-way ticket. No doubt, he's now ranked amongst the largest importers of mica to the West, but for him to rise to such prominence from those humble beginnings, it wasn't easy. He made it the hard way."

Up to that point in time, there were no special surprises in it for me. It sounded very much like another of those remarkable success stories that one hears from time to time. Fine, Uncle Haroon was a self-made man. So were Howard Hughes and Robert Maxwell. What did all that have to do with me? I was not even ambitious.

"About an year or so ago," continued Mr. Rao, "when he came here in search of a suitable match for his daughter, he had only one thing in mind: he wanted someone who was prepared to set up home in England, somewhere close to him. As you know, Rehana is his only child, and make no mistake about his love for her, which she's received in plenty. She knows it, and so do some of us who are close to the family. Therefore, if he settled for you out of such a vast choice, it couldn't possibly be because of marriages being made in Heaven, could it?"

"Why *did* he settle for me, Mr. Rao?" I asked him once again, more firmly than before. "Looking at the gap that has opened up between his aspirations and my priorities, I hardly seem to fit the bill. Don't you think he should have made sure he was getting value for money *before* dishing it out?"

"He did make sure, Mr. Quraishi, in every other way except one: instead of talking things over with you face-to-face, he resorted to *tradition* and dealt with your father. Seems like he stepped on a banana skin there, don't you agree?"

The moment he dragged my father into the equation, I became extra cautious. Papa was no longer around to speak for himself. It would be too easy to put all the blame upon a dead man and get away with it. Besides, the conversation had moved away from the main issue. Whatever happened in the past was no longer relevant. My concern was for the future, which did not seem to be receiving much attention.

"What did my father do, Mr. Rao?" I asked him. "Apart from negotiating the dowry and other inconsequential details, he did not concern himself with anything else. At least, not to my knowledge."

It seemed I was mistaken, for he swiftly got to his feet, took out a folder from his filing cabinet and thrust it under my nose.

"If you care to read through the contents of this folder," he snapped relentlessly, "I'm sure you'll come across plenty to the contrary."

I stared at him, utterly flabbergasted. There was no need for me to go through the folder; his word was good enough. We were not fighting out a lawsuit; no one was on trial; no one was making any repudiations; his office was not a courtroom; I was not researching into the origins of my marriage but merely trying to protect it against unfair encroachments.

"Tell me in plain English, Mr. Rao. What is all this?" I asked him point-blank.

"Some facts which might change your thinking," he snapped again, still in a rotten mood. "I began with asking you if you knew why Abdallah chose you for his daughter. I'm now trying to answer the same question. He did so because your father gave him a written undertaking that you *will* emigrate to UK and pitch your tent there."

There it was, the real explanation that had been eluding me for such a long time! In other words, my father, *as party of the first part*, offered to exchange my life through a *non-negotiable instrument*, and Uncle Haroon, *as party of the second part*, took up the offer. As a result of the *deal* between the two *parties*, not only did capital change hands, but Yusuff's spermatozoa also fertilized Rehana's ovum. Papa thus became richer by around two hundred and fifty thousand rupees, Uncle Haroon by a subservient son-in-law, and Rehana and I by a child. Now, I was being called upon to discharge my contractual obligations!' Inside the folder was my *bill of sale*, and the man whom I had mistaken for a friend reading out the book to me!

"A pact of honour," continued Mr. Rao, "is as good as the men who make it, Mr. Quraishi. Your father-in-law kept his end of the bargain in full. Can you blame him for trying to make sure that your father's end of the bargain is also kept?"

I could not question the validity of his argument; it was absolutely flawless. Neither could I doubt his word that Papa, in desperate need of money at the time, had given them such an undertaking. Besides, it was not entirely his fault; I had been educated for a career; I had not succeeded in finding it; and at one time I did take a keen interest in going abroad in pursuit of a career. Uncle Haroon offered an easy solution to all of those. My father got the much-needed capital and I got the long awaited opportunity of putting my qualifications to good use. A wife like Rehana was just *icing on the cake*. Taking all that into account, I did not seem to have fetched too bad a price. An insignificant, inconsequential, good for nothing *bum* like me, I stood paid in full. Uncle Haroon owned me—lock stock and barrel, a settee in his lounge, a vase on the mantelpiece, a sack of potatoes in the kitchen and I in his daughter's bedroom! The fact that I had a will of my own; a mind that could reason; a heart that could feel; a conscience that could evaluate, did not matter one bit. There was a stamp printed upon my back that said *sold* and I was! If I backed away, my father's name would be tarnished; I could not thus disgrace him because he was dead. There could also be another grim consequence resulting from my backing out: I was at risk of losing the woman I loved the most. And Mr. Rao, given a special power of attorney by his client-cum-friend to ensure my home delivery in excellent shape, was not inclined to spare any scruples. What if I was refused the permit; the matter could be taken up with the tribunal. In the meantime, the flames in which I was burning here, and in which Rehana was burning over there, could wait. Our dreams could wait, our hopes could wait, our conjugal vows could wait; our mutual loyalties could wait. And I had thought Mr. Godfrey was being despicable!

"I'm sorry, Mr. Rao," I conceded the point to him, finding my voice somehow. "Until now, I was under the impression that my father merely *used* me. I didn't know he *sold* me."

"Well, you know now," he said, still without letting up the pressure. "Suppose, soon after the delivery, Abdallah confronted his daughter with the same details. What do you expect her to do?'

An extremely sensitive detail, it had completely missed my attention. What would she do? On one hand, there was *her* father, and on the other hand, there was *my* father. Given those facts, I could hardly see her disappoint the one or discredit the other; both of them were equally important to her. A young woman of limited experience but strong affiliations, she would simply persuade herself into making all the obvious decisions, the easy ones, the ones that stood out: she would 'render unto *Caesar* whatever belonged to *Caesar*,' setting me and all of mine aside until some other day!

"I see what you mean," I stammered.

"I'm glad you do."

"What do you think I should do?"

"One of two things. Either wait until Mr. Abdallah confronts his daughter and see what she decides to do, or don't leave the decision to her. You make it *before* she has to. Write to her and tell her that you've changed your mind about living here and have decided to immigrate to England on your own accord. Then, whenever the authorities permit you to, go there and sort things out with her father yourself. Whether you wish to settle there or return here along with your family, *you* decide and *you* work it out. Am I making sense?"

He was. Just like his logic, his advice was also flawless. Based upon it, I asked him to go ahead with the appeal in the event of Mr. Godfrey's ruling going against me and came home.

Later that night, after everyone went to bed, the house plunged into silence, all lights went off, a dull moon began to clamber up the horizon and the myriad young buds of *night queen* in the garden were tickled awake by an invisible spray of mist, the hushed solitude in my room suddenly made me aware of how lonely I really was even in the midst of company; how desperate was my craving for my partner; how tall had the Himalayan and the Alpine Peaks grown in order to prevail between the East and the West! As I lay sinking and surfacing in the turbulent undulations of my gloom, dearest Shabbu turned up with a hot mug of Horlicks to ease me into sleep. Accepting her kind hospitality as well as the tasty beverage with gratitude, I told her whatever happened at Mr. Rao's office. As usual, she listened to me without making any comments.

"Is this fair, Shabbu?" I asked her in a shallow voice. "Uncle Haroon comes to Hyderabad waving a few thousand rupees in his hands in order to buy himself a son-in-law. Not a *husband* for Rehana but a *slave* for himself. Papa sees the money and grabs it; not for Rehana and me but to buy Riaz for you and Khaleel for Rox. Uncle Haroon tells me where to sit and where to stand, how to brush my hair, which toothpaste is good for my teeth, what is the ideal length for my toenails; Mr. Godfrey says I can't go to England, Mr. Rao says I must. And not one amongst them courteous enough to ask me what I want."

"What do *you* want, Bhaijan?"

"Just live and be happy, that's all. Is it too much to ask?"

"No, it isn't."

"Then why do we have to bid for it? To match offers? To pay prices? Why are we being required to compete? To fight? To win? To justify?"

"I don't know. What've you decided to do?"

"What else can I do? Just like Mr. Rao has suggested, I will write to Rehana and tell her that I've decided to immigrate to her country. And I will too, if there's no other option."

"Don't you want to?"

"No, I don't. But then, I can't live without Rehana, either. Can you, without Riaz now?"

"No, I can't."

"There you are, then!"

She kept quiet. An otherwise pleasant night, it should have been one of bliss and contentment for me too, but nights had lost their charm and cheer. Of late, they had only been coming to take their toll.

It took me two whole days, but I managed to finish writing the crucial letter, keeping the matter as simple as possible. She already knew that my job at the institute had come to an end and why. Building upon the same theme, I wrote that I had been making applications up and down the country for a decent break in my own speciality but without any luck because of scarcity of vacancies, nepotism, graft and so on. It was not true, but in my situation, I could not afford to be too candid. After a lot of unsuccessful attempts, I told her I had come to the inevitable conclusion that finding an appropriate career in this country was like *pie in the sky*. No doubt, there was other work available, but nothing geared to ensuring a worthwhile career. Then I reminded her that we were both at a stage in life where prudence was the *by word* in order to get along. Three from two now, and probably four and five in due course, we were increasing in numbers, and thereby also, multiplying our duties and responsibilities. Even if I was married to the only daughter of a wealthy mica importer, I said I would prefer to stand on my own two feet and not live off other peoples fortunes. I had already wasted enough golden years of my youth and had no wish to waste anymore, chasing gold at the bottom of rainbows. As she knew it quite well, with Papa already gone, Mamma being taken care of by reliable hands and both my sisters well settled in life, there was nothing else holding me down to Hyderabad. Whereas my responsibilities towards one family had come to an end, those towards another were in desperate need of attention. Making use of yet another harmless bluff, I wrote that property market in the city was picking up momentum and it was getting a lot easier to sell larger properties. Even though no one was demanding me to do it straight away, I must not forget that it was Papa's final admonition to me to sell the house at the earliest opportunity and pass on to Mamma and the girls whatever share in the proceeds were theirs according to the *Shariyyah*. I was, therefore, honour-bound to fulfil his most ardent wish without too much delay. Taking all that into account, I wrote that I had decided to heed Uncle Haroon's advice to pitch my tent in England where I could fulfil my career ambitions as well as give our kids a decent break in life. Making a passing reference to the issue of the entry permit, I explained to her that I made a big cock up at the embassy due to inexperience, but that, if they rejected my application because of it, Mr. Rao was already preparing to appeal to a tribunal on my behalf. No doubt, such a course of action would necessarily mean delays, but what were a few months when compared to our entire lives? Thus coating it nicely with sugar, I administered the bitter pill.

Two weeks later her reply arrived. As usual, a good 90 percent of it was devoted to the baby, without any reference to the main crux of my letter. She talked at length about all the activity that was going on inside her; about pre-natal nursing in Bradford; about her new gynaecologist; about this and about that. Why a name for the baby has not yet been finalised? What exactly was holding things up? How am I coping without her? How is Mamma? How are Shabbu, Rox, Riaz and Khaleel? Why is there still no news of the girls being in *the family way,* etcetera and etcetera. 'I read the bit about your decision to emigrate,' she finally got to the point. 'Like you said, the appeal will take time. Meanwhile, soon after the baby's born, I'll be back. We can then thrash the whole thing out face-to-face. What's the hurry? ...'

That was all she had to say about a topic that took me two whole days to cover! If she was aware of her father's intentions to coerce me into making the move and had guessed that it could simply be my way of sparing her the *test of loyalties,* then the dispassionate attitude which she had taken towards an issue as contentious as that was nothing short of brilliant! If she gave him such a simple and down-to-earth reason for coming back here along with the baby, there was not much he could do to dissuade her. 'Sure, sure, why not?' I could almost hear her say to him. 'As soon as we get permission from the embassy to settle here, we'll catch the first available flight and come back.' What could he say to that? How could he openly mistrust her and yet expect her loyalty? How could he possibly *force* a person who was not offering *resistance?* If I knew him any, he would not even try. He was crafty and devious but not stupid, and she had an inborn ability to deal with people like him, 'to render unto Caesar what belonged to Caesar, setting aside God's for God alone!'

In due course, Mr. Rao received a letter from the embassy to the effect that my application for an entry permit had not been successful. Secretly, I welcomed the news. It meant the matter would now inevitably go before a tribunal, putting everything on hold for the foreseeable future. Time, which had so far prevailed like a curse between us, suddenly turned into a blessing. There was no chance of Uncle Haroon either trying to hold Rehana back, or of his forcing me into going there.

Pleased to learn that the tide had swerved in my direction at long last, Riaz commenced preparations for Rehana's return to Hyderabad along with the baby. What was once my courageous bluff to Mr. Godfrey began shaping up into reality. First of all, *Kalim Manzil* was converted into two self-contained apartments and put in the hands of a reliable estate agent for leasing. With that, I was not only a family man but also a man of means to support it. Next, he proceeded towards providing a roof over our heads. Being an architect himself, he designed a cute little bungalow for us, obtained planning permission and handed over the contract of its construction to a known builder. Money towards the project came from Khaleel. Mamma gladly agreed to come and live with us after Rehana returned. Back in familiar surroundings, her mind focussed upon her cherished hobbies and her hands filled with the care of an infant, she could not have hoped for a better way of spending her old age.

Not content with all that, Riaz also offered me a full-time job in his office as a manager. Because of his honesty, integrity and professional competence, his practice was expanding month by month, with two more new partners teaming up. He did need someone like me to look after the administrative side of the work as well as be loyal to him and I did not mind working for him. Until only a few months ago, he was a total stranger to us all and yet his favours were beginning to pile up. We had a common bond between us in the form of Shabbu because of which I, too, was given a very special place in his heart.

Soon after all the hectic activity connected with sorting out my own problems came to an end, I started work. It was not at all difficult to handle. Apart from making some extra money, I also had something to keep my mind occupied with. Besides, there was no other way in which I could pay something back to dear Riaz in return for all his kindness and generosity. My implicit loyalty to him in the handling of his practice covered it all.

Matters were progressing very smoothly until one morning when I received an unexpected letter from Uncle Haroon. He mainly concerned himself with details of yet another application his solicitors had made to the Home Office on my behalf for the same entry permit, requesting the home secretary to set aside Mr. Godfrey's decision for any one of the umpteen reasons which they listed. 'Rehana has developed some sort of a freak fever,' he wrote towards the end, 'on account of which she's spending a few days at the hospital. I mention this merely to ease your mind in case there are any unexpected delays in her letters. With the date of delivery also being so close, she might not be able to stay abreast of her correspondence. But don't worry. Either your auntie or I …'

I could not bear to finish the rest. It was more or less on a similar note that Uncle Saleh had once summoned me to Azra's bedside. *A freak fever* had cost me so much the very repetition of those words jerked the rug from underneath my feet. I knew there was no such thing as Small Pox in England; I knew my wife would not be given anything less than the best by way of medical attention; I knew whatever happened to me once simply could not happen again in the same span of life. But then, I was a man without a *God,* I had no one to look up to; I had no one to scream at; I had no one to beg from or to blame upon this time around. I had lost my utmost support; I had renounced my best friend. I had relinquished my strongest hope. So I panicked … .

CHAPTER (25)

I made up my mind to go to Bradford whether by *hook* or by *crook*. I must admit it was a rather emotional and hasty decision but the only one acceptable to me. Different people said different things; Riaz thought I was overreacting; Khaleel said I ought to give myself some time and think things over; according to Sal I was being utterly childish and according to Mr. Rao, it was all a storm in the tea cup. As always, Shabana sheltered behind silence and Roxana behind tears, but I did not heed any of them. All I wanted to do was just to be by my wife's side in the moment of her need, no less and no more. As far as I was concerned, *freak fevers* do only one of two things: they either come and *go,* or they come and *get.* True, it was not in my hands to dictate destinies or to rewrite them, but that was neither here nor there. I simply wanted to be near Rehana, wait until the baby was born and then bring both of them back with me. What Uncle Haroon had to say, what Papa had done, what Mr. Rao would think, none of it mattered to me anymore.

To be able to concentrate and act unhampered I desperately needed complete privacy. So, packing up my bags, I shifted into the bungalow first. It was not yet furnished but Riaz had got our old telephone reconnected to it, which was all I needed.

Time, by my watch, had just gone past two in the afternoon. Around six hours behind us, GMT would be eight in the morning, early enough to catch people indoors. Direct dialling had come to Hyderabad recently, which made things a lot easier. Making a start with Rehana's house, I dialled their number. It took me a while to obtain a free line because of the peak hour but I did manage to get through. Only, the bell kept ringing but no one was around to answer it.

Next, I tried Uncle Haroon's office. According to the lady who spoke to me, he was out of station. She did not know where he had gone off to or for how long nor did she have any idea of what was going on in his house. Apparently, he never discussed private affairs with his employees.

I could try again, but in the mean time, I had to work out a plan of action. To be able to travel abroad in such a big rush, I needed money as well as contacts. Who could help me with those? Sal, Riaz, Khaleel and Mr. Rao could, but no one had come forward with any offers because they did not approve of what I was doing. It left me pretty much on my own.

The only other name that sprang to mind was Mr. Vadkar, the gentleman whom I had run into at the British Embassy and who had offered to help me out if I needed any help. I was fairly certain that, when he mentioned 'moving Mountains to Mohamed,' he could only be hinting at *illegal passage.* If nothing else, it seemed at least worth a try. Getting through to Bombay was not so difficult either. In less than five minutes, I had his office on the line. They said he was not yet in. Then I tried his house. They said he had just gone out. Dead-end again.

Concentrating upon the next most important subject, I paused to think. I needed money too, and in plenty, without any delays, without any fuss, without any questions asked. How would I cross that bridge? The State Bank of Hyderabad was all I could think of. I had personally dealt with the manager in connection with Papa's loan, paid off the interests as promised and had finally repaid the debt too in full. The title deeds of the house were still in my possession. No doubt, the property did not have a single owner anymore, but if he had any idea of our family ties, he must know my signature would speak for all. I hoped he would accept that. It was pointless contacting him yet as I had no idea of how much money was going to be involved, but at least having put him down as a viable source, I left it at that for the time being.

All my hopes towards travel arrangements were banked upon Mr. Vadkar alone, whom I had met only once and quite by chance. Even he was not a particularly reliable source. For a man who mostly hung around the British Embassy to pick his vulnerable targets, the distance between him and jail could be virtually measured in yards. All those smart clowns who made a living out of illegal immigration in a place like Bombay must be living dangerously. No wonder he could not be found either at his office or at his house.

What about obtaining a *visitors' visa?* Why should I not get one from the British Embassy? How do all those crooks and smugglers who trot around the globe at the drop of a hat manage them? Moviemakers, politicians, millionaires, black marketers, mobsters, cheats, thugs? If they could call their shots with such ease, why not me? I could raise as much capital as I needed for financing my trip; frankly, I could purchase any amount of sterling currency from clandestine dealers at around 20 percent premium. So, why should I not get the same treatment from the British or any other Embassy for that matter? My cause was better than theirs; better than the rich getting richer; better than pleasure seekers having their fill; pornographers hunting for outlets; drug pushers making their killings. How do they get their visas and who gives them out?

That too seemed well worth a try. So I rang up the British Embassy, got through to the relevant department and explained to them what I was after. Instead of getting a quick answer, I got a long story. Bla…bla…bla… They kept beating around the bush for so long, I ran out of patience and hung up.

At around 4 p.m., Shabbu dropped in with some snacks and hot tea. She saw what I was doing but made no effort to dissuade me. "Any luck?" she asked instead.

Tea and *sympathy* came hand in hand. Dear old Shabbu! She knew when to push and when to give way.

"Not even a silver lining in the cloud," I replied, letting out a cold sigh.

"What about Uncle Haroon?"

"No one is answering their phone. Makes you wonder, doesn't it?"

"Perhaps they're all at the hospital with Bhabi?"

"Perhaps. I wish I were there too. It's *my* place, you know."

"Have a bite. I also brought some aspirin, in case you've developed a headache from strain."

"Bless you."

"Rox wanted to come too. But I thought two's company while three's crowd and asked her to defer her visit for a while. She said she'd bring you supper, instead. Is that all right?"

It was. I had not only developed a splitting headache but was also famished. Helping myself to a *samosa*, I asked her to sit down and tried Uncle Haroon's number in her presence once again. Still no luck, no reply, no response, no break through, not even a glimmer of hope. Then I dialled Mr. Vadkar's office and got him on the line. What a relief!

"Mr. Vadkar?"

"Yes?"

"My name's Quraishi. Yusuff Quraishi. We met at the British Embassy in Bombay several weeks ago."

"Did we?"

"Yes, we did. You offered to help me if I needed help."

"Help you with what?"

"You know? That. *Mohamed and the Mountain.*"

"Who and the what?"

"Well, about going to England. My wife is there. I came to know she's developed a freak fever. I'm worried sick. My application for the entry permit has been turned down. You're the only one who can help me."

"How?"

"I don't know. You said you could. Don't worry about money. I can pay. Doesn't matter how much. Will you?"

"Will I what?"

"Help?"

"I don't know what the *dickens* you're talking about."

The line went dead. Completely perplexed by his astonishing attitude, I stared at Shabbu aghast. The very man upon whom I had banked so many of my hopes cut me off without even discussing the matter further. Perhaps he did not like the idea of transacting business over the phone, which was perfectly understandable; his game was full of tripwires and pitfalls. For all he knew, I could be bait set up by the vice squad or the Interpol. But he could have at least said something, asked me for either a phone number or an address. He did not know a thing about me; I was neither a celebrity nor was my surname uncommon. How would he possibly get back to me even if he wanted to?

I told Shabbu what happened. At the very mention of *illegal passage,* her jaw dropped, her face shed much of its colour, her eyes slightly widened from disbelief and her breathing came to a momentary halt before taking off again. But she did not pass any comments one way or another. It must have been pretty obvious to her from my grimace that I was in intense pain.

"He hung up!" I screamed, just to get it off my chest. "The son of a bitch actually hung up!"

As if I was the Emir of Oman! Impotent rage, not enough even to impress my younger sister! Try this out inside a swimming pool once and see how it feels: hold your breath, loosen your limbs and just let go, straight down to the bottom, ears cupped, vision blurred, a curious awareness of immense weight upon you, of total loss, of an awesome void. Call it immersion, call it submersion or call it drowning. That was precisely how I felt. Plain sunk!

"What next?" Shabbu asked, "Anyone else you can try?"

"There must be plenty of others in the trade. This sort of thing goes on every day. But how does anyone find out about these *gurus*? They certainly do not advertise in the Yellow Pages?"

"Isn't it a bit dicey?"

"What do you think Rehana is worth to me, Shabbu?" I asked her point-blank.

No comment. But I could see the lines of deep concern on her expressive face.

"Listen, pet," I said, a reasonable explanation to her very much owed. "I know it's a risk, and a damned expensive one too. But I'm determined to see this through. It isn't just a question of being by Rehana's bedside anymore. I want to put an end to the madness once for all. And if I succeed in my efforts, I want only one thing out of it: I simply want to bring my wife and my child back here with me. Uncle Haroon better not get in my way because, right now, I'm like a test tube filled with volatile TNT. I might explode smack in his face and change its shape beyond the scope of recognition."

She listened to my outburst intently and then just nodded.

"What sort of risks are we looking at, dearest?" I asked her, my impatience showing. "If I get caught, they'll put me on board another plane and send me home. They can't send me to the gallows in the Tower of London for this, can they?"

She nodded again, her worried eyes still glued to my face. A lot seemed to be going on in her mind though.

"True, Shabbu," I said in a much softer tone. "My family's all I want. I don't know why everyone is making such a big deal out of it. I could've done with some company, you know. I feel so terribly, terribly alone, I feel marooned, ostracised, recanted, and I feel let down."

"I understand how you feel, Bhaijan. I wish I could help."

"You already have, more than you realise. I got things off my chest, at least. Do me one more favour, if you can. Don't let anyone worry because there's no reason to. To tell you the truth, I could do this sort of a thing for fun, for a laugh, for a kick, and then talk about it all through the coming summer."

After a while, she left. As expected, Rox brought me supper later on. We ate and talked. Probably reassured by Shabbu to some extent, she neither showed any signs of undue stress nor made any reference to Rehana's *freak fever*. But she did make quite a lot of plans for the immediate future. After Bhabi returned home from Bradford, they would do this and they would do that. In course of our conversation, two superb names for the baby also turned up—Inayat for a son and Tabassum for a daughter. Both Persian words, one means a blessing and the other a smile. They sounded so appropriate, I accepted them with pleasure. Very much at ease, she, too, left.

Without any idea as to what on earth was I doing alone in the bungalow, I stayed on. I could just as well have gone back to Riaz's house and kept trying from there; at least, I would have had some sympathetic company to listen to my moans and to prop up my courage. Disapproval expressed by him and Khaleel related only to my going to England without adequate travel documents, whereas concern for Rehana's well-being was shared alike. They were equally anxious to find out how she was. But of that, there were no indications as yet. That was what made the entire spectrum so damned prognostic. Where had they gone off? One word from them would have eased my mind; perhaps even prompted me to give up the crazy idea at least for the time being.

Over the next three days, no news arrived from Bradford at all. In order to give myself some freedom of thought and action that I desperately needed, I stayed on at the bungalow. I also sent two cables to Uncle, phoned his office thrice, explained the situation to his secretary and sought her help. She promised to inform him the moment he got in touch with her. Mr. Rao also did his utmost to contact his client, but without any luck. Complete silence from Rehana worried Sal too. They all continued to oppose the idea of my breaking the law, but efforts at contacting her were never slackened by any of them.

On the third night, however, a most extraordinary incident occurred. At around 11 p.m., all the lights in the apartments went out. In the pitch darkness that prevailed outside, I could merely see vague silhouettes and contours of big trees. Toads hid inside potholes and parlayed with each other in a hoarse twaddle; a full moon climbed up the ashen sky, playing hide and seek behind random thickets of rain bound clouds; the flux of the mist was soundless; swarms of glow-worms moved quietly from one bush to the other; and tempted by the silence and the solitude, mongooses ventured out of their secret burrows and raced around without shattering the profound hush of the quiet night. My mind plagued by all sorts of uneasy thoughts, I sat on the floor, restlessly shifting my weight from one lap to the other.

It was more or less as I prepared to abandon hope once again and hit the sack when suddenly some sort of a dim glow appeared in the distance. Obscured by the thin haze of mist, the only clue it gave away about itself was a swinging movement, as though someone was heading towards the house with a torch in hand. As I was not expecting any company myself, I thought it could be a visitor for one of the tenants, but nevertheless, in order to make absolutely sure that it was for them and not for me, I carried on looking outside, my attention fully focussed upon the curious glow.

As the person carrying the light got closer to the house, a somewhat unsettling doubt entered my mind. Was it really a torch or was it a hurricane lantern? In my state of nerves, under such emotional stress, such mental confusion, such endless worries and daunting premonitions, was I going to receive a visit from that mysterious old man who had once persecuted poor Azra out of her wits in her dreams? If so, what was he doing on my property? How did he know where to find me? What could he possibly want? Was he coming there to tell me that Rehana had also gone the same way as Azra had?

Suddenly breaking into a cold sweat, my breath held and my limbs frozen, I sat rooted to the floor. When the gravel in the drive crunched underneath his feet, his destination became pretty obvious. He was after me. He knew precisely where I was; he must have brought bad news about Rehana. Anyone as close to tragedy as him could only bring bad news. The very thought sent cold shivers running down my stiff back. My heart pumping blood faster than my veins could circulate it, a major tussle broke inside me.

After a nerve-shattering wait, I heard a knock on the door. Reluctantly heaving myself on to my feet, I crossed the room in hesitant strides and answered it. There was a man standing on the doorstep, waiting. The light in his hand, much brighter now than it had seemed from a distance, dazzled my vision. But behind the glare, I distinctly saw his hefty figure in a silhouette. There was absolutely no room for error about it; he was clad in a long robe, wore a turban, and if I could see past the glare of light which was hampering my vision, he might also have a white beard!

"Mr. Quraishi?" He accosted me with a pleasant smile.

"Yes?" I replied in a hoarse voice completely taken aback by that mysterious encounter.

"I am sorry, I seem to have caught you unawares. May I come in?" he asked, speaking in fluent Urdu.

Reluctantly, if inevitably, I let him in. Confusion inside my mind about the man was infinitesimal. Who was he? How did he know my name? How did he track me down to the correct address? What did he want? Why so late in the night?

"Is there something I can do for you?" I enquired, pulling myself together with a great deal of difficulty.

"There might be something which *I* can do for you, sir," he replied without toning down the charismatic smile, "My name's Bux and I was asked to contact you by Mr. Vadkar."

Had he said he was from Allah and was on his way to collect Rehana's soul at His instructions, it would have certainly been a lot easier for me to believe. Mr. Vadkar was the last person under the sun with whom I could have associated him. My eyes literally tore apart out of utter incredulity.

"I see," I barely managed to mumble. "How did you know where to find me?"

"Well," he replied, further accentuating the winsome smile, "you don't really expect us to go around broadcasting the tricks of our trade, do you?"

Mr. Vadkar certainly seemed to know his tricks well. Not only did he pick clear targets, he also scored bull's-eyes!

"Sorry, I withdraw the question," I said.

"I gather you want us to make travel arrangements for a quick visit to London?"

A rather subtle way of putting it! What I really wanted to do was to give Mr. Godfrey a *licking* as well as put Uncle Haroon in his place.

"Yes, if you can. I'm in a hurry."

"So I hear. How soon?"

"The sooner, the better. Is it possible?"

"Anything is possible—at the right price."

"What sort of *dosh* are we talking about for a return fare to London?"

"Fifty thousand rupees, in advance."

"That's a lot of money."

"Ah, well," he said, almost on the verge of going away. "We are all entitled to our opinions. Sorry to have wasted your time."

"Wait a minute," I swiftly intercepted him. "I only said it's a lot of money. I didn't say I ain't coughing up."

"It's entirely up to you. If you don't have the cash on you right now, I'll be happy to call again tomorrow."

"Why can't I bring it to you?"

"Our motto is complete satisfaction. We do all the work."

"Fifty thousand rupees is a great deal of money, Mr. Bux," I somehow managed to put it across to him without causing him any offence. "I don't know who you're and where you live. Don't you think I need some proof of authenticity, at least?"

"That I can give you in plenty," he replied, without taking any offence, "You were interviewed on the twenty-seventh of March at the British

Embassy by Peter Godfrey. Our agent, Mr. Vadkar bumped into you soon after you came out of Room 608. You were given his card; you phoned him three days ago; your wife's a citizen of UK; lives in Bradford; and since your application for entry permit has been turned down, you want to join her through our services. Is that enough, or do you need more?"

He seemed to have a complete *dossier* on my life! I was so impressed by the sheer professionalism of the man I dared not question either his credentials or his competence.

"Brilliant!" I applauded, admiring his ingenuity. "Say no more. I'll take your word for the rest. Do come back tomorrow night and I'll have the money ready for you."

Just like I had thought, borrowing a secured loan from the bank once again did not pose any insurmountable problems in spite of the joint ownership. But a sensible purpose for the loan was required. If I told the manager the truth, I was hardly likely to get even a single paisa. So I lied. Although the money towards the construction of the bungalow had come from Khaleel, there was no need for me to tell him that. I said it was required for settling the builder's bill and the manager swallowed it. As soon as the paperwork was sorted out, I got the cash in my hand.

Without breathing a word to anyone, I waited for Mr. Bux to come on the following night. He did as promised and picked up the money. I knew I was taking a big risk but went ahead. The house, once so courageously saved by Rehana's timely intervention, was back to square one again. I did not give a damn. If it could buy me safe passage to Bradford and the pleasure of seeing her radiant face one more time, I did not mind it in the least bit. For one look at her, I would do the same thing ten times over. There was nothing to it, really. At the most, I might lose the apartments and their income. So what? Lives are known to have been lost for the sake of love, kings are said to have forsaken their crowns in the name of love. One such great king belonged to England too. When they could throw away such a lot, my risk was trivial.

If Mr. Bux had walked out of the house with the *dosh* and never showed up, there was not a thing I could do to catch him. But like they say, there is honour amongst thieves. We were both thieves, engaged in a common conspiracy to flout the law. He did it for a living whereas I was forced into it by people beyond me and by circumstances beyond my control. In all my life, I had never so much as walked on the wrong side of the road, in a manner of speaking. I was always taught to respect rules, whether they were made by my parents or by my rulers. The principle is what matters the most. But mine had been flushed down the drain, thus turning me into a daring criminal. I should have kept the money I got towards my dowry and kicked Rehana out after a night or two of *khushi;* I should have blown it all upon myself and then joined the queue of suitors for some other rich heiress. Others are known to have done it. But I did not. Instead, I fell in love with my wife. I made her pregnant. I decided to set up home with her; I made plans for the morrow; I aspired for the status of a family man; none of which went down well with people like Mr. Godfrey. Or, with people like Uncle Haroon. One thought I was a *fortune hunter* and the other a mere *stud.* To the one, the child inside my wife's womb was no more than the biological outcome of sexual intercourse, and to the other, just a *yield* returned by capital investment!

Mr. Bux worked absolute miracles. I was given a new passport. According to it, I was born in Calcutta. My name was no longer Yusuff Quraishi but Bilaal Agha. Why Bilaal Agha and why not Ullull Tuppoo? Who knew, who cared! By my new profession, I was an overseas merchandiser working for M/s Choudhary & Choudhary Conglomerate of Calcutta who, frankly, did not exist. But I had all the necessary documentation to prove that they did—business cards, letterheads, invoices, rubber-stamps, the lot. And more important than all those, my passport contained visas issued by several Europeans countries, including Britain. I had a long list of clients and contacts to meet along the way, presumably bogus. I was given a book of Travellers Cheques in the sum of about two thousand pounds issued by a well-known travel agency, also bogus. In addition to it, I was given one hundred pounds in cash, which were genuine. Apart from that, the only other genuine thing was my photograph inside my passport. For the rest, the hoax was so incredibly foolproof; it did not leave much to be desired. And all that, within a matter of five working days! How was it done? Your guess is as good as mine. Mr. Bux himself never revealed the *tricks of his trade* to his clients!

Meanwhile, five desperate people continued to exert nonstop efforts at establishing contact with Uncle Haroon. But it seemed as if the entire family had vanished from the face of the earth. To where and for what? We wished we knew. Neither Rehana wrote to us nor did her parents. Not even the courtesy of a measly phone call was extended to any of us right through the week. Perhaps, in terms of such distant correspondence, *just a week* was not a particularly long duration, but to me it had felt like eternity. The inexplicable silence alone increased my motivation to go ten fold. I was so annoyed, I swore to myself I would not stand for a similar thing happening ever again. Frankly, on that particular occasion, Rehana had also given me a cause to complain for the first time. Unless a satisfactory explanation was forthcoming, I had no mind to condone the matter. The damage done to my feelings was virtually implacable. At times, I had gone dangerously close to insanity.

As the day of my departure began to approach, it no longer seemed like fun. All those arguments about ends justifying means, or playing down the element of risk did not hold water anymore. I knew I was setting out on a perilous and unpredictable journey. So did my family, even though I did not reveal to them any of the sordid details about the mysterious Mr. Bux, or about how it was all arranged. Their anxieties concealed, their grief hidden from sight and their tears courageously held back, they went through hell.

On the due date, Riaz drove us all to *Begumpet Airport.* Prayers on their lips and tears in their eyes, they wished me luck. They also urged me to let them know as soon as I reached my destination. The money that I had given to Mr. Bux was nowhere near the price of their distress and their anguish. That was the real cost: tearing apart the hearts of those who loved us. Over what? One man's bigotry and another man's intransigence!

We changed flights at *Santa Cruz* Airport. Once on board the nonstop Jumbo to Heathrow, I stopped thinking about Hyderabad. Our journey progressed bit by bit. First of all, the Himalayas went past. After that, the Great Desert was crossed. Soon, the Alps were all that remained. And, of course, the immigration authorities at Heathrow. The very thought made me shudder. But as soon as it did, Rehana quietly crept into my mind and took over. Just like a teenager with a crush, I secretly thought about her. In her country, under her protective eye, I had nothing to worry about, really. Taking care of people had always been her passion. And I was not just people—I was her *one and only*. She would not let even a fly land on me. Suddenly, I felt past caring. Only one fear kept nagging at the back of my mind. If I was apprehended by the authorities and repatriated before I could see her, it would be a terrible blow to me, indeed. I hoped it did not happen.

Our seat belts fastened and spirits held, we touched down at Heathrow around quarter past ten. By then, all the concerns that I left behind were forgotten and my thoughts fully focussed upon those that were about to begin. My feelings were mixed. On one hand, the joy of a reunion between Rehana and me was something well worth looking forward to; on the other hand, the chances of getting caught raised a volley of fears. The helping hand of dear Mr. Bux was no longer available to me. I was completely on my own, in for a penny, in for a pound. Playing with fire on home ground was something entirely different; but on foreign soil, I could easily end up with an awful lot of blisters.

As soon as the aircraft came to a halt, we all got off, cheerily thanked by the air hostesses and pleasantly welcomed by the ground hostesses. A comfortable coach picked us up outside the aircraft and dropped us off at the arrivals bay of Terminal 4. I walked through the long corridor leading to the exit at my own pace. Both my ears, which had cupped at the time of landing, remained cupped. Impaired hearing did help; I was glad I could not catch other people's conversation. Anything to trigger off panic was all I needed for a give away.

I finally entered the crowded lounge where passengers had formed into five queues, three of them for commonwealth citizens only. Choosing the right one, I took my place and waited. With so many others ahead of me, a prolonged delay seemed inevitable and I reconciled to it. The dead weight of the shoulder bag began to hurt my shoulder on which it hung, my knees kept shivering, more out of tension than from strain. Our progress was painfully slow. From the few glimpses I could steal of the checkout counter, I noticed with a growing sense of unease that most passengers were being detained for immigration checks. The somewhat disconsolate sight sank my spirits further. The security guards pacing around put more fear into me. I wondered what they did with us *felons*. Send them back they must, but what happened between arrest and expulsion? Would they lock me up in a police cell like a common criminal? Would they let me see my wife at least?

It took a good hour or so before my turn came up. When it did, I handed in my passport to the officer at the counter. Not even bothering to take another look in my direction, he started to scrutinize it carefully, especially the pages on which all those visas were endorsed. The expression on his face gave away nothing, but he was taking his time, which looked rather ominous. In the end, when he added my passport to the large pile that had already built up on the counter, I knew my game was up.

"Go over there and wait until you're called in," he said, pointing towards the Immigration section with his chin.

Suddenly, all those hopes of seeing Rehana, being by her side in the moment of her need, holding her hand, listening to the first wail of our baby, putting Uncle Haroon in his place, the whole lot fizzled into thin air at a stroke. Dragging myself as far as the nearest empty chair *over there*, I slumped in it. No one paid me any attention, everybody engrossed in his or her own worries and preoccupations. The sheer embarrassment of getting

362

caught felt overwhelming. The questions that would be fired at me, and my stupid answers! Apart from my wits and my ability to improvise instant lies, I had no other recourse. And of that, there suddenly seemed a big dearth. At a time when I could do with some courage, it fled; at a time when I badly needed some steady nerves, they collapsed!

I have no recollection of how long the painful wait lasted. When my name was announced on the loudspeakers, it did not even register in my mind as I was subconsciously waiting to hear the name *Quraishi*. But the moment it did, I wished the ground split apart and swallowed me; I wished I had listened to sound advice and given up the idea of that wild adventure; I wished a carrier pigeon had flown to Bradford with my message of distress and a flying carpet had brought Rehana back to my side. Frankly, just one interrogation by a member of Her Majesty's Civil Service was enough to last me for a lifetime. And that was, when I did not have the burden of guilt straddled upon my conscience! Now, the tables had reversed completely. Not only was I guilty, but about to be found so on Her Majesty's own soil!

Supporting myself on false dignity, I approached Cabin Three, which was designated as my destination by that eerie voice over the loudspeakers. The man who encountered me from behind a small desk had auburn hair; a wooden face as neutral as a piece of rock; granite hard features that made him look incredibly sinister, completely devoid of feelings or of emotions, not even extending to me the courtesy of a smile.

"Mr. Agha?" he said, reading out the name from my passport.

No, he was not Mr. Godfrey. But then again, neither was I Mr. Quraishi anymore. So, what's in a name?

CHAPTER (26)

"Uncle Haroon?"

"Yusuff! Where on earth are you speaking from?"

"From Heathrow Airport. I tried to sneak into the country through the back door but got caught."

"You what!"

"Yes, Uncle. They've got me."

"But...but...but why?"

"Why what? Why did they catch me? Or, why did I get caught?"

"Why did ..."

"One of the few dark secrets about me that Papa probably didn't tell you is, all sorts of bizarre things start happening to me on every full moon. It all began on the fourteenth of Rajjab two years ago. The pundits call it *Lunacy*."

"What!"

"Please stop wasting time, Uncle. I've been allowed just one phone call and I want to know just one thing. How's Rehana?"

"Rehana's fine. But..."

"Please tell her I love her very much."

"All right, I will. Don't put the phone down yet. Where are they holding you?"

"For the time being, at their detention centre in Heathrow, pending further enquiries."

"You dumb, stupid, arrogant, hot-blooded scatterbrain! Why the hell did you have to do a silly thing like that!

"Well, I've done it and it's too late for regrets."

"For God's sake, don't you open your mouth and say anything to anyone until I get there. Did you hear what I said?"

Loud and clear. The news I gave him seemed to have dealt him a really nasty blow. I could feel the agony in his voice.

Now, then. How did I get caught and how did I manage to set up contact with Uncle Haroon as easily as that? Two main issues that need some explaining before we proceed.

The first is pretty straightforward. When put through the acid test by the immigration bosses, I muffed. The auburn-haired man in Cabin 3, born with the instincts of a slug, did not let go of my skin until the last drop of blood in my veins was sucked out. His inquisition was so thorough he made Mr. Godfrey look like a toddler at the Montessori! The more smoke screens I tried to raise, the more rigorously he penetrated them; whenever I hid, he found me; whenever I paused for a breather, he punctured my lungs; wherever I puked, he rubbed my nose into it. He was like a heavy-duty rubber band, resilient enough to be stretched out of all proportions and yet returning to his original size instantly. As soon as I quit playing games, he got hold of me by the scruff. Then he laid me on the table, face downwards. Out came a knife and a fork from inside his pockets with which he cut me into four slices. On one slice, he applied French Mustard; on the other, he spread Anchor Butter; on the third, he gave a good helping of Robertson's Strawberry Jam. And on the fourth, he emptied a whole tub of Philadelphia Cheese. With that, I was good and ready for consumption. Smacking his lips with great delight, he picked me up slice by slice, put me in his great big mouth and carried on munching until I turned into pulp. At that stage, I submerged in an ocean of saliva, and after a brief somersault in the vicinity of his adam's apple, went down his throat. That was how I came to be caught!

And how did I manage to contact Uncle Haroon as easily and as quickly as that? I would have given my right arm to find out. Averaging around twenty tries per head per day by five people, we had moved heaven and earth to trace him. We had beaten the brains out of his wretched secretary; we had blown away a small fortune in unanswered cables; we had spent an awful lot of restless days and sleepless nights trying to figure out their whereabouts! It was long enough for the bank manager to approve as well as dish out a big loan; it was long enough for Mr. Bux to come up with a fake passport; for seven European Embassies to endorse visas on it; for a reputable travel agency to issue two thousand pounds of bogus Travellers Cheques; for M/s Coudhary & Choudhary Ltd. to come into being and then disappear from the face of this earth. But it had not been long enough for Uncle Haroon, or for Auntie Zeenath, or for Rehana to drop us a brief line. Yet, soon after the auburn haired man in Cabin 3 had me for breakfast, I made contact with him at the very first go! Do you think I was not curious to find out how? Of course, I was. Only, what with the strain of having gone through a full digestive process, and what with two security guards flanking me on either side, my thoughts roamed elsewhere. So I did not bother with such trivialities. The good news that Rehana had not been struck down by Small Pox was rewarding enough to overcome all the other concerns. I no longer cared whether they pickled me in vinegar or flushed me down the loo. I was on the same land on which she was born; breathing the same air that she was breathing; together with the Himalayas and the Great Desert; the Alps had also been crossed. Only two armed but otherwise amiable guards, a restraining order passed by the irate immigration officer, a certain matter of a confiscated passport, a few pending enquiries, the possibility of a judicial reprimand in due course and, if nothing else, about five hundred miles of Motorway was all that prevailed between her and me … .

The guards escorted me to a detention centre situated within walking distance of the immigration enclosure and handed me over to its warden. In his early sixties, tall and sprightly, smartly dressed and incredibly soft-spoken, with a handlebar moustache that suited his mesmeric personality so well, and a genial smile right below it that inspired respect and exuded confidence, he was remarkably reminiscent of some of those high ranking military officers in the Colonial British Army one sees from time to time in the movies. Nothing in his attitude or manners suggested that he was dealing with a possible felon.

"Come on in and sit down, old chap!" he chimed quite affably, offering me a seat across the table in his cosy office room.

"Thank you, sir," I replied, bringing out the best in me.

"Well, Mr. Agha," he said after I sat down, "what brings you to this neck of the woods?"

"My real name isn't Agha but is Quraishi, sir," I replied, unable and unwilling to maintain a lie that had already turned sour on me and had also outlived its usefulness. "I tried to cheat the authorities, which I regret very much. I do acknowledge that two wrongs don't make a right."

"Indeed, they don't. Is your family here?"

"A good 90 percent of me is here, sir. Most of what is mine is here. My wife, and a baby on its way."

"Does she know where you're?"

"I think so. I just spoke to her father on the phone with the kind permission of the security guards who escorted me here."

"Let's hope he knows what to do."

"May I ask you a question, sir?"

"Go on. Fire away."

"Now that I'm caught, is it likely that they might send me back before I could see my wife and have a chat with her?"

"I don't think so. I'm almost sure of it. We *do* respect all decent family values here."

"Thank you very much, sir. That's all I wanted to know."

"Good. My assistant, Timothy, will show you to your room. If you need anything, feel free to ask. I try to run this place with the least amount of inconvenience to the detainees."

Mr. Timothy Collins, an equally smartly dressed civil servant with impeccable manners showed me to my room. My baggage, which bore clear signs of having been thoroughly gone over by cstoms, had already arrived and was left in it. Meals, I was told, were served twice a day in a common mess where Halal meat as well as vegetarian menus were served for those who preferred them. Each wing of the building had its own communal toilet facilities, and a well-stocked library was also available to us for intellectual stimulation, catering to the needs of over one hundred and eighty people detained in it by immigration for one reason or the other, pending *further enquiries*. The centre, Mr. Collins was at pains to emphasise, was not intended to play the role of a penitentiary and, therefore, must not be viewed as one.

The warden's assurance that I was unlikely to be repatriated without the chance to see my wife set my mind at ease. Whether or not Uncle Haroon succeeded in getting me out of that place did not matter too much. I had only one aim in view and that was to sort things out with my wife face-to-face. Tired as I was from the strain of the tedious journey as well as the nightmare that followed it, I took a quick shower, had a hot meal and went back to my room.

At around four o'clock, I was informed by someone from the reception that I had a visitor. It could only be either Rehana or Uncle Haroon. In all honesty, I wished it was she rather than he. If trying to hoodwink the authorities had not yet landed me in a real cell, grievous bodily harm done to the Mica King certainly would.

Luckily for both of us, it was Rehana and not the latter. As soon as she saw me, she flew into my arms. Colour rushed to her cheeks; eyes lit up; lips relaxed in a smile of welcome; breath speeded from excitement; her entire physiognomy underwent a sharp metamorphosis. Holding her in a firm clasp so close to my eager heart after such a long time and after all that aggravation felt exceedingly good. Her familiar and much missed fragrance entered my lungs and quickly settled in them; a strangely soothing warmth subsided most of my aches and my stresses; all those tender words of endearment which I had forgotten to utter even in my dreams returned to my mouth; a buoyant love that was beginning to sink in the quicksand of blighted hopes instantly revived. For once it occurred to me that my fate also had a hidden side to it, a propitious side, a positive side, which made matchless reading!

At some stage, both of us simmered down. Uncle Haroon seemed to have knowingly given us a head start that was good thinking on his part. Unwelcome faces were not acceptable at a time like that; I had paid too high a price for it.

"Nice to see you again, Rehana," I said, finding my tongue.

Instead of drawing her into some lighthearted conversation as it was meant to, the remark exacerbated her grief even more and she broke into sobs.

"Come on, Rehana," I urged. "Let's talk before the warden changed his mind about this visit, or before his bosses changed the rules about the visitors."

"What've you done!" she exclaimed as soon as she found her tongue, watching my face with a bemused expression, seemingly at a loss to determine whether my stupidity was to be condoned with an indulgent laughter or to be rebuked with a stern reprimand.

"Just got caught with my hand stuck inside the proverbial chocolate jar."

"But why did you do it?"

"For this," I said, squeezing her even harder in my arms.

"We waited for so long, couldn't we've waited for a few more weeks?"

"I ran out of patience. You know what sort of crazy things I do when that happens ..."

"Well," she remarked, inclined to condone my indiscretion rather than rebuke me. "Whoever thought I'd come here one day to meet you!"

"Does it matter where we meet, Rehana?" I asked, planting a gentle kiss on her forehead. "Isn't it enough that we have?"

She looked at me with her affectionate eyes and reciprocated the smile. It was a smile with which a thousand wrongs done to me had been restituted within the blinking of an eyelid; a smile that had healed so many of my wounds, subsidized all my losses, enriched my life and had added to it a whole new dimension. That million-dollar smile of hers, which had no substitutes.

"Gosh! Never suspected I'm married to a hardcore hoodlum!" she exclaimed again, the happy side of her gradually taking over from the other one. "Are they treating you well?"

"Like I'm the Maharaja of Patiala," I replied in the same jovial vein. "The Maharani is all that's missing. Why don't you come and bunk in with me, eh? The bunk's large enough for the three of us ..."

"I'm so glad you're here!" she said soon after a cold sigh of relief and returned to my arms. I drew her as close to me as she could ever get physically. Emotionally, she was already submerged.

"Know something?" she whispered in my ear. "Reading about human reproductive system at school was something else. But the very thought that a real baby would soon emerge out of me has an entirely different feel to it. A living miracle, isn't it?"

"Indeed, it is! Love begotten by love."

"You're going to stay with me until this whole thing's over, aren't you?"

"Lloyds wouldn't dream of selling insurance to anyone who's thinking of stopping me."

"Good. Whatever we *incurred* together, let's also *discharge* it together."

"I don't think it would work out that way, sweetheart ..."

"What wouldn't work out?"

"This business about *discharging* together whatever we've *incurred* together."

"Why wouldn't it?"

"Well, it didn't work out for the duchess."

"For who?"

"For the duchess."

"Which duchess?"

"This duchess who met God one day and bitterly complained to Him that He had been most unfair to women by making women suffer all the consequences of sex and letting men get away scot free."

"And what said God to her?"

"He asked her if she had a *fairer* solution in mind."

"Did she?"

"Yes she did. She said He ought to let women go through the delivery but make men suffer the pain, thus discharging together whatever they incurred together."

"And?"

"Her wish was granted, until it was time for her to deliver her own baby."

"Go on. I'm listening."

"The poor duke was in hot soup. So, anticipating that the pain would strike him any moment, he kept restlessly pacing the veranda outside her royal chamber."

"Did it strike him?"

"No, it didn't. Instead, he heard her *chauffer* screaming his head off inside the garage!"

She burst into laughter. That was the whole idea. We were meant to live happily, without regrets, without remorse. We did not owe anyone anything. Whatever was ours, we were born with it, an unchangeable line on our palms that had brought us together, and a resolute determination in us to be forever together.

"So, you see, my precious," I carried on with my joke, "God has a jolly good reason for keeping these matters arranged the way they are!"

"Thank you very much."

"That doesn't mean I'm not willing to be the chauffer. I am. Provided, of course, your old man knows how to get his eggs boiled. Where's he, anyway? I thought he's on his way to my rescue?"

"He is. Getting jailbirds out of the pen takes time, you know."

"Yes, it does," I conceded readily enough. "And by the way, what about this small matter of a certain *freak fever,* eh? What happened to it?"

"It's gone! But how did you know about it?"

"From Uncle's last letter," I replied, getting a bit serious from there onwards. "Since then, five resourceful well wishers did their utmost to get in touch with him but couldn't. There was no trace of any of you, not a line, not a word. Have you any idea how close I got to insanity? Why, Rehana? Why? Couldn't you at least be bothered?"

She sat up tensely. The smile on her lips disappeared and blood receded from the face. She knew I was not joking anymore.

"Is that why you came here like this?" she asked me after a pretty long pause. "You took all these risks on account of what Daddy had written in his letter about my fever?"

"You didn't think I would?"

The question rendered her speechless. She shut her eyes and then bent her head. The tears resumed. Her torment became utterly agonizing.

"Listen, Rehana," I delivered those words straight into her ears without altering the level of my voice. "Whatever happened in course of the past few days must never happen again. These are just the sorts of things that can wreck our lives. You've no idea what the words *freak fever* represent to me up here in my mind. Don't ask me, because they can only bring back a flood of painful recollections. I simply can't endure such a lot of grief all over again. Whenever I look at you, I only see the years ahead of us that we're yet to spend together. If anything threatens those years, our future, our plans, our love, I freak out. So, please. I've already lost so much I want to hang on to whatever I've got. And that, by itself, is one heck of a lot, believe me.

After listening to it, she did not even attempt to offer explanations. Neither did I press her for one. Instead, I tempted her into some conversation on less controversial topics. Soon she unwound and asked me how Mamma was keeping. I told her that she got over the shock of Papa's departure and had settled in with Riaz's brothers and sisters. Then she asked me why there was no news of Shabbu and Rox being in the 'family way.' I said I had absolutely no idea. She drew me into details about the job, the bungalow, the apartments and the tenants. I filled her in with all the information there was. The weight gone from her mind, she cheered up to a great extent.

As we sat chatting, Uncle Haroon walked in, looking tired and worried. Soon after greeting me with an affectionate hug, he looked at Rehana's swollen eyes with a crease of concern on his face. "What's the matter?" he asked her. "Is anything wrong?"

She did not answer him and I was glad that she did not. It was a pretty simple equation. Whatever had gone wrong between us, we had sorted it all out; she had made me a little angry, and in turn, I had made her weep a little. My grievance was gone and so was her distress; we were both on friendly terms again. Was it so difficult for him to grasp?

The news he brought was not one of instant solutions to the daunting problem I had unwittingly set up for him. He said he had seen the MP for his constituency and sought his help towards getting me out of the detention centre on a temporary visitors' visa, at least until the delivery. Unfortunately, as there were several moral issues at stake apart from the legal ones, it was not going to be easy. By making a deliberate attempt to cheat the Home Office, I was in contempt of prevalent legislation and had rendered myself beyond the scope of compassion. The minister in charge of immigration took a pretty grim view of people like me who had no compunctions in making use of any number of lies in order to get what they want. The trust was gone from the equation and nothing I do or say could be taken at face value anymore. No matter how sympathetic the MP was to me and how extenuating my circumstances, there was no way in which the rules could be bent in my favour. Understandably, if they let me get away with what I did, others would make an example out of me and try the same tricks. There would be no end in sight to the unacceptable practice of breaking the law and then taking shelter behind the cover of compassion. A firm line had to be drawn somewhere, which had already been drawn, and I had crossed it.

Upon listening to it, I realised for the first time that the *fire* I had ventured to play with on foreign soil was not going to be put out without inflicting more blisters upon me than I had bargained for. Nobody likes the idea of being taken for granted, neither they nor us. In letting myself be carried away by silly sentiments, it seemed I had dislodged a crucial boulder, setting off nasty upheavals. There were unambiguous indications that the Home Office was getting battlebound to make sure *he who dares is not always allowed to win*. If so, I could clearly see the enemy I had woken up was not going to be so easy to placate; the game I had started to play was not going to be within my means to end; the joke I had cracked was not necessarily going to conclude in laughter. Until such time as a decision was made about what to do with me, whether to let me out, or to keep me in, or to let me go home, I would remain a prisoner at the centre. Having brought it upon myself, I did not mind being one, but it was the thought of Rehana making those daily trips between Bradford and Heathrow to see me that set my head reeling. Only a few weeks from delivery, her tummy stretched to the limit, she was in no fit condition to go through such a lot of strain without either putting herself at risk or putting the baby in serious jeopardy. But how was I going to stop her?

"Look, Rehana," I tried to put it across to her as gently as I could. "Rightly or wrongly, I managed to get here somehow. I've seen you and you've seen me, I know you're okay and you know I am okay. Can we not leave it at that without pushing our luck until Uncle can sort things out? I mean, is there some way in which I could persuade you to refrain from making daily visits to see me in your condition?"

"You can try but that doesn't mean I would yield."

"Come, come, Rehana. Don't be silly. You mustn't do it. You know you must not."

"I want to be where my husband is, or I want my husband to be where I am.

Either leave the *Mountain* near where *Mohamed* is, or let Mohamed stay by the Mountain. Period."

When she put it across to me so bluntly, my spirits began to sink. The *Mountain* and the *Mohamed* she was talking about were not the same as what Mr. Vadkar had talked about; her mountain was somewhere up in the clouds and she did not have any wings to fly. Unless the precarious stalemate was resolved sensibly, one of us was going to have to pay a high price in the end, and I hoped it would not be the baby in her womb. Scared by the very thought, I rested my pleading looks upon Uncle.

"What can I say!" he exclaimed with a helpless shrug. "I was against the idea of her coming here even today. She just wouldn't budge. But at least, Bromley isn't as far as Bradford."

"What do you mean?"

"After she caught a bug and gave us some cause for concern, all of us moved over to our house in Bromley. According to the terms of her medical insurance, BUPA made arrangements for her to be admitted to a private hospital here in London, and with the date of her delivery also being so close, we decided to stay on."

"I see. I didn't know that."

"No one does, including my office. To free myself from other preoccupations and concentrate upon her alone, I've deliberately dropped out of circulation."

"I see. Is that why we couldn't contact you?"

"Yes," he said with an apologetic smile. "Yesterday, I drove over to Bradford just to pick up my mail when a call came through from Riaz quite by chance. I came to know from him for the first time whatever transpired in Hyderabad during the past two weeks, and also that you are already on your way to London. Since that moment, I've been sitting tight at home waiting for you to call. I'm very sorry about the breakdown in communications. Nobody was expecting matters to reach this far."

That, at the very least, satisfactorily explained away why none of us had managed to establish contact with the family even after making so many efforts. But it did not resolve the issue I was trying to grapple with. The situation had become so awkwardly complicated, apologies and exculpations were no longer enough to put matters right.

"And how far is Bromley from here?" I asked him for what it was worth.

"About forty miles," he replied.

Forty miles was forty miles, far enough to compound the element of risk and endanger their safety, hers, the baby's or both. But there was nothing I could do to prevail upon her, at least not on the spur of the moment. For as long as I remained locked up at the centre, she would carry on taking those risks, which suddenly turned an ordinary drama into a crisis of extraordinary proportions. If only I had taken into account all those ramifications behind the ramifications of one foolish act and yielded to sound advice while the time was still available for introspection. But it was too late for regrets.

"Well, Uncle," I said, addressing myself to him over another equally sensitive issue before it too turned into a crisis. "Do you think you could send Riaz a cable for me?"

"Why cable?" he replied, "I'll phone him as soon as we get home. I'm sure Rehana too would like to say hello to them."

"No, Uncle, please don't," I quickly intercepted him. "If you talk to them on the phone, you'd also have to tell them about the soup in which I've landed. But in a cable, you can stick to the bare minimum and just say what *you* want to."

"I see what you mean. Okay, I'll send them a phonogram. What do you want me to say in it?"

"How about: PARCEL ARRIVED SAFE BUT INTERCEPTED BY CUSTOMS? That way, you wouldn't be lying to them but only being *economical* with the truth …"

He looked somewhat uncertain, while Rehana turned her face aside for a surreptitious smile. Resumption of diplomatic ties between us seemed to be working quite well; we were back on the same wavelength again.

My first week in detention passed away without any serious problems. In spite of protests, Rehana visited me every day and spent as much time with me as she was allowed to. Uncle Haroon's political contact promised to do his utmost to get me out—in consultation with the home secretary. In addition to it, he started to explore other venues of his own. I had no reason to grumble and took matters in my stride.

CHAPTER (27)

Towards the end of the week Rehana herself delivered to me the devastating news that, more or less as feared and cautioned by the MP for Bradford, it seemed the junior minister in charge of immigration had refused consent for my temporary release from the centre in order to be with her at the time of delivery. Apparently, having found out my real identity, his office got in touch with Mr. Godfrey and obtained the entire audiotape of his interrogation of me. After listening to it, he decided that I was to remain in detention until further investigations were carried out regarding how I managed to obtain the fake passport, together with all those visas endorsed in it, especially one from UK too. He was determined to discover how those clandestine activities were being perpetrated at their embassy in Bombay, by whom and to what extent before he would even consider what to do with me.

"What happens now?" she asked me, for once forsaken by the cool and confident woman behind the woman, her face gone ghastly pale, both from strain as well as from worry, and then broke down into muffled sobs.

"Please stop crying, Rehana," I beseeched her, watching the tears dribble down her cheeks with growing concern."This isn't doing anyone any good. You are bearing a child,remember? Both of us happen to have a responsibility towards it."

Instead of subsiding her grief, my admonition increased it even more. Her mind in complete chaos, her feelings badly hurt, the extent of her distress immeasurable, she was going through hell since the moment she set eyes upon me at that centre. Gone was the self confident, resourceful and inspirational *Shahzadi* of the recent past who had successfully organised two simultaneous wedding ceremonies in *Kalim Manzil* with such competence; earned the respect and adulations of all and sundry; taken one crisis after another by the horns and resolved them without a crease of worry on her face; given Papa the love he needed; given Mamma the attention she deserved; given my sisters the backing they expected; dragged me out of the doldrums in which I was sunk; flooded my life with brighter lights and given me a clear sense of direction; now replaced by a scared, nervous and vacillating stranger, no longer in control of herself or the chain of events that were tossing her around. In addition to all that, the severe blow dealt by the Home Office simply crushed her. Frankly, having brought upon myself the debacle in which I was trapped, I did not mind paying the price of my folly, but its effects upon here were absolutely devastating.

"So far, I was under the impression that coming here in the face of all those overwhelming odds was the cleverest thing I did in all my life. Now it seems it wasn't so clever after all, was it?" I mumbled in her ear.

Soon her eyes swelled up from constant weeping, her eyeballs flared red, the nose dribbled and the sobs turned into incessant hiccups. It was so painful to watch her torment, especially in the certain knowledge that there was no need for either of us to suffer like that. Surrounded by people who loved us, our bread and butter secured in our own backyard, safe underneath a modest shelter, ours should have been a golden era of peace, bliss and contentment. We were young, we were in love, and we were married and were about to have our first child. Our fruitful life read like a complete book with all its chapters in their proper places. But people had started to tamper with the pages, to tear them apart, to deface them, to alter their text, some out of selfishness and others out of sheer malice.

"Did you ever try your hand at fantasising, Rehana?" I asked her. "I mean, making up things in your mind you know aren't true? Did you?"

"Why?"

"Just pretend that I'm not here, that I'm still in Hyderabad and eagerly waiting for you and the baby to join me?"

After giving the proposal some thought, she shook her head. She was not a child anymore, and by not being a child, she was at a painful disadvantage; the blessings of childhood were no longer available to her.

"What're you planning to do, Rehana? Travel eighty miles a day in this condition?"

"I need you! I need you so much!" she mumbled in between the hiccups. "I was counting on taking you home today, I was banking on it, I was looking forward to your company, to have you around, fussing over me, taking care of me."

"So was I, Rehana," I whispered again, feeling rotten deep inside. "But we can't have everything the way we want it all the while. We must learn to accept our disappointments as evenly as we grab our good fortunes. Everything in life has a price tag on it. Our meeting ahead of time was an unexpected joy, but now, it seems there is a hitch. So what? Just a matter of time, that's all. You can speak to me on the phone for as long as you want to and as often as you like. And what's more, looking at it from the positive side, there're only forty miles between us. Not a lot of distance to conquer, is it?"

Probably realising that, apart from causing more distress, tears were not going to accomplish much else, she stopped crying and managed the smile that had forsaken her earlier. "You're right," she agreed. "One must be satisfied with whatever one has got in hand. Like you said, I can talk to you on the phone more often now than I could have, if you were in Hyderabad. Even that is enough to keep me going."

"There's a good girl!"

"If I become too depressed sometimes, is it all right for me to drop in just for inspiration?"

"So long as you think it's safe. You decide for yourself. I am here because you're here, and I'll sit tight until all this is over. Then we can go home together, you, me and whatever else is ours."

"What're you hoping for? A son or a daughter?"

"You asked me once before and I told you. One's as welcome as the other. I mean it."

"You haven't yet told me the names which Rox suggested."

"I'm saving the surprise for a more appropriate moment, if you don't mind."

"No, I don't mind."

"All right, then. I'll look forward to your phone calls."

"So will I. Are they still treating you like the Maharaja of Patiala?"

"Yes, they are."

"Kiss me quickly when people aren't watching."

I kissed her. Resting her head upon my shoulder, she let out a cold sigh of hidden despair. For quite a while, I sat running my fingers through her hair and she kept picking scuds of wool stuck here and there to my jumper. Quiet moments trickled away in pensive brooding.

A phone call from reception to the security guard informing him that Uncle Haroon was waiting in the main foyer to collect Rehana interrupted us both. It was time for her to say good night to me and go. Left with no other choice, both of us cheered each other up with fake smiles. Wiping her drenched cheeks with my handkerchief, I rearranged her dishevelled hair, planted a final kiss on her forehead, helped her to her feet and escorted her as far as the exit door. Beyond that point, I was not allowed to go. I had been through so much hassle in order to be by her side in the moment of her need; I was there, if not by her side, barely forty miles away from her, and yet we no longer had any access to each other … .

After she left, I returned to my room. That day, I really had a tremendous need for privacy. No, not to cry. Only to gather my thoughts and put them in the right perspective. To pick myself up from the dumps in which I felt sunk. I had no reason to cry or to feel sorry for myself. Emotionally, there was never any distance between my wife and me. Physically there was, but a lot of it had been cut down. For the price of a felony, it had been; at the expense of my freedom, it had been. What was there to cry over?

Soon the centre plunged into a profuse silence, interrupted only by the trickle of water travelling in and out of central heating radiators, or by the traffic of aircraft in the distance. Time simply refused to budge. Each punitive moment of solitude and retrospection felt like eternity. All sorts of crazy thoughts plagued me. I wondered how everything was back home in Hyderabad. Rehana had told me that she wrote a confidential letter to Shabbu with all the details, asking her to keep things under covers for the time being. I wondered what sort of effect it had on her, I wondered if she managed to do it or was constrained to disclose the secret to the others. Thinking about my family drew me to tears. I wished Rehana and I could go back where we belonged; I wished the battle was brought to an end there and a truce drawn; I wished the nightmare were nipped in the bud and peace restored. At that particular moment in time, most probably several Oxford and Cambridge graduates were busy trying to uncover all sorts of evidence against me. Not that with which I could be exonerated, but that with which I could be incriminated. For, had they really wanted the former, there was no need for them to search for the latter. Whatever evidence they needed to justify my deeds or my misdeeds was available to them in the Whitehall itself. But they were not satisfied with it because it spoke for me. They must be looking for Mr. Vadkar and for Mr. Bux, for Choudhary & Choudhary Conglomerate of Calcutta, for the bogus travel agency who issued those fake Travellers Cheques to me. The most incontrovertible proof of my innocence had come to the detention centre and gone from there many a time in the form of Rehana, but no one had even bothered to take a look at her.

Somehow, the night wore out. All through the following day, I eagerly waited for Rehana's phone call without stirring from my room even for food. When there was no response from her at all, I naturally got into a panic and tried to call her myself. But the switchboard informed me that no outgoing calls from the internal extensions could be put through, as detainees were not allowed to contact anyone outside the centre without a convincing reason. I had one; to me, it was no less than a matter of life and death. But to my captors, it did not mean a thing. They said I was overreacting. That was precisely what Riaz had also told me way back in Hyderabad when I started getting worked up over a very similar situation—Rehana's uncharacteristic silence. Only, being a free man at the time, I had chosen my course of action by my own free will. Now, I no longer had that freedom.

Towards the evening, Uncle Haroon arrived and put me out of my misery. "I'm sorry, I couldn't come earlier," he apologised, settling down in a chair in the visitors lounge, "We had to take Rehana to the hospital."

"To the hospital? Why?"

"Just a routine check up by her gynaecologist. She did try to phone you several times in order to put your mind at ease, but couldn't. It seems we aren't allowed to talk to the detainees on the phone. They refused to put her through."

"Who refused?"

"Security. Calls go straight to them from the switchboard. They didn't agree even to give you a message."

That was more or less as what I had gathered in course of the day. It meant that I had no contact with the outside world whatsoever. For as long as I remained a prisoner at that centre, there was no chance of my being able to communicate with my wife, or with anyone else for that matter. The first taste of captivity went down my throat rather bitterly

"I see," I said, weighing the information in my mind. "In other words, no one from your side would be able to tell me how things are, unless you make a special journey?"

"More or less. Except, of course, in serious emergencies."

"A mere matter of opinion, isn't it? What you and I consider to be a *serious emergency,* they might not. In which case …"

"In which case, someone or the other from our side will rush here to fill you in."

"And then what? You'll either run an hourly courier service between Bromley and here, or I break down from nervous debility?"

"You're making too many assumptions. In the first instance, there is no reason to anticipate an emergency; by the grace of Allah, nothing has gone wrong so far. But even if there's one, we can cross that bridge when we come to it. Or, have you lost faith in me completely?"

Frankly, I had, even though I did not like to insult him to his face. After all, he had been going through a lot of pressure on account of me, knocking around from place to place, talking to solicitors, negotiating with politicians, sometimes visiting me himself and sometimes driving Rehana over to see me, his business left to the winds.

"Looks like coming here was a stupid mistake. A daily trunk call to Hyderabad would've been less strenuous and one heck of a sight cheaper," I mumbled.

"Too late for regrets. And looking at the situation from a positive side, it isn't altogether a waste either. For one thing, you and your wife saw each other. It has done you both a lot of good. For the other, the very feeling of proximity by itself can be quite rewarding. But above all, your detention here does add a great deal of strength to her reapplication to the Home Office for your entry permit in the light of the altered circumstances."

The observation gave me a nasty jolt. I could clearly see a new crisis shaping up. When I wrote to Rehana that I had made up my mind to emigrate to UK, the situation at the time was entirely different. Mr. Godfrey had recently rejected my application and an appeal to the tribunal was a long way off. On account of it, even she had taken a casual view of the suggestion. But now, things had changed dramatically. There was no longer a question of she and I *sorting it all out face-to-face* at leisure in Hyderabad; I was already there, *face-to-face* with Uncle Haroon himself. In saying what he just did, he brought the entire issue out into the open.

"I see," I said without much enthusiasm. "Does it make such a big difference to her reapplication? I mean, my presence here and my detention?"

"Of course, it does. So far, we've been asking them to let you come. Now, we can simply ask them to let you stay. Whatever evidence is needed to back up her application has already been submitted to the Home Office by her solicitors."

"What about the investigations being carried out by the Home Office?"

"Sir Ralph Bellamy, Rehana's barrister whom I appointed for her, knows all about it and feels confident that he would be able to persuade the home secretary to treat the things which you have done as mitigating circumstances and drop the investigations. He happens to be a leading civil rights campaigner and a real thorn in the home secretary's flesh."

"Is he, really?"

"Yes. Apart from that, ministerial decisions can always be challenged in courts where they are often reversed by judges if a clever solicitor with the right experience and a sharp mind is in a position to establish due cause. All the professionals I've got working on the case are absolutely brilliant jurists with lots of amazing ideas."

"And how long do you think all this could take?"

"A few months, I guess. And if the matter gets referred to the European court, it could even drag on for a year or two."

I felt a big explosion inside my head. If I stayed in that dreadful dump for two months, let alone two years, I could see myself swallowing spiders, eating ants, munching cockroaches and asking for more! The only time I would ever willingly surrender to such a long and painful punishment was upon murdering him!

"Two years!" I exclaimed, which was the best I could do by way of a substitute for screaming. "How the hell do you think I'd be able to endure this terrible torture for as long as that? Two years happens to be about one-twelfth of my entire life to date, you know?"

"Don't be absurd."

"Am I being absurd? Is that what it sounds like to you?"

"Yes," he said, brushing aside my strongest objection with a mere wave of his hand. "Your assumption that I'd let you rot here for the next two years does."

"But you do agree that staying in this place for any length of time— whether two years or two months—is beyond the scope of anybody's endurance?"

"Of course, I do."

"And what happens if I start running out of patience before your solicitors run out of their amazing ideas?"

"It's a very hypothetical question."

"But it's also a very possible state of affairs."

"If you look at the situation from where I sit, I'm sure you will see things differently."

He was not answering me. If I pressed him too hard, he might simply make promises without any intentions of keeping them, just to stall the issue. The very thought scared me. At a time when we should have been talking about Rehana, about the delivery, about the baby, about the arrival of a new guest in our midst, we were sinking deeper and deeper into futile arguments. I really had my back up against the wall this time. Without any friends, without much guidance, without an iota of support and without a minimum measure of help from someone who cared about me, I felt pretty much like one of those wretched Roman slaves who get thrown into rings packed with hungry lions just for fun. In my case, no one was even paying towards the fun.

"From where you sit, just what the heck is it that you see, Uncle Haroon?" I demanded in sheer desperation. "Take a good hard look and then tell me. What do you see? Just a heap of ruins—one here and one in your own house. You weren't present in this room yesterday when Rehana and I took leave of each other. You should have seen us. We were quite a spectacle for you to watch."

Shifting his weight from one lap to the other, he braced up. He knew I was on the verge of exploding. He also knew when to talk and when to keep his mouth shut, the prime quality of a good businessman.

"Ask yourself a simple question, Uncle," I carried on in the same belligerent mien. "Why is Rehana stuck over there in Bromley and I am stuck here in this Goddammed dump? I agree that physical distance between us is now no more than forty miles. But have you any idea why it's beginning to feel much farther away than forty thousand? Because the hurdles in between are more unconquerable than the Himalayas and the Alps could ever be. You on one side and Mr. Godfrey on the other, both extremes of the same rod; you, obsessed with your mad love, and he, with his petty prejudices, both adding different fuel to the same fire. A fire that the two of you are keeping alive, but in which the two of us are burning alive. When is this going to end?"

He went pale in the face but still refused to break the seal of silence. By then, I had already spoken so much there seemed no point in my holding anything back. So I kept up the assault with a devil may care attitude.

"Things weren't like this before you snatched Rehana away from me, Uncle," I said, biting harshly upon the words. "We were a family held together with unbreakable bonds of love. We didn't have material assets but we cared for each other; the food on our table was seldom rich but we shared whatever we had. In a matter of a few unforgettable months, we've accumulated so many golden memories I just can't find their parallel anywhere. And you had to come charging out of the blue and take them away! Why, Uncle, why?"

"Because," he said in an astonishingly restrained voice, his first few words since my onslaught began, "a part of that golden dream happens to belong to me too, my friend. I, too, have similar stories of family bonds and mutual loyalties to tell, the saddest of them being that of the foolish old man who sowed all his corn seeds on far-off farms and then watched the others reap his rich harvest."

His remark was so asinine it sent a series of shivers down my back. "Are you sure you are talking only about a share in the rich harvest, Uncle Haroon?" I demanded arrogantly. "Or, is it your *pound of flesh* that you seek?"

"And what the hell is that supposed to mean?"

"I don't know. When you say *your* harvest on *our* farm, I presume you're hinting at *your* daughter now being a part of *our* family. Unless, of course, the reference is to that so-called *pact of honour* between yourself and my father. I know all about it: Mr. Rao told me everything. If so, then please level with me, Uncle. Are you now calling upon me to make good Papa's word?"

"At the moment, I'm only referring to the letter you wrote to Rehana last month. You did say in it that you've decided to emigrate to this country by your own free will, didn't you?"

I was afraid he would say that. It was not Rehana's fault; in my anxiety to spare her the test of loyalties, I remembered how convincingly I had expressed myself in it. She probably did what she thought was the right thing to do and mentioned it to him.

"I never had the will to emigrate, Uncle," I clarified the misunderstanding for what it was worth. "I was only acting upon your friend's advice. I just wanted to spare her the distress of having to take sides, having to choose between her *husband* and her *father*."

"What's different now?"

"Now, she doesn't have to do any more than *obey* me. One heck of a reason why we all take our conjugal vows, isn't it? Can you blame her, if she does what I command her to do?"

I must have scored pretty high on that, for he fell into brooding.

"Why don't you leave the choice to us, Uncle?" I urged him in a much softer tone. "Let's decide on which branch to build our nest. We both know there's one going towards the *East* and there's another going towards the *West*. We'll think it over at the right time and make up our minds. If we decide to live here, we'll come back as soon as an entry permit is given to me by the

Home Office to settle in this country. But if we decide not to, then bear us no grudge. Is it so difficult to concede?"

"Very well," he conceded after giving the suggestion some thought. "Do it your way. I won't interfere," and then walked away in a huff.

For the next seven days, there was no sign of him. Neither could Rehana phone on account of the security restrictions. How was she? What was happening? Did the gynaecologist set a date for the delivery? I did not have the foggiest notion. The element of uncertainty began to take its toll upon me. I soon lost my sleep and my appetite. My active imagination did not spare any scruples either. All sorts of poignant visions rose in front of my eyes, of coffins wrapped in green cerements, of desolate graves, of rose lattices, painful, disturbing, frightening. If staying there at the centre was so fraught with tensions, going back to India in such a state of nerves was even worse. I dared not go away in such a rush, without taking one more look at Rehana, without telling her, without asking her permission. My sudden departure could so easily crush her heart. I could not even think in terms of forsaking her side. It was a time for us to stick together; it was a time for us to make sacrifices; it was a time to take tests and to win them all.

On the eighth day, I was summoned to the warden's office to receive a phone call. Nothing short of an extreme emergency could have persuaded security to make such a major concession. The very thought froze the blood in my veins. With the help of Mr. Collins who had come to escort me, I staggered on unsteady feet as far as the warden's office. The only thing that caught my attention in it was the telephone on his desk, waiting for me. Picking it up with a trembling hand, I listened.

"Yusuff?" said Auntie Zeenath.

It was the first time she had bothered to speak to me since I arrived at Heathrow. That, coupled with the fact that she had been put through to me by security, rocked the ground underneath my feet

"What's it, Auntie?" I asked her in a hoarse voice, giving her my undivided attention. "Is anything the matter?"

"Listen," she said, for some reason noticeably lowering the pitch of her voice. "I got through to you with great difficulty to tell you something extremely important. Rehana's is so upset at not being allowed to contact you on the phone, she's setting out on a collision course with the Home Office. I don't know all the details, but whatever they are, I feel it's a dangerous step to take. Making such powerful enemies could cost her dearly in the end."

"Why's she doing it?" I mumbled incoherently. "Is it really because she hasn't been able to contact me on phone? Or is there anything more to it than that?"

"I don't know," she replied, sounding immensely exasperated. "All she said was, time had come for her to take the Home Office to the launderers, no longer through lawyers and judges, but by publicly embarrassing them. I don't know the full details, except that she spent most of the week locked up in her room, weeping as well as using the phone, presumably drawing up her battle plans."

"Doesn't she realise that I'm a prisoner here because of my own folly, and prisoners can't expect to have the same rights as free people?"

"I said the same thing to her, but she's too upset to listen to reason. For the first time in her life, she's turned a deaf ear even to my pleas."

"So, what do we do?"

Before she could answer my question, someone who had been quietly listening in to our conversation either at her end or at my end abruptly cut us off … .

CHAPTER (28)

"Is anything the matter, Mr. Quraishi?" the warden asked me, obviously taking due note of the intense pallor upon my face. His soft voice echoed in the quiet room. I looked at him. He sat wearing an expression of deep concern. Mr. Collins relieved me of the phone and put it back on the cradle. The sound of its bell exploded in my ears like the toll of Big Ben. The disconcerting news that Rehana had decided to set upon a collision course with forces beyond her scope frightened me to death. Just like Auntie Zeenath had felt and expressed, it was, indeed, a very dangerous step to take.

"May I sit down for a while, sir?" I asked him.

"Yes, of course. Do sit down."

I sat down. Mr. Collins quietly left the room.

"What is it? That's—if you don't mind my asking," the warden said again.

"Not at all, sir. That was my mother-in-law on the phone. She said that my wife is planning to 'publicly embarrass the Home Office.' Any idea what it could mean?"

"Not the foggiest. I hope she isn't thinking in terms of *Satyagraha*. You now? Like Mahatma Gandhi used to do. Is she?"

"I don't know."

"I'm afraid that sort of thing won't work in this country. Several IRA prisoners tried and failed. Some gave up while the others ..."

He did not finish the sentence but I knew precisely what he was hinting at.

"If I remember right, she's due for her delivery any time now, isn't she?" he asked.

"Yes, sir," I replied.

"Why don't you talk to her and find out what exactly is she planning to do?" he suggested out of goodness of his heart.

386

"But how? I'm not allowed to contact anyone on the phone and neither can I send her a message without its being—"

"I know what you mean. Do you reckon she's likely to carry out the threat?"

"If she's made one, I'm sure she will. But I don't know what exactly my mother-in-law meant when she said—well, what she said."

If only there was some way in which I could talk to Rehana. There was no need for her to do anything; I had already brought her father up-to-date with the real situation and made my views known to him without any uncertainty or ambiguity. Whether or not he liked what I told him, he knew I meant every word I said. After the delivery, we could go back to Hyderabad, talk things through between ourselves at leisure, consult with our well-wishers too, reach our own decisions and then act accordingly. What was the rush? Unless … .

The possibility of Uncle Haroon's hand being behind all the newfangled upheaval seemed pretty strong. Having failed to get my backing for his plans, or to motivate me in the slightest degree to follow in his footsteps, he might have provoked her himself. In order to detonate her feelings, adding just a tiny flame to the fuse was quite enough. But would he take such a risk? At a time when she was extremely vulnerable and so dangerously poised on the very edge, would he consciously put her life in danger by provoking her to launch that kind of a perilous mission? Was my immigrating to England of such importance to him that he would bid for it at any price?

"Why don't you drop her a line?" the warden suggested. "Just ask her to come and see you once? It might take a day or two for your communication to reach her because of the complicated state of affairs over here, but I'm sure it'll get through eventually."

The suggestion was quite sensible, provided there were no impetuous obstacles in between. A letter as simple as that was hardly likely to be stopped by security at my end, but if any of my suspicions about Uncle Haroon were right, it was more than likely to be intercepted by him at the other. For how long could I wait for her response? How much time could I afford to waste? If she did not come despite my writing to her, how would I find out why did she not turn up?

"Yes, sir. You're quite right. I'll do that straight away. And thanks for the kindness," I said and left his office.

Back in my room, I began to think hard. Writing to her was not difficult. The simpler the text, the better stood its chances of getting past security.

Whether or not it would get past Uncle Haroon's hands was another matter. Never before had I experienced a greater need for freedom in all my life. Brooding brought along with it its own share of frustrations. *'The worst that can happen to me if I get caught,'* I remembered having told Shabbu that day, *'is an instant repatriation. Who cares?'* But suddenly, I realised it was not as simple as that. By trying to sneak into the country unlawfully, I had stirred up a hornet's nest; I had given rise to a storm that was not even there on the horizon; I had forced a change upon the course of events.

Hence, on the following morning, when Mr. Collins informed me that my wife had arrived and was waiting for me in the visitors' lounge, I could not believe my ears. Let alone mailing, I had not even written the letter. Why did she suddenly decide to visit me? What could have prompted her to make such a hazardous journey at that particular juncture? I did not have the foggiest notion. She either had a pretty strong ESP, or I was a damn sight luckier man than I had thought myself to be. Whatever the case, I rushed over to the lounge to see her.

As plain as daylight, she was really there, waiting for me. Holding her in my arms, I did not utter a word for some time. I just could not. I felt completely overwhelmed by anxiety and by concern towards her safety. For two people who had committed no premeditated crimes either against God or against mankind, we were paying an unjust and unjustifiable price. She in my arms and I at her service was the long and short of our expectations. But we hardly seemed to be getting anywhere on account of one reason or the other.

After recovering myself with a great deal of effort, I gazed at her. She looked tired, drained and exhausted. If the idea of crossing swords with the Home Office was hers alone, I did not have any insurmountable problems; I could control her, beg her, beseech her, and if necessary, I could even command her. She was within my means. And since she had come to the centre to talk to me on her own accord, she must have come prepared to listen, to negotiate, perhaps also to conceded and compromise. I ventured to take that much for granted. Both of us were partners in the same enterprise, heading in the same direction, aiming to accomplish the same goal and were walking shoulder to shoulder. We were not at cross purposes, like Uncle Haroon and me, like Mr. Godfrey and me, like God and me.

"Come along, Rehana," I whispered to her gently. "Sit down. Relax. Rest your head on my shoulder. You look worn out. Must be because of the long and tedious journey."

Resting her head on my shoulder, she loosened up a bit.

"Are you all right?" I asked her in a while.

"Now, yes. And you?"

"Me too. You must be pretty oracular to have found out that I was desperate to see you."

She stared at me with a slight hint of surprise in her eyes.

"Someone from the centre phoned Dad last night and asked him either to send me or to bring me here today. Didn't you know who it was?" she asked.

I did not. But if it was who I thought it was, may he live to be an hundred! "Never mind who. How's Uncle?" I asked her, deliberately changing the topic.

"He's fine. Making up on lost time."

"And how about our unknown guest in here?"

"Rather restless, but fairly well behaved on the whole."

"Who drove you to this place?"

"Mum did."

"Is she waiting outside?"

"Yes, she is. Let her."

Both of us paused there for a while. The next part of the conversation was not going to be as casual as that. Whether or not she knew it, I did.

"What's all this rumour I hear about you wanting to take on the Home Office?" I asked her without beating around the bush.

Once again she looked at me with that same hint of surprise in her eyes. "How did you know?" she asked.

"Auntie phoned the other day and told me. And sounded rather upset too. Since then, I was getting pretty desperate to see you and to talk this through."

"Yes, she's. So is Dad. Are you too?"

"Not upset but worried sick. Why do you want to quarrel with them?"

"A matter of principle, that's all."

"Can't it wait? At least until after the delivery?"

"After the delivery, we've got a plane to catch."

"Plenty of them fly homewards every day, Rehana."

"And if I promise you I won't do anything foolish, can't you trust me?"

"You—yes. But I don't trust fate. It scares me to death."

"Don't be afraid. Good luck's on its way," she said, holding my hand and running my palm over her bulging stomach.

"Let's not do anything to delay it," I said.

"I won't. I swear I won't," she assured me.

It should have sufficed and satisfied me; I knew she always kept her promises. But I simply could not let matters rest there. The stakes had gone too high.

"Please, Rehana. Forget about the Home Office. Let's go back first and then talk things over. We can always return if we want to, after the permit is issued. These things take time. You said so yourself in your letter, remember? We aren't in any particular rush, are we?"

"If it's all the same with you, we aren't coming back here."

"Fine. In that case, there's no need for you to quarrel with the Home Office anymore, is there?"

Sunlight filtering in through the windows ignited her eyes. Suddenly, her mouth flexed, her jaw locked, her fists clenched, her breathing speeded, her entire physiognomy underwent a curious metamorphosis. She looked possessed by a force outside her. I had never seen her overcome by so much anger all at once.

"Yes, there's," she replied, savagely biting upon those two words.

"What's the need, Rehana?" I asked her.

"A few days ago," she replied in a voice that was barely louder than a whisper, "Uncle Rao phoned Daddy and informed him that your application for the entry permit was turned down by the E.C.O. in Bombay. To them, it was just another of those awful things that happen from time to time. But to me, it was the worst injustice I was ever dealt."

That was the need; hitting back, retaliating, setting right an inexcusable wrong, seeking justice from those who did not know what it means to be just, asking the leopard to change its spots, expecting honey in a cobra's fangs, reaching out for oases in a mirage! She was talking about a belt of mountains that had never been shifted, about rivers that are never known to have altered their course, she was talking about restitutions, about reforms, about reawakenings!

"I see," I said, gulping down a bitter lump, "Because the E.C.O. in Bombay turned down my application, you've now decided to throw a punch at him. Is that right?"

Without saying yes or no to the question, she simply sat there staring at me, her face masked behind a dense cover of silence.

"Did it not occur to you that there might be some other and a much simpler explanation to it?" I asked her.

"Is there?" she wanted to know.

"Yes, there's," I replied quite bluntly. "You're looking at the other explanation. Me. The incompetent lowbrow, the invincible gauche. All I needed to do was to convince the man of my bona fides. Butchers from Baroda and peasants from Punjab are known to have fared better, no offence intended. But I couldn't handle even that much. If anyone's to blame, I'm to blame. Go on, blame me, mock at me, and scoff at me, laugh at me. I won't mind it one bit. But don't try to reform the establishment, Rehana. It will not work."

I put it across to her as emphatically as I could. If only she could accept my self-ridicule with an indulgent smile and nip the matter in the bud. But she did not. Instead, she made me put my hand upon her head and said, "Now swear and tell me. Is that the real truth?"

Frankly, it was not. I was not given a fair treatment by the E.C.O. in Bombay. He had shown no inclination whatsoever towards discovering the real truth. In his efforts to punch holes in my story, he had stopped at nothing; he had called our marriage into question, he had mocked at our conjugal vows, he had impugned me with insensitive allegations that were not true, he had saddled me with untenable imputations that had no basis. Yet, if that was what it took to dissuade her from her chosen course of action, I did not mind giving even him some credibility.

"Technically, yes, although I won't swear to it," I replied. "The E.C.O. claimed he was merely doing his duty. Perhaps he was. Why can't we give him the benefit of the doubt? Besides, whatever happened in the past is no longer important, no longer relevant, and no longer of any consequence or of significance. Uncle said a new application has been made to the home secretary on your behalf by your solicitors aiming to accomplish the same thing. The rest is just history."

"That's what I thought, until I saw you locked up here in this detention centre."

"I'm here because of what I did; I took the law into my own hands, which's wrong. No one likes to be taken for a ride, neither they nor we. It was a very foolish thing to do; I behaved like an imbecile; I asked for some trouble and I was given some."

"No, that isn't why you're here," she said without altering the pitch of voice in the slightest. "I know everything now, I've sussed it all out. Daddy wrote to you that I wasn't well and you lost your head. You panicked because you loved me. You wanted to be by my side because you thought I needed you. Is that breaking the law? Is a husband's desire to be by his wife's side when she needs him, or a wife's craving for her husband's arms around her when she wants to, breaking the law? Is it?"

I could not say yes to her question. In a moment or two, her eyes filled up with tears. Anger turned into grief and began to spill drop by drop. The lounge plunged into a precarious silence; outside the room, woolpacks of white clouds that had gathered in the sky seemed at an absolute standstill. My heart kept ticking in a weak flutter; a spasm of pain rocked my body. There was a child inside her, waiting to be welcomed; a new human being was getting ready to take its place amidst the fraternity of mankind. And what were we doing? Instead of running with outstretched arms to welcome it into our midst, we were turning our faces away; we were surrendering ourselves to our weaknesses; we were upsetting our priorities; vitiating our surroundings; rendering the world unacceptable for incarnation; turning life into a sad punishment; sinking deeper and deeper into virulent pits, some of hatred and some of its aftermath!

"They locked you up for it!" she continued, dwelling upon the same theme. "I still remember the day I saw you here for the first time. Know how I felt? I felt as though I was naked, I was stripped, I had no protection; I did not have any shelter to take refuge in. And do you know why? Because I did not have any rights. Before I walked in through that door, a security woman searched me inside out. I was allowed to enter this room because she thought it was all right for me to do so. When you asked me to go home that day, I did not want to; I was not yet satisfied; I wanted to spend some more time with you but I couldn't because visiting hours were over. We had met after such a long time and after such a lot of hassle; money shrank the distances and yet it could not buy us satisfaction. Just like you yourself said, the Himalayas and the Alps were overcome, but one man in Cabin 3 could not be. The sanctity of wedlock, handed down by one generation to the other since the times of Adam and Eve was suddenly brought to a grinding halt inside the perimeters of Heathrow Airport!"

As she spoke, the tears kept dribbling down her cheeks in an endless succession. I realised at once I was not up against a woman's frailty but her most unconquerable strength. Rehana was not surrendering herself to her emotional turmoil as a prisoner. On the contrary, she was on the battleground, in full armour and with her swords drawn. When they get there, they seldom retreat; they either go down, or they take you down!

"You know something?" she asked me, her flared eyes shot in my direction, her brow dented by a deep frown, her mouth drawn in an angry grimace. "Being born in this country was not a matter of my choice. I did not elect to do it. No one cautioned me of its grim ramifications while I was still gestating in my mum's womb. Or asked me to wait for a more convenient time and place before taking birth. Or warned me that I could get myself into this kind of trouble if I took birth here. Was it my fault?"

I sat speechless, just gazing at her and listening to her. For some reason, she chose that particular moment to cover her head with the edge of her *sari*. The pink background of the fabric lent an additional tinge to her flushed cheeks. Tears soaked the welter of lashes and washed down the mascara. Her nose began to run and her chest heaved from deep breathing. Having discovered an outlet, her pent-up emotions kept spilling one after another. I let her talk without any interruptions. The tide had settled on a course. Changing its direction at that stage was beyond me.

"I grew up in the country of my birth," she continued after only a short pause to recover her breath. "I went to school, made friends, played with them, shared secrets with them, enjoyed many a Christmas and birthday party, saluted the Union Jack, stood to attention whenever I heard *'Long Live the Queen'*, applauded our cricket teams and our tennis players. When I came of age, I cast my vote in the hope that my country would protect me in times of need; I believed in the concepts of democracy, of freedom, of justice, of equality and of fraternity. I learned how to read the *Qur'aan* at a very early age; I offered *Namaaz* as regularly as I could and I always respected my parents and my peers. One day, Mum and Dad told me they were contemplating a traditional marriage for me. I did not object to it. I went to Hyderabad with them, I let them choose you for my husband, I accepted you as my lifelong partner without any qualms, I gave you my best, I always strived to please you. Not long after that, I became pregnant. I did not object to it, I did not have any regrets; I did not look back. Where did I go wrong? Which law did I break? What crime did I commit? Would someone please explain to me?"

I did not utter a word. I could not. Any effort on my part to restrain her would have triggered off even more uncontrollable outbursts. Like a river in spate, calm but outstretching, gaining ground inch by inch, wave after wave, she progressed relentlessly.

"Have you any idea how I felt upon listening to the sordid details of your interrogation at the British Embassy in Bombay?" she carried on. "I spent three whole days locked up inside my room just crying. Every insult thrown at you landed upon me like a leash; every affront you suffered at their hands turned into red-hot cinders and charred my soul. It left my pride in tatters and it turned my faith into a mockery. What am I worth, in my own country, in a civilized community? My husband, born in a decent home, brought up by caring parents, loved by his kith and kin, respected by his colleagues, a man of honour and self respect, driven out of my own country's embassy by a fellow countryman of mine? On what grounds? Why's it that no one seems to care? Why do I have to make applications here and there; why should my father go knocking around from door to door, either currying favours from politicians or commencing legal proceedings on my behalf? Haven't I been married long enough? I am about to have my first child, for God's sake!"

She was right. When Mr. Godfrey rejected my application for entry permit, my grievance was entirely different. I could merely complain of one man's inhumanity towards another, but not of one citizen's utter disregard towards the rights of a fellow citizen. The most I could have expected from him was fairness, a minimum measure of compassion, and a little bit of understanding. But it was not the same with her. She was a victim of prejudice, of racial bias, of bigotry. A law that had been passed to protect her was invoked against her; those who were being paid to guard her robbed her.

"When Daddy came to know from Riaz Bhaijan that you are on your way, and phoned us through to Bromley," she carried on. "I went mad with joy. I made all sorts of plans to welcome you at Heathrow. I had already tasted a measure of hospitality that was extended to me by your family in Hyderabad and I looked forward to showing off some of ours too. I rang up all my friends and told them you're coming. I went to the shops and bought many new clothes for you, decorated the bedroom, sorted out the bed, spent hours and hours watching myself in the mirror, trying out so many different ways of concealing the awkward tummy, because I wanted to look my best. For what! Can you imagine how disappointed I was when Daddy phoned again and broke the dreadful news that you've been apprehended and locked up at the detention centre? My heart broke. Do they know that? They know how to throw the book at us, how to read out rights and how to interpret legislation. Do they also know how to interpret the grief of a broken heart? How to translate the silent language of my tears? How to give a voice to the muffled whisper of my sighs?"

Drained and worn out, she rested her head on my shoulder again. Her hand searched for mine and she held it tight.

"You're here, barely forty miles away from where I live and yet I can neither see you nor speak to you. Why? Why's it that I can't speak to my own husband? What're you doing *here* when I need you *there?* What's stopping you from coming to my side? Why've you been stripped of your freedom?

What is your fault? What is your crime, your sin, and your guilt? Marrying me? Is that all I'm worth?" she asked.

"Why must you care what you are worth to someone else, my precious?" I said, opening my mouth at long last, "when to me, you're a million times worth the Crown of Great Britain?"

"The decision to bring me into this world was Allah's. The decision to unite us both in holy wedlock was our parents'. The decision to prevent us from reuniting was Mr. Godfrey's. And yet you say they're irrelevant?"

"I'm sorry. I was wrong."

"I'll tell you what's wrong. It's wrong to give one man too much power over another. It's wrong to be allowed to take away without the ability to restitute. It's wrong to be permitted to pronounce judgements without being required to pursue justice. It's wrong to deprive without the means for recompense. That's what's wrong. But it isn't wrong for a wife to seek comfort in her husband's arms, nor is it wrong for a husband to come forward and offer his wife that comfort. Is it?"

"No, it isn't."

"I want to look squarely into the eye of every free and free thinking woman of this Egalitarian Society and ask her two simple questions. How would she have felt in my place and what would she have done in my plight? I'm just as proud to be British as you're to be an Indian. I want to know what price my fellow citizens are willing to put upon that pride. It isn't true that I want to take on the Home Office; I've no bones to pick with them. I don't want to ask them to let you come into the country. I want to know why you were stopped in the first place. I don't want them to issue you with an entry permit now. I want to know why it was refused. When I go back to Hyderabad along with you, I don't want to be underrated as some sort of a Babylonian Slave in a Roman Court. I want to be able to walk around with my head raised high. The privilege of my birth in this country guarantees me that right. I want to fight for it, I want to take it and not be given it. How can anyone give me what I already have? Or, don't I?"

As things stood, it seemed she did not. When she saw me for the first time at the detention centre, no wonder she felt naked. A woman without rights is more vulnerable than a woman without clothes. Like a chic outside its eggshell; like a pupa without its cocoon.

"Since yesterday, Mum and Dad have started waging a war of nerves on me. Are you too intending to do the same?"

"No, I'm not," I promised her.

"Thanks. It's a load off my mind. I swear I will not do anything foolish or take any unnecessary risks."

"I'm sure you won't."

"You are not going to go back to Hyderabad *without* me, are you?"

"No way."

"I'll promise you one more thing. The day I'm fit enough to travel, we're catching the first available homeward flight and go, come hell or high water."

"All right."

"I won't let you rot in this dreadful dump even for a single moment after that."

"Good."

At that stage, suddenly overcome by yet another upsurge in her run away emotions, she circled her arms around my neck and broke down again saying, "I wish we could go to Bromley together, now, right now, this very minute …"

We did not have such luck. I had no idea how she was planning to accomplish her tough mission, and neither did I ask, but that was beside the point. For one reason or another, I was not going to be available to her for lending a hand. It was one battle she was going to have to wage on her own; it was *her* battle, for *her* cause and by *her* choice. I could applaud her if she won; mourn her if she fell; but I would not be alongside her while she fought. I remembered the vow I had taken at the time of our wedding to stand by her 'in sickness or in health, in sorrow or in joy, in poverty or in affluence, until prevented by death alone,' a vow which millions of people take day after day and many are also lucky enough to keep. Given the chance, I, too, would have kept mine. One small concession was all I needed, one kind thought, one kind word, one stroke of the pen, one gesture of goodwill, one decent man like the warden at the top. We would have waited until our baby arrived and then gone back, blessing the queen, blessing those who governed the kingdom in her name, blessing the kingdom of which she is the sovereign. We would have taken back with us not only our child, but also a lot of pleasant memories to ruminate upon—I with my everlasting gratitude, and Rehana with her pride in tact. But it was not to be so.

Wiping her wet cheeks with my handkerchief, I rearranged her tousled hair. On that particular day, I could not do anymore than that for her. Suddenly, my service to her had become severely curtailed.

"Go home now, Rehana," I whispered in her ear after kissing her head, *"Visiting hours are over."*

She nodded and got to her feet. We walked together up to the exit door. That was about as far as I could go. There I stopped. After taking a few more steps without me, she paused and turned round to take one parting look at me. As she did so, a thin film of moisture in my eyes blurred my vision.

CHAPTER (29)

Within two days since Rehana set out on her arduous mission, most of the detainees at the centre came to know what was going on. In their opinion, she was not only fighting for herself, but also for all the other women who shared a similar plight. As a result of it, she attracted an instant following both inside as well as outside. They praised her courage; they prayed for her success; they wished her well. The sense of solidarity was so strong, they saw in her a champion of their own cause too. Some saluted her, some eulogized her, and some even wrote poems in her honour, all anxiously waiting to see the outcome of her toils.

They also brought an unexpected measure of comfort for me. Some lady or the other always visited the centre at most times of the day. The men passed on Rehana's telephone number to them so that they could ring her up regularly, talk to her, find out what sort of progress she was making, what problems she was coming up against, strengthen her resolve with their own faith as well as bring me messages from her. Such solidarity often made me wonder if she was not on to something useful after all. Perhaps she was. Perhaps she was the solution to their problems too. Perhaps they needed someone like her to lead the way. Perhaps, in her search for her own exits and accesses, she might throw open the doors for a lot of others too. That alone would make her fight worth its while.

Towards the end of the week, none other than Uncle Haroon himself brought the very first piece of solid news about her plight and her progress to me.

"That daughter of mine!" He exclaimed with a great deal of relish and satisfaction, settling down in the chair. "Do you know how far she's gone without moving an inch out of the house?"

He was no longer hostile, which considerably eased my mind. The feud between us seemed to have lost its puissance in the wake of all those exciting developments.

"Today," he informed me with a glint of pride in his eyes, "the first part of her exclusive interview has been published in *Womanity*, a leading women's weekly in the country with a strong accent on egalitarian issues. What a sensation it has caused!"

"Why didn't you fetch a copy with you, Uncle? It would've brought a great deal of comfort to no less than one hundred and eighty young men right here at the centre?"

"Really? Has she already made that many fans?"

"Yes, she has."

"Wonderful! God alone knows how many more people she has impressed today. I did bring along with me a copy of the magazine but those dreadful chaps working in security confiscated it."

"Why did they do that? If the entire country is reading it, what harm was there in our doing the same?"

"Not my fault. They just took it."

"How's Rehana, anyway?"

"She's exerting herself a bit more than she ought to, but not bad on the whole. And what about you? How are you keeping."

"As well as I can be expected to, under the circumstances."

"Don't worry. If she continues to achieve a similar measure of success in the days to come, you'll be out of here before you can say: 'Jack's my brother'."

"Do you really think so? In time for the delivery?"

"There're pretty strong possibilities. This interview that has been published today is expected to mobilize a lot of public sympathy in her favour. Besides that, Channel 4 Television have also come forward with an attractive proposal to make a short but quick documentary about her case and broadcast it on their *Asian Eye* slot next week. As you know, television happens to be a more effective medium than printed material and hence has a much wider popular appeal. "

"Indeed, it has."

"Apart from that, a lady called Mrs. Brown has contacted Rehana on behalf of the Asian Welfare Association in Birmingham. Her proposal is to come up with a petition addressed to the home secretary and get it endorsed by as many women as possible from his own constituency. Obviously, politicians being vulnerable people, they can't afford to take the risk of displeasing those who put them in power."

"True."

"And Rehana's plea has a novelty of its own, you see. She isn't seeking any concessions from the Home Office or making any sort of unreasonable threats by way of retaliation. All she wants is for people to acknowledge that her grievance is fair."

"Yes, that's what she told me she'd do."

"Just a matter of getting through to the masses with the right words, spoken in the right tone. That's all she needs to do. Just get through. And judging from the turbulent storm she has stirred up already, she certainly seems to be."

"I agree."

"Did you know that Sir Ralph Bellamy, the successful London barrister and a leading campaigner of human rights whom I had mentioned to you once before, is already preparing to fight the Home Office in the European court rather than at the Old Bailey? Yes, he is. It's only been a few days since she got to work and look how far she's reached! That's what I call real progress!"

"Sure."

"You've no idea what it means to me—getting you out of this place and making you a lawful resident of this country."

If he was talking about the principle behind it, I could not agree with him more. But I had a sneaking suspicion he was not.

"Oh?" I said, sitting up.

"I don't know if you're aware of this, but upon my death, Rehana stands to inherit the bulk of my estate, including the business. Can you see her running a show as big as mine on her own? Making trunk calls here and there, going around on business tours in India, negotiating deals with so many of our suppliers, satisfying the requirements of our customers?"

"No, I don't. "

"Neither do I. But someone has to. Otherwise, a lifetime of toils could get wiped out within a matter of days."

"And who's that someone? Me?"

"If you don't do it, who else will?"

"I see," I said somewhat tensely. "In other words, as far as you're concerned, Rehana's campaign has nothing to do with the academics of right and wrong, or with missions and with causes. It's either the availability of a successor to run your business after you're gone, or its non-availability. Isn't that so?"

When I put it over to him in those words, he studied me for a while with a distasteful look, but offered no sort of comment one way or another, either agreeing with the question or disagreeing.

"Does Rehana know about this?" I asked him quite bluntly in order to force him into the open and take a clear stand.

"No, she doesn't."

"Precisely what is she trying to accomplish, Uncle Haroon?"

"You know it very well. She told you all about it herself."

Asking him that question was most unfair on Rehana, but it was vital for me to find the truthful answer. The platform from which she was waging her battle needed to be clearly defined and identified. Fighting for her rights was one thing, but using that fight to accomplish her father's personal ambitions was entirely different. One was a mission while the other was just a pretext, which made a difference of heaven and earth. If Rehana's struggle had anything at all to do with the latter, then she was fighting for herself and not for anyone else, least of all for the hundred and eighty detainees at the centre who had been writing poems in her honour and whose womenfolk had been running errands between Bromley and Heathrow. What Uncle Haroon wanted and whether or not he got it was beside the point. All said and done, I might agree to fulfil his dreams in the end, or I might not. One had nothing to do with the other. It was his bringing up that topic in that particular context which had triggered off those doubts in my mind. No one can restore a crack in the mirror and I did not want any such abrasions to exist between my wife and me. Until then, I had genuinely believed that she was waging a crusade. Without it, there was no question of pride. Business empires are built and lost ten times over in all parts of the world every day. One can only associate either success or failure with them and not pride.

"Yes, she did," I said with considerable relief, even though what he told me was merely a reassertion of a known fact. "But I would be most grateful if you could kindly clear a few more of my doubts, Uncle. These chaps from this *popular women's weekly* who've got involved; have they entered the picture out of genuine sympathy towards her cause, or are they doing it merely to boost the circulation of their *Womanity?*"

"How can I answer that question? I don't know what their real motives are, I couldn't possibly sneak into their minds and read their secret thoughts, could I?"

"What about this Mrs. Brown? It wasn't you who put her on to Rehana by any chance, was it?"

"Certainly not! Look here …"

"Please, Uncle. I promise you I won't ask you any more questions after this one. This leading human rights campaigner, Sir Ralph Bellamy, whom you said you retained to fight for Rehana. Is he taking the matter to the European court to uphold a principle, or is it merely because you gave him a whiff of your bank balance?"

"I haven't made a single contribution towards your wife's campaign. If anything, I had been against the whole idea from the start. She's doing it all by herself. Give her some credit, for God's sake! That poor girl has been wearing herself out for the sake of a principle."

"That's all I wanted to know, Uncle," I said, letting out a sigh of relief. "Now, listen. About this matter of my taking over the business from you; I wouldn't like to commit myself to you at this stage and in such hurry. This is a major decision that could affect the rest of our lives. Would you mind if I slept on it for a while?"

"Take your time. Make your mind up at your own pace. In one form or the other, my daughter will inherit most of what's mine, anyway. Nothing can change that. If I can't pass on the business to her, I can always sell it off and let her have the money in its place. What do I care what happens to it after I'm gone?"

So saying, he abruptly shot to his feet in a temper. Things had not been working out between us from the start. I felt very sorry about it. For one with such an incredible flair for success, he had made an utterly ludicrous mistake in choosing me for his daughter's hand. I was not quite the type to run such big business enterprises, solicit buyers, service customers, satisfy clients. All my life I had been taking orders either from one or from the other.

"Wait a minute, Uncle," I said, quickly stopping him. "Does this mean you won't come here to see me again?"

That was my worry. Rehana, her health, her well-being, her safety. His obsession was different; he also had a choice. If he could not pass on the business to his daughter, he could let her have the money instead. But I did not have any such choice. For me, it was either Rehana all the way or just Cipher. His bringing news of her was different from strangers doing the same. I could rely on it. I could learn more from him than from anyone else. As her father, he was also closer to her. Seeing him was almost like seeing one half of her, which in itself was a distinct advantage.

"Whatever gave you such a preposterous idea?" he asked me instead of answering me.

"Uncle, please. This is no time for feuds. Take any promise from me that you like. I'll give you a *blank cheque*. But please don't stop visiting me. I could go mad with worry," I implored.

"Rest assured," he said, softening up a bit. "I'm not going to exploit you by accepting any *blank cheques*. Can't say when exactly, but I'll drop in as soon as possible."

With those words he left. If he meant what he said, he would come again; if not, there was nothing I could do to change his mind. I returned to my room in a much worse state of nerves. By then, some clever lady had managed to smuggle a copy of *Womanity* into the centre in which Rehana's interview was published. Out of deference to my feelings, her husband passed it on to me first. A professional journalist, quoting her from time to time, wrote the article. Skilfully designed to arouse the sympathy of the readers, appropriate words were used in a practical vein. Her first childbirth, my presence in the country, her disappointment and my helplessness had all served as useful ingredients towards the making of an emotional human drama. I could tell it must have stirred the cockles of everyone's heart.

By that evening, our special courier service began to relay more news of the outside world. Response from public had picked up momentum; a *hotline* set up by the publishers of the magazine to monitor the reactions of their readers had been jammed all day. Most of the callers were outraged women asking them if there was anything they could to help Rehana. The colour of her skin receded into the background completely. Whatever be the policy of politicians on immigration, harassment of those who were already living in the country was not acceptable to most of them. Apart from readers, several voluntary organisations and pressure groups had also come forward to lend her support.

That was not all. Apparently, pressure had also begun to build up on the home secretary from his own constituents, and many grass route supporters of the ruling party, alarmed by the way public opinion was mobilising in her favour, were exerting pressure on their respective MPs to do something about it quickly before the adverse publicity could do too much damage to their own standing with the rank and file. Grave concern was being expressed by the backbenchers too, and more or less as expected, the opposition parties were *cashing in*. If whatever I gathered from her ardent fans was accurate, Rehana undoubtedly seemed to have made a major breakthrough so quickly.

Anxious days began to pass, in suspense, in restlessness, in uncertainties. Uncle Haroon did not come to see me after our most recent encounter. Apart from what the visitors to the centre told the detainees, no more news of Rehana reached me. I wrote to her several times, but there were no replies. Anything written was not getting past security, whether inward or outward. I heard about her along with the rest of the nation and no more than what was relevant to the campaign. Her personal well-being remained a grey area, which made my days utterly unbearable and turned my nights into sheer nightmares.

As expected, Channel 4 Television soon broadcast the much-publicised documentary on their *Eastern Eye* slot. But inside the centre, however, the programme was blacked out. If I saw her face and heard her voice, I would have been able to guess the extent of stress she had endured and assessed the amount of damage she had sustained. I would have also had the joy of watching her move and talk. But that joy was denied to me quite bluntly. Along with me, my partners in misfortune also felt bitterly disappointed by the unfortunate choice of censorship, which inevitably caused a great deal of disquiet. Tempers flared and spirits jarred, but there was not a lot anyone could do other than wince and moan. The warden was not available for comment and Mr. Collins unable to cope with the crisis on his own initiative. All of us pulled long faces and returned to our rooms, our zeal deflated, our hopes thwarted, our morale lowered.

Ever since the television broadcast, news about her became even scarcer. Only two more things emerged. One was that, some other solicitor retained by Uncle Haroon was lodging a complaint with the ombudsman of London against Peter Godfrey, and the other was, more women than she was expecting had signed Mrs. Brown's petition to the home secretary. Consequently, it was passed on to the junior minister in charge of nationality and immigration for closer attention and an immediate response.

Meanwhile, the second part of Rehana's interview was published in *Womanity*. On that occasion, Security decided not to confiscate any of the incoming copies. I was given one by some of my friends. There was a small measure of consolation in it for me too; on the right hand corner of the centre page, underneath her photograph, a personal message from her was printed. She wanted me to know that she was as well as could be expected in those sort of daunting circumstances, and also that she had not been taking any avoidable risks. 'Our child *will be born here*,' she asserted in it with a renewed passion, reinvigorated by the success she had made so far, 'and if her or his rights are trifled with by some other Godfrey some other time, we will do the same all over again … .' That too must have stirred a lot of emotions.

The flow of events, however, abruptly changed course one day when our courier service failed to contact her. Apparently, her phone was not being answered by anyone. By inference at least, it could only be on account of the delivery but no one was certain. Information coming by word of mouth varied from person to person. Uncle Haroon, who should have taken some steps to put me in the picture, showed no signs of doing it. What I really wanted to know, my fellow detainees could not find out for me; and those who knew that, they did not bother to tell me.

Its effects upon me were utterly devastating. Since making a spectacle of myself in front of all those people hurt my pride, I suffered in solitude. The nearest thing to Rehana I could lay my hands upon was her photograph published in the magazine. I spent endless hours gazing at her tired face, talking to her, wishing her well, wishing the ferocious storms in which she was temporarily trapped blew over and ushered a much-needed peace in her life soon, wishing she could emerge out of those whirl blasts unharmed and unscathed one day and be back in my arms. In return, the most she could give me was just a neutral smile, shackled in the inflexibility of print. Other than that, I did not have even the vaguest clue of how things were with her. For all I knew, the entire family might have been quietly locked up in a prison cell in order to silence her outcry and divert attention. Such crude things happening in a modern democracy was unthinkable, but with my kind of active imagination, I could think almost without any limitations. Sometimes, I saw visions of Rehana behind iron bars, weeping, bashing her head on stone walls and screaming for help; sometimes, I saw her give birth to our baby inside a dark dungeon crawling with large spiders and fierce rats; sometimes I even saw her being tortured, defiled and violated by the wicked villains guarding her cell!

The speed with which I sank alarmed everyone at the centre. My fellow detainees, who were not aware that I suffered from such a severe *persecution-phobia* panicked at the sight of pallor on my face. Getting a bit uneasy over the deteriorating situation at the otherwise calm and quiet centre, Mr.Collins at once appraised his boss. To be on the safe side, the warden sent for a doctor to look me up, and at the same time, alerted security. I was put on tranquillizers straight away. In response to his call for help, a fresh squad of guards was deployed immediately who began to come in ones and twos in order to keep the situation under control. The abrupt acceleration in the pace of activity inevitably made the detainees somewhat nervous. Abandoning their routine pastimes in the library, the recreation hall or the diner, most of them went into their rooms and locked themselves in. The hustle bustle and the warm social intercourse between comrades in misfortune that had once marked the ethos of the place were no longer in evidence. Silence reigned supreme everywhere, tension became the order of the day, and cordiality and optimism were replaced by discontentment. Wives continued to visit their husbands but no longer brought any news of Rehana.

Then, one morning, the warden summoned me to his office once again. When I encountered him, the grim expression he wore on his otherwise genial face took away my breath. I could clearly read his thoughts; somewhere along the line, something seemed to have gone wrong.

"I'm afraid I've some very bad news for you, Mr. Quraishi," he said after a nerve-shattering pause.

Upon hearing those words, shivers of panic ran down my spine.

"The police," he told me without beating around the bush, "have decided to bring criminal charges against you. Forgery, fraud and impersonation, amongst others. I've received orders from my superiors to hand you over to them. I'm sorry."

Whatever else I had feared and expected, that was not it. I went dumbstruck. In all my life, I had never been in any kind of trouble with the law. If I were in my own country and my town, it would have been another matter. At the very least, I had powerful friends and dependable contacts to bail me out. But facing those sort of serious charges on foreign soil was something entirely different. Suddenly, I reached the end of my tether. There was no word from Rehana, her father had deserted me just when I needed him the most, and her mother had spoken to me only once and never bothered again. Who was I to turn to for help? How was I going to organise my defences? Where was I going to get the courage from in order to live through such a phenomenal crisis? What would happen to me if I failed? Who would pay towards my cerements, my coffin and my grave if I hung myself from the ceiling and died? Who would shed some tears for me, who would bring me wreaths, who would absolve my troubled soul?

"But why now?" I asked the warden, desperately groping for some support, for a little bit of comfort, just a word of advice if nothing else.

It did not come forth. Whether or not he liked it, whether he was in favour of it or against it, whether he thought it was the right thing to do or it was not, the warden had to carry out his orders without questioning those who issued them for as long as he sat in that chair and behind that desk.

"I don't know," he replied, extremely ill at ease. "but I wish I did …"

CHAPTER (30)

My doom was sealed within the batting of an eyelid. Even as I sat in the chair gaping from shock and shivering from fear, the wrden buzzed the reception on his intercom and asked the police to come in. In response to it, a middle-aged man in plain clothes arrived. Without further ado, he informed me that he was placing me under arrest on a series of criminal charges, which he read out aloud from the charge sheet. He also advised me of my statutory rights and warned that anything I said could be taken down and used against me as evidence in court at the time of trial. After that, he placed handcuffs on my wrists and signalled me to get up on my feet. The sheer horror that rocked my entire body at that particular moment is something I have never been able to forget in all my life.

His job done with simplicity and professional competence, he wrapped a piece of cloth around my wrists to conceal the steel cuffs and unceremoniously ushered me out of the warden's office. In spite of dark shadows obscuring my vision, I could not help noticing that the corridor was thronged by several detainees who had lined up with white faces and dazed eyes to watch my abrupt departure from their midst. I felt my ears cupped, except for a shrill whistle mercilessly piercing my eardrums. Either pressed for time or trying to assert his authority, my escort all but dragged me behind him without letting up the relentless pressure upon my wrists until we reached the car park and I was safely deposited in the back seat of his unmarked car. A colleague of his who sat behind the wheel waiting for us to arrive started the engine without saying a word and drove out of there.

My captors took me to the remand centre where I was locked up behind bars. It was a small cell containing two narrow bunk beds and a washbasin. If I had a cellmate in it, there was no sign of him. For the time being at least, I was allowed to wear my own clothes, presumably because I was not yet tried and convicted. But what was the difference? The dangerous game that I started to play had drawn to an end and I was now caught up in its aftermath. Unless someone did something to rescue me from the quagmire in which I was stuck, my very life was in peril.

After what felt like eternity, two men arrived at the cell. One of them was in uniform and the other in plain clothes. While the former opened the door and let me out, the latter signalled me to follow him, which I did. The images of people I came across along the way looked blurred and indefinable, like silhouettes set into motion. Corridors resembled tunnels, rooms looked like cysts drowned in crepuscule and voices produced a curious echo inside my ears. It all conveyed the impression that I was moving around in some sort of an underground maze, enclosures concealed within enclosures, shapeless furniture, and shadows gliding.

Our journey came to a temporary halt in one of the rooms and someone else took over from there. There was important business to be done and they got on with it. First of all, I was asked a question. I heard it quite distinctly but could not grasp what was said. Suddenly, it seemed I had forgotten my English. I could neither understand them nor could I answer back.

From there I was taken into another room and made to sit in a chair across a large desk, behind which sat their boss smoking a pipe as well as concentrating on paper work stacked in front of him. No one bothered with introductions or explanations. It was all so down-to-earth routine for them they did everything like puppets on a string. The conversation was triggered off by their inspector with reading out to me the same charges I had already heard several times before, if only to comply with legal formalities. I was not expected either to admit to them or to repudiate them at that stage. They did not even bother to wait for a response and moved on to the next stage of explaining to me my statutory rights. That, however, was conducted in some detail, presumably because they were required by law to make sure that I understood them without any scope for ambiguity or misconception. I had a right to remain silent; I had a right to defend myself; I had a right to be legally represented in court; I had a right to waive all those rights; a lot of rights I had never asked for, probably to compensate for the one that Rehana had.

The second and third stages of the proceedings were worse than the first two. One of the men took me back into the larger room for fingerprints. Well versed in his job, he pressed each of my fingers on a pad of black dye and obtained the prints in a hefty ledger. With that, I was on record. Even if the court acquitted me later on, no one would ever be able to erase those testimonials from police files. Guilt or innocence was not the criterion any more; mere prosecution was sufficient to perpetuate dishonour. As I sat gaping at the striations of my skin on their ledger with startled eyes, I had a feeling Papa's body must have turned upside down in his grave!

After the fingerprints, I was taken into another room for mug shots. Behaving more like a radiologist than a photographer, the same man carefully adjusted my face in front of the camera. He took four pictures in all, two portraits and two profiles to be on the safe side. With that, my fingerprints were also given a face. Very soon they would probably be circulated around the country's major police stations; they might even be passed on to Interpol in due course, as the charges against me were serious enough to arouse international concern!

When all those formalities were concluded, I was passed on back into the hands of the prison staff. Before returning me to the cell, a doctor checked me thoroughly to make sure I was not suffering from any contagious skin diseases that could be passed on to my cellmates on contact. It was followed by urine and blood samples taken for all sorts of tests. Then, standing naked underneath the shower while two orderlies stood guard and watched everything I did, I washed myself half-heartedly in its lukewarm torrents. The clothes they gave me to change into were still my own. After putting them on, I was taken to the cell and locked up once again.

As the night rose, almost everyone fell asleep, except me. I just could not. All sorts of disconsolate thoughts entered my head and raged havoc in it. What a shame! All that support from public that Rehana had mustered in so short a time with such a lot of tireless efforts stood on the verge of being washed away. My image as a *fraud* would very soon overshadow my image of the *wronged husband*. There was a great difference between being unfairly driven out of the country by the Home Office and being expelled in dishonour by a judge and his jury. Clearly, that must have been the reason why the police chose that particular moment to bring in all those criminal charges against me. It was a well-calculated and clever move, designed to produce the most damaging results. Suddenly, Rehana's fight for a principle had plunged me into a struggle for survival; her pursuit of justice had launched my career in crime; her appeal for the restoration of wrongs done to her was being answered with an assertion of wrongs done by me; her righteous grievance was being vetoed through the medium of my misdeed, her triumph was being neutralised by my defeat! Like in a game of chess, one move was being held at bay with a countermove. We were simply pawns, being shunted around from one square to the other according to the will and skill of the players and according to the rules of the game. Rehana had made the mistake of asking her fellow countrymen what price were they willing to put upon her pride. They put that price; only, I was paying it!

First thing in the morning, I was asked to get ready for an appearance before the magistrates. Quickly rinsing my mouth in the washbasin I straightened the creases of my crumpled clothes and waited. When it was time to go, they handcuffed me first and then boarded me into a police van. Our journey began without delays—my first *conducted tour* of London! For a long time, it had been my precious dream to see that city of past memories and historic associations; but who thought that I would see it riding in a police van! I could not help remembering what Rehana told me once. 'When we go visiting *my country*,' she said wearing a proud smile, 'I will drive you around London. We can feed the pigeons in Trafalgar Square; stroll down the Victoria Embankment hand in hand and watch the dance of the Flamingos in Hyde Park!' But that was not how things had turned out to be. The price of her pride was so heavy my head was bowed in shame.

Shortly after we reached our destination, I was taken inside the courtroom. Standing in the dock with bated breath I looked around me. The amphitheatre of my trials was very large; partly filled with performers and partly filled with spectators. I did not know if I had any friends amongst them, or at least one or two sympathisers. If my court appearance that morning was given adequate publicity by the press, surely Rehana and Uncle must have also come to know about it. Were they present somewhere in the crowded galleries, with a thought to spare at long last? Were there tears in my wife's eyes? Was her father struck by a sense of guilt? Was there a least measure of solidarity, coming from those who should have cared? Was my child also present, to witness its father's public humiliation; to get the first bitter taste of the world into which it had arrived?

As those painful thoughts kept rolling in my mind, I stood in the dock motionless. When the clerk got to his feet to read out the charges, the courtroom hushed. They were the same as had been spelled out to me twice before. Then I was asked whether I pleaded guilty or not guilty to the charges.

What was I guilty of! A strange hunger, a painful thirst, a thing called *love*. I was guilty of loving my wife, perhaps a bit more than I should; I was guilty of that much excess. Upon coming to know that she had gone down with a *freak fever* I had worked myself into frenzy over nothing. Even if she had really fallen victim to some deadly disease, I could not possibly have rescued her from the jaws of death, anyway. I would have simply shut my eyes and run away. That was how futile my entire adventure was right from the start. Giving in to emotions was my only guilt. As a citizen of the commonwealth, my travelling to England was not a crime. As Rehana's husband, my coming to see her was not a crime. As a would-be father, my wanting to see my child was not a crime. With no more than the indiscretion of a silly schoolboy, I had tried to be clever and got caught. In order to be put back in my proper place, I was not even in need of a caning, let alone prosecutions and committals. What was I guilty of, to plead for the one or for the other?

When the clerk repeated the same question again, I still could not answer him. Several members of the bar as well as many amongst the spectators craned their heads in my direction and gazed at me, either in surprise or from curiosity. I, however, remained dumbstruck. Hence, resorting to standard procedure, the magistrate adjourned the proceedings for a month and finalised a suitable date with the prosecutor for the trial thereafter.

Next came the question of bail. There were enough voices to oppose it, but none to contest them. The prosecutor immediately drew the magistrate's attention to the serious nature of offences I was accused of committing. Keeping it in view, bail was refused and I was released back into police custody until the date of the trial. It was all over in a matter of minutes.

After we came back to the remand centre, they locked me up in the same cell once again. If I spent an entire month inside it, the chances of my going mad looked pretty strong. I had no idea how much coverage was given to my court appearance in the tabloids but even a minimum measure of publicity distinctly held the prospect of bringing Uncle Haroon to my rescue at least then. Without his intervention, I could not see myself emerging out of the quicksand in which I was sunk. It was all very well to say that I had a right to be legally represented. But who would agree to represent a pauper like me? Probably none—not even for glory.

On the following morning, at around eleven o'clock, the prison staff informed me that I had a visitor and that permission was granted for me to see the person. Keeping my fingers crossed, I accompanied the policeman who came to escort me. I was more or less certain it must be Uncle Haroon. Until then desperate for his company, I suddenly felt an irresistible urge to punch him in the face. His behaviour towards me had been utterly outrageous to say the least. He had brought me no end of misery from the start. Along the way, I decided to have a showdown with him and prepared a mental scenario of what I was going to say.

The room in which my escort took me had the typical outlook of a prison amenity. The access and the exit were the same, both heavily guarded. The meagre furniture in it comprised a table and two chairs facing each other. The man who occupied one of them was white and a total stranger to me. Upon seeing me, he got up and introduced himself as Harry Harrison, a solicitor retained by Uncle to represent me in court. I was glad to hear about it, but at the same time aspersed by the lukewarm attitude with which help was sent. The fact that I was married to Rehana never seemed to reflect in anything her father did. Courtesy demanded he sent a solicitor, which was the least he could do, and had settled for it!

"Before we talk about other matters," I said, going straight to the subject of utmost importance to me, "there's one thing I'd like to ask you, Mr. Harrison. Do you happen to know how my wife is?"

"I'm afraid not," he replied with a mild frown. "Why? Is there a cause for concern?"

Plenty of it. But if he did not know, there was no point in asking him.

"And what about Mr. Abdallah? Do you know where he is?"

"He's outside, waiting in his car."

"Is he planning to see me? Or, is he merely waiting to take you back?"

"Of course, he'll be seeing you. Even though it is he who has retained me to defend you, I wanted to talk to you alone first for reasons of confidentiality. Is that all right with you?"

Why not. The trial being the next most important thing on my mind, I settled down to answering his questions. Going through the contents of a folder, he went over all the facts relevant to the issue. He had already gathered quite a lot of those, mostly accurate. I did not have much to add.

"Well, so far so good," he said, shutting the folder.

"Does this mean I'll have to remain here for a whole month until the trial comes up?"

"Can't say. No doubt, pressure is being exerted on the home secretary to set aside the criminal proceedings, but we can't take it for granted that he'd yield.

"A month is a long time. I hope I can survive."

"I agree. And if the barrister defending you isn't satisfied with the facts I prepare and present to him, he might ask for a further adjournment. It could then take even longer. Perhaps you ought to know."

I simply stared at him lockjawed.

"By the way," he said upon reflection, "I heard you're not interested in pursuing the matter of entry permit. Is that true?"

"Yes, it is. I just want to get the hell out of here. I've had enough."

"If that's all you want, you might be released from custody sooner, probably upon giving an undertaking to the Home Office to that effect. Will you?"

"Ten times over. If only someone asked."

Wishing me good luck, he instructed me to wait in the room for Uncle and left. I waited. The room plunged into a precarious silence. Once or twice, the policeman guarding the door looked in to see what I was doing. I simply sat bolt upright in the chair, restlessly drumming the tabletop with my fingers. If anyone had asked me to guarantee good behaviour at the time, I would have refused. I was angry enough to wring Uncle Haroon's neck, without regard to its consequences. Until that day, no one had done the sort of wicked things to me as he had. It seemed the time had finally arrived for us to settle our scores. Never one better.

In due course, he was let into the room. There were no affectionate reunions this time, no fond hugs, no blessings. His otherwise smart appearance badly impaired by an unshaven beard and unkempt hair, he looked in a shambles. Charisma was gone from his face, and the impeccable manners, which were a benchmark of his ethos, totally neglected. The eyes, however, were moist with what looked to me like crocodile tears. If he really felt for me half the concern as he had suddenly begun to demonstrate, I would have been twice as lucky a man. Whether it was guilt or grief, he seemed muffled in it. So, I waited until he sat in the chair, my fiery eyes glued to his face.

"All right, Uncle Haroon," I said, viciously grinding my teeth. "Save the histrionics. Are you going to tell me anything about Rehana, or isn't it time yet?"

His reply did not come quickly. After shimmering in his eyes for some time, two large tears rolled out. If it was merely some sort of a performance aimed at melting my heart, he was doing a damn good job of it. But the grudge I bore him needed a lot more than that to be placated. To think that he could hurt me so much and then get away with it by shedding a couple of fake tears! For a man of his stature, weeping did not become; he looked ludicrous.

"Uncle, please," I growled. "Don't try my patience anymore. You've no idea what I'm going through right now. Just tell me whatever you can about Rehana and go away."

"She's in the hospital," he replied in a hoarse voice.

"I know she's in the hospital. Half the nation has been telling me that, except you. Why's she in the hospital?"

"She ..." he said and then choked.

My heart suddenly fell into loud poundings. Looking at the way the veins in his neck swelled and the eyes came bulging out, I could swear he had something worse to tell me than whatever I expected.

"What's it, Uncle?" I demanded nervously. "For God's sake, come clean, will you? Just level with me!"

"She...she ... had ... an ... accident," he finally revealed, making a tremendous bid at self control and then broke into noisy sobs.

If he had any idea at all as to how those words landed upon me, they were better never uttered. Suddenly provoked beyond the scope of restraint, I got to my feet. Once or twice my mouth did open but words did not come out. My mind completely declined to absorb those tidings. It was too painful to be true, too cruel to be real.

"Accident! What accident?"

"Three days ago, she fell down the stairs in the house," he replied in between gasps, squeezing a phenomenal tragedy into the brevity of those words, "She hasn't come round so far ... Not even for one moment ..."

"And—what about the baby?"

"According to the doctors, only one of them is in with a chance. They don't know which one, they can't say yet ..."

On the day when I bade goodbye to Allah, my loyalties to Him had stood paid in full. He had taken from me all He wanted to and I had given Him all I could. Since that moment onwards, I did not owe Him a thing. I had never asked Him for one happy day or one great night. Whatever came along my way, I was quite content with that much, on that day, at that moment. My father found Rehana for me and her father gave her to me strictly on the strength of my own merits and demerits. Suddenly one night, clad in red and concealed in red, I found bliss; I found hope; I found my dream. It was not as though I gained her cheap and easy, either; I was footing a tall bill; I was suffering; I was burning; I was bleeding; I was going through one ordeal after another without a groan or a grumble. She was the reward of my toils; she was the goal of my race. For her love, for her heart, for her hand, for her companionship, for her loyalty, I did not owe Him a thing. Even a scratch on her body without my consent was a trespass, a sacrilege, a violation, and a crime!

"Take me to Rehana, Uncle," I said first, keeping my voice as low as I could manage.

He did not move, but his eyes filled up with fresh tears all over again.

"Take me to my wife right now, Uncle Haroon!" I screamed this time. "If you know what's good for you, better do what I'm asking you to …"

I shouted so loud, the walls shook up. A couple of guards, startled by the loud outburst, came rushing into the room at once and grabbed hold of me. But I could not restrain myself; I could not think straight; I could not control my anger. I had never been dealt a more merciless blow; I had never experienced a greater pain; I had never been called upon to accept my fate so blindly; I had never surrendered either to God or to man so very helplessly.

"I came here for my wife and my child, Uncle Haroon, and I'm not going back until I have them both. Did you hear what I said? I said *BOTH*. I will not concede this time, I will not reconcile, I will not compromise. Damn you all! Leave us alone! Just leave us alone! Stop somewhere! Make room! For Heaven's sake, let's get on! What's the matter with you? I want Rehana! I want my baby! I want my dream! I want just a little bit in return for such a lot. Oh, please! Please! Please!" I kept on shouting at the top of my voice.

The scuffle which broke out between the guards and me as a result of that insane outburst was disgraceful, to say the least. I had no idea where I got the strength from to handle two men twice my size but I did as though my life depended upon it. Even after being physically subdued with brute force, I kept screaming. I felt possessed; I went mad; I lost myself completely. The pale face of the man who sat staring at me with stunned eyes brought out the worst in me. I could not stand him; I could not put up with him any longer; I let out whatever filth came to my mouth; abuse as I had never learnt to speak, and in a language that I could not recognize as mine. There was no other way of getting it off my chest. I kept screaming and screaming until I felt the taste of blood in my mouth … .

CHAPTER (31)

The guards who managed to stop me from physically assaulting Uncle Haroon did not take me back to the prison cell from where I was brought. Instead, I was dragged over to some other place and locked up in isolation. It was an extremely small room in which, most probably, demented people like me were left for a while in order to get over themselves. I, too, had become totally incapable of reasoning, of judgement, of review. Ninety percent of me was gone to the dogs; I had to make do with the remaining ten, which was not enough. When up against the sort of odds that stared me in the eye, it was nowhere near being enough. I was desperately in need of being subsidized, reinforced and revamped; I needed to be rescued from the undercurrent that had swallowed me, put on the shore and resuscitated; I needed to be exhumed from the cyst in which I felt buried, resurrected and reincarnated.

Who was there to help me at a time like that? From whom to ask and of whom to expect? I did not have a clue. There was no time for me to think, to postulate, to engineer, to improvise; there was no time to plan, to prepare, to manage, no freedom to act. My wife as well as my child were both stuck in the jaws of death. That was not just two people, two lives, two entelechies; that was 90 percent of me, now left at the mercy of the remaining ten percent for retrieval; that was the sum and substance of all my hopes, now waiting to be recovered by whatever was left of my courage; that was the small shelter I had found in the midst of storms and tides, now waiting to be washed ashore by angry waves. All going to none; infinity tumbling down the chasm of nix; life being swallowed by death; an entire universe being crumbled into dust by an invisible fist. I could not let it happen. I could not sit back and watch the perpetration of such an injustice, such an irreconcilable tragedy, and such an unacceptable cruelty. If whatever I gathered from Uncle Haroon was right, it meant that my wife was lying in a coma for the past three days, and our child, trapped inside her womb, was probably gasping for breath. It was all very well and easy to say that only one of them was in with a fighting chance. But who could decide which one? Who had the prerogative to exercise an option in the matter? Who had the power to decide who must live and who must die?

I had no idea for how long I remained in isolation. Days looked no different from nights and nights seemed no different from days. I refused to eat or to drink. My mind, unable to cope with the enormity of my thoughts, gave up on me completely just like it had done once before at the time of Azra's death. That helped a lot. The less conscious I was of pain, the better it felt; the farther I was from the next human being, the safer it seemed. Only one thing kept me going. Rehana was not yet dead, at least not to my knowledge, and I had no wish to be advised to the contrary. If truth could be as grievous as that, I would rather survive in a lie; if time could be spent better in hopes, I would rather go on hoping.

One day, some day, next day, this day, that day, salvation arrived; viciously kicking open the door, two huge men barged in. Authority was not spoken in words but demonstrated to the eye. One of them got hold of me by the scruff and stood me up on my feet. Two blazing blue eyes stared into mine, accompanied by a derisive leer.

"Fuck off!" he said.

Confused by the sudden intrusion, I simply gaped at them.

"You can go home now, Mr. Quraishi," said the other, a shade more polite between the two, "your solicitor is waiting for you at the reception."

When I heard what he said, the thought of Rehana obviously stirred fresh concerns in my mind. I hoped I was not being set free on account of her demise. Nothing could be more cruel than release me from one imprisonment, only to be locked up once again in another—even more agonising.

Mr. Harrison met me in the outer foyer. He was not alone. The gentleman who accompanied him had already collected my suitcase from the police. All three of us walked as far as the parking lot without any conversation and got into a waiting car.

"Is there anything you could tell me about my wife's plight, Mr. Harrison?" I asked him, the first between us to break the portentous silence.

"I'm afraid she's still in a coma and on the critical list," he replied.

It seemed my ordeal had not ended but just begun. She was in a coma and on the critical list. Was it good news or was it bad news? Which was better for me between the two: Rehana dead or Rehana dying? How would I prefer things to be: harbour futile hopes or discard them altogether? How different could Rehana's motionless body be from Rehana's motionless corpse?

"I'm sorry I don't have better news for you," he added out of sheer pity towards my pitiful fate.

No one could be sorrier than I was. At that moment, I could have had everything. I was free. Were it not for that wretched accident, our baby would have already been born. And for going home, I did not have any favours to seek; any visas to get; any Vadkars or Buxes to rely upon and any Godfreys to contend with. Rehana was the only one missing. If she moved, I could take on the world; if she did not, everything would go a total waste.

"Well, Mr. Quraishi," continued Mr. Harrison, "we applied to the court for your bail, which the magistrate allowed as you were not legally represented at the preliminary hearing. Abdallah has since posted it. The home secretary has also yielded to pressure from all sides and granted you a temporary visa, subject to the outcome of the trial. It means you're a free man, at least for the time being. This gentleman with me is Mr. Bishop who works for your father-in-law. He'll drive you to the hospital in which your wife is admitted. I must take your leave now as I've several other pressing engagements to attend. I hope your wife and child will make it. I hope, one day, the three of you will be able to put this sordid saga behind you and go home happily. For now, just good luck from me."

There is no surer way of forcing more grief upon a grief stricken man than by kindness. His words spilled on me like acid. Luck was the only thing that I needed. All of those trials and tribulations I had faced and overcome so far were on one side; luck was on the other. Never before had I become so inescapably dependant upon luck. The very feeling of helplessness resulting from the notion sent my head reeling.

Soon after Mr. Harrison left, Mr. Bishop started the car and emerged out of the forecourt. Probably realising the strain I was going through, he kept his attention focussed upon the road most of the time. The journey was quite long, Bromley no longer our destination, my feelings no longer the same as they would have been if I knew that Rehana was going to be at the other end to greet me.

All along the way, I kept on thinking. Why did she have to embark upon that wild adventure? Why did she decide to play with fire just when we could have done without it? Why did she have to start fighting for something that already belonged to her? With so many friends who loved and respected her, what was she short of? Why did she get her priorities confused and put pride above safety? I had never looked upon her as a *'Babylonian Slave in a Roman Court'*; no one had. We never even thought about it. Her being Rehana was enough for us, whether she was British or was Brazilian. Why could she not be satisfied with that? She promised me she would not take any unnecessary risks. But it was not up to her, was it? Without stepping out of the house, she waged wars and raised storms; without stepping out of the house, she also came tumbling down. On one day, she was riding the crest; on another day, she went rolling with the ebb. What purpose did it serve? What did she accomplish? If she died, there would be rejoicings in the enemy camp; those who begrudged her an inch of her motherland while she lived, would gladly concede to her six square feet after her death. Was that what she fought for and staked so much upon? A heap of soil, a dark ditch, an endless silence till eternity? Surely, she could have found a happier place to rest in my arms than that; a better time with me than without me; a better future to look forward to? Surely, I had so much more to give her than just a notion; whatever rights she wanted; whatever status she aspired for? Surely, my world needed her more than Britain did; my throne needed a greater queen than Her Majesty; my home needed a worthier mistress?

Long before my thoughts wore out, we reached the hospital. After parking the car in the parking lot, Mr. Bishop escorted me straight to the Intensive Care Unit. Auntie and Uncle were both present in the visitors' lounge, their faces languid, their eyes swollen from weeping, their noses running, their lips quivering. Seeing them in that condition worsened my fears but I carried on walking like a somnambulist. A curious hum began to echo in my ears. I could not even see the way ahead of me clearly. My limbs were in motion but I felt numb.

Rehana's bed was screened from all sides. Except the face, the rest of her body was concealed underneath a blanket. Saline drips were being let into her bloodstream through a plastic tube from a bottle close by and oxygen was supplied from a cylinder. A small display screen above her head constantly monitored her heartbeat. Her face had gone frighteningly pale; eyes were half closed and her mouth flexed. There was not a sign of life in her. I stood holding back my breath, my mind refusing to absorb the painful spectacle, my senses within inches of abandoning me.

What could I do! What could I say! There she was, neither dead nor alive; neither stuck in the present nor gone to the hereafter; neither denying nor yielding; aloof from me; away from me; beyond my reach; beyond caring;

beyond response; cast in the lap of death; poised on the brink of annihilation! There she was, the woman I loved more than anyone else in the world; about to be robbed from my side. How would I live without her? What would I do with the baby she might give birth to before going away—her parting gift to me, her memento, a little bit of herself stashed away inside a little being?

"What're her chances?" I asked the nurse who stood by my side, as if her answer was the last word.

"I'm afraid I don't know," she replied and added no more to it.

Just like my life, her reply was also incomplete; just like my fate, her words also had an air of doom to them. It was all so unfinished, so unpredictable, so uncertain—Rehana's will to stay with me, and my good fortune to keep her, as if it were up to us.

The nurse waited patiently until I had my fill. What was there to fill or to be filled with? Nothing. A painful image, sinking and surfacing in an ocean of grief; a desperate hope, giving way to the odds against it; a shocking reality, pushing everything else into the background. There was not much for me to do in the ward. I could not touch her, I could not hold her hand, I could not kiss her lips. I could not even expect to be allowed to stay by her bedside, look after her, tell her stories, amuse her with jokes, strengthen her courage, reduce her suffering, assuage her wounds, assure her that everything would be fine at the end of the day!

I came out, reluctantly but unavoidably. Overcome by a surge of sudden grief, Auntie Zeenath clung to me and broke down just like she would have clung to her own son if she had one. I let her. And Why not! Her family had unexpectedly fallen short of a very important member. If I could fill that space even in the smallest of measures, she was welcome to shed all the tears she could on my shoulder.

Uncle Haroon drove us to Bromley in his car. Right through the long drive, no one spoke. The glass on the windows had cut down the outside noises completely. In the profuse silence that resulted from it, all I could here were auntie's incessant sobs. The sky was overcast and rain spitting. The wipers on the windscreen oscillated relentlessly but quietly. I sat hushed, absorbed in my own pensive thoughts. We were all caught up in the same crisis, in the same nightmare. A piece of Rehana belonged to each of us in equal measures. We loved her in our own different ways but we loved her just the same. And that love was in danger of being robbed from our side.

After reaching home, hospitality took precedence over other matters for a while. Uncle Haroon, who had not uttered a single word so far, carried my

suitcase upstairs. Auntie asked me if I would like her to run me a bath or preferred the shower. I said the latter would do. She showed me the bathroom and then gave me some new clothes to put on.

"Rehana had bought these for you to wear after you came out of detention," she said, breaking down again, "I'm sorry it has turned out this way … I'm sorry … I'm sorry …"

"So am I, Auntie. But it isn't your fault."

"Yes, it is. To a very great extent. I should've woken up a long time ago."

"I, too, should've."

"Forgive me for not coming to the centre to see you. I did not have the courage to watch you in such a miserable situation. Hearing the details by itself was trying enough for me."

"Don't worry, Auntie. No offence has been taken."

"Listen. I might not get the opportunity to say this again. If Rehana … if she makes it, go away from this place. I don't mean this house but this country as a whole. And don't let anyone ever tell you what to do. You have already put up with enough of messing around. It isn't fair. It just isn't fair …"

Forcing the clothes in my hand she hurriedly went back to her preoccupations in the kitchen. But I stood by the door for a while, weighing whatever she said in my mind. Whether in time or too late, it looked as though we had at least one sincere friend in that house; at the end of the day, a mother seemed at pains to prove herself to be a mother.

Quickly finishing with the shower, I put on whatever things she had forced into my hands. Wearing new clothes on that day of all days felt painful, but I went ahead. A line had to be drawn somewhere beyond which it was not pragmatic to stretch sentiment.

When I was ready, Uncle Haroon showed me to the dining room and kept company while Auntie served the food. I did not refuse; I was hungry enough to eat a horse. Conversation around the table was sparse; they were laconic in whatever they said and I brief in whatever I did. Frankly, we were all falling short of topics, none inclined to broach upon the subject that mattered the most; details of Rehana's accident were deliberately omitted.

After the meal, while she became busy in the kitchen and he disappeared somewhere else, I found my way into their lounge. It was unoccupied and plunged in darkness. Without bothering to turn on the lights, I sat in a chair and lost myself in thought. There was so much to come to terms with, a lot of blame resting upon my own shoulders too. If only I had listened to Riaz and given up the crazy idea; if only common sense had prevailed whilst there was still time. It was on account of my detention at the centre that Rehana's pride was hurt and her anger provoked. Upon seeing me locked up, she became strongly aware of her being wronged and just as determined to balance the scales tilted by the treatment I was getting. I should have anticipated her reaction; I should have realised what sort of storms such a contingency could stir; I should have assessed the real outcome of my stupidity. After all, we had been married for a whole year and knew each other pretty well.

"What on earth are you doing alone in the dark?" I heard Auntie say after a while and raised my head.

She switched on the lights. Without realising, I had started to cry. "I wish Shabbu was here, Auntie," I said, expressing the first thought that sprang to my mind. "I wish Rox was here and so was Mamma."

"I know how you feel," she said, putting on a brave front. "There's no point in distressing yourself too much. Miracles can always happen. I've made coffee. Would you like some?"

I would have preferred to be left alone and allowed to get on with the brooding, but she would not let me and brought some freshly percolated coffee.

"Tell me about the accident, Auntie," I asked her at long last, accepting the mug she gave me. "I still don't know what exactly happened."

The recollection must have been pretty painful, for she sat wearing a grim frown on her face for quite a while before opening her mouth. "Oh, what a day it was! What a nightmare!" she finally mumbled to herself and began to give me the sordid details of the dreadful day and the horrendous nightmare it unfolded. At around ten on that portentous morning, Rehana had an appointment at the hospital with her gynaecologist for a routine checkup. As usual, Uncle drove them there and dropped them back before going away to his office. Mother and daughter sat around the dining table for a quick bite, talking about my plight and me most of the time. It was not in the least bit a pleasant conversation. Rehana was still pretty upset at not being allowed phone calls to me. The daily visits to Heathrow had already put a lot of strain upon her health, not to mention the tireless efforts of fighting the Home Office, but above all, the proximity of the delivery had also given rise to fresh concerns in her mind. For a young and frail person like her, the pressure was getting to be a bit too much.

After they finished eating, Rehana decided to take a nap in her room, excused herself and went out of the dining room while she became engrossed in her other culinary preoccupations. Only a few moments later, as she stood washing the dishes, she suddenly heard the noise of Rehana's fall, followed by her shrill screams. Dropping the plates in the sink, she rushed to see what happened. By then, Rehana had already come tumbling down the stairs and was sprawled on the floor motionless.

"When I saw her sprawled like that," she continued, "I was struck dumb. The entire house of cards went blowing out of the window within the batting of an eyelid. Where they go after they shut their eyes, aeroplanes don't go there; for all my money, I couldn't have made one trip to see my child, if that's where she had gone away. Somehow or the other, I managed to phone for the ambulance and then phoned your uncle. After that, I stood by her side, gaping. Her face had gone absolutely white, eyes rolled back and body limp. There was no movement of any sort in her at all, not even the sign of breathing. I thought she was dead. It wasn't just her, you see. There was the baby too. If the mother was dead, what chances could the baby have? I couldn't bear to think about it. Rehana represents my whole life. It's different with your uncle. After all, he's a man and has seen some nasty things in his time. But me? I spent my entire married life doing only one thing: I just took care of Rehana, that's all. I slept for her, I woke up for her, I breathed for her, I lived for her. Her joy's my joy, her grief's my grief, her triumphs my triumphs, her defeats my defeats."

She paused for a while as her eyes began to stream. Then, recovering her breath, she continued. "The ambulance and your uncle arrived one behind the other. After making a minimum effort at reviving her, they gave up and boarded her into the vehicle. All along the way she neither moved nor breathed. When we got to the hospital, the doctors took over and did everything possible to bring her round, but without any success. From that day to this day, she hasn't batted an eyelid. No one is able to predict what'll happen to her. Allah's her only hope. I keep beseeching Him alone day and night. What else can I do? Every morning, I go to the hospital with fresh hopes and come home at night bitterly disappointed. Then I lie in bed staring at the ceiling, telephone in my lap, prayers on my lips, waiting, waiting, waiting. It's so painful … it's so painful …"

Putting the mug on the coffee table, she dug her face in her palms and broke down again. When I tried to speak, words failed me too. I could neither stop her nor comfort her.

"I've prepared your bed in Rehana's room," she informed me, recovering herself after a while, "but if you don't feel up to it, there's another spare room in the house."

Running away from Rehana in her own house was impossible. I told her there was no need for it. She showed me the room, asked me to try to catch some sleep if I could, committed me to *Allah's* care for the night and went back to her duties. Shutting the door behind me, I let out a deep sigh and looked around me. Rehana had put her stamp upon everything. The room had a distinct profile of its own, so characteristic of her, so reminiscent of her. It clung to her recollections; it reeked of her perfume; it reproduced her images. Her clothes hung inside the wardrobe; her cosmetics were arrayed on the dressing table; her footwear neatly arranged on the shoe rack. I could feel her presence; I could hear the rustle of her *sari*; I could recognise the thumping of her footfalls; I could reach out and almost touch her. I remembered the bedroom in our house back home that she had similarly effused with her aura, her ambience, and her exuberance. A part of her always stayed behind even after she was gone, in vestiges, in reflections, in analogues. She cast such spells; she generated such charisma.

First thing in the morning, we rushed over to the hospital. While Auntie and Uncle waited in the lounge, I went straight to Rehana's bedside. She was still being supported by oxygen and her heartbeat was constantly monitored. The ward sister put a chair close to the bed and said I could stay with her for a while. Thanking her from the bottom of my heart for her kindness and compassion, I sat in it. Rehana's hand lay within my easy reach, absolutely motionless. I brushed my lips on her fingers first. Whatever I wanted to say to her, I said it below my breath. I begged her to open her eyes and look at me. If she did not come back from where she had gone away to, I threatened to drown the entire universe in my tears. I reminded her of all those promises she had made me, the dreams she had shown, the plans she had drawn, the route she had charted out for her journey through life. "Come on!" I passionately exhorted her, "and wake up from your slumber! Days are turning into nights and nights are turning into days; so many precious moments of our youth are slipping away through our fingers. No one gets a second chance. We're in the prime of our lives and can't afford to waste them. Each and every one of those rolling moments is irretrievable and irreplaceable. Hurry up!"

She did not yield. If I knew how to perform miracles, I would have woken her up just by snapping my fingers. I would have set the clocks backwards; I would have redesigned our future in accordance with our own wishes and our dreams; I would have drawn a huge pentacle around us to ward off all evil; I would have made the Everest grow as far as the Seventh Heaven and keep the East forever inaccessible to the West! I would have prevented love from being vitiated by hate; happiness from being overshadowed by grief; life from being conquered by death. I would have grown roses in our garden that never withered; I would have created days on which the sun never set; I would have filled the sky with stars that never lost their shimmer! I had all the right ideas in my head but without the power to make them come true. If only I could! If only I could!

In course of the next several days, not much happened that was worth mentioning. Rehana did not show any signs of recovery whatsoever. I spent as much time by her bedside as I was allowed to by hospital rules, weaving my chaotic thoughts into patterns; gathering my diehard hopes on strings; collecting my priceless wishes in caskets of dreams; sometimes watching the tiny dot on the display screen go bobbing up and down; sometimes holding her cold hand in my colder hand; sometimes kissing the icy tips of her fingers, sometimes pressing her dishevelled tufts in place; all the while helplessly trying to transmit my own soul into her.

During those few agonising days, Auntie Zeenath stuck to my side loyally. Every morning she brought me to the hospital, let me have my fill of the livid face before it disappeared from sight just like another face had, and went home only when I was ready to go. In the house, she forced me to eat regularly, saw to it that I had a daily shower, gave me more clothes out of the huge stock Rehana had built up for me, regularly dusted my room and changed the bed linen. Sometimes she brought me hot drinks in the middle of night fully aware that I spent most of it wide-awake and gazing into the voids. She did not like to see me grieve and wane like that all the while. Once or twice, she even exhorted me to belt up and get a hold upon myself. Her faith in Allah was firm. She offered *Namaaz* whenever she could and prayed constantly for Rehana's recovery. My indifference towards *Divine Mercy* often surprised her, although she never tried to preach me sermons. Her strength of tolerance was admirable, her courage in the face of all the odds amazing. Once up on her feet, she stayed up and kept marching, a laudable trait of character which Rehana had doubtless inherited from her.

Unfortunately, it was not the same with Uncle Haroon. He did keep in touch with what was going on at the hospital through his wife, but came and went as he pleased. It would have been another matter if he went back to work, but he did not. Instead, he spent most of his time trying to promote Rehana's almost forgotten and forsaken campaign against the Home Office, drafting all sorts of petitions, tapping every source he thought could help, collecting videotapes of interviews between irreconcilable politicians and disillusioned journalists, of promises made today and forgotten tomorrow, of sermons preached abroad without ever been practiced at home. My continued indifference towards his crusade hurt him, but I deliberately and resolutely kept away from it. What he did with himself in his own house and in his own country was entirely up to him.

In a way, I would have liked to see him succeed, as far as the principle was concerned. His triumph was Rehana's triumph. Whether or not it served any useful purpose, her grievance was fair. She was trampled upon; she was taken for granted; she was stripped and shorn. Unlike him, her aim was not to gain but only to get back. Something that belonged to her was unjustly taken away from her and she had set out to repossess it, which was quite understandable. If he, too, was sincerely aiming for the same goal, he certainly had my goodwill behind him. Nothing could give me greater joy than to tell her one day that the mission she launched was eventually accomplished by the will and resolve of her father; nothing could give me greater satisfaction than to see her laugh in the faces of those who had laughed in mine. But the aggressive element in his behaviour remained too pronounced to be ignored, the deviousness of his mind too demonstrative to be misread, his personal goal too different from Rehana's to be confused with.

A few week or so later, I was informed by the nurse that Mr. Jenkins, the consultant gynaecologist looking after Rehana, was asking to see me at once as a matter of urgency. Something seemed to have come up, something crucial and confidential on account of which he was trying to see me alone instead of either one of her parents. It scared me out of my wits, but I rushed to meet him. Even though there was no prior appointment made, I was taken into his office immediately. A biggish man in his late fifties with a kind face and excellent deportment, he calmed me down first and then broached upon the topic without beating around the bush.

"A few days ago," he explained to me in a clear voice and slow speech to make sure I understood him without any room for error, "when your wife was brought to the hospital, she had not only gone into a coma but was also having a very severe internal hemorrhage. We've, no doubt, managed to stop the bleeding, but we haven't quite succeeded in bringing her out of the coma. We can keep trying for a while, and if she doesn't respond in time for a natural childbirth, or if the baby shows any signs of distress, we can easily resort to a Caesarean delivery with least amount of risks to the mother. But the sticky problem we're up against is something entirely different."

"And what is that, Mr. Jenkins?" I asked him, suppressing a sudden shiver that ran down my back from sheer prognosis.

"As a result of the fall," he continued after only a brief pause, "she's also sustained considerable damage to her spinal chord. We know we can repair it, but not without subjecting her to major surgery."

"I see."

"If it was just a question of Caesarean delivery, we can cope and be more or less certain of positive results. But I'm afraid we can't be sure of a similar measure of success with the other."

"What do you mean?"

"If we subject her to major surgery whilst she's still in a coma," he carried on without mincing his words, "there's a remote possibility that she might not—well—she might not make it."

"Why can't you wait until she comes out of the coma? Surely, she isn't likely to remain unconscious forever?"

"No, she isn't. But whether or not she'd come round in time for the surgery is the main question."

"You sound as though there's a deadline for performing the operation. Is there?"

"I'm afraid there is. We would either have to go ahead with it pretty soon, or give up the idea completely."

"What happens if you give up?"

"It could result in a permanent paralysis of the bottom half of her body, waist downward."

The staggering blow sent me reeling and a sudden spasm of pain rocked my body from head to foot. If I heard him right, what he was asking me to do was to choose between a sort of voluntary Euthanasia and lifelong incapacity. Major surgery while she was still in a coma could result in her death; but on the other hand, without such surgery in time, she could become a cripple for life and end up in a wheelchair. The scope of my options was so very limited, I could stand in the middle and touch both the extremes. The odds had suddenly multiplied beyond comprehension. We were on the brink of a real disaster. We would not be able to realise the least of our expectations, fulfil one hope, and carry out a single plan out of the many that we had made. How could I let them go ahead with the surgery knowing fully well that she might die on the operation table? Or, how could I let them condemn her to a lifetime of misery and grief? I could not point in either one of the directions. If she died, I could sit weeping by her corpse, shoulder her coffin, carry her to the grave, and commit her to dust and mourn her parting for the remainder of my days. On the other hand, if she became crippled, I could continue to love her as I always did, look after her and serve her. But I could not possibly sit there and declare which of the two I preferred!

"You sound final and unchangeable," I nervously mumbled in a voice choking with grief. "Does this mean there's no other way at all? Nothing else?"

"None," he replied, firmly shaking his head. "What I want to know from you is, when the time for making a decision arrives, we can either act according to our professional judgement or your personal wishes. Which way would you prefer us to look?"

If left to me, there was only one way to look: Rehana alive, Rehana breathing, Rehana talking, Rehana sharing, visible to the eye, responsive to touch, whether crippled, paralysed, blinded, disfigured or cut into pieces. I might never be able to put her back together, but love her I would, my heart, my soul, my body, my mind, everything dedicated to bringing just one smile to her blessed lips.

"There's only one thing I can say, Dr. Jenkins," I said in answer to his question. "Apart from making a decision, if you can also play God on that day and spare her life, I'll worship you for as long as I breathe."

"I don't know about playing God," he replied, winding up the conversation. "But I will certainly look up to the One above me for inspiration when the moment of reckoning arrives."

I came back to the I.C.U. Rehana lay on bed as before, with Auntie sitting in a chair close by. Probably struck by the grim expression I wore, she asked me if anything was the matter. I did not tell her. I could not break to her such a shattering piece of news in so many words. At that moment, Rehana was still visible to the naked eye; on that afternoon, she was still defying death and defeating destiny. But for how long would she be able to keep up the fight? What sort of tenure was I left with in her life? How much share did I have in her rapidly disappearing moments? I did not have a clue.

On the following morning, at around half past nine, I phoned Mr. Harrison for an urgent appointment. He asked me to come along right away. Uncle Haroon heard me but dared not pry; the question to which I needed an answer was not up his street.

Somehow finding my way to Chancery Lane with the help of the A-Z in

London, I reached Mr. Harrison's office. After a brief wait at the reception, I was sent into his room to see him.

"Hello, Mr. Quraishi," he said with ample courtesy. "Do sit down and make yourself at home."

"Thanks. I hope I haven't caused you any inconvenience?"

"None at all. In fact, I was glad you phoned. I was going to send for you early next week, anyway. How's your wife?"

"No improvement yet."

"I see."

"I came to find out one or two things about the trial. Since the last time we spoke, has anything changed?"

"No. Your defence is ready and will be presented to the court by Sir Nigel Hopkins QC."

"Any idea of its outcome?"

"Not a clue. If I were you, I'd try not to speculate."

"I remember having heard something about a Sir Ralph Bellamy and proceedings in the European Court of Human Rights. Is it true? Or, was it just talk?"

"A suggestion was made at the time but I gather it's been dropped by the barrister."

"Do you know why?"

"There's a backdrop to it," he said, explaining the matter to me in some detail. "You see, some time ago, three coloured young ladies married to Indian citizens whose applications for the entry permit were similarly turned down, lodged a complaint against the Home Office in the European court on grounds of sex discrimination. The court did find the Home Office guilty as charged, but so what? It's neither here nor there."

"Why?"

"Because the home secretary has a cosy choice; in order to balance the scales tilted by the ruling, he doesn't necessarily have to add to women's rights. He can accomplish the same thing by taking some away from men's, which is what he has done."

"Oh? I thought two wrongs don't make a right."

"Depends very much upon who's doing the adding up."

"I had also heard rumours about a complaint to the ombudsman of London against the Entry Clearance Officer in Bombay. Any news on that?"

"It was our idea. But I'm afraid it, too, has been dropped in the light of fresh evidence."

"What sort of evidence?"

"In a similar complaint made by some other aggrieved party, the ombudsman did find the E.C.O. in question guilty of bigotry and racial bias. Consequently, the Home Office recalled him from Bombay."

"And?"

"Peter Godfrey was sent as his replacement. Where do you go from there!"

"I see. So, all that remains is the trial?"

"Yes. And its outcome hardly likely to be favourable to you."

Mr. Harrison was so candid, he almost hurt me with the truth. Letting out a sigh of anguish I told him whatever Dr. Jenkins had explained to me about Rehana's plight.

"In the circumstances," I put it across to him with equal condor, "if I'm expelled from the country by the magistrate before she came round, I can't leave her on the deathbed and go away."

"You aren't thinking of jumping bail, are you?" he asked, staring at me with startled eyes.

"I might do just that. For her sake, I've already broken the law once, and if I have to, I might break it again. As you know, my father-in-law is rich enough to absorb the financial loss."

"What you really want is some extra time, isn't it?"

"Yes. Until I either bury her here or take her back with me.

"Well, look," he said, making up his mind swiftly, "since time's all you want, we can enter a plea of 'Not Guilty' on your behalf and ask the magistrate for a trial by jury."

"What will that accomplish?"

"The matter will then have to be referred to the Crown Court for a trial by jury. The hearing will automatically be postponed until a new date is finalised and a jury is formed. It could take several weeks, even months."

"And then?"

"At that stage, if you want more time, we can interrogate some of the jurors and raise objections about their suitability to come up with an impartial verdict. They would then have to form a new jury. We can thus keep dragging our heels at least for a while."

"I would appreciate it very much if you could do it, please"

"So long as you remain on the right side of the law, I'll do everything possible to help you out. Do I have your word on it?"

"Yes, you do, Mr. Harrison. And thanks."

"You're welcome. I will write to you nearer the time of the hearing. For now, good luck with your wife's situation."

I shook hands and left.

CHAPTER (32)

It was a quiet night. All three of us were assembled in the living room for a round of hot drinks before retiring. Uncle sat in the armchair, nervously drumming on its arm with his fingers. Auntie was lost in thought, waiting for the kettle to boil before making the drinks. I, too, began to brood. Flames crackled in the fireplace; water gurgled in the kettle; steam came puffing out of the spout; the mood was ponderous and the air seemed fraught with tension. I would have been better off inside my bedroom, but if only because etiquette demanded it, I kept company for a while.

"I gather you're trying to extend your stay in the country," Uncle Haroon remarked, making it sound neither like a question nor like a statement.

"Yes," I replied and added no more.

"I hired Mr. Harrison," he suddenly snapped. "You shouldn't have gone to see him without me and he shouldn't have taken any instructions from you in my absence."

Rightly or wrongly, instructions were given by me as well as taken by him in good faith. I doubted very much if the situation would have changed in any way on account of how he felt. I simply shrugged.

"What makes you so sure that Rehana would recover, or even come out of the coma before the date of the trial? With the best of intentions on Mr. Harrison's part, it can not be put off until eternity, you know," he said sarcastically.

Neither would she, in the Intensive Care Unit. Frankly, her time was at risk of running out a lot sooner than Mr. Harrison's tactics.

"One hopes she'd make a speedier recovery," I said.

"Good heavens!" he exclaimed and sat up. "You aren't, by any chance, suggesting that I wish ill to my own daughter, are you?"

I was not, but it was up to him to draw his own conclusions. I neither withdrew the observation nor tendered any apologies. When he saw no response coming from me to that ill-judged remark, he sat back in the chair and reverted to the drumming once again, now more listlessly than before. A poignant silence ensued in the room. Conversation tended to enhance tension instead of bringing relief. I had half a mind bidding them good night at that stage and leaving, but his next question pinned me back.

"What's eating you, anyway?" he said, throwing up his arms. "You don't consider me fit for even a simple consultation. If it comes to being naive, no one can hold a candle to you. Did anyone tell you that?"

Taking due note of his truculence, Auntie quickly intervened. "Is this necessary?" she asked.

"You keep out of it," he shouted back at her.

She got up and stormed out of the room.

"What's that supposed to mean, Uncle?" I asked him.

"Have you ever done anything right in your life, Yusuff?" he said and then elaborated on it. "See for yourself. You've excellent academic qualifications, you're married to a British citizen and you've my full backing. If you want a career, I can find you the right job. If you want to be your own boss, I can provide you with the best opportunity. But do you? Oh, no, you don't! Instead, you prefer to be an office boy in your brother-in-law's practice.

"Take another thing. When I brought Rehana back here, I had done it on purpose; I was making arrangements for you to come to this country lawfully. But did you wait long enough? No, you did not. Instead, you sneaked here unlawfully and got arrested, as a direct consequence of which she's now ended up in the hospital fighting for her life.

"That isn't all. For some reason best known to yourself, you suddenly decide to extend your stay in the country. But do you come to me for help? No, you don't. Instead, you go to a lawyer hired by me and make your own arrangements. I hear about it quite by chance.

"I've been waging Rehana's battle at the expense of my work. I am moving heaven and earth to accomplish what she had herself set out to. You don't even bother to take notice, let alone help out. But behind my back, you run to Mr. Harrison and swallow his suggestions without asking any questions. For how long do you think he can keep the boat from sinking; the bridge from falling and the lion from making a meal out of the goat? When I ask you about it, you talk as if I don't possess any paternal feelings. I raised Rehana from a tiny baby in the cradle to a pretty bride in the palanquin, for

Pete's sake! But you suddenly emerge out of nowhere and write me off like I'm just a fistful of trash. Can't we at least work together? Be on the same side of the fence for a change?"

Most of what he said was true; I had often thought about it myself. If I worked alongside him, I could improve my chances of staying with Rehana for longer, and if by some unexpected stroke of good luck he also succeeded in his efforts, the rest of my problems, too, could come to an end. I could then wait until Rehana made a full recovery and return home at my own convenience rather than on account of a court order.

"I'm sorry I blew my top," he said, himself interrupting my thoughts. "You've no idea what's going on in my mind. At this moment in time, my only child is lying in the hospital fighting for her life, and here I sit, quarrelling with her husband. How unlucky could one get to be!"

It seemed my misfortunes were beginning to rub off on him too. I noticed his eyes were glued to my face, probably to read my thoughts, search for a response, trace my reaction. But I did not have anything on offer. My mind was cast backwards; I was regretting the mistakes I had made and mulling over the painful present that resulted from them. I was still not looking ahead at the future.

"If only we could put aside our feuds and work out some sort of a compromise," he continued, musing to himself than talking to me. "Whether or not we're aiming at the same goals, we certainly happen to have a lot of common enemies. Why can't we at the very least fight shoulder-to-shoulder? Is it so difficult for you to stand up for the things in which your wife believed? Are you insensitive to her wishes because she isn't able to speak them out? If she opened her mouth and asked you to, wouldn't you have responded? Don't you want to avenge those who silenced her? What more do you need for motivation, for God's sake? Her corpse? Her coffin? Her grave? Her epitaph?"

At that stage he became so emotionally carried away his neck swelled, his face turned red and his eyeballs came bulging out. I thought he was going to have a heart attack and drop dead any moment. But it was all done just to squeeze out a couple of tears. Such was the man's revulsion to weakness he needed an incredible effort even to succumb to it.

"That's all right, damn you!" he finally conceded. "Go on and do what you like. Go to the hospital every day, sit by her bed and watch her die. Then sit by her grave, beseeching her to come out. From what I hear, you seem to be pretty good at that sort of thing …"

If it was his intention to draw me into a duel, he damn near succeeded. As though passing ill-omened remarks about Rehana was not bad enough, he dragged poor Azra into the slush. At any other time I would not have let him get away with it, but on that night I had to. Relations between him and me had deteriorated to such an extent, only a fresh start could put us back on the same level again.

"Dr. Jenkins," he then said, coming at me from a different direction, "told us whatever he told you. Your auntie and I know all about the great choice that Rehana's got: between death and a life worse than death. I heard you agreed to their professional judgement superseding your personal wishes. In other words, you gave them a license to kill her; you put your seal of assent on her *death sentence* and *deputised* Dr. Jenkins to carry it out on your behalf. But did you ever pause to think about what Rehana's own choice would've been in the matter? No, you did not. It's her life, but you determine its quantity as well as quality; it's her suffering, but you stipulate the extent to which she must endure; it's her nightmare, but you decide for how long she must carry on watching it. And then you talk so bitterly about humans playing God!"

The imputation shook me up, but I could not argue against it. When Dr. Jenkins asked me, I did agree to their professional judgement superseding my personal wishes. But who was I to make such irretrievable decisions? I wanted Rehana to live because I loved her far too much to think of anything else for her. But what about her? Would she have chosen for herself what I had chosen for her? Like he said, it was her life, her suffering, her nightmare, and therefore, it must be up to her to decide how far to go, how long to endure, how much to bear. Yet, when I agreed to let Rehana's fate rest in Dr. Jenkins' hands, I had done precisely what Uncle Haroon was accusing me of, I had endorsed my consent on her death sentence and deputised her doctor to carry it out on my behalf, I had performed the role of *God* for her.

"All right, play it your own way, dammit," he continued, "and do whatever you like to do. I know what I will. If anything happened to my child, I will blow up the White Hall; set fire to No. 10 Downing Street and gun down all the bloody politicians that I come across; I will foster every coloured young lady in the land who is suffering the same plight as Rehana, hire the best lawyers in town and give them back their husbands. I will fill the place vacated by my daughter with a thousand others; find my happiness in their happiness; and substitute my child's love with their love. I will search for my Rehana in their eyes, I will … I will … I will …"

He could not go on anymore. Grief choked him. What could blowing up the Whitehall or setting fire to No. 10 Downing Street or gunning down the politicians accomplish? If I knew it changed things; improved Rehana's chances by a mere fraction; performed that one miracle for which all of us were waiting; I would have done it myself; I would have turned into a reactionary and taken to the hills. If it reformed mankind; if it melted hearts; if it made brick walls bleed; if it ended one man's inhumanity towards another; if it cleansed souls; if it purged our conscience; if it annihilated sin; if it made the world a better place to live in; a lot of the others would have already done it. But we, who have learnt to hate one another since the times of Cain and Abel, are not in the market for reforms and requitals. If one Whitehall were blown up, ten towering skyscrapers would come into existence; if No. 10 Downing Street were destroyed, a new marble palace would be built to take its place; if one politician were shot dead, ten others would rush to occupy his empty chair. Bottles and labels might change but the contents would remain the same; people would continue to behave in the same way; hate would never come to an end; inequalities inherent to mankind would never be dispensed with. How could anyone bring perfection to an imperfect world?

That night, Uncle Haroon did his utmost to stir and motivate me but I did not budge. Far from changing my mind, every argument he put forward forced me into deeper thoughts. The more he tried to blindfold me, the clearer I saw: the harder he attempted to convince me the sharper became my vision. Frankly, neither of us was playing the roles cut out for us. We were interfering with nature's law, we were trying to swim against the current and were trying to manipulate the events instead of letting them take their own course. We were both wrong.

In the morning I went to the hospital as usual. There was still no change in Rehana's condition. Her face was white as a sheet; her mind incapable of thought; her body unresponsive to touch. For quite some time I simply sat gazing at her. Moments gathered weight and dragged; the tiny dot on the cardiac monitor kept bobbing up and down tirelessly; the oxygen mask swelled, deflated, swelled, deflated; saline drips travelled through the length of the plastic tube one behind the other. I felt terribly lonely and became desperate for her company. I wanted her to sit up, look at me, talk to me, sort it all out with me face-to-face just as she had written in one of her letters. I wanted to know whether or not she, too, loved me enough to stay in my life without any stipulations. The ones that I had made, I had withdrawn them all.

I was quite prepared to abide by her wishes; as much as I looked forward to the joy of her company, I was also willing to reconcile with her parting

"Rehana!" I whispered to her as though she was listening, "please help me. Tell me what to do. Sooner or later, someone's going to ask me a question. Until last night, I thought I knew the answer. But I'm not so sure now. I want you to live because I love you; I cherish you and I need you, but only if you too want the same thing for yourself. So tell me, please. Are you coming back to me, or are you going away for good? Are you willing to suffer such a lot for so little that I can give you? If you are, I'll do my best to make up for it. But if you aren't, I won't complain. Just as we used to sort out all our crises together, let's sort this one out too—together. This is the biggest to date and I don't quite know how to resolve it by myself. I can't ask them to let you die; neither can I let them force you into a life for which you don't particularly care. Can you see what sort of a fix I'm in? Do you honestly believe this is something I can handle alone? Please join me at least for one moment. Wake up for one look; open your mouth to say one word. Bless me or damn me. Save me or destroy me. Accept me or reject me. Do whatever you like, but do something. The burden of life's beginning to wear me out. Let me pause for a while to recover my breath. Then I'll get going again, as far as I can, as fast as I can, whether or not you travel with me, my angel!"

Without so much as a blink, she kept me waiting for three days, merciless in her indifference, uncompromising in her attitude, unyielding in her resolve. I began to age so fast, half of my hair turned grey. I lived in constant fear, on the run all the time. Days never seemed to pass; nights never seemed to end. The sound of footsteps threw me into a panic; silhouettes on the other side of the screen surrounding Rehana's bed gave me a start; whenever Dr. Jenkins' name was mentioned in front of me, scorpions crawled over my back. I avoided coming across Uncle Haroon; spoke less and less to Auntie Zeenath; and wore the outlook of a man haunted by devils. I also felt like one, tense, scared, dumbstruck, quick at losing temper, slow at regaining composure.

Then, suddenly, Dr. Jenkins did send for me again. I could guess why; a decision must have been taken about Rehana. I would either be consulted or simply told. What was I supposed to say? If the issue were taken up with Uncle Haroon, it would have been another matter. He knew all the answers; he had been making such crucial decisions most of his life. He could tell people what to do, and if there was a conflict of opinion, he had the ability to prevail. With me, it was a different situation altogether. I was reconciled to the idea of accepting rather than soliciting. I had lost the courage to foster any hopes; I had lost the strength to harbour any despair. I would be around for as long as Rehana was around; I would fizzle into thin air when she too fizzled into thin air. If she wanted to go, I would bid her farewell; if she wanted to stay, I would extend her a welcome. If someone saved her, I would be eternally grateful; if no one saved her, I would be forever miserable. I could, however, make my wishes; I could wait, I could watch, I could wait, I could watch, without daring to stretch my hand and without having to say a word. Why did Dr. Jenkins send for me? Why was I being asked to participate in a debate in which either her death or her life long incapacity was the only thing that could feature?

The new venue to which I was taken was not the same office where I had met Dr. Jenkins on a prior occasion. This one was a much larger room, and instead of only one person, there were five people present, two on either side of a table and the fifth one presiding.

First of all, we were introduced. Besides Dr. Jenkins, there were two orthopaedic surgeons, a consultant anaesthetist and a nursing administrator. I sat down and faced them. My heartbeat accelerated and my mind went a total blank but I pulled myself together. Whether or not I participated in that crucial debate, it was important that I heard what was being said. If at all there was a silver lining in the cloud, it was my last chance of being shown where to look for it.

"Mr. Metcalfe," said Dr. Jenkins, leading the conversation, "is a prominent orthopaedic surgeon in the country and has been closely following your wife's case. He feels sure he'd be able to carry out the operation on her with least amount of risks."

I simply nodded, unable to determine whether it was good news or bad.

"It would've been better, and obviously a lot safer, if Rehana had come out of the coma," he continued, "but since she hasn't, the decision to operate has been based strictly upon ratios. This is something we work out in every surgery; we weigh the benefits against the element of risks involved. The same thing has been done in your wife's case too. In our opinion, what she stands to gain is far greater than what she might lose in an extremity."

He paused there to let it sink in. There was nothing new in what he had said so far. Applying clear logic, they had felt that her death on the operation table would be a lot better than her life confined to a bed. They were willing to take the risks and go for the sweepstakes rather than not gamble at all. That was what it boiled down to, just a game with so much to bet with, so much to lose and so much to gain. There was no room in it for emotions.

"Having said that," Dr. Jenkins proceeded, "I must point out that this is only a recommendation. The final choice would have to be yours. If you don't want us to take the risk and go ahead with the surgery, please say so now. We can continue with the present course of treatment and then hope for the best. Do you understand what I'm saying, Mr. Quraishi?"

"Yes," I replied, barely managing that one word.

"If there was time, I would've let you think it over. But unfortunately, we've reached a stage where we can either perform the surgery and give her the only chance she's got of a total recovery, or take it away from her for good. There's no middle ground; we've used it all up," he said.

My voice choked. I must have committed some heinous sin in my life to have brought upon myself a weight as heavy as that. It simply crushed me.

"What do you say, Mr. Quraishi? Is it a 'yes' or a 'no'?" He pressed me in a soft but firm tone.

I tried to answer him but just could not. My voice remained muffled in my throat.

"Or, let me put it to you in a different way," he said, obviously well experienced in facing and resolving many a similar crisis, "Do you have any objection to us doctors exercising our professional discretion?"

I simply shook my head. Anything was better than sealing her doom with my final word.

At that stage, the five solemn faces turned away from me and towards each other, exchanging meaningful glances. Dr. Jenkins got to his feet and escorted me as far as the door, neither pleased nor displeased. He would have probably behaved in the same manner if I had nodded my head instead of shaking. To him, it was just another step in a day's honest work.

The long walk from there to the I.C.U. stretched infinitely. People I came across along the way passed me by like shadows. Everything became suddenly too much for me to cope with. I could not think, hear or talk. I felt so scared I would have broken into a run to get away from there. Only a total lack of physical strength prevented me from running.

Rehana lay motionless on the bed just like I had seen her last. Whether she would still be around in the morning had become a matter for speculation now. It could easily be my last chance to look at that face, touch those hands, kiss those feet, sink in that image while she was still alive. The shrine was damaged, but the deity I worshipped was not yet gone.

I kissed her on the forehead, held her hand, pressed it on my eyes and then gently put it back. There she lay, a victim of bigotry, a casualty of racial bias. The woman who wanted so much for herself that her country could not afford to give it to her. The one for whom the heads of great politicians failed to nod; on whom their books were closed; at whom all sorts of rules were waved. By daybreak tomorrow, she might become yesterday's news. An inconsequential storm, which had raised a whiff of dust in the backyard of the Whitehall would subside and everything return to normal. Until there was one more Rehana, one more stir, one more whirl, one more splash, all to be followed by yet another lull. Elephants would carry on roaming, unhampered by barking street dogs; prayers of St Francis would continue to echo in Downing Street, while grief and despair go wherever the meek and the humble are. Jesus Christ would continue to draw crowds into churches and chapels for the Sunday Mass, while only those who run the farthest inherit the biggest share of the earth; Divine Healers and Messiahs come only once, but lepers, cripples and blind babies are born forever and forever!

I came out of the ward in a state of trance; I was driven home in a state of trance; I was left inside the bedroom in a state of trance. What was my recourse? In which direction was I to face? To whom could I turn for help? Who would lend me a kind shoulder to shed my tears upon? Who could take over the helm and steer my sinking ship away from the doldrums? Who could make a slit in the overwhelming darkness around me and send in a ray of light? Who could call off the advancing clouds, the dazzling flares of lightning, the deafening roar of thunder, the endless torrents of rain, and usher into my life a much-needed peace?

In moments of such immense frustration and helplessness, there is only one direction to look at; there is only one source to go to; there is only one hand to lean on, and that is *Allah's*! But how could I? I had renounced Him, I had rejected Him, I had forgotten Him. I had quarrelled with the best friend man has got. Just because He turned away from me once, I had turned away from Him forever; just because He robbed me of my love at one time, I had robbed Him of His glory for all times; just because He did not listen to me once, I had stopped listening to Him forever; just because He did not recognize my existence upon earth, I had refused to recognize His presence in Heaven. Frankly speaking, within a matter of one year since Azra's death, my life had been methodically reconstructed; my emotions rehabilitated; everything that was taken away from me was given back to me. I was blessed with a caring partner; I was about to be blessed with a child; I was granted a shelter over my head, assured of my daily bread. Every wrong done to me was paid back in full, every grievance restituted, every wish granted. Yet, too bitter to acknowledge His kindness, I had stuck to my complaints. Having gone away from Him once, I had stayed away from Him at all times; having withdrawn my faith in Him, I had continued to put it elsewhere; I had made up my own gods and offered them worship.

Where were they now! Out there somewhere, poor Rehana was fighting for her life. Who had the power to save her? Who had the ability to spare her? Who could protect her against death, who could heal and restore her? If I needed a miracle, who could make one for me? If my world fell apart once again, who could reconstruct it for the second time? Who could prevail upon fate, alter destinies, redesign life, and turn ends into new beginnings? Above all, who cared about a husband's love for his wife or a child's need of its mother? Who tied such lasting bonds between one human and another and who gave them perpetuity?

He alone! Our Father in Heaven; our Guide upon earth. The Omnipotent, the Omnipresent, the Ubiquitous, the Metamorphic. The one who loves; who cares; who forgives as well as gives. The one to whom kings bow; the one into whose arms the meek and the mighty go alike; the one to whom we all belong and to whom we all must return one day! He was right there next to me, waiting to be sought, willing to oblige. I did not have to open my mouth; a thought was enough to invoke His mercy. That was what I had been denying myself so far; His love, His mercy, His favours. I could not afford to make the same mistake once again. Hence, without wasting any more time, I kneeled on the floor, raised my hands and looked heavenwards.

"*Ya Ilahi!*" I said, addressing Him in all humility, "I have come back to you for the *fatted calf*. I had strayed away from you in ignorance, I had denied myself your love, I had withdrawn my faith in you. I know now that it was wrong. So, let's both forget the past. All that is over and done with. The grudge I bore you so far and for such a long time is gone. I've returned to my senses, the blindfold has come off my eyes, I've learnt my lesson, I regret my folly and I apologize. Here I'm, on my knees, at your mercy, in total submission to your will. For the second time in my life I'm facing a similar crisis but without half the strength which I once possessed. Please don't put upon me any more burden than what I can lift; don't take me any farther than I can walk. I've reached the end of my tether. I beg you as I had never begged before. Take pity upon me, accept what little I can give you in return for such a lot that I need from you, because you're bigger than me, you're the biggest of all. My need is desperate. I'm not alone now. I'm about to be blessed with a child. Please spare Rehana for the both of us. Help us; watch over us. Forgive us our failings and shortcomings. You gave us life, and hence you tend to it; you nurture it; you make it flourish. Bless us with your compassion; protect us against evil; guide us through our troubled paths. We've no one to look up to but you; we've no one to seek from except of you; we've no need of anything other than what you bestow upon us. Please open the door and let us enter your kingdom. Extend your arms and take us to your bosom. Look at us, listen to us, and respond to us. Give us just a little out of your abounding bounties of which there is never a dearth. Give us your blessings as you gave those before us, and as you will give those after us. Give us your love in a greater measure than you taught us to give one another. *Aamin, sum aamin!"*

With those words I rested my forehead head on the floor. I had no intentions of lifting it until there was some sign of His response, a gesture of His forgiveness, a reward for my trials. That night, the scores between us had to be settled one way or another, the scales had to be balanced, a truce drawn. I was not negotiating anymore; I had surrendered! It was now up to Him to decide what to do with me and how to deal with me!

CHAPTER (33)

On the following morning, Rehana was subjected to major surgery. Auntie Zeenath, Uncle Haroon and I waited outside the operation theatre. He kept nervously pacing the floor, while she sat in a chair, her head covered by the *sari,* her eyes shut, her face a complete blank, rolling the beads of her rosary, in solemn communion with Allah, in total submission to His will, all her hopes banked upon Him alone.

I, however, felt strangely subdued. Fear and bitterness were both gone from my system. Neither tempted into premature rejoicings, nor sunk in needless despair, I was able to strike a healthy balance between the two at long last. I knew what was going on inside the operation theatre; I was aware of the odds; I was conscious of the perils; I was wide-awake to reality. Yet I did not feel under pressure. The name Allah remained on my lips right through the anxious moments. A silent conversation took place between Him and me. I made Him many promises. A holy pilgrimage to Mecca and Medina with my family was the foremost amongst them.

'And if we can afford it,' I added, 'we'll also visit as many shrines of our saints as possible. Mamma and Papa had done the same thing; after they lost three children successively, the doctors told them one thing and the Ulemas quite another. But they put their faith in you and were amply rewarded."

The operation lasted until two in the afternoon. As soon as we heard signs of activity, we knew it had ended and braced up. I would be less than honest if I said the moments that followed were not filled with anxiety. They were, of immense anxiety and tension. They were moments when the earth seemed to have stood still. Yet, I did not harbour a single negative thought. I waited to see Rehana and not her corpse; I waited to be told how well the operation had succeeded and not how miserably it had flopped. I waited for good news and no longer for bad news.

In due course, the door to the operation theatre slid open. Then a stretcher emerged, surrounded by several nurses. Behind it came the full team of doctors, known and unknown. One look at their serene faces was enough to reaffirm the extent of Allah's mercy. Through their hands and by means of their expertise, we had been duly rewarded. Even though Rehana was still unconscious and wrapped in white sheets, her eyes were no longer half open as before, revealing the glazed pupils. They were firmly shut, as if she was in deep sleep. I rushed and caught up with her. Now she was not only visible to the eye but her hand was also waiting for mine. My dream was in tact, never again to be trifled with. The crucial lessons that I learnt from my recent experiences were unforgettable.

Upon reaching the ward, she was transferred on to a freshly made bed. Moments later Uncle and Auntie also joined me. Their joy too, just like mine, knew no bounds. The sister suggested that it would be better if we could keep the interruptions to a bare minimum for a while. We agreed and came out.

Dr. Jenkins, on his way to check upon his patient, saw me and stopped for a brief chat. We went into a small consultation room adjoining the visitors' lounge and sat down.

"The risk," he informed me with a great deal of relief, "was well worth taking. Your wife's going to be all right."

I had no reason to doubt it. On that occasion, Allah had not only heard my prayers but also answered them without a moment's delay. If my understanding of the situation was correct, there was a distinct chance that I would be able to speak with Rehana very soon. What had looked like a lost cause to all of us barely twenty-four hours ago was now an expectation I could venture to harbour without any misgivings.

"I've some good news and some bad news for you," Dr. Jenkins said next. "Let me dispense with the latter first. In course of the operation, we were forced to perform a hysterectomy too, which means your wife won't be able to bear any more children. But I hope the good news will more than make up for the loss. You're now the proud parents of a healthy and absolutely adorable baby daughter. Happy?"

Just happy? Ecstatic! One is better than none.

"If we can hang on to whatever we've already got, Dr. Jenkins, that alone is more than enough," I said.

"Indeed, it is," he agreed with me wholeheartedly.

Did Rehana come out of the coma in time for the surgery? Was she unconscious merely from the effects of Anaesthetics, which would soon wear out? How long was it before she walked again and before she was discharged from the hospital? None of those questions had any significance anymore. I neither bothered to ask him nor did he attempt to explain.

"Come along," said Uncle Haroon as soon as I joined them in the visitors' lounge. "Let's go to the maternity ward and see your little girl. She's simply gorgeous!"

If I could, I would have preferred to wait for a few more days and seen our *Tabassum* along with Rehana. We had made so many plans and preparations to welcome our baby together. Keeping that unique moment of joy to myself pinched, but how could I help it? The father in me had suddenly woken up and run out of patience. I desperately wanted to hold my baby in my arms, open the doors of my heart and lock her inside. Rehana was already there. I could not think of a quicker way of uniting the mother with her child!

Without further ado, all three of us made for the maternity ward in rapid strides. Along the way, I felt immensely excited. I had experienced the same sort of tremors on our wedding night when Rehana sat on the nuptial bed covered in red and concealed from sight. At that time, she was an *unknown factor*, a million images of her projected in my mind on the strength of just one hurried glimpse in the mirror conceded to me by dearest Rox. But when we came face-to-face, she had gone beyond my wildest expectations. Now, it was Tabassum's turn. Dr. Jenkins described her as absolutely adorable, and according to Uncle Haroon, she was gorgeous. I had built up a sketchy image of her in my mind to my own fancy. How well would she measure up to it? Did she have hair as dark as rain clouds? Did she have cheeks as red as vernal cherries? Were her eyes shaped like almonds? Was she fair like her mother? Could she, too, make the roses blush? Had she brought along a heart big enough to feed both parents with love? Was there a message of joy and goodwill carved upon her forehead?

When we reached the ward, a cheerful nurse came out and took us in. My heart kept leaping into my throat and endless currents of excitement rocked my body. Suddenly, there were no more gaps in the story of my life. All those pages and chapters that had been tampered with were back in their proper places. Not only did it make sense but it also made matchless reading. An auspicious beginning was developed into a coherent plot and given a smooth progress in the right direction. Rehana and I, bonded together by love, had brought into being our Tabassum by the will and consent of a God in whom both of us believed! It was as definitive and straightforward as that. The rest of the trimmings did not matter anymore. They had served their purpose and become superfluous to requirements!

Just like her mother, Tabassum surpassed all my wildest expectations. If seeing her was a dream, holding her in my arms its pleasant outcome. I felt so replete and content, there was no room in me for anything else. I had never carried an infant as little as that in my whole life, but all of a sudden, I seemed to know everything there was to know about tiny tots! I held her as if she was made of fragile glass, exerting no more pressure on her than absolutely necessary for fear of hurting her. A gentle brush of my lips on her forehead served the purpose of that much-awaited kiss. Her eyes were shut but I could visualise an entire milky way lit up inside the lids; her lips were sealed and yet I could hear the chorus of a million promises made. Her faint moan rang in my ears like the sweetest melody I had ever heard in my whole life. My heart was concealed somewhere inside my cage of ribs, but I saw my baby toddle straight in and lie down in her mum's lap. Mother and daughter safely together where they ought to be; I hoped they remained there uninterrupted for as long as I breathed.

From there, we went home. It was time for all of us to relax a little. If we were in Hyderabad, I had a feeling Auntie Zeenath would have treated every beggar that roamed around the streets to a decent meal, arranged for teams upon teams of people to recite the Qur'aan over and over again, lit candles in every shrine, laid wreaths at all the pious tombs inside them, distributed clothes to orphanages, provided shelter to destitutes and given alms with both hands. Such was the extent of her joy that she could not contain herself. The sober, quiet and sagacious auntie I had known so far was no longer in her. She kept bursting into laughter whether or not there was an occasion for it; fussed over me as she had never fussed before; cooked rich dishes and stuffed me like a pig. While doing all that, she did not neglect her duty to Allah for His boundless mercy, either. Whenever her time was not taken up by earthly preoccupations, she spent every moment of it in silent supplications and solemn thanksgivings.

That day, the tension that had built up between Uncle and me also showed signs of lifting. For once, he spoke to me without making any reference either to the home secretary or to his mica empire. And for the first time since I set foot in that house, much of his erstwhile charisma and charm also returned to his face. Right through the day, we made several phone calls to the hospital to check on Rehana's progress. The news was consistently encouraging; her condition was stable and the baby was also fine.

On the following morning, we went to see them both. There was a dramatic improvement in Rehana's external appearance; all those artificial aids that had been supporting her life until then were withdrawn. The nurses had washed her face, put on some powder and brushed her hair. There were no signs of movement in her yet, and her eyes were still shut, but she had started to use her own respiratory system, which truly made a difference of heaven and earth. I could see she was heading my way in rapid strides.

Pulling a chair close to the bed I sat in it, held her hand and whispered to her. "Hello, Rehana!" I said, anxiously watching the expression on her face. "If you can hear me, please press my hand."

She did. The pressure was not much, but enough to acknowledge an appropriate response. "Come aboard, partner!" I urged her in similar whispers. "It is getting to be too lonely without you!"

There was no answer yet, but her grip on my hand tightened. After a while, two large tears swelled at the corner of her eyes and rolled down. Drying them with my handkerchief, I kissed her hand with which she was holding mine and pressed the tousled hair in place.

"I hear the season of yellow flowers has started back home," I mumbled. "Crickets are squeaking in grass, frogs are perched on lotus leaves, black clouds have begun to scatter raindrops hither and thither, and the smell of spring is in the air! Come along, my *Shahzadi,* and hurry up! Let's go and trip the rainbow; let's swing in it; let's gather all those golden moments that slipped away through our fingers; let's pick up the threads of our lives! Tabassum needs you, I need you, a little bungalow in Asifnagar needs its mistress, a small kingdom is desperately short of its sovereign. Wake up and rise!"

It was too soon for her to do anymore than give me faint signals of her homebound journey from the unknown, but in the days that followed she made steady progress. As soon as the wounds resulting from surgery healed and the sutures came off, she was put in plasters. Shortly afterwards, a carefully planned diet was introduced, which began to restore her strength in small measures. Her blood pressure went back to normal, she was able to move her hands, sometimes opened her eyes and looked at us, on some rare occasions even managed a word or two. Since Dr. Jenkins had told me that she was not yet ready for holding the baby in her arms, I chose an appropriate moment and told her about Tabassum. Mother's love woke up whenever the name was mentioned. I could distinctly see the time for our reunion was not too far away. She knew it too; her resolve strengthened tenfold and she began to recover in leaps and bounds.

Meanwhile, the date of my trial caught up. As there was no longer any need for me to trouble Mr. Harrison for buying time, I let him go ahead with it. Uncle Haroon drove me over to the Old Bailey and kept me company throughout the lengthy proceedings. The legal battle lasted for two whole days, neither side prepared to concede easy defeat. On the third day, after a brief summing up by both the barristers, the dogfight came to an end.

Before relieving the jury to consider their verdict, the judge gave them some tips. The charges against me, he pointed out, were crystal clear. If, in their opinion, the prosecution had proved them beyond a reasonable doubt, it was their duty to return a verdict of guilty. On the other hand, if they thought that the balance of probabilities was tilting in my favour, it was equally their duty to return a verdict of not guilty. Their decision, however, must not be based upon any of the mitigating circumstances contained in the defence. He would take them into consideration at the time of passing the sentence.

At the end of two nail-biting hours of tension and waiting, the moment of reckoning finally stared me in the eye. The jurors reassembled, their foreman rose to his feet and faced the judge. Then the clerk asked him if they had reached a verdict. He said they had. I was found guilty as charged on all the counts.

That, in itself, did not bother me too much. No doubt, it left a bad taste in my mouth, but that was all it did, just left a bad taste. For one who had never harboured any illusions to the contrary, there was no question of being disillusioned. It was, in fact, the fear of the sentence that had been raging no end of havoc on my nerves.

Before passing it, the judge dwelled at some length on the offences I was proved to have committed. If I was allowed to get away with it too easily, others could be tempted into making an example out of me. Justice, he said, was one thing and law quite another. Those who broke the latter could not expect to bargain for the former. Therefore, after taking into consideration all the extenuating circumstances which had been so robustly outlined by the defence, he said he had decided to sentence me to serve two years in Her Majesty's prison, but the sentence suspended for a period of twelve months on condition that I left the country within five working days from the date of the sentence and did not attempt to defraud Her Majesty's government ever again.

By the time we finished all the routine formalities with the court and got home, it was about four in the afternoon. I did not know how and when Uncle had managed to send Auntie a message, but she was back from the hospital and was waiting for us. From the troubled expression on her face, it was clear that she also knew the outcome of the trial.

"What next?" Uncle asked me as soon as soon as the three of us gathered in the lounge for a quick coffee following the late lunch.

There was no need to put the obvious into words. I simply shrugged.

"Mr. Harrison thinks we can go for an appeal," he said, his diehard hopes still gasping for a breath of fresh air. "Today's judgement doesn't have to be taken as final. At least, give it some thought. You've got five whole days in which to make up your mind."

I firmly shook my head, leaving him in no doubt that I was not interested in breathing the air that had turned foul for me.

"Are you going to tell Rehana?" he asked, fishing for other pretexts.

That, I had every intention of doing. In course of the four tense days of strenuous preparation for the trial, and then the trial itself, I had not seen her at all, because if I saw her, I could not have lied to her. What sort of excuses Auntie made up in order to explain away my preoccupations, I did not yet know. But going back to Hyderabad without the courtesy of telling her and taking her leave was simply out of the question.

"Of course, I'll tell her," I replied.

"She might not be willing for you to go," he pointed out. "Ever thought about that?"

I had, and several times too. But it was a chance I had to take, sooner or later. I was sure of one thing; Rehana knew me well enough to decide for herself where a line must be drawn. I had already crossed that line.

"If she isn't, it would be too bad," I told him without adding any flavours or sweeteners to it.

"Well," he said, giving up at long last, "I'll phone Mr. Harrison in the morning and tell him you're going. Would you like to spend here whatever time's at your disposal, or don't you want to do even that?"

"You mean, the five working days conceded by the judge?" I asked him pointedly, to make absolutely certain that he was not toying with the idea of unauthorised extensions to the measly time given. "I won't say no to a few days with my family, so long as they remain within the stipulated time."

Realising that there was no temptation under the sun that could possibly persuade me to change my mind or change the date, he gave up trying. After that, only one thing remained for me to do, and that was to thank Auntie Zeenath for all the support she had given me in course of those trying times, the hospitality she extended to me, her affection and attention, her incredible patience, so much she had done for me in so short a time, and I did it on our way to the hospital.

"I don't quite know how to thank you, Auntie," I said to her sincerely and truthfully. "With you around, I never once missed Mamma, believe me."

"Same here," she replied with a cheerful smile, "with you around, I never fell short of a son."

"I hope Uncle can forgive me and forget this whole affair."

"I'm sure he will. Whatever be his faults, he isn't the type of person to carry over one day's grudge into another. And by the way, Rehana's been transferred to a private ward this morning."

"Has she seen Tabassum?"

"Not yet. But she knows all about the trial, and about the judgement."

"You told her?"

"Yes, I did. She has to know, sooner or later."

"Of course, she has to. What did she say?"

"Not a word so far. But she's done quite a lot of crying since."

"Why?"

"Well, she has her pride. This happens to be her country too, you know. Going away from it is one thing, but being asked to get out of it is quite another. Don't you think?"

"Yes."

"But you don't have to prove anything to anyone. At his age, your uncle ought to know that those who can hear seldom need to be shouted at, and those who play deaf, they never respond. You do only what you want to do and stick to your own plans. As soon as Rehana and Tabassum are fit to travel, I'll see to it that they join you without a moment's delay."

"Will you?"

"Yes, I will. I swear I will."

"Thanks."

Upon reaching the hospital, she proceeded to the maternity ward and I went to see Rehana. Her room was small, bright and breezy. She sat on the bed, armed with tears, but not to fight me. The message in her eyes was too clear to be misread. It did not have anything to do with winning or losing. It contained no stipulations; it offered no explanations; it did not lay any claims and neither did it make any concessions. It simply said that she loved me and ended there.

As soon as she raised her arms in my direction, offering me the best substitute to universe, I rushed into them. That was my Paradise. That was my shrine in which my God sat beaming. That was where my havoc ended and my peace began. That was where one half of me joined hands with the other half. That was the only place where dreams and realities rubbed shoulders and coexisted. That was where I had resurrected from the voids one unforgettable night and was given a new mould to wear. That was the cocoon in which I could hide, and that was also the doorway through which I could gain access to lasting freedom ... .

"Are you going back?" she asked me.

"Yes," I replied, gazing at her with anxious eyes. "My pride is at stake. Are you going to be upset?"

"No, I'm not. Your pride is my pride."

"Thank you."

"It'll be rather difficult for me to spend the time of day without you or the nights without your arms around me, but it'll soon pass."

"The same sun which shines on you will shine on me too," I deliberately whispered in her ear the things that we had said to each other on the night before her departure from Hyderabad.

"When the geese fly East," she too responded with a cherubic smile, taking the cue, "I'll cajole one of them to whisper an *'I love you'* from me in your ears ..."

"And if you let me know when you're ready to come," I said, continuing the same theme, "I'll despatch a Flying Carpet for you all the way from Hyderabad ..."

At that moment, interrupting our silly chat, Auntie Zeenath stepped in, holding in her hands what looked like a bundle, but the smile on her lips and the sparkles in her eyes had their own story to tell. It had fallen into her share of luck to pass into our hands the most coveted of gifts which any man or woman could ever hope to receive: our child, brought into being with love, brought into the world with love, love begotten by love! For, a child born is Divinity multiplied; a child born is the kingdom of God reasserted; a child born is human love perpetuated! May those who say words to the contrary be damned!

Suddenly overwhelmed by an upsurge of joy and excitement, the force with which Rehana tried to break out of her plasters and go for the baby was stunning. Auntie Zeenath' s eyes tore open from apprehension. Letting out a mild scream of caution, she signalled her to lie back and rushed closer. Then she gently put the bundle into her eager hands. In it lay our sweet Tabassum, eyes closed, lips drawn, cheeks full, legs arched, hands stuck in air, the tiny body wrapped in soft flannels, as salubrious as a rose bud washed in dew, looking as though she had just been brought down upon earth straight from Heaven by the angels!

"My baby!" Rehana screamed, somehow managing to hang on to the bundle in spite of the plasters.

Another moment like that was not going to be repeated in our lives. But the one in hand was enough to last us for as long as we breathed!

THE END

Printed in the United Kingdom
by Lightning Source UK Ltd.
103557UKS00001B/238-270